HEMISPHERIC COMMUNICATION: MECHANISMS AND MODELS

HEMISPHERIC COMMUNICATION: MECHANISMS AND MODELS

Edited by

Frederick L. Kitterle
Stephen F. Austin State University

LEA

LAWRENCE ERLBAUM ASSOCIATES, PUBLISHERS
1995   **Hillsdale, New Jersey**   Hove, UK

Lawrence Erlbaum Associates, Inc., Publishers
365 Broadway
Hillsdale, New Jersey 07642

Library of Congress Cataloging-in Publication Data
Hemispheric communication : mechanisms and models /
   edited by Frederick L. Kitterle.
           p. cm.
   Includes bibliographical references and index.
   ISBN 0-8058-1144-3 (acid-free paper)
   1. Cerebral hemispheres. 2. Corpus Callosum. 3. Cerebral
dominance. I. Kitterle, Frederick L.
QP381.H46   1994
612.8' 25--dc20
                                    94-1958
                                      CIP

Books published by Lawrence Erlbaum Associates are printed on acid-free paper, and their
bindings are chosen for strength and durability.

Printed in the United States of America
10 9 8 7 6 5 4 3 2 1

Contents

LIST OF CONTRIBUTORS

Francisco Aboitiz
Department of Anatomy
University of Chile
Santiago, Chile

Marie T. Banich
Department of Psychology and the
Beckman Institute, University of Illinois
Urbana-Champaign, IL 61820

David B. Boles
Department of Psychology
Rensselaer Polytechnic Institute
Troy, NY 12180

Christine Chiarello
Department of Psychology
Syracuse University
430 Huntington Hall
Syracuse, NY 13244

Stephen D. Christman
Department of Psychology
University of Toledo
Toledo, OH 43606

Jeffrey Clarke
Department of Psychology
University of North Texas
Denton, TX 76203

Jorge S. Conesa
Department of Psychology
University of Toledo
Toledo, OH 43606

Lauren Julius Harris
Department of Psychology
Michigan State University
East Lansing, MI 48824

Joseph B. Hellige
Department of Psychology
Seeley G. Mudd Bldg., Room 501
University of Southern California
Los Angeles, CA 90089-1061

David Kaiser
Department of Psychology
University of California
405 Hilgard Ave.
Los Angeles, CA 90024-1563

Frederick L. Kitterle
Department of Psychology
Stephen F. Austin State University
Nacogdoches, TX 75962

Susan C. Levine
Department of Psychology
University of Chicago
Chicago, IL 60637

Rana Matteson
Learning Disabilities Center
Northwestern University
Evanston, IL 60201

Lynn C. Robertson
University of California
Center for Neuroscience
Davis, CA 95616 and
Veterans Affairs
150 Muir Road
Martinez, CA 94553-4695

Justine Sergent
Montreal Neurological Institute and
Hospital
3801 University
Montreal, Quebec, Canada
H3A 2B4

Sandra F. Witelson
Department of Psychiatry
Faculty of Health Sciences
McMaster University
1200 Main Street West
Hamilton, Ontario, Canada
L8N 3Z5

Eran Zaidel
Department of Psychology
University of California at Los Angeles
1282A Franz Hall
405 Hilgard Ave.
Los Angeles, CA 90024-1563

Preface

Research on cerebral laterality continues to capture the interest of a broad range of scientists. Recent work (Hellige, 1990; Hellige, 1992; Kitterle, 1991) has summarized the contributions of researchers across areas as diverse as neurochemistry, neuroanatomy, higher level perceptual and cognitive processes to our understanding of hemispheric differences. Work from these various areas - using normal human subjects and those with brain damage, as well as research with animal models - has deepened our understanding of the functional asymmetries between the left and right cerebral hemispheres. These insights have been facilitated by more sophisticated measurement techniques at both the micro and molar levels. With the steady increase in data, our understanding of cerebral function has gradually shifted away from characterizing the processing of each hemisphere in terms of broad, mutually exclusive dichotomous categories. In addition to considerations about the nature of hemispheric processing, attention has also focused on the nature of visual input because the quality of the input, and the nature of the task appear to determine jointly which hemisphere will dominate in a given situation. With the advent of computational modeling, more probing questions have been asked about the nature of the task itself and the processing components or modules necessary for such processing. According to this view, information processing can be seen as the result of distributed processing within these modules, and, depending on the specific nature of the task, the left or the right or neither hemisphere may dominate. A number of these topics were discussed at a symposium held at the University of Toledo and published in *Cerebral Laterality: Theory and Research* (Kitterle, 1991). The primary focus of that conference was on hemispheric differences in information processing.

The present volume extends that work and presents chapters based on a recent conference on hemispheric communication and interaction held at the University of Toledo. In contrast to the earlier Toledo Conference, this conference addressed research on interaction between the two hemispheres in the functioning of the whole brain. The idea that information processing is distributed in the brain implies coordination of processing between and within the hemispheres. The chapters presented in this volume contain research at the behavioral, anatomical, and electrophysiological levels that characterize the nature of interhemispheric communication and interaction and the substrates that subserve these functions.

Harris (chapter 1) presents an historical overview of theory and research on the corpus callosum and hemispheric communication, recounting the ideas, discoveries, and events that have influenced current research. Because there are a number of strands to the history of this topic, Harris discusses the developments in this area as separate subtopics with multiple chronologies and points out some of the linking events along the way. First, he addresses the question of hemispheric communication and intergration. He then reviews the lesion studies of the corpus callosum, as well as an account of the effects on mental health believed to be caused by a breaking down of communication between the hemispheres. He reviews early research on individual differences in the size of the corpus callosum and the implications for mental functioning. Finally, he provides an historical review of the studies addressing the importance of the role of the corpus callosum in integrative functioning. This review contrasts research in the 1930s and 1940s, which suggested a minimal role for the corpus callosum, with later studies supporting the importance of this structure.

In chapter 2, Witelson discusses studies that are beginning to reveal what the neuroanatomical substrates of functional asymmetry may be and how they may bear on the origins and mechanisms of functional asymmetry. In part, the conclusions reached in this chapter are derived from studying relationships between the variation in several gross neuroanatomical and histological measures derived from the study of postmortem brains, and variation in neuropsychological measures of functional asymmetry in cognitively normal people. One focus has been on the corpus callosum, whose size, Witelson notes, varies with a behavioral index of functional asymmetry in men. Given that the varying size of the corpus callosum could indicate a concomitant variation in the total number of axons, Witelson discusses the role of axon loss as a developmental factor in asymmetry and suggests that axon loss in the human brain may occur completely or mainly in the prenatal period. Witelson considers, also, the implications of these findings for sex differences in handedness. Moreover, because the relationship of callosal anatomy to hand preference exhibits a sex difference, Witelson suggests a two-factor (genetic and hormonal) model of functional asymmetry.

Hemispheric competences and regional callosal connectivities differ across individuals. Therefore, individual differences in behavioral laterality effects can reflect differences in hemispheric competence only if the lateralized tasks do not require interhemispheric exchanges (direct access) or they can reflect both hemispheric competence and callosal connectivity, if the tasks do require such transfer (callosal relay, interhemispheric interaction). Both types of tasks need to be sampled systematically before general conclusions about group differences in interhemispheric relations can be reached. That has not been done in the study of sex differences and is the purpose of chapter 3, by Zaidel et al. In particular, the authors ask whether there are consistent sex differences in hemispheric abilities for word recognition and in the connectivity of callosal channels that interconnect cortical word processing modules in the two hemispheres. In considering this question, Zaidel et al. first address the critical issue of what, for example, a right visual field (RVF) or right ear advantage implies. They consider several possible alternatives, and then review research and present data from tachistoscopic experiments and anatomical studies bearing on this question. Zaidel et al. relate these findings to the question of sex differences in terms of four different views that have been put forth:

    1.   Interhemispheric.   Females have greater callosal connectivity than males.

    2.   Intrahemispheric.   Females and males have different language organization in the two hemispheres. This has two aspects: First, females have greater language competence in the RH (right hemisphere) than do males, especially for lexical processes.   Second, within the LH (left hemisphere), females' language functions are more focally organized.

    3. Strategic. Females use verbal (LH) strategies to perform spatial tasks, thus showing reduced left visual field (LVF) advantages relative to males. More generally, females may exhibit a more dynamic deployment of available resources, resulting in more frequent shifts of dominance for direct access tasks.

    4. Mediated. Sex differences in laterality are mediated by some other trait variables. They consider various candidate variables including handedness, familial handedness, cognitive style, reasoning ability, age at puberty, and levels of circulating hormones.

Typically, two roles have been associated with the corpus callosum. One of these is the transfer of information from one hemisphere to the other. The other role is the inhibition of processing in the opposite hemisphere. In chapter 4, Chiarello explores another conceptualization of the corpus callosum, the *homotopic inhibition theory*. According to this theory, the corpus callosum functions to produce complementary, rather than duplicate, sets of information in the two hemispheres. The motivation for this approach is that it may account for some of the counterintuitive effects of semantic priming. For example, it may explain why in some semantic priming experiments, word meanings are activated in the RH, but not in the language-dominant LH. Based on the homotopic inhibition theory, certain meanings would be highly accessible in the RH because they are suppressed or inhibited in the language-dominant LH. Her results do not support the homotopic inhibition theory, but, rather, are consistent with the *callosal duplication* view: Whatever within-hemisphere meaning suppression occurs as a consequence of the first presentation, prime-target processing is shared with the opposite hemisphere. Thus, although there is some evidence that activation and suppression of ambiguous word meanings occurs in a complementary fashion across hemispheres, the homotopic inhibition theory of commissural function does not appear to be an explanation. Chiarello discusses the implications of these results for the hemispheric representation of word meanings and the functions of the corpus callosum.

    In chapter 5, Sergent examines the use of positron emission tomography (PET) of cerebral blood flow to explore the issue of functional cerebral asymmetry in face identification in the context of a more global and comprehensive framework. From this perspective, the functioning of the two hemispheres is viewed in terms of a highly connected and integrated system. Within this framework, two themes are evident. One is that the integrated functioning of the whole brain reflects coordinated activity and cannot be viewed simply as the sum of the activities of each hemisphere. The other, which embodies the approach of computational modeling, is that mental functioning should not be viewed as a unitary process, but, rather, as a number of subprocesses or suboperations organized in a specific fashion (e.g., serial, parallel, hierarchical, etc.). With these considerations in mind, Sergent contrasts the PET approach to face identification with other techniques and provides examples of how different approaches to the problem of hemispheric asymmetry constrain one another in the interpretation of findings that may, initially, appear contradictory.

In chapter 6, Boles presents parametric research on the *bilateral effect,* in which larger field asymmetries are found using bilateral displays compared to unilateral displays. This phenomenon generalizes across modalities, stimulus types, and dependent measures and, thus, represents one of the fundamental phenomena of lateralization research. A critical feature of the effect is that the display must have an aspect of bilaterality, even if only at the midline. Boles considers a number of possible explanantions for this phenomenon and concludes that the most likely cause of the effect is the activation of homologous areas of the two hemispheres by stimuli requiring similar processing, which disrupts communication between the hemispheres through a process of hemispheric interaction. He suggests that the locus of the interaction appears to be anterior to the occipital areas, perhaps in the parietal and temporal regions. The parametric data presented in this chapter indicate that the bilateral effect may be the second largest influence on field asymmetry, after that of stimulus type. It is also of empirical interest that bilateral displays produce visual field differences more reliably than do unilateral displays.

In chapter 7, Christman explores the functioning of the two hemispheres using foveal presentations, as opposed to lateralized stimuli, with both right- and left-handed subjects. His working hypothesis is that sinistrality is associated with both less lateralization and a thicker corpus callosum, suggesting that there should be greater interhemispheric interaction in left-handers in the coordination between RH and LH processes. Thus, one would expect relative advantages for situations that require coordination of subcomponents of a task in which some processes are localized in the RH and others in the LH. However, one would expect processing disadvantages in dual-task situations in which LH and RH processes need to be carried out in parallel, without interaction or interference. Additionally, subjects exhibiting lesser degrees of lateralization should be relatively superior at complex tasks requiring integration of LH and RH processes; conversely, subjects exhibiting greater degrees of lateralization should be relatively better in dual-task situations, which require independent execution of LH and RH processes. These hypotheses were investigated in two pilot studies. The first examined handedness among musicians as a function of the instruments they play. The goal of the study was to determine if the relative roles of the left and right hands in playing a musical instrument that requires bimanual activity were related to the direction and/or degree of handedness. For example, keyboard instruments require that the activities of the two hands be independent, whereas, for woodwinds and strings, the activities of the two hands need to be coordinated. A second study provided evidence for greater interhemispheric integration in those with personal or familial sinistrality using a task that required same-different judgments. In two of the tasks subjects decided whether a verbal component of a fovally presented stimulus was the same as or different from the spatial component. For example, subjects saw a line drawing of a face with the word *happy* or *sad* written across it, and judged whether the facial expression matched the word. Another experiment involved a Stroop test, in which the subjects had to indicate whether the color name matched the actual color of the stimulus. A related task involved the judgment of whether a local component of a stimulus matched a global component. A final task was designed to determine whether or not the left and right halves of complex geometric objects were mirror images of each other (i.e., symmetrical). Because verbal, local, and right-hemispace judgments are typically performed better by the LH, whereas spatial, global, and left-hemispace judgments are performed better by the RH, these tasks presumably require interhemispheric integration. Therefore, subjects with personal or familial sinistrality were hypotheized to be better at performing them. The verbal-spatial and local-global tasks supported the hypothesis: Reaction times for both left-handers and right-handers with familial sinistrality were faster than for right-handers for the local-global, Stroop, and face tasks. The symmmetry task yielded no differences between subject groups. Christman discusses the implications of these results for understanding hemispheric interaction and the role of individual differences in the cognitive psychology literature.

In chapter 8, Levine considers the question of whether individual differences in asymmetry scores on laterality tests are related to individual differences in cognitive functioning. Previous research has failed to uncover a consistent relationship between measures of hemispheric specialization and cognitive functioning in normal subjects. In contrast, the studies reported by Levine appear to yield more positive results and support the hypothesis that perceptual asymmetry on a standard laterality task is a joint function of hemispheric specialization and characteristic arousal asymmetry. Moreover, this research also indicates that hemispheric specialization is relatively stable, both across dextrals as a group and within individual subjects. In contrast, characteristic arousal asymmetry is hypothesized to be highly variable across subjects, but highly stable within individual subjects. The research reported by Levine indicates that individual differences in characteristic arousal asymmetry are related to individual differences in cognitive functioning. Levine also discusses why the relationship between hemispheric involvement and performance level in normals may have been elusive in past studies.

Banich (chapter 9) explores mechanisms of interhemispheric interaction and unified processing. Her work indicates that interhemispheric interaction cannot be characterized simply as a shuttling mechanism, in which information is passively transported between the hemispheres. Rather, interhemispheric processing provides an advantage and is most clearly observable when all the information required for performance of a task is available simultaneously to both hemispheres. Banich suggests that the collaboration between hemispheres aids performance when tasks are computationally complex and the processing load is high and discusses methodological problems in testing this hypothesis. In addition, Banich indicates that predictions of interhemispheric interaction may not follow directly from knowledge of the functioning of each hemisphere in isolation.

Neuropsychological investigations of functional hemispheric differences in patients have long shown that LH damage disrupts performance on the "details" of a visual pattern, whereas RH damage disrupts performance on the "configuration." Cerebral laterality studies with normals using hierarchical stimuli in which a global letter is constructed from local letters, have revealed faster reaction times (RTs) for local information presented in the RVF, and faster RTs in the LVF for global information. In addition to local and global precedence, hemispheric asymmetries are found in global interference. That is, RT to identify a local letter is interfered with if the global letter differs from the local letter. In chapter 10, Robertson discusses these findings and their application to a broad range of issues that cross the disciplinary boundaries of neuropsychology, cognitive psychology, cognitive science, and cognitive neuroscience. As she indicates in her chapter, the relevance of the results to the different areas can be represented best by a series of questions: Do the hemispheres differentially compute gestalts and parts or wholes and details? What anatomical regions in the right and left hemispheres produce a global-local hemisphere asymmetry (a long-standing question in neuropsychology)? Is there evidence for parallel processing within processing modules that is biased toward global or local levels as parallel distributed processing models in cognitive science would predict? If so, what computations occur within each module and what cognitive and neural systems support them (a question most pertinent to cognitive neuroscience)? The discussion of research presented by Robertson is organized into sections structured around each of these issues.

In chapter 11, Kitterle, Christman, and Conesa present experiments designed to determine the nature of spatial-frequency information transferred between the cerebral hemispheres. In one series of experiments, we show that a low-spatial-frequency adapting grating can increase RT for detection of a low-contrast grating of similar spatial frequency presented in the contralateral visual field. However, adaptation is not found when the adapting and test gratings are of high spatial frequency. Moreover, other studies have shown that adaptation does not occur when the adapting and test gratings are spatially adjacent and are both presented in the same visual field, regardless of spatial frequency. The fact that it occurs when the adapting and test gratings straddle the vertical midline supports the conclusion that adaptation is mediated through interhemispheric communication. Thus, it appears that low spatial frequencies are transferred more readily than high spatial frequencies. A second experiment utilized a redundant signals paradigm and compared the cumulative frequency distribution (CDF) of RT to bilateral targets with the CDF to unilateral presentations to the LVF or RVF. These results indicate that low-spatial-frequency information from each visual field is summed to conjointly determine RT. This is not found for high-spatial-frequency stimuli. The finding that activation from low-spatial-frequency channels in each visual field can combine on bilateral trials, and thus coactivate a response, provides additional evidence for selective hemispheric transfer of low-spatial-frequency information.

In chapter 12, Hellige presents research that addresses the question of which hemisphere dominates when both have equal access to the incoming sitmulus information. One possible mechanism is *metacontrol,* which refers to the neural mechanisms that determine which hemisphere will attempt to control cognitive operations. His work indicates that the hemisphere that dominates is not necessarily the one with the greater ability, that there is a clear dissociation between hemispheric ability and hemispheric assertion of control. Hellige reviews the nature and reliability of this dissociation. He describes studies using rotated consonant-vowel-consonant stimuli that provide further insight into this dissociation and also indicate reliable individual differences in which hemisphere's mode of processing is utilized when both hemispheres are given an equal chance to process the stimuli. Finally, Hellige concludes with a discussion of the conditions under which metacontrol mechanisms might serve to coordinate the different processing biases of the two hemispheres in the intact brain. Thus, whether separate processing of the hemispheres must converge on a common set of neural structures that underlie the preparation and organization of a motor response might or might not favor the application of control mechanisms. A review of the literature indicates that competition between the hemispheres at the response production level can lead to blocking of processing in one hemisphere. Alternatively, blocking of one hemisphere's preferred mode of processing may occur because both hemispheres must converge on the same set of neural structures that control the distribution of attention across space.

I hope that the work presented in this book and our earlier one contributes to continued interest in understanding the role of the cerebral hemispheres and in motivating new research directions as we celebrate The Decade of the Brain.

REFERENCES

Hellige, J. B. (1993). *Hemispheric asymmetry: What's right and what's left.* Cambridge: Harvard University Press.

Hellige, J.B. (1990). Hemispheric asymmetry. *Annual Review of Psychology, 41,* 55-80.

Kitterle, F.L. (1991). *Cerebral laterality: Theory and research.* Hillsdale, NJ: Lawrence Erlbaum Associates.

ACKNOWLEDGMENTS

I would like to express my appreciation to the many individuals whose involvement facilitated the preparation of this book. I am especially grateful to the contributing authors for their patience, and to Lynn Robertson, Steve Christman, and Joe Hellige for their comments on selected chapters. This book would not have been possible without the generous support of the State of Ohio Academic Challenge Grant to the Department of Psychology and the continued encouragement of the administration at the University of Toledo.

The continued support and encouragement of my wife, Janet, helped to make the conference and the resulting book a successful venture.

Frederick L. Kitterle

1 The Corpus Callosum and Hemispheric Communication: An historical survey of theory and research

Lauren Julius Harris
Michigan State University

I am glad to have been invited to contribute to this collection of papers on hemispheric communication: mechanisms and models. I am especially pleased that the editors have thought it appropriate to begin with a consideration of historical issues, themes, and questions. Too often, the historical perspective is treated as a luxury to be dispensed with in favor of more reports of new data.

WHICH TYPE OF HEMISPHERIC COMMUNICATION SHOULD BE EMPHASIZED?

Any historical account of theory and research on hemispheric communication poses several problems and challenges. The first is to decide which type of communication to emphasize: between hemispheres or within? Neuropsychologists know that an understanding of within-hemisphere communication (between, say, the temporal and frontal or parietal and occipital association areas) is critical to understanding higher-order cognitive functions, including memory, attention, language, visuospatial perception, and praxis. Nevertheless, when we say "hemispheric communication," we invariably think of communication *between* hemispheres, and that will be the focus here. It is the understandable, if not the only or even necessarily the better, choice for two reasons. First, at an accelerating pace since the 1950s, neuropsychologists have been providing ever more detailed accounts of what each cerebral hemisphere contributes to higher-order functions. Indeed, these accounts have brought theory and research on lateral specialization to the attention of a broader array of scientists, as well as to the general public, than have most other scientific topics over this same period. But, having made so much progress in describing hemispheric differences, we have increasingly come to appreciate that this takes us only part of the way toward understanding the neuropsychological bases of higher cognitive functions, and, indeed, that for certain topics — for example, attention, cognitive development, and individual differences in motor and cognitive skill — the focus on interhemispheric *communication* may be paramount. Some neuropsychologists and some philosophers also see research on interhemispheric communication as raising thorny philosophical questions about consciousness and personhood, such as "Do two minds exist in one head following split-brain surgery?" "Do the mental properties of the normal brain exist in duplicate, so that disconnecting the cerebral hemispheres creates two separate consciousnesses?" (e.g., Churchland, 1986;

Dennett, 1991; Gazzaniga, 1970; Puccetti, 1981; Sperry, 1969, 1983). More and more, then, we are asking how the hemispheres actually communicate. The word *communicate*, from the Latin *communicatus*, means "to impart, share,"literally 'to make common." How, then, do the hemispheres impart, share, and make common the information they take in about the external world and then process in their respective ways? How do they coordinate their work to achieve normal cognition and action? Neuropsychologists pursuing these questions use a variety of invasive and non-invasive techniques on a variety of subject populations. These include normal persons, individuals with callosal agenesis, neurological patients with callosal lesions (infarcts and tumors), and epileptic patients who have undergone partial or complete callosotomies.

In addition to what we are convinced it will add to our understanding of psychological phenomena, a second reason for emphasizing interhemispheric communication is that the commissures, more than the association fiber tracts, constitute an anatomically clearly defined system on which we can focus our attention and frame questions about mechanism. Understandably, contemporary theory and research regarding interhemispheric communication have concentrated most on the forebrain commissures, the corpus callosum in particular by virtue of its exclusive neocortical origins and its massive size. Less attention has been paid to the other forebrain commissures (anterior and hippocampal commissures) and less still to subcortical commissures such as the posterior commissure, the habenular commissure, or the commissures of the superior and inferior colliculi.

A Long and Winding Road

A more difficult challenge in doing an historical analysis is one common to historical treatments of any scientific topic. It is that, in recounting the ideas, discoveries, and events leading up to our own time, we must take pains not to make the story sound more "progressive" than it really is. Science is progressive, but hardly unremittingly so, and the real story of any scientific enterprise, as every working scientist knows, will recount many more errors, blind alleys, and failures than successes. Often, too, we find some work elevated and other work neglected for reasons related as much to circumstance as to merit. The story of hemispheric communication is no exception.

How to Tell the Story?

The last challenge is logistical: There are a vast number of elements, or strands, in the story, some of them separate, others intertwined, some appearing in the same historical periods, others not. So many time lines makes it hard to tell the story straightforwardly, even if we followed a strict chronology. My strategy is to present the different strands more or less individually, meaning that there will be multiple chronologies, and to point out some of the linking events along the way. The organization is as follows: First, I note the longstanding interest in the question of hemispheric communication and integration; next, I provide a review of the anatomical study of the corpus callosum (here, in particular, we see coincidently developing ideas about function); then, I review experimental and clinical studies of the corpus callosum in animals and humans. This is followed by an account of theories linking mental illness to the supposed breaking down of communication between the hemispheres. I then describe early research on individual differences in the size of the corpus callosum and what these differences were said to reveal about mental functioning; finally, I summarize the "negative" studies of commissurotomy patients in the 1930s and 1940s and the "positive" reports of the decades that followed.

Hemispheric Communication: A Venerable Question in the Science of Mind

I have suggested that the question of hemispheric communication, or integration, looms large today because, having learned much about hemispheric differences, we now better appreciate the need to understand how the hemispheres work together in the service of normal cognition. But questions about communication and integration predate the discovery of lateral specialization. They even predate the two fundamental steps establishing, first, that the brain and not the heart is the source of mind, and second, that the critical brain structure is the soft tissue rather than the fluid-filled ventricles as the physician Galen of Pergamon had taught. If our story has a true starting point, it would be in the recognition that, although our sensory organs come in pairs — two eyes, two ears, two nostrils, two hands — our perceptions of the world are singular. The further recognition that the doubling of sensory organs is repeated in the bipartite structure of the brain itself, and that the processing of the sensory information occurs there, changed the perceptual question into a neuropsychological question.

Among the philosophers and scientists who grappled with this question, two are especially noteworthy. In 1649, in his *The Passions of the Soul*, René Descartes puzzled over the fact that, although "all the organs of our external senses" are double, so that they register spatially separate images of the same scene or event, "we have only one simple thought about a given object at any one time ." (Descartes, 1649/1988, p. 230). Descartes' explanation was that the immaterial rational mind was itself unified. By "rational mind," Descartes meant the soul, a gift of God. Descartes therefore looked for a structure in the brain that could unite these disparate images, a place where the single immaterial mind, or soul, and the double images of the physical body could come together. For Descartes, the best candidate was a "certain very small gland" ("la petite glande") in the "innermost" part of the brain: the epiphysis cerebri, or pineal gland. Descartes made this choice for several reasons, two in particular. First, in contrast to the double brain itself, the pineal was a unitary, midline structure, the only such structure that Descartes could find in the brain (Descartes, letter to Father Mersenne, April 21, 1641; in Adam & Tannery, 1896-1910, Vol. 3, pp. 119-123; cited in Brazier, 1984, p. 23). Second, the pineal was suspended between the ventricles, or "cells" of the brain, which, following Galen's doctrine, held the animal spirits ("suspendue entre les cavitez qui contienent ces esprits . . . "). The animal spirits, in turn, were thought to transmit messages to and from the nerves, which originated in the walls of the ventricles. The pineal, therefore, appeared to be the only structure that could receive and also unify and control sensory impressions. As Brazier (1984, pp. 23-24) has expressed it, Descartes likened the pineal to a control tower. Moving on its base, it directs the flow of spirits to the appropriate pores in the walls of the ventricles, pores that it then opens to allow the spirits to flow out and down the nerves. From the same set of considerations, Descartes (1664/1972) also identified the pineal gland as the seat of imagination and, literally, 'common sense'.[1]

In 1860, the German psychophysicist Gustav Fechner became engaged in fundamentally the same issue. In *Elemente der Psychophysik*, Fechner observed that despite a "physical multiplicity" of sensory input, the psychological result was unity of consciousness (Vol. 2, p. 526). Unlike Descartes, Fechner also believed that each neural structure (the spinal cord, the basal ganglia, the cerebral hemispheres) might have its own stream of consciousness. Unity of consciousness, therefore, must depend on the spatial continuity of the nervous tissue itself at every level of the neuroaxis. Surmising that, for the cerebral hemispheres, the most relevant nervous tissue was the corpus callosum, Fechner predicted that if the cerebrum were divided by cutting through the corpus callosum, each half brain would have a separate consciousness. Fechner even supposed that if the brains of two men were joined by a bridge of nervous matter, in the same way that the hemispheres of one man are joined by the corpus callosum, the two men would have a single consciousness (and see Footnote 10, further on).

ANATOMY

In designating the pineal gland as the means for uniting the disparate images of the external senses, Descartes chose a gray matter structure. Today, we understand (as Fechner already did in 1860) that integration is the responsibility of the fiber tracts that comprise the cerebral white matter. In recounting early anatomical studies of the corpus callosum, I show that this history is part of the larger story of the study of cerebral white matter and the localization of function.

The players in this part of the story are great in number, so only the most prominent are mentioned.[2]

---

[1] It is routinely suggested that Descartes also chose the pineal as the seat of the human soul because he believed it to be a uniquely human structure. In other words, it has been suggested that Descartes saw animals as having no need to integrate mind and body because animals were mere automata: marvelous but mindless (and soulless) organic machines. In fact, Descartes knew that animals had a pineal gland; indeed, his description of the structure was based on his own dissection of a sheep brain in an Amsterdam slaughterhouse (see Brazier, 1984, p. 21). As far as its "controller" function was concerned, then, Descartes attributed the same role to the pineal in both animals and man (see Brazier, 1984, p. 24). He, therefore, chose the pineal as the seat of the human soul because he assumed that only the pineal, by virtue of its physical singularity and proximity to the ventricles, could support this additional and uniquely human attribute above and beyond its species-wide function.

[2] Many of the earliest scholarly and scientific works on this topic have been collected and also translated, either in whole or in part. A major collection can be found in Edwin Clarke and C. D. O'Malley's work, *The Human Brain and Spinal Cord* (1968), a compilation of translations and

Classical Period

Galen. In the ancient world, Aristotle, Eristratus, Hippocrates, and other Greek savants provided descriptions of the brains of animals and man and commonly referred to the brain's *doubleness*, or bipartite design. The first reference to the corpus callosum, however, evidently had to await the work of Galen, who, though born in Pergamon (now Turkey), lived and worked chiefly in Rome as physician to Emperor Marcus Aurelius. In the year 177 C. E., Galen offered this description:

Examine the region exposed [the corpus callosum][3]. It is like a callus, so that there appears to be a natural hollow there which receives from the overlying and surrounding tissue incompletely concocted nutriment (Singer, 1956, p. 231).

Although Galen seems to be referring here to the corpus callosum as we define it today, his "corpus callosum" was a more extensive structure than our "corpus callosum." As Clarke and O'Malley (1968, p. 577) have noted, the term could include not only the midline connections of the white matter (i.e., the interhemispheric commissure) but also the white matter in the cerebral hemispheres that it connects — in other words, the whole of the medullary center (centrum semioval). This more extended usage persisted into the Renaissance period and even through the 18th century. Galen's specimen most likely was an ox brain, not a human brain ("Ox brains, ready prepared and stripped of most of the cranial parts, are generally on sale in the large cities"; Galen, Book IX, Chapter 1, # 709; quoted in Singer, 1956, p. 226). Even for his general anatomy, Galen relied predominantly on animals, now, however, monkeys and great apes. As Singer (1956) pointed out, the text generally describes "the soft parts of the ape imposed on the skeleton of man" (p. XIX).[4] Finally, Galen's description referred to location and physical appearance but said nothing about function.

---

annotations of excerpts from neuroanatomical writings from the classical, Renaissance, and modern periods (through the late 19th century). My account of the early anatomical study of the corpus callosum, along with direct quotations from these works, draws extensively from this collection. For the work of Galen and Vesalius and their contemporaries, I also have drawn on Charles Singer's translations and commentaries (1952, 1956). I also have been aided by Mary A. B. Brazier's *A History of Neurophysiology in the 17th and 18th centuries* (1984), and by Max Neuburger's *The Historical Development of Experimental Brain and Spinal Cord Physiology Before Flourens* (1897/1981), which was written in German and translated into English and annotated by Edwin Clarke. References to Neuburger are to Clarke's translation of the original text; references to Clarke are to his annotations.

[3] Except where noted otherwise, all inserts in brackets are those provided by the translator/annotator from whose work the passage has been quoted.
[4] Singer (1956) added that Galen himself "had perhaps some slight direct knowledge of human anatomy, certainly of the bones. He also noted that Galen, evidently, made no drawings of the brain. According to Singer, neither Galen nor any of the ancients appreciated the value of

The Renaissance

Vesalius.   Although rudimentary and making no reference to function, Galen's description remained virtually the last word on the subject for more than a millenium. Finally, with the Renaissance came a rebirth of the scientific study of anatomy and the brain, along with what appears to have been the first extensive description of the corpus callosum in its modern sense but also the first description in man. Its author was the anatomist Andreas Vesalius, who also was the first to point out that because Galen had dissected only animals, human anatomy had to begin anew (Clarke; in Neuburger, 1897/1981, p. 366). Here is part of Vesalius' description from his great work *De humani corporis fabrica* (1543):

> If you look at the right and left brain, the lower part of the middle of the base of the brain, the very highest region of the brain, and also if you compare the front and rear, the corpus callosum is observed to be in the middle of the brain; for the part of the corpus callosum that is farthest to the rear is a little nearer to the front of the brain than the forward part is to the rear. It comes into view of those dissecting when they manually separate the right side of the brain slightly from the left, for with the brain so separated, that which unites its parts there, the corpus callosum, is observed gleaming white, long, and arched . . . (Vesalius, 1543, in Clarke & O'Malley, 1968, pp. 578-579).

Vesalius' description marked a clear advance over Galen's. Unlike Galen, Vesalius also explained what the corpus callosum did:

> . . . it relates the right side of the cerebrum to the left; then it produces and supports the septum of the right and left ventricles: finally, through that septum it supports and props up the body formed like a tortoise [fornix] so that it may not collapse and, to the great detriment of all the functions of the cerebrum, crush the cavity common to the two [lateral] ventricles of the cerebrum (Vesalius, 1543; in Clarke & O'Malley, 1968, p. 579).

From this description, Clarke and O'Malley (1968, p. 578) concluded that, for Vesalius, the corpus callosum served a purely mechanical role: it connected the two halves of the brain, "preserved the patency of the ventricular cavities and

---

graphic methods in anatomy: "He never indicates that he used figures in our sense of the word and he very seldom employed even diagrams" (p. xxii). Galen believed, instead, that the three-dimensional impression created by directly viewing and handling the dissected parts was the only way to appreciate their form and relationships. Clarke and Dewhurst (1972, p. 5) called this a "laudable attitude by modern standards."

supported the fornix."[5] Of course, preserving the patency of the ventricles was important because, for Vesalius as for Descartes and their contemporaries and immediate successors, the ventricles, not the soft tissue, were the brain's true functional units.

Malpighi.   Anatomists in the Late Renaissance made many further contributions to the developing picture. Among them was the Italian biologist Marcello Malpighi.   Like Galen, Malpighi used the term *corpus callosum* synonymously with *medulla cerebri*, meaning the cerebral white matter. Noting that the white matter ("that rough substance") also appeared to be more solid than the cortex and to be surrounded by veins and arteries, Malpighi observed that "it seems to be for filling the intervening space." But Malpighi rejected this "supposition" after demonstrating, with a crude microscope, that the cerebral white matter was composed of "fibers," which he could trace from the brainstem to the cortex, where they were embedded "like the roots of a plant."[6] (Malpighi, 1664/1665; all quotations from Clarke & O'Malley, 1968, p. 580).

Willis.   After Vesalius, the most important anatomist was the English physician Thomas Willis, coiner of the term *neurology* an eponym for several anatomical structures, most famously the *Circle of Willis*. Willis' greatest work was *Cerebri Anatome*, first published in Latin in 1664 and translated into English in 1681 by Samuel Pordage under the title, *Anatomy of the Brain and Nerves*. In this work, Willis described the brain as being composed of "double hemisphere" and "double substance," with the hemispheres joined together in several places "either by a contiguity, or by processes setforth," so that "every impression coming this or that way, becomes still one and the same." Willis here referred to the corpus callosum along with the corpus striatum and optic decussation. His description of the corpus callosum, or "callous body," suggests that he saw it as having a

---

[5] In saying that for Vesalius the corpus callosum served a purely mechanical role, Clarke and O'Malley (1968) evidently saw the first part of Vesalius' three-part account of function ("it relates the right side of the cerebrum to the left") to mean that if the corpus callosum is to hold up the ventricles, it must connect ("relate") the left side of the cerebrum to the right. Clarke and O'Malley presumably attached no further significance to the word *relates* in Vesalius' description.

[6] These were not necessarily "fibers" in the modern sense. As Clarke and O'Malley (1968, pp. 576-577) noted, the nerve fiber was not identified with certainty until 1781 with the work of Felice Fontana (1781; see Clarke & O'Malley, pp. 36-38), although the terms *nerve fiber*, *filament*, and *thread* had been in use for centuries. These terms referred to bundles of primary fibers or to the theoretical fiber in the same way that reference was made, in antiquity, to the postulated but unidentified *atom*. As another example, Descartes had suggested the presence of tubes ("tuyeaux") in the brain, passing from the pineal body to certain of its parts. These tubes, Clarke and O'Malley went on to say, were almost certainly speculative and "satisfied a demand that most seventeenth century investigators felt for structures to conduct the still accepted animal spirits of antiquity. It is often impossible for us to know what early authors had in mind when using the word *fibre*, but it is essential to recognize that their concept of it was certainly not equivalent to ours" (p. 577).

communicative role: "[Within the brain substance] . . . may be observed many white parallel lines, which cut the partition of the brain in right angles, as if they were certain tracts or footsteps, in which the animal Spirits, travel from one hemisphere of the brain to the other, and return back again" (Willis, 1664/1965, p. 61).

In referring to the corpus callosum, Willis, like Galen and Malpighi, designated all of the cerebral white matter, even while others had already begun to use the term in the more limited, modern, sense. In so doing, Willis probably would have won the approbation of his contemporary, the Danish anatomist Nicolaus Steno. In a section of his *Lecture on the Anatomy of the Brain* entitled "Meaningless and worthless terminology," Steno wrote that "The corpus callosum, according to common usage, means the white substance of the brain that is seen when the two lateral parts are separated," and that he found "little obvious reason for giving a specific name to part of this substance" inasmuch as "this part is completely similar to the remainder of the brain's white substance" (Steno, 1669/1965, p. 138).

Willis' statement also shows that he clung to Galen's ventricular doctrine, as modified by Descartes. In his account of localization of function, however, he broke with Descartes and with convention. Rather than follow the ventricular, or cell, doctrine, as it had come to be known, Willis followed Descartes' contemporary, Pierre Gassendi (1858) in localizing sensory and cognitive functions in the brain substance itself (see Meyer & Hierons, 1965, a, b). To the corpus striatum, he assigned the "sensus communis" (common sense); to the cerebral cortex, "memorativa" (memory); and to the corpus callosum, "imaginativa" (imagination; see Clarke & O'Malley, 1968, pp. 332-333; and Willis, 1664/1965). Willis' "dynamic" analysis changed accordingly, so that, in contrast to the cell doctrine, which conceived of cognitive processes (in the form of animal spirits) as undergoing a variety of transformations while moving through the system of ventricles, Willis envisioned the animal spirits as moving between the different parts of the brain substance itself.

Like Descartes (1649/1988), Willis was searching for the place where the disparate images and processes of mind could be brought together and made whole. Descartes' pineal gland theory had come to grief following criticism from Nicolaus Steno, among others (see Steno, 1669/1965, pp. 129-133).[7] Willis' description of callosal structure and function suggests that, for Willis, the corpus callosum was the better choice for this integrative role. Steno was no more impressed with this choice than he had been with Descartes':

---

[7] As Brazier (1984, p. 50) pointed out, Steno's criticism was based partly on the position of the pineal gland as shown in illustrations in the various editions of Descartes' works. The illustrators, evidently through their own misconceptions of Descartes' views, were led to depict the pineal gland as standing on the floor of the ventricles rather than suspended between them as Descartes had described them (see Brazier, p. 21).

What assurance can [Willis] have . . . that would be credible to us, that these three operations exist in the three bodies to which he assigns them? Who can say whether the nerve-fibers begin in the corpus striatum or pass rather through the corpus callosum as far as the cortex or grey substance? Indeed, the corpus callosum is so unknown to us that anyone with the least inclination can say what he pleases about it (Steno, 1669/1965, p. 127).

Lancisi. Steno's criticism was not entirely unfair and, indeed, was echoed by a 20th-century historian who said that Willis was "giving free rein to his fancy" (Garrison, 1929; quoted in Meyer & Hierons, 1965a, p. 7). Insofar as the corpus callosum was concerned, Steno's criticism did not deter the physician Giovanni Maria Lancisi from proposing a similar functional analysis:

It is quite clear that the part formed by the weaving together of innumerable nerves is both unique and situated in the middle [of the brain]; and so it can be said it is like a common marketplace of the senses, in which the external impressions of the nerves meet (Lancisi, 1712; quoted in Neuburger, 1897/1981, p. 50).

Lancisi went on to say, however, that "we must not think of it as merely a storehouse for receiving the movements of structures: we must locate in it the seat of the soul, which imagines, deliberates, and judges" (Lancisi, 1712; quoted in Neuburger, 1897/1981, p. 50).[8]

Transition to the Modern Era

Vicq d'Azyr. Willis' abandonment of the ventricular, or cell, doctrine marked a crucial step in the development of theories of functional localization. His proposal that the corpus callosum allowed for animal spirits to "travel from one hemisphere of the brain to the other, and return back again" (Willis, 1664/1965, p. 61) also seems to anticipate, in some sense, the modern concept of interhemispheric communication. In the late 18th century, the French anatomist Félix Vicq d'Azyr (1784) came even closer to the modern view. Vicq d'Azyr was perhaps among the first to use the term *communication* in reference to the commissures: "It seems to me that the commissures are intended to establish sympathetic communications between the different parts of the brain, just as the nerves do between the different organs and the brain itself . . ." (quoted in Clarke & O'Malley, 1968, p. 592). Unlike Willis, he distinguished between two distinct classes of connecting fibers, both of which he called *commissures*:

---

[8] Lancisi continued to envision a role for the pineal gland — to strengthen the movement of the animal spirits: "what is developed and perfected in the corpus callosum and directed and prescribed by the whim and judgment of the soul for the movements of the members and organs receives on its way a momentum of force and a new energy of direction, when and where it is necessary" (Lancisi, 1712, quoted in Neuburger, 1897/1981, p. 50).

[T]he first run from one hemisphere to the other, the second between different regions of the same hemisphere; . . . I include in the first class the corpus callosum, . . . the quadrigeminal bodies [i.e., the collicular commissures], the anterior and posterior commissures . . . [Without them] the brain would be completely divided into two absolutely independent parts, the one from the other (Vicq d'Azyr, 1784, pp. 535-536; quoted in Clarke & O'Malley, 1968, p. 592).

Reil.   In the early 19th century, a further contribution came from the German anatomist Johann Christian Reil (1809).   Reil was the first anatomist to use preservatives and hardening agents consistently (alcohol, potash, and ammonia), and to write about their use.   This was an important technical advance because it allowed anatomists to dissect firm organs rather than jelly-like specimens that decomposed rapidly.   It also enabled Reil to include more anatomical detail in his description of the corpus callosum (Clarke & O'Malley, 1968, pp. 593-594).

Gall.   Finally, an important advance was made by Vicq d'Azyr's and Reil's contemporaries, the Austrian physician Franz Josef Gall and his associate Johann Caspar Spurzheim (1810-1819).   Gall's neuroanatomical work is often overlooked or underestimated because of the notoriety attending his (subsequent) organological theory of mind.   His neuroanatomical work, however, included a clear statement on the integrative role of the corpus callosum as well as (furthering the work begun by Vicq d'Azyr, Reil, and other anatomists) a clear distinction between what later came to be called *projection fibers* and *association fibers.*   Gall also had special interests in Vicq d'Azyr's two classes of *commissures*, the interhemispheric, or "transverse layers of fibers," and the intrahemispheric (i.e., association) fibers.   In his organological theory, Gall had postulated that each cerebral hemisphere contained 27 cortical organs, each one the site of a distinct psychological faculty, and that each organ in one hemisphere was matched by a "congenerous" organ in the other.   Recognizing that the congenerous pairs had to act coordinately for mental activity to be coordinated, Gall saw that there had to be physical connections between them.   This led him to propose the existence of two systems of fibers, one diverging ("divergent" or "sortant"), the other converging ("convergent" or "retrant").   As Clarke and O'Malley (1968, p. 599) pointed out, the divergent system corresponds to our afferent and efferent projection fibers, which run to and from the cortex in a radiating mass, out from and toward the brainstem.   The convergent system corresponds to our association fibers, which are entirely intracerebral.   Gall included the corpus callosum with the convergent, or association, type:

We have demonstrated . . . that the congenerous systems of the two sides [of the brain] are joined together and placed in reciprocal action by transverse layers of fibers [commissures].   We call this organization *apparatus of connection or of junction*, though we do not doubt that they contribute to the formation of the whole, like the *mechanisms of formation*.

All parts of the cerebrum are connected with analogous parts of the other hemisphere by a similar mechanism and are thus united for mutually influencing and the attainment of a common end. (Gall & Spurzheim, 1810-1819; quoted in Clarke & O'Malley, 1968, p. 600)

Similar views are reflected in the work of other anatomists of the day. For example, John Bell and Charles Bell (1827) wrote: "Betwixt the lateral parts there is a strict resemblance in form and substance: each principal part is united by transverse tracts of medullary matter; and there is every provision for their acting with perfect sympathy" (p. 26).

The Modern Era

Meynert. The work of Vicq d'Azyr, Reil, Gall, and others was groundbreaking, but in the first half of the 19th century, much confusion and vagueness remained about the intracerebral white matter. Further progress had to await the development, beginning in the 1830s, of better microscopes and new methods of preparing and staining brain tissue (Clarke & O'Malley, 1968, p. 604). This set the stage for the work of Theodor Meynert, Professor of Neurology and Psychiatry at the University of Vienna. Meynert (1872) extended Gall's relatively crude division of the fiber systems and, for the first time, used the terms *association* and *projection* in their modern sense. He also clearly distinguished the intrahemispheric association pathways from the interhemispheric commissural systems. Finally, Meynert contested the view of the French psychiatrist Achille Foville (1844) that the corpus callosum consisted of decussating fasciculi of the projection system entering into the ganglia. Meynert (1872) instead cited new microscopic studies of the brains of small mammals as demonstrating "the truth of the statement made by Arnold, that the system of the corpus callosum consists exclusively of commissural fibers between corresponding and identical regions of the opposite sides of the cortex, . . ." (p. 405). Meynert was referring to the German anatomist Friedrich Arnold, presumably to his *Tabulae anatomicae* (1838-1840).

Over the next decade, Meynert's (and Arnold's) analysis found wide acceptance. We see this reflected in a statement by D. J. Hamilton, Professor of Pathological Anatomy in the University of Aberdeen:

The almost universal idea at the present day is that the corpus callosum is a commissure — that it is composed of fibres which run between the two hemispheres, thus uniting their cortical centres, and so bringing corresponding areas on the two sides into functional harmony. It is held that the fibres, which concentrate in the corpus callosum from the cortex of one side, spread out in a fan-shaped manner in the opposite centrum ovale, and ultimately become attached to parts of the cortex corresponding in situation to those from which they have arisen (Hamilton, 1885, pp. 385-386).

Flechsig. Another major figure in the anatomical part of the story is Paul Emil Flechsig, the histologist and professor of psychiatry in Leipzig. Flechsig's contribution was twofold. By the close of the 19th century, localization theory had progressed to the point where primary sensory cortex was distinguished from association cortex. Flechsig's first contribution was his proposal of a "general law" according to which callosal projections link the latter but not the former (Flechsig, 1901).[9] His second was his research on myelogenesis. After it was established that medullated fiber tracts carry nerve impulses more quickly and efficiently than non-medullated tracts, Flechsig significantly advanced functional analysis by showing that nerve fibers in different parts of the developing nervous system become myelinated at different stages of development (Nielsen, 1963).

Giovanni Mingazzini, Ramón y Cajal, and Others. The 1890s and the early decades of the 20th century saw further, more sophisticated anatomical and physiological studies of the corpus callosum, assisted by new cell staining techniques in combination with new retrograde cell degeneration methods (e.g., Beevor, 1891; Dejerine, 1895; Forel, 1907; Kölliker, 1896; Langelaan, 1908; Lévy-Valensi, 1910; Ramón y Cajal, 1909-1911). Among the new contributions was a monograph on the corpus callosum by the Italian neuropathologist Giovanni Mingazzini (1922). The monograph provided a great fund of data and bibliography, making it "the standard work on the subject" (Ferraro, 1970, p. 348). The new research provided an improved understanding of the development of the corpus callosum and of the origin and termination of its fibers, although even in this new era, many questions remained uncertain: whether the commissures connect only homotopical or also heterotopical regions; from which cells and in which cortical lamina its fibers arise, to which cells and in which lamina they go; whether or not all brain convolutions, except those of the olfactory region, are connected (see Van Valkenburg, 1913).

Among the new generation of researchers, at least a few saw the corpus callosum's role much as Fechner (1860) had. One was the great Spanish histologist Santiago Ramón y Cajal, who wrote, "The bilateral disposition of the perceptual centers, and the unilaterality of memory, justifies in our opinion the corpus callosum . . ." (Ramón y Cajal, 1909-1911/1960, p. 266). Mingazzini (1922), likewise, regarded the corpus callosum as essential to the integrating, or harmonizing, of thoughts and ideas.

---

[9] Flechsig's principle must be qualified with respect to the midline of space. As Kinsbourne (1974, pp. 251 ff.) has pointed out, although the cortical somatosensory representations of hands and feet and of the lateral extremes of visual space are not directly inter-linked (as Flechsig's principle stipulates), the cerebral representations of axial body parts (e.g., Jones, 1967) are directly linked, as is the median vertical meridian (e.g., Hubel & Weisel, 1967).

Comparative Anatomical Studies

In the anatomical research cited so far, I have not systematically distinguished between research on human brains and animal brains. Comparisons across species, however, contributed to the presumptive functional significance of the corpus callosum by showing that the structure varied regularly in size in mammals, being largest in the higher mammals and largest of all in man. In the words of the anatomist Richard Owen, "The brain in Mammalia is essentially characterized by the complexity and magnitude of the apparatus by which its different masses are brought into communication with one another" (Owen, 1837, p. 87). Owen also uncovered a remarkable discontinuity within the mammalian line when he found that the corpus callosum was present in placental mammals but not in marsupials. Thomas H. Huxley (1898) presumably had Owen's (1837) report or later reports in mind (e.g., Flower, 1865; Symington, 1892) when he called this "the greatest leap forward anywhere made by Nature in her brain work. For the two halves of the brain being once thus knit together, the progress of cerebral complexity is traceable through a complete series of steps from the lowest Rodent, or Insectivore, to Man . . . " (Huxley, 1898, p. 132).

The comparative anatomist Pierre Gratiolet, himself a contributor to the study of species variations, saw special significance in the commissures. By the "intermediary of the corpus callosum," he wrote, the two hemispheres are not merely linked but made interdependent ("l'une commande à l'autre et réciproquement") (Leuret & Gratiolet, 1857, p. 177).

17TH- AND EARLY 18TH-CENTURY STUDIES OF CALLOSAL FUNCTION

So far, I have reviewed highlights in the growth of anatomical knowledge about the corpus callosum and have shown how this knowledge developed apace with speculation and theory about its function. What of real empirical study of function as distinct from, say, Gall's suppositions about callosal function, or Fechner's "thought experiment" about the effects of commissurotomy? Clinical neurologists and experimental physiologists alike recognized that one way to assess callosal function was to find out what happens when the corpus callosum is damaged or missing. Clinicians drew on "experiments of nature": on psychological examinations, often followed by post-mortems, of human beings with callosal agenesis or with infarcts or tumors; experimental physiologists studied the effects of deliberately damaging, sectioning, or in some other way "disturbing" all or part of the structure in animals.

The use of clinical evidence to study human brain functions goes back to ancient times. True experimental studies of cerebral functions in animals, however, were not undertaken until the mid-18th century. Only then, according to Neuburger (1897/1981), "did it become generally recognized that science gained nothing from deceptive ideas spun from the mind, that it was enriched by conclusions derived only from experiments" (p. 48). Neuburger perhaps had in mind certain rationalist philosophers who eschewed empirical study. Neuburger (p. 18) also credited the long delay to the continued dominance of the Cartesian view on the difference between animals and man. Animals, being mindless, or soul-less, automata (according to Descartes), could shed no light on the supposedly uniquely human higher cortical functions. Animal research therefore could not verify theories about human cerebral, meaning higher cortical, function.[10]

Clinical Studies

Ironside and Guttmacher (1929) consider the first two verified cases of callosal tumors to have been reported in the 17th century (that these were also the first verified cases of callosal injuries of any kind, including infarcts, remains to be seen). In both instances, certain mental changes were noted. The first report was published in 1614 by Felix Plater, Professor of Medicine at Basle, in his "Observationum" under the heading, "Stupor or Obfuscation from a Globular Tumour Occurring in the Brain" (Vol. 1, pp. 13-16). According to the report, "Caspar Bonecurtius, a Knight, gradually, over the course of two years, became mentally deranged, until finally he was utterly incapable of any reasoning . . . occasionally, he uttered a few words but they were hardly relevant" (quoted in Ironside & Guttmacher, 1929, pp. 443-444). The autopsy revealed a globular tumor, "the size of a small apple," over the corpus callosum and "composed of masses of tortuous venules" (p. 444), which Ironside and Guttmacher (1929) suggested was probably a hemiangioma of the falx, involving the corpus callosum.

The second report was by Johann Jacob Wepfer, Professor of Medicine at Tübingen. Ironside and Guttmacher (1929) identified Wepfer's 1675 work, *Observationes anatomicae*, as its source.[11] The subject was a young woman who "suddenly had a sensation as though something had burst within her head." Although the immediate effects were negligible, 6 months later she became hemiplegic on her left side, with both the arm and leg affected. Speech was unimpaired. Death followed 12 months later. In his examination of the cadaver,

---

[10] As far as the callosal hypothesis is concerned, this would be true only if one followed the Cartesian doctrine that consciousness (along with will) was peculiarly human, and, in addition, that it was uniquely a property of the brain rather than of the entire nervous system, including the spinal cord. In the early 19th century, both propositions figured in the debate between the German physiologist Eduard F. W. Pflüger (1829-1910), who argued that consciousness is a function of all nervous activity, in the spinal cord as well as in the brain, and Rudolf Heinrich Lotze (1817-1881), who denied this (cf. Fechner, 1907). The neuropsychologist Jeffrey Gray (1979, pp. 9-10 ff.) wrote that for Pflüger, that meant that if the spinal cord of a cat were divided into two parts, the cat would acquire two "minds." The German word is *die Seele*, which Gray suggested probably should be understood more in the sense of the English word *mind* or *consciousness* than the word *soul* (see also Clarke & O'Malley, 1968, p. 354).

[11] This was the second edition of a work that first appeared in 1658, the complete title being *Observationes anatomicae, ex cadaveribus eorum, quos sustulit apoplexia, cum exercitatione de eius loco affecto*. It is a remarkable document, replete with accounts of Wepfer's anatomical discoveries, including (in both editions) a detailed description of the Circle of Willis, one of several accounts before it was described by Willis himself (see Meyer & Hierons, 1962, p. 119).

Wepfer found a cystic degenerating tumor of the posterior part of the corpus callosum, extending into the right lateral ventricle and the right internal capsule (Ironside & Guttmacher, 1929, pp. 442-443).

These first reports, although coming before Lancisi's time (1712), can be seen as bearing on his view that the corpus callosum was the seat of the soul and the prime source of the life force. They also would challenge his prediction that callosal injuries therefore would be instantly fatal. In his own time, however, Lancisi's theory found an influential champion in François (Gigot) de La Peyronie (1678-1747), Chief Surgeon of the Charité in Paris and first surgeon to Louis XV. In a lecture in Montpellier, France, in 1708, and then in reports published in 1741 (a, b), La Peyronie offered two kinds of supporting evidence: surgical observations, amended by autopsy findings, showing that injury or pathological degeneration of the cerebral hemispheres, corpora striata, thalami, pineal gland, or cerebellum did not necessarily result in death; and evidence that in those cases that did, the corpus callosum was always involved as well. For La Peyronie, it followed that the corpus callosum was critical to life (cited in Neuburger, 1897/1981, p. 51).

Experiments With Animals

Only a few years following La Peyronie's report, Lancisi's theory came under further scrutiny, this time through what may have been the first tests on living animals. The investigator was the German physician Johann Gottfried Zinn. Zinn was the favorite pupil of Albrecht von Haller, the great physiologist at the University of Göttingen, and later became Professor of Medicine there himself (Neuburger, 1897/1981, pp. 40, 373). (He also was a botanist of note: the zinnia is named after him [Espy, 1978, p. 308].) In research for his medical thesis, Zinn (1749) set out to test Lancisi's theory through experiments on cats and dogs. In one kind of experiment, Zinn thrust a trocar[12] through the animal's skull in various directions so as to cause trauma to the corpus callosum. In another, he opened the skull with a saw, removed the brain in layers until he reached the corpus callosum, and then cut through the structure. Although the procedure produced lethargy and paralysis, at first confined to one side and later on both sides, Zinn concluded that "the corpus callosum may be damaged and cut, yet the senses and power of movement remain intact" (quoted in Ironside & Guttmacher, 1929, p. 449). According to Neuburger (1897/1981), Zinn's experiments also showed that such injuries were no more dangerous than those to other parts of the cerebral hemispheres, which led Zinn to conclude that there was no part of the brain, injury to which did not occasionally result in death. What, then, of the principle of the soul? Zinn did not reject it. Instead, he proposed that its seat, rather than being in the corpus callosum, was "extended through all of the brain's substance" (quoted in Neuburger, 1897/1981, p. 137).

In rejecting Lancisi's theory, Zinn also made a reasonably accurate guess as to the corpus callosum's principal function, noting that it was "most likely . . . to

---

[12] A stylet, usually with a triangular point; from the Latin *tres* + *carre*, the side of a sword blade.

bring about some communication of motion and sensation between the hemispheres" (Zinn, 1749, p. 117; quoted in Neuburger, 1897/1981, p. 137). If Zinn's statement does not seem fundamentally different from Lancisi's, which likened the corpus callosum to "a common marketplace of the senses, in which the external impressions of the nerves meet" (Lancisi, 1712; quoted in Neuberger, 1897/1981, p. 50), the difference is that Zinn, unlike Lancisi, did not see this role as associated with any functions essential to life itself.

LATER EMPIRICAL STUDIES

Experiments With Animals

Zinn's experiments refuted Lancisi's view that the corpus callosum was essential to life (and, by imp'' ation, was the seat of the soul), but they did not unambiguously support Zinn's surmise about its true function. The reason is that, in cutting into the corpus callosum or in cutting through it, Zinn undoubtedly damaged other structures, which means that any motor or sensory effects could have stemmed from injury to those other parts of the brain as much as to the "disconnection" itself (see also Neuburger, 1897/1981, pp. 133-134). It has also been said that these and other early experimental studies "were almost certainly marred by the occurrence of secondary infection" (Ironside & Guttmacher, 1929, p. 449). Nevertheless, the idea of directly disturbing the corpus callosum would figure in many more experimental studies of animals beginning in the early 19th century.

Electrical Stimulation. Experimental physiologists recognized that one way to disturb the corpus callosum, without permanently damaging it, was to stimulate it with electric current. The idea of studying the brain by observing the effects of electrical stimulation originated with Luigi Galvani's (1797) first experiments on electrical phenomena and *animal electricity.* In Galvani's time, the conventional view was that the brain, especially the cerebral cortex, was unexcitable. One of the first to challenge this view was Galvani's nephew, the physicist Giovanni Aldini. Aldini discovered that all parts of the brain were excitable, especially the corpus callosum and cerebellum, which, following stimulation, resulted in facial or bodily contractions. Aldini (1804) tested a variety of freshly killed animals (cows, goats, dogs, and horses, among others) as well as human beings executed by guillotine (cited in Neuburger, 1897/1981, p. 198). According to Brazier (1984, p. 193), Aldini found that passing a current through the ear and mouth or through the exposed brain and mouth evoked facial grimaces. Finding that "the fresher the head the more remarkable the grimace," he stood close to the guillotine in order to receive the heads of his human subjects "in as fresh a condition as possible" (Brazier, 1984, p. 192).

Aldini's experiments, however dramatic, did not change the conventional view about the inexcitability of the cerebral cortex. It was the experiments in the 1870s by David Ferrier in England (1876, 1890) and by Gustav Fritsch and Eduard Hitzig in Germany (Fritsch & Hitzig, 1870) that accomplished that change. Their work also showed that the motorically excitable regions were in the frontal, or pre-

Rolandic, cortex. This landmark advance in the study of localization of function changed the focus of tests of the corpus callosum because such tests could now be used to address functional and anatomical questions jointly. That is, if it could be shown that direct electrical stimulation of the corpus callosum elicited movement of the body or limbs, it would mean that callosal fibers could carry an electrical stimulus. It also would provide behavioral evidence that the newly discovered motor areas were among the cortical regions linked by callosal fibers, consistent with anatomical data from studies showing that cortical lesions produce secondary degeneration of nerve fibers that pass through the corpus callosum (cf. Sherrington, 1889; and see Footnote 14 further on).

Among the first to try this new kind of stimulation study was the French-American physician Charles E. Brown-Séquard (1887). Brown-Séquard applied faradic stimulation to a Macaque and concluded that every part of the corpus callosum had fibers capable of producing movements on faradic stimulation. The current, however, had to be stronger than that needed to excite the Rolandic area (the motor strip, or precentral gyrus) directly.

Subsequent experiments were performed by Mott and Schaefer (1890) at the Physiological Laboratory of University College, London (see also Mott, 1890). Using a faradic current, they applied electrodes to the upper surface of the corpus callosum of a variety of species of monkey. Finding that the animals made bilateral movements of the head, trunk, and limbs, Mott and Schaefer concluded that the corpus callosum connected motor regions. They also were convinced that the movements "are due to excitation of fibres in the corpus callosum and not to a spreading of the electric current to the 'motor' surface of the cortex" (p. 174), in other words, that they were not the result of electrical stimulation of the motor cortex directly. First, the effects were obtained with very weak currents; second, if the electrodes were withdrawn slightly from the surface of the corpus callosum, the movements immediately ceased, even though the excitation was then being applied at a point nearer the motor surface (p. 174). A later study of callosal stimulation of monkeys and dogs by Lévy-Valensi (1910), using a weak current, also found movements, but only of the face, neck, and trunk. To elicit limb movement, strong current had to be used, and, under these circumstances Lévy-Valensi could not eliminate diffusion to the cortical motor centers. Animal studies of this kind also were seen as holding important clues to understanding the phenomenon of generalized epilepsy. In 1907, the neurologist Max Lewandowsky proposed that the corpus callosum was the central mechanism of generalized epileptic seizures, that is, the means by which a seizure starting in the motor region of one hemisphere potentiates seizure activity in the motor region of the opposite side (cited in Spiegel, 1931, p. 600).

Commissurotomy. Both the older and the newer electrical stimulation experiments supported Zinn's (1749) conclusion that the corpus callosum played a role in the mediation of motor functions. Even this modest conclusion, however, appeared to founder in the light of further commissurotomy studies. The British physician and surgeon James Paget (1846) cited three such studies ending in the middle 1840s. One was by the physician and anatomist Anne-Charles de Lorry (1767), as quoted by the anatomist and physiologist François Achille Longet (1842, vol. 1, p. 534);[13] another was by Longet himself (1842, vol. 1, p. 534); and still another was by the German physiologist Gabriel Gustav Valentin (1841, p. 361). According to Paget (1864), all found that "neither pain nor convulsion is excited by irritation of the corpus callosum, and that, after its complete longitudinal division, sensation and voluntary motion are retained" (p. 69). Two other studies from the middle 1840s were reported by the French experimental physiologists François Magendie (1841) and Marie J. P. Flourens (1842). According to Ironside and Guttmacher (1929, p. 449), each investigator made total commissurotomies in animals and obtained "negative" results. Ironside and Guttmacher suggested, however, that mortality was probably very high in studies like these, suggesting that the amount of time and the number of surviving animals would have been insufficient for adequate tests of function. Magendie must have been aware of these and other methodological problems: Only a few years earlier, in the last edition of his *Précis elémentaire de physiologie* (1844), he had written, "the *corpus callosum, septum lucidum, cornu ammonis*, the *anterior* and *posterior commissure*, the *pineal gland*, the *pituitary gland*, and the *infundibulum*" all "no doubt execute important functions, but so defective has been the method of studying the cerebral functions that we are quite ignorant of them" (p. 141).

Later commissurotomy experiments did not change the picture dramatically. Some found symptoms following callosal section; others did not. For example, the French experimental physiologists Carville and Duret (1875) made a total section of the corpus callosum of a dog and found no motor difficulties: "It was perfectly able to move its four limbs; none of them were paralyzed" (p. 447). Van Valkenburg (1913, p. 123) cited two other late-19th century studies — by the English neurophysiologist Charles Sherrington (1889) and by the Russian scientist Wladimir Muratoff (1893) — that Van Valkenberg described as involving "section" of the corpus callosum (or perhaps only the anterior callosal fibers), each with "no permanent effects."[14] Likewise, in the early 20th century, Lévy-Valensi (1910, 1911) performed commissurotomies in monkeys and dogs and observed apathy and some loss of acquired habits, but no other abnormalities. Later, in research at the Ramón y Cajal Institute in Madrid, Lafora and Prados (1923) did the same with monkeys and cats, as did Seletzky and Gilula (1929) with cats and dogs. In Lafora and Prados' study, the acquired habits were certain movements of the left forelimb performed while the animals reached for food with the right.

---

[13] In addition to the 1767 work cited by Longet, the primary account presumably is in an earlier publication by de Lorry entitled "Sur le mouvements du cerveau" (1760).

[14] Van Valkenburg's reference to Sherrington (1889) is perplexing because Sherrington's experiment was not a commissurotomy study; it was instead aimed at discovering which nerve tracts degenerate following cortical lesions in monkeys and dogs. Among other things, it showed that lesions to the "cord-area" of the cortex produced secondary degeneration in fibers that pass through the corpus callosum into the opposite hemisphere (Sherrington, 1889, p. 432). Perhaps Van Valkenburg was conflating Sherrington's anatomical results with other findings, though not by Sherrington himself, judging from the apparent absence of any commissurotomy studies in his bibliography (see Denny-Brown, 1979, p. 516 ff.).

According to Alpers and Grant (1931), "symptoms" appeared, mainly following section of the genu and anterior portion and consisted of apathy, inactivity, and lack of interest in the environment, although the animals sometimes showed periods of excitement and great anxiety, as indicated by dilated pupils and pilo-erection. Both studies also found motor signs, including apraxia. No such signs, however, were found by Hartmann and Trendelenburg (1927) in their study of monkeys taught to obtain food by a complex series of bimanual movements requiring the simultaneous use of both hands. Following total callosal section, there was "not the slightest evidence of apraxia" (cited in Armitage & Meagher, 1933, p. 456). As for Lewandowsky's (1907) proposal, mentioned earlier, naming the corpus callosum as the mechanism of generalized epileptic seizures, the evidence was inconclusive. In dogs, local cortical stimulation produced generalized seizures despite, in the words of the investigators François-Franck and Pitres (1883), "la section longitudinale complète du corps calleux" (p. 120). Karplus (1914; cited in Erickson, 1940, p. 430) reported the same for dogs and monkeys.

In several of the newer studies, methodological problems persisted. For example, Lafora and Prados (1923) reportedly had "uncommonly bad fortune" with their surgical results, the surviving animals going through such a stormy convalescence that the procedures taught had been forgotten (Ironside & Guttmacher, 1929, p. 452). Kennard and Watts (1934), however, had far better surgical success in monkeys with sections of the anterior two thirds of the corpus callosum. Although the operation failed to produce motor weakness or reflex grasping or to affect previously produced syndromes of the motor or premotor areas, the animals did show inertia and slowness in initiating purposeful movements. The authors therefore concluded that fibers crossing through the corpus callosum "must carry impulses which are concerned in motor performance", (Kennard & Watts, 1934, p. 168).

After so many negative reports, it is not surprising that even the more positive of the later reports had limited impact. Apart from the sort of postoperative problems mentioned by Ironside and Guttmacher (1929), the major reason may have been that the motor symptoms tended to "disappear after a relatively short time, leaving no trace of their former presence" (Alpers & Grant, 1931, p. 85), much as Van Valkenburg (1913) had said of the late 19th-century studies.

Commissurotomy and Conditioning. A different test of callosal function through commissurotomy was introduced in the early 1920s in St. Petersburg (then Petrograd) by the great Russian physiologist Ivan P. Pavlov. In his conditioning studies of dogs, Pavlov (1928) had shown that conditioned reflexes established on one half of the body were "obtainable to exactly the same degree from the stimulation of corresponding symmetrical points of the other half of the body" (p. 326). The phenomenon — which Pavlov referred to as interhemispheric "irradiation" — had first been demonstrated by his student, N. I. Krasnogorsky (1911), and later confirmed by G. V. Anrep (1917), among others (cited in Pavlov,

1927, pp. 152-166; 351-352; p. 416; Pavlov, 1928, p. 326; see also Anrep, 1923). For Pavlov, who had long been interested in questions about hemispheric coordination, the question thus arose whether the corpus callosum played a role in mediating interhemispheric transfer of sensory impulses. To find out, Konstantin M. Bykov and Aleksei D. Speransky (1924), working in Pavlov's laboratory, tested for interhemispheric irradiation in corpus-callosum-sectioned dogs. The test provided what appears to be the first unmistakable experimental evidence of interhemispheric communication of sensory information via the corpus callosum. First, it showed that dogs trained to salivate in response to a tactile conditional stimulus (CS) on one side of the body would eventually salivate when the CS was presented to the corresponding spot on the opposite side of the body (which Pavlov, Krasnogorsky, and Anrep had already demonstrated). Then it showed that "section of the corpus callosum completely abolished the whole phenomenon" (of irradiation of the "reflexogenous zone") so that conditioned reflexes to tactile stimulation of the two sides became "entirely independent of one another" (Pavlov, 1927, p. 352).

This was a powerful demonstration, which, especially in light of Bykov and Speransky's association with Pavlov[15], ought to have lent considerable credibility to the "callosal hypothesis." It clearly had this effect on Ironside and Guttmacher (1929), who said that the conditioning studies had "done more [than previous studies] to clear our ideas" about callosal functions (p. 452), and then went on to speak of their "great importance in showing that the bilateral synergic activity of the hemispheres may be dependent on the corpus callosum, and indicating the part which the corpus callosum plays in the development of symmetrical reproduction of function in the hemispheres" (p. 453).

Ironside and Guttmacher (1929) were not alone in their appreciation. At the Montreal Neurological Institute, the neurosurgeons Olan Hyndman and Wilder Penfield (1937, p. 1258) said that the negative reports of Hartmann and Trendelenburg (1927), among others, "may rectify false conclusions, but they leave unanswered the question of what may be the function of this large structure." By contrast, "The experiments of Pavlov [meaning those from his laboratory] are more constructive" in suggesting that afferent pathways from peripheral receptors to their representation in the contralateral hemisphere also reach areas of homologous representation in the ipsilateral hemisphere "by way of the corpus callosum" (Hyndman & Penfield, 1937, p. 1258).

In the early German literature, Bykov and Speransky's work was cited by Seletzky and Gilula (1928, pp. 59-60), among others. Understandably, it was, and continued to be, well-known to Soviet scientists (e.g., Bianki, 1958). It also appears to have been well-known to Japanese scientists, several of whom carried out successful replications (see citations in Wada, 1951).

---

[15] Pavlov, a Nobel laureate for his work on the digestive system, was already a legendary figure, regarded as the greatest experimental physiologist of the day and as an immaculately careful and thorough researcher. He was also a surgeon of remarkable speed and skill and enjoyed uncommon success in bringing his animals through surgery alive and well (see Babkin, 1949, pp. 13-14).

Despite the endorsements from Ironside and Guttmacher (1929) and Hyndman and Penfield (1937), Bykov and Speransky's experiment does not appear to have left a strong impression in the long run (the Japanese studies seem to have left none at all, at least in the West). Given the actual citation record, however, Bogen and Bogen's remark, in 1969, that it had been "overlooked for more than thirty years" (p. 192) was off by at least a few years.[16]

If Bykov and Speransky's experiment was overlooked or undervalued, the reasons are not clear. One possibility is that, endorsements notwithstanding, the primary report never became so widely known in its own time as it might have been. If so, the problem may have been its publishing history.[17] Another possibility is that the impact of the results became diluted amid the welter of more ambiguous data from other contemporaneous animal studies (e.g., Hartmann & Trendelenburg, 1927; Lafora & Prados, 1923; Seletzky & Gilula, 1929). There also were those who assumed that the animal studies were, in principle, of no relevance for human beings. As Armitage and Meagher (1933) said, although without citing Bykov and Speransky's study, "Such observations on the lower animals are of dubious value since the elaborate association mechanism which Mingazzini [1922, *V. supra*] regarded as essential to the harmonious exteriorization of ideas is hardly to be looked for in anything lower than man" (p. 456). Whatever the reason for overlooking Bykov and Speransky's (1924) experiment (not to mention the Japanese replications), we shall see that it was not the only positive report to have less weight than it now would seem to have deserved.

---

[16] Bogen and Bogen evidently were referring to the citation by Ronald E. Myers in 1956 in one of his own seminal reports on commissural functions (discussed further on). Myers clearly appreciated the historical significance of Bykov and Speransky's work. In a later essay, he wrote, "This early, clear and beautiful experiment led to the conclusion that, for the dog, the neocortical commissures play an important role in the generalization of sensory learning between the two sides of the body" (Myers, 1965, p. 3).

[17] A full account, by Bykov and Speransky, was included in 1924 in *Collected Papers of the Physiological Laboratories of I. P. Pavlov*. An abstract in German also appeared in 1924-1925 in the *Zentralblatt für die gesammte Neurologie und Psychiatrie*. Pavlov himself gave a very brief account in Lecture 20 of a series of lectures that were delivered in 1924, published in Russian in 1926, and translated into English by Anrep in 1927 under the title *Conditioned Reflexes: An Investigation of the Physiological Activity of the Cerebral Cortex* (see Pavlov, 1927). In Gantt's English translation of Pavlov's own collection of his lectures from 1903 to 1927, entitled *Lectures on Conditioned Reflexes*, the study is cited in the bibligraphy (p. 404) but not in the text (see Pavlov, 1928).

Of these different sources, Ironside and Guttmacher (1929) cited the 1924-1925 German abstract (with "Bykoff" named as sole author) and the account in Anrep's translation (Pavlov, 1927); Hyndman and Penfield (1937) cited Anrep's translation (Pavlov, 1927); Seletzky and Gilula (1928) cited still another account, by Bykov alone, in the 1925 *Pavlov Jubilee* volume, which I have been unable to trace. The German abstract was also cited by Myers (1956). The Japanese papers (cited in Wada, 1951) referred to a Russian-to-Japanese translation (1937) of Pavlov (1926).

Clinical Studies

Of the clinical and animal studies discussed so far, several were conducted prior to the first great period of theory and research on *localization* of cortical function initiated early in the 19th century by Gall (Gall & Spurzheim, 1810-1819) and also, of course, prior to the modern era of *lateralization* of function initiated in the 1860s by Paul Broca (e.g., 1861, 1863, 1865). They also preceded the work of Theodor Meynert (1872), who, as noted earlier, was the first to bring real clarity to the various fiber tract systems, and who endorsed Friedrich Arnold's (1838-1840) statement that the corpus callosum bundles unite "corresponding and identical regions" of the neocortical hemispheres (Meynert, 1872, p. 405).

Meynert contributed to the study of hemispheric communication in human beings by inaugurating a new way of thinking about white matter lesions. With respect to *intra*cerebral lesions, recall that one of Meynert's medical students in 1870 was Karl Wernicke. Meynert's anatomical studies of intracerebral white matter, together with the new evidence showing that the Rolandic fissure divided motor from sensory cortex, figured critically in Wernicke's studies of aphasia. Following Broca's discovery of a "speech center" in the left frontal lobe, Wernicke predicted a new kind of aphasia, a "disconnection aphasia" produced by a lesion to the fiber tract connecting Broca's area with the posterior-temporal language zone that Wernicke himself had discovered (1874).[18]

The predicted effect of a lesion to *inter*cerebral fiber tracts was no less remarkable. Whereas the corpus callosum had once been seen as permitting the coordination of two presumably functionally symmetrical hemispheres, now the corpus callosum could be seen as providing for communication between hemispheres with different psychological capacities. For the first time, one could ask, what would happen if information sent to the "silent" right hemisphere were prevented from reaching the language zones of the left hemisphere? This question figured prominently in further clinical studies of the corpus callosum.

Callosal Lesions From Cerebral Infarcts: The Work of Dejerine and Liepmann. In the lateralization era, the work of two eminent neurologists is paramount: in France, Joseph Jules Dejerine, and in Germany, Wernicke's student Hugo Karl Liepmann. In 1892, Dejerine reported the case of an intelligent, well-educated 68-year-old man who, on October 25, 1887, suddenly discovered that he could no longer read letters, words, or musical notation. Although still able to write, he could not read what he had written. There were no signs of general intellectual disturbance. The man was examined first by an ophthalmologist, and then, over a 4-year period, by Dejerine. In 1892, a second cerebral vascular accident left the man paraphrasic and agraphic, and he died soon after. The autopsy, conducted by Dejerine, indicated that the more recent lesion involved the angular gyrus and adjacent parts of the parietal lobe and temporoparietal junction,

---

[18] Wernicke, however, supposed that the fiber tract linking the two areas coursed through the insula, or Island of Reil; later, Constantin von Monakow (1914) demonstrated that the more likely route was by a superior pathway, the arcuate fasciculus.

and that the initial lesion had destroyed the left visual area (striate, or calcarine, cortex) and the splenium of the corpus callosum. The autopsy led Dejerine to reason that the destruction of the left visual area had disconnected, or isolated, the intact visual area of the right hemisphere from the language area in the left hemisphere, thereby rendering the man alexic but not agraphic. At this time, Dejerine did not emphasize the damage to the splenium but supposed, instead, that the destruction of the white matter in the left occipital lobe was enough to disconnect the right visual area from the language area (for an account of this case, see Geschwind, 1962; 1965, pp. 277-280). Within a few years, the English neurologist Henry Charlton Bastian (1898) cited several similar cases in his treatise on aphasia and other speech defects.

A few years after Dejerine's report, Liepmann and his colleague Oscar Maas (Liepmann, 1900, 1907; 1905/1908; Liepmann & Maas, 1907) described a new syndrome: motor apraxia to verbal commands in the left hand in right-handed patients with lesions of the anterior four fifths of the corpus callosum. Liepmann and Maas concluded that the language-dominant hemisphere controls the motor cortex of the right hemisphere in the performance of skilled hand movements, and that this control is mediated through the corpus callosum. Confirming clinical reports followed, including one by the neurologist Kurt Goldstein (1908) and another by the Berlin psychiatrist Karl Bonhoeffer (1914). The latter reported finding motor apraxia in a patient whose cortical speech area was preserved but who had a capsular lesion on the left side and a callosal lesion.

Given the strength of Dejerine's, Liepmann's, and related demonstrations, one might expect them to have lent considerable credibility to the callosal hypothesis. According to Geschwind (1974), however, they did not have this effect. The reasons are hard to pin down, but one reason that can be dismissed outright is that the studies were not well known at the time. For example, Liepmann's work appeared in prominent journals, garnered considerable acclaim in its own day, and was cited in later reviews. These included Ironside and Guttmacher's (1929) review, which said that Liepmann's "series of brilliant papers" had identified "the predominant influence exerted in man by the left hemisphere, and the value of apraxia as a diagnostic sign of callosal damage" (p. 450). Liepmann's studies were also fully discussed in Lange's (1936) article in the standard German neurological reference, the *Bumke-Foerster Handbuch* (1936; cited by Geschwind, 1974, p. 8 ff.).

One of the likely factors weighing against broad acceptance of the work has already been mentioned: the mixed evidence of apraxia following commissurotomy in experimental studies of animals (e.g., Hartmann & Trendelenburg, 1927; Seletsky & Gilula, 1929). There also were prior, as well as subsequent, reports on human patients whose callosal damage produced no symptoms at all. For example, according to Mingazzini (1926; cited in Elliot, 1969, p. 761), apraxia following anterior callosal lesions was reported in less than 10% of the cases. Furthermore, because infarcts causing callosal lesions also often caused cortical lesions, it was possible to suppose that any symptoms were due to the cortical lesions rather than to the callosal disconnection per se.

Tumor Studies.   The co-occurrence of callosal and cortical lesions was particularly evident in new studies of callosal tumors. The resulting confusion is illustrated in the contrasting interpretations of an early paper by the British physician John S. Bristowe. In a report in *Brain* (1884), Bristowe described four cases of tumor of the corpus callosum (anterior half or two thirds, confirmed by postmortem), all accompanied by certain mental and physical symptoms that Bristowe suggested were regular enough to constitute a true syndrome. These were the symptoms' "ingravescent" character (i.e., gradually increasing in severity — something found in common with other kinds of cerebral tumor); the gradual coming on of hemiplegia; the association of paralysis of one side with vague hemiplegic symptoms of the other; and the supervention of "stupidity" associated, mostly, with extreme drowsiness, puzzlement, and cessation of speech. This last, however, was not a sign of aphasia or "loss of articulating power," that is, not definitely a sign of injury to cortical speech centers (p. 318), but seemed to be due mainly to "stupidity and irresistible tendency to sleep."

Bristowe's account was very influential. Ransom (1895) noted that his summary "has been copied into text-books as diagnostic of tumours of the corpus callosum" (p. 536). Ironside and Guttmacher (1929) even credited Bristowe with the "establishment of the "Callosal Syndrome" (p. 444) and regarded his report as "the inspiration of all subsequent work on this subject" (p. 444), indeed, as leading ultimately to Liepmann's description of apraxia in 1907. Ironside and Guttmacher, however, appear to have conflated two different ideas. Having proposed a callosal syndrome, Bristowe concluded by saying that the symptoms "were due chiefly, if not altogether, to the extension of the disease into the hemispheres, and to the diffused pressure on important parts caused by the great collective bulk of the tumour . . . " (pp. 318-319). In other words, although Bristowe did propose a set of symptoms associated with callosal tumor, his concluding statement indicates that he saw the symptoms not as the result of a cortical disconnection but as due to cortical injuries directly.   This was fundamentally different from Liepmann's conceptualization of the nature of commissural apraxia.   This latter reading of Bristowe's concluding statement seems to be how the British neurologist Sir William Richard Gowers understood Bristowe's report.   In his authoritative *A Manual of Diseases of the Nervous System*, Gowers (1893) wrote:

> The chief lesion that occurs in the corpus callosum is tumour, but this almost always extends into one or both hemispheres. Mental dulness and stupor, with weakness in the limbs, greater on one side, have been present in many cases, and in some there has been disturbance of speech and locomotion; but it is probable that these symptoms (with the possible exception of the mental dulness) are due to the pressure on, or extension into, the cerebral hemispheres. We do not yet know of any symptoms that are the result of the damage to the callosal fibers (Vol. 2, p. 314).

Gowers (1893) went on to say that it was "certain that the symptoms that have been present are indistinguishable from those produced by multiple tumours" (p. 314), here citing Bristowe's (1884) cases and noting that the "diagnostic indications" formulated by Bristowe "are no exception" to Gowers' own statement (p. 314). Gowers ended by saying that the "complete interruption (by softening from embolism)" of the corpus callosum "has caused no symptoms" (p. 314), referring here to a study by Kaufmann (1888).

In the early decades of the 20th century, more and more accounts of patients with callosal tumors appeared until, by the 1930s, there were well over 100 cases on record. These became the subject of numerous reviews (e.g., Ayala, 1915; Armitage & Meagher, 1933; Lévy-Valensi, 1910, 1911; Mingazzini, 1922; Vorhis & Adson, 1935; Vorhis, Adson, & Moersch, 1935; Vorhis, Kernohan, & Adson, 1935). According to a pathologic and clinical analysis of 38 such cases by Vorhis and Adson (1935), as part of a series of 314 cases of microscopically verified tumor of the frontal lobe (Vorhis, Kernohan, & Adson, 1935; Vorhis, Moersch, & Adson, 1935), certain symptoms were indeed associated with callosal tumors, although not quite the same ones as those proposed by Bristowe (1884). Vorhis and Adson's list included convulsions and other motor manifestations, unilateral or bilateral paralysis, reflex disturbances, and apraxia. Like Bristowe's cases, however, in all or nearly all instances, there also was frontal lobe involvement, with additional involvement of the parietal lobe in a few cases. In fact, Vorhis and Adson (1935) reported finding only 2 cases where the tumor was grossly confined to the corpus callosum.

On the basis of a new study of 5 patients with callosal tumors, Alpers and Grant (1931), in a more positive report, described what they regarded to be the clinical syndrome of the corpus callosum in the human brain. The outstanding symptoms were, in decreasing order of importance and regularity of occurrence: mental signs (especially an inability to concentrate and maintain attention), motor signs (hemiparesis or weakness in the limbs), and apraxia, which Alpers and Grant acknowledged was "unfortunately . . . not often present in tumors involving the callosum" (here, citing Mingazzini, 1922). Nevertheless, they concluded that when it *was* present, "it almost certainly points to an involvement of the corpus callosum, especially if it is unaccompanied by hemiparesis and [certain] mental signs" (p. 85). These symptoms also closely corresponded to those observed in experimental studies of animals. The difference, as noted earlier, was that the symptoms in animals disappeared in time, whereas those in human patients persisted (see discussion in Baker & Graves, 1933).

CALLOSAL AGENESIS

As we have seen, the callosal hypothesis was hard to test in human beings with callosal infarcts, and even harder to test in those with callosal tumors, because of the frequent co-occurrence of *cortical* pathology. It also had come to be recognized, however, that another test was offered by persons with callosal

agenesis. The first such report may have been the one by the Italian physician
Giovanni Battista Bianchi (1749) in his study of monsters. The case is frequently
cited in the early literature on the corpus callosum. As described by James Paget
(1846) and by William Turner (1878), the latter drawing on an account in
Mihalkovics' (1877) textbook on neural development, the subject was a child with
"no corpus callosum" and with "scarcely a trace of pons, or medulla oblongata"
(Paget, 1846, p. 61), and whose "hemispheres had grown together in the mesial
plane, so that the lateral ventricles presented a single, common cavity" (Turner,
1878, p. 252). Paget noted that the child was "quite senseless and motionless" (p.
61) and cited numerous other reports of "idiocy" associated with still greater
malformation of the rest of the brain.

By the late 1800s, several dozen agenesis cases had been reported. For
example, the physician Alexander Bruce (1889-1890) listed 30 cases, which he
arranged into four groups: 15 with total agenesis; 6 with partial agenesis; 3 more
with partial agenesis involving only the anterior portion; and 6 in which the
agenesis was obviously secondary to a tumor (see also Eichler, 1878; Jolly, 1869;
Knox, 1875; Turner, 1878).

The evidence from these reports gave scant encouragement to supporters of
the callosal hypothesis. In many cases, the total or partial absence of the corpus
callosum did seem to affect cognition and intelligence inasmuch as, like the child
described by Bianchi (1749), the condition was associated with gross mental
retardation ("idiocy" or "imbecility"). The problem, as already noted, was that,
just as with callosal tumors, the agenetic brains typically showed other anomalies.
These might include abnormally distended ventricles[19], polygyria, an embryonic
arrangement of sulci, the absence of olfactory nerves, hydrocephalus, an enlarged
anterior commissure, and incomplete separation of the frontal lobes or even of the
entire cerebrum (as in Bianchi's report and the later report by Turner, 1878). As
Paget (1846) surmised, where agenesis *was* associated with cognitive deficits, it
was, therefore, reasonable to attribute the deficits to the other neurological
defects. For this reason, Paget regarded all such cases as "uninstructive" about
callosal functions (p. 61). Later writers were largely in agreement on this point.

What was required, therefore, was information about individuals whose
deficits were confined, or at least largely confined, to the corpus callosum itself.
There were a number of such reports. Perhaps the first and most frequently cited
was one by Johannn Christian Reil in 1812, just 3 years following publication of his
first anatomical study of the corpus callosum. Reil (1812) described a "woman
about 30 years old, who was otherwise healthy, but dull in intellect." The woman
"was able to do errands in town for others from her village" (p. 341). After a fall
from a baker's loading ramp, she suffered an apoplectic seizure and died. The
autopsy disclosed "ventricles moderately full of water," and a corpus callusum
"divided longitudinally in the middle," the hemispheres being held together only by
the anterior commissure, optic chiasm, isthmus of crura cerebri in front of the

---

[19] Turner (1878), in commenting on cases reported by Knox (1875), regarded this condition of
the ventricles to be the main factor arresting callosal development.

pons, and corpora quadrigemina (pp. 341-342; see also Paget, 1846, p. 62; Bruce, 1889-1890, p. 176).

Reil's case thus seemed to indicate that the corpus callosum *was* important for normal intelligence. Other reports, however, gave few or no such indications. Paget (1846) himself described a 21-year-old woman, dead from pericarditis, whose brain showed "only a rudiment or a remnant" of a corpus callosum (p. 56). Missing also were the septum lucidum and middle part of the fornix. Otherwise, the brain was normal and unexceptional, as had been the woman's mind and intelligence according to the testimony of her family, teacher, and neighbor. Said Paget, "I could not find otherwise than that this girl's mind was one of the least remarkable kind" (p. 61). Her only "peculiarity" was what Paget called her "vivacity, and a want of caution, showing themselves in an habitual rapidity of action and want of forethought, deliberation and attention," but Paget dismissed this in consideration of her scanty education and "natural heedlessness" (p. 61).

Similar results appeared in later reports of agenesis without associated gross cerebral anomalies. Bruce's (1889-1890) first category of persons with total agenesis included 5 such cases. One case, reported by the Italian physician S. Germano Malinverni (1875, French abstract; original report in Italian, 1874), was that of a soldier who died at age 40 of "gastro-intestinal illness complicated by pulmonary congestion," and whose autopsy revealed "absence absolue" of the corpus callosum as well as the septum lucidum and gyrus fornicatus. According to the French abstract (1875), during his life the soldier had "never given proof of a derangement of his intellectual faculties." In military service, his conduct had been "excellent." In private life, he was gentle and hard-working. He also showed a tendency for melancholy and taciturnity, but never to a pathological extent (p. 33). Another case, this time in Bruce's second category — "primary partial development of the corpus callosum" — was reported by Friedrich Jolly (1869) (also cited in Douglas-Crawford, 1906, p. 57). The subject was a railway servant, "mental powers normal," who died at age 58 from stomach cancer, and whose autopsy revealed a corpus callosum "about 1 inch in length." Likewise, William Ireland (1886) noted that William Hitzig, "who has studied the question carefully, observes that no well-marked disorder of motion or sensation follows atrophy of the corpus callosum, nor is there any characteristic mental defect attendant upon this lesion" (p. 317). Ireland also mentioned negative cases of his own (p. 318).

The authors of these reports all came to essentially the same conclusion. For example, Paget (1846) said that "a corpus callosum is not necessary for the mental reception of sensations, or for the ordinary exercise of the will upon the muscles, or for the natural movements of any internal organs, or for due nutrition or secretion in any part" (pp. 68-69). Nor could its functions be found "among the higher and more internal functions of the brain . . . for the facts do not even show that its existence is necessary to the possession and average development of any of the admitted faculties of the mind" (p. 70). Malinverni (1875) concluded that the corpus callosum does not seem to play "un rôle indispensable en ce qui concerne l'intégrité des facultés, l'harmonie des actes de l'intelligence" (pp. 33-34). Ireland (1886) said that it was "impossible to avoid the conclusion that the two hemispheres of the brain can perform their usual functions without this structure.. " (p. 318). For Douglas-Crawford (1906), it was "obvious that absence of this commissure is not incompatible with mental efficiency" (p. 58), a view also expressed by Erb (1885), Ransom (1895), and Bruce (1889-1890), among others. Bruce (1889-1890) also drew on this negative evidence to attack what he called Meynert's (1872) "opinion" about the corpus callosum's anatomical connections, which Bruce credited as the basis for the callosal hypothesis:

> It is right to state that Meynert's opinion is based on no proof whatever and the physiological view is equally speculative. It was supposed to account satisfactorily for the idiocy or imbecility of most of the [agenesis] cases. But examination of the literature shows that where there has been imbecility there has always been some other grave brain defect. On the other hand, the cases of Eichler [1878], Paget [1846], Malinverni [1874/1875], Jolly [1869], and that recorded by me, and the second case of Kaufmann [no reference; probably 1888] and that of Erb (*Virch. Arch.*, 96) [no date; presumably 1884; see also Erb, 1885], show that where the brain is otherwise well developed there may be 'no disturbance of mobility, co-ordination, general or special sensibility, reflexes, speech, or intelligence, whether the defect of the corpus callosum be primary or secondary" (Bruce, 1889-1890, p. 190).

In France in 1890, the neurologist Gabriel Descourtis sought to explain the negative reports by pointing out that the two hemispheres of the brain possessed the same hereditary dispositions and had lived through the same experiences. It was therefore understandable that they normally should feel and react in a unified fashion, whether or not they were joined together (cited in Harrington, 1987, p. 153). Descourtis even compared the hemispheres to the Siamese twins[20], who, though able to show their independence, essentially shared a single personality.

There was one fundamental problem with Descourtis' analysis. In saying that the hemispheres possessed the same hereditary dispositions and had lived through the same experiences, he made no mention of functional asymmetry, which, by 1890, had become a bedrock principle of medicine and neurology. The analogy to the Siamese twins was problematic too. From childhood, they were said to have had quite different personalities; indeed, later in life, they reportedly did not get along very well (I. Wallace & A. Wallace, 1978).

At Oxford University, the psychologist William McDougall, in his essay *Body and Mind: A History and a Defense of Animism* (1911/1918), welcomed Bruce's (1889-1890) report that callosal agenesis "afforded no indication of 'dual consciousness'" (McDougall, p. 296). For McDougall, this undermined Fechner's (1860/1907) entire psychophysical scheme, especially his doctrine of psychophysical continuity (it "remains utterly obscure, a metaphor of extreme

---

[20] Descourtis meant the Siamese twins, Chang and Eng (1811-1874), conjoined twins born in Siam (Thailand) to Chinese parents.

vagueness merely" [McDougall, p. 296]). It also showed, McDougall believed, that Fechner was mistaken in his answer to his (Fechner's) own thought experiment about the effects of splitting the human brain. Above all, McDougall saw the evidence as refuting the materialistic doctrine that the unity of consciousness depends on the unity of the brain's physical connections, and as affirming his own animist doctrine that the mind and body are different and distinct. Many years later, Oliver Zangwill (1974) recounted an amusing story about McDougall and Sir Charles Sherrington as told by the British psychologist Cyril Burt. Burt recalled McDougall:

> saying more than once that he had tried to bargain with Sherrington . . that if ever he [McDougall] should be smitten with an incurable disease, Sherrington should cut through his corpus callosum. "If the physiologists are right" — and by physiologists [Burt said], I suppose he meant Sherrington himself — "the results should be a split personality. If I am right," [McDougall] said, "my consciousness will remain a unitary consciousness." And he seemed to regard that as the most convincing proof of the existence of something like a soul (Zangwill, 1974, p. 265).

One may ask why callosally agenetic persons showed so little indication of mental "disconnection," "split personality," or "dual consciousness," in the sense meant by McDougall. It is not that the reports cannot be trusted; the "null" effects have been essentially corroborated by later reports (see Jeeves, 1986). More likely, these agenesis cases exemplify the familiar principle that congenital chronic conditions typically have less dramatic consequences than later acute injuries, presumably because congenital injuries allow for substitution or compensation by other neural centers. For callosal agenesis, it has been suggested that compensation for visual transfer is partly mediated by hypertrophy of the anterior commissure (see Loeser & Alford, 1968), a condition mentioned in the early literature, as already noted. For tactile integration, it has been suggested that acallosals make use of cerebral plasticity by reinforcement of existing ipsilateral and/or subcortical connections of the somatosensory system (Lassonde, Sauerwin, Chicoine, & Geoffroy, 1991). Finally, such "disconnection" effects that do exist probably could not be detected by the relatively gross observational methods used in most of the early clinical studies. The same problem arises in other early studies, as we shall see later.

THE CORPUS CALLOSUM AND MENTAL ILLNESS

So far, we have seen how those who affirmed or denied the callosal hypothesis emphasized either the effects, or lack of effects, of callosal infarcts, tumors, or agenesis on cognitive and motor functions. The principals in this part of the story were, as I said, experimental physiologists and clinical neurologists. In the early 1800s, before the emergence of cerebral lateralization theories, the importance of neural integration also began to be remarked on by "mad doctors" (alienists, or psychiatrists) as well as by general practitioners. These physicians believed that because unity of mind and consciousness depended on the cerebral hemispheres working symmetrically and synchronously, any breaking down of this balance would lead to mental illness. Those favoring this view frequently found inspiration in Gall's organological theory, which assumed that the two cerebral hemispheres had symmetrical functions. Recall that Gall's original 27 organ scheme stipulated that every faculty on the left side had its duplicate on the right.

Several reports were by Gall himself. One was of a Viennese minister tortured by insulting sounds on his left side, so that he was constantly turning to look in that direction, "although he knew distinctly with his right side [of his brain] that those insulting sounds were the simple result of a disease on the left side of his brain." In Paris, Gall also had treated a young woman who confessed to him her fear of going mad on one side of her head "because she had noticed that the course of her ideas was not the same on this side as on the other." A third patient, described by Gall as "a woman of great talent," said that she perceived everything differently on the left side than on the right, that sometimes her power of thinking would cease on the left side and an "icy torpor" would grip half her skull, and that (as she explained to Gall) "from the forehead to the back of the head my brain is divided into two distinct halves" (Gall, cited in Elliotson, 1847, pp. 212-213, and Harrington, 1987, p. 18; see also Ireland, 1886).

Following Gall, several more cases were recorded. In France, reports were filed by the psychiatrist Jean Esquirol (1845), the physician-in-chief of the Maison Royale des Aliénés de Charenton. In his treatise *Mental maladies*, Esquirol described persons who, in an extreme state of passion, or "delirium," are "drawn away *irresistably*" to commit heinous, irrational acts. Aware of their condition and able to deplore their acts, they nonetheless are "drawn away" again. Such an individual "has lost the unity of his mind. He is the *homo duplex* of St. Paul and of Buffon; impelled to evil by one motive, and restrained by another.[21] This lesion of the will, . . . can be conceived of, as resulting from the duplicity of the brain, whose two halves, not being equally excited, do not act simultaneously" (Esquirol, 1845, p. 363).

In America, the pioneer American psychiatrist Benjamin Rush (1981) reported similar cases in his lectures at the College of Philadelphia from 1795 to 1811. One such case was of a young man who, while seized by a fit, perfectly remembered things that occurred in the preceding fit but nothing that had happened in the interval. He "seemed to have *two distinct minds* which acted by turns independently of each other" (p. 669), leading Rush to wonder whether such cases could be ascribed "to all the mind being, according to Dr. Gall, like vision a

---

[21] The *homo duplex* of St. Paul refers to *Romans*, Chapter 7, verses 14-15: "For we know that the law is spiritual: but I am carnal, sold under sin. For that which I do I allow not: for what I would, that do I not; but what I hate, that do I." Buffon (George Louis LeClerc Comte de Buffon, 1707-1788), in his essay "De la nature de l'homme" (1971/1750), likewise describes man as a being compounded of two distinct and conflicting natures, body (flesh) and soul.

double organ occupying the two opposite hemispheres of the brain, . . . " (p. 670; see also Harrington, 1987, pp. 18-19).

In England, the physicians Arthur Ladbroke Wigan and Sir Henry Holland weighed in with still more evidence. Wigan was the author of a remarkable book entitled, *A New View of Insanity: The Duality of the Mind* (1844a; see also Wigan, 1844b; Harris, 1985b). There, he proposed that, "When the disease or disorder of one cerebrum [that is, one hemisphere] becomes sufficiently aggravated to defy the control of the other, the case is then one of the commonest forms of mental derangement or insanity . . . in the insane . . . it is almost always possible to trace the intermixture of two synchronous trains of thought, and . . . it is the irregularly alternate utterance of portions of these two trains of thought which constitutes incoherence" (pp. 126-127; quoted in Harrington, 1987, p. 24). Wigan also proposed a scheme to overcome madness and insanity. Because disease and injury rarely struck both hemispheres of the brain with equal severity at the same time, it should be possible for someone on the verge of madness to override or to inhibit the deranged thoughts being produced by the diseased hemisphere by using the other, healthy hemisphere. In other words, each hemisphere could act as a "sentinel and security for the other," steadying its fellow in health and intervening in order to correct the "erroneous judgments" of its fellow when disordered (quoted in Harrington, 1987, p. 27).

Wigan was a general practitioner from Brighton, and his book was his only claim to fame. Holland, by contrast, was a celebrity: a Fellow of the Royal Society, Physician Extraordinary to Queen Victoria, and Physician in Ordinary to Prince Albert (Harris, 1983). Holland presented his views in 1839 in his essay "On the brain as a double organ," reprinted in *Chapters on Mental Physiology* (Holland, 1852). Like the others, Holland believed that unity of mind depends on the two halves of the brain functioning in a symmetrical, synchronous fashion and that "some of the aberrations of mind, which come under the name of insanity [could be] due to incongruous action of this double structure . . . " (Holland, 1839/1852, p. 172). For examples, he described deranged persons who appeared to have "two minds, one tending to correct . . . the aberrations of the other," and persons torn between two contradictory impulses, leading to "a painfully exaggerated picture of the struggle between good and ill" (Holland, 1839/1852, p. 185). As Harrington pointed out, Holland rejected the materialistic implications inherent in the phrenological view of the brain's functional duality. Instead, he favored a dualistic analysis according to which the human brain was double but "standing *over and above* that brain," there was a single immaterial mind (Holland, quoted in Harrington, 1987, p. 21).

Given the times, it would seem that the corpus callosum would have figured prominently in investigators' explanations of their observations. Gall, however, did not mention the corpus callosum in this context, even though he had emphasized it in his general anatomical and functional (i.e., organological) theory of mind. Wigan went further, dismissing the corpus callosum as "an organ of no importance, and not necessary to the functions of the brain" (Wigan, 1844a, p. 49). It was left for Holland to be the first, evidently, to name the corpus callosum directly as the means for affording sanity (in the sense of wholeness of mind) when the corpus callosum was healthy and, by implication, as the cause of the mind's disintegration when the corpus callosum was damaged or diseased:

> On the connexions afforded by the Corpus Callosum and the other commissures depend, it may be presumed, the unity and completeness of the functions of this double organisation, as well as the translation of morbid actions from one side to the other. And any breach in the integrity of the union, and of the relations thus established, may tend no less than disease in the respective parts themselves, to disturb the various actions of the brain and nervous system (Holland, 1839/1852, p. 165).

Holland acknowledged, however, that his own statement was not justified by clinical data: "researches made, through lesions of these commissures, give results quite as equivocal as those on other portions of the brain" (p. 165). Here, Holland referred to the "observations of Reil [meaning, presumably, Reil's 1812 report on callosal agenesis], [Luigi] Rolando, and other physiologists," which "though valuable, cannot be considered as leading to any assured conclusions" (pp. 165-166). Even so, Holland remained convinced of the importance of the integrity of the commissures, saying that "it is probable, or even certain, that many phenomena of sensorial disorder have their origin in these connecting parts more especially, as the seat of disease" (p. 166). Holland's confidence was understandable. As Harrington (1987, p. 22) observed, the conception of the commissures "as so many fibrous bridges grafting the two brain-halves together and providing a means for communication between them was so utterly logical — just by *looking* at the brain — that it was hard at this stage to be overly troubled by the lack of empirical evidence actually supporting the idea" (p. 22). Nonetheless, Holland had "unwittingly put his finger on an empirical lacuna that would not go away, that would continue to vex and perplex the best minds of neurology throughout the whole of the nineteenth century and well into the twentieth" (Harrington, 1987, p. 22). Holland, evidently, was less troubled by the lack of evidence than some others had been or would be in the future, as we have already seen.

SIZE OF CORPUS CALLOSUM

I have traced the development of several lines of theory and research on the role of the corpus callosum in hemispheric communication. Today, there also is interest in the possible functional significance of individual differences in commissure size. For example, does a larger corpus callosum mean better interhemispheric integration? Might size differences help to explain individual differences in lateral differentiation of function and cognitive skill? Of course, interest in the size of neural structures may be as old as the study of the brain itself. Differences in the overall size of the brain figured in Aristotle's heart-centered theory of mind (which viewed the brain as a kind of radiator to cool the blood), were a key ingredient in

Gall's organological theory, and were the major focus of analysis and debate for Broca and his fellow members of the Societé d'Anthropologie de Paris in the 1860s and thereafter. One, therefore, might have expected to find a similar interest in the size of the corpus callosum size by Broca's time, if not by Gall's. As we have seen, much significance was attached to the size difference across mammalian species (Owen, 1837; Huxley, 1898). The question of *intra-species*, more particularly intra-human, differences, however, does not seem to have been addressed until the early years of the 20th century. The one to raise the question was the American physician Edward Anthony Spitzka, a professor of general anatomy at the Jefferson Medical College in Philadelphia.

Spitzka's major account of his work appeared in 1908 in an article entitled, "A study of the brains of six eminent scientists and scholars belonging to the American Anthrometric Society, together with a description of the skull of Professor E. D. Cope" (Cope was America's leading paleontologist and evolutionary biologist). But first, let us recount how Spitzka came to be interested in this question.

Starting with Gall, anatomists, anthropologists, and other students of the brain had begun to create collections of skulls and brain casts. Gall's own vast collection included specimens from a broad class of individuals, which he offered in support of his organological theory. In Paris in 1881, the Mutual Autopsy Society was founded for the purpose of securing what Spitzka (1908, p. 175) called "élite brains for scientific study." In America, in 1889, the American Anthropometric Society was founded on similar lines. This was followed by the Cornell (University) Brain Association, to which about 70 brains of "educated orderly persons" had been bequeathed (Spitzka, p. 175). Still other collections were in Munich and Göttingen.

The chief object of these societies was to preserve and to study the brains of its members. Among the "élite brains" donated to Spitzka's American Anthropometric Society were those of the morphologist Joseph Leidy, the physician and surgeon Philip Leidy, the comparative anatomist Harrison Allen, the neuroanatomist A. J. Parker, and the poet Walt Whitman.[22]

Like his predecessors, Spitzka was interested in the straightforward question of whether great men had great brains, as indexed by absolute overall size as well as by other indexes, such as the "cerebro-cerebellar ratio" and the depth and extent of the convolutions. Spitzka also chose to study the corpus callosum because of what he regarded as undue emphasis placed on the gray matter at the expense of the "very notable researches of Flechsig in the field of myelin-development" (p. 301). In Spitzka's (1908) estimation, this emphasis lost sight of the most important clue to the analysis of mind:

---

[22] Whitman, like many other members of the Society, was inspired to donate his brain because of his ardent belief in phrenology (see Kaplan, 1980, pp. 146 ff.). The poet's brain, however, was not destined for enrollment in Spitzka's study: "together with the jar in which it had been placed, [it] was said to have been dropped on the floor by a careless assistant. Unfortunately, not even the pieces were saved" (Spitzka, 1908, p. 176).

Were it not for the manifold connections of such [nerve] cells with each other, as well as with the periphery by means of the millions and millions of fibers, such a brain . . . would be as useless as a multitude of telephone or telegraph stations with all inter-connecting wires destroyed. The bulk of (normal) white matter in the brain therefore signifies elaborated gray matter and hence the significance of brain-weight in relation to brain-power. . . So characteristic is this preponderance of white matter in the brain of man, and so needful is such an elaboration and amplification of the cerebral architecture to the workings of the human mind, that it is only necessary to glance at the cross-sections of the brains of lower animals as compared with that of man . . . while we pause to think that, after all, it is this enormous coördination of the separate units of thought and action which constitutes the somatic basis of the highest mental functions. (pp. 301-302).

As Spitzka saw it, the best evidence that the corpus callosum was important for this coordination came from the reports linking mental deficiency to callosal agenesis or to callosal tumors (". . . every case of deficiency or disease of this structure is attended by more or less profound weak-mindedness or downright idiocy, not to speak of hemiparetic and other affections" [p. 302]). (Spitzka did not cite specific cases, and he evidently had overlooked the negative reports by Bruce, 1889-1900, and Douglas-Crawford, 1906.) Spitzka also drew support from his own anatomical studies. Compared with "ordinary men, individually and collectively," Spitzka found that notable men had larger callosa; indeed, that of the morphologist Joseph Leidy was larger than "any other in this series or recorded in literature" (p. 303). "Here again," Spitzka said, "we have an index in somatic terms of how we may distinguish the brain of the genius or talented man from that of persons of only ordinary abilities" (p. 303).

Spitzka studied only men's brains (no women having been invited into the Society), and, in his statements about brain size and commissure size, he had not raised the possibility of sex differences. This question was taken up by a young American anatomist named Robert Bean (1906). While working at The Johns Hopkins University, Bean had undertaken the study of over 150 brains. Bean's initial purpose was to compare the brains of blacks with those of whites[23], but, in the course of this work, he discovered both race- and sex-related differences in the corpus callosum. The "most striking" differences were "in the anterior and posterior lineal halves," the anterior, or genu, being larger, in proportion to the posterior, or splenium, in the whites than in the blacks, and larger in the males than in the females (1906, p. 391). From the brain's overall appearance, including the shape or size of the corpus callosum, Bean reported being able to determine race

---

[23] Bean credited the original suggestion for studying race differences to his mentor at Johns Hopkins, the distinguished anatomist Franklin Mall, as a result of information provided by the anatomist A. Hrdlicka, of the United States National Museum, suggesting racial differences in the brain (Bean, 1906, p. 354).

and sex correctly 60 times, one or the other 15 times, and neither only 4 times (p. 411).

Bean explained the racial differences and, by implication, the sex differences, as signifying differences in the corresponding parts of the brain itself. That is, the larger anterior:posterior ratio in the size of the corpus callosum in the brains of whites as compared with the brains of blacks implied similar differences in the ratio of the anterior to posterior cortical association centers. In consideration of the "deduced differences between the functions of the anterior and posterior association centers and from the known characteristics of the two races," Bean (1906) concluded that "the Negro has the lower mental faculties (smell, sight, handicraftsmanship, body sense, melody) well developed, the Caucasian the higher (self-control, will power, ethical and aesthetic senses and reason)" (p. 412).

Bean's mentor, Franklin Mall (1909), evaluated both Spitzka's and Bean's claims. In the case of Spitzka's work, Mall agreed that the callosum of Joseph Leidy was the largest on record, "but regarding the rest he is in error" (p. 8). Mall asserted that all the rest of the callosa of Spitzka's notable men were not above the average for brains of the same weight, whereas the figures for Spitzka's ordinary men were much below the average of Mall's own data. (It may be relevant that Spitzka's "ordinary" men were electrocuted criminals.)

As for race differences, Mall repeated Bean's measurement, but with a more accurate instrument. Unlike Bean, Mall also controlled for what was called the "personal equation": he made all of his measurements "without my knowing the race or sex of any of the individuals from which the brains were taken" (Mall, 1909, p. 9). The results confirmed Bean's findings that callosal area increased with brain weight, and that callosal area minus splenium area increased with the weight of the frontal lobes. However, there was great individual variation, and it was comparable in the brains of whites and blacks. As for the female callosa, they were "somewhat different from the male, but this is due no doubt to the lighter [brain] weight of the former" (Mall, p. 9). Mall therefore concluded that "there is no variation in either genu or splenium of the corpus callosum due to either race or sex" (p. 11).

Mall's report was influential in the often bitter psychological debate about race and sex differences in sensory and cognitive skills. The American psychologist Helen Thompson Woolley (1910) called it "the single most important contribution to our knowledge of the facts of the case," namely, that "there is as yet no reliable evidence for the variation of anatomical characters with either race or sex" (p. 335; for an account of these early debates, see Harris, 1985a).

COMMISSUROTOMY STUDIES OF THE 1930S AND 1940S: A NEGATIVE PRELUDE TO THE MODERN ERA

By the 1930s, then, the callosal question had been pursued in a variety of ways: by the anatomical study of white matter (including between-species comparisons), experiments on animals, retrospective accounts of the behavior of deceased persons whose postmortems disclosed callosal agenesis, clinical evaluations of patients with callosal tumors or infarcts, psychiatric studies of the mentally deranged, and studies of individual differences in callosal size. Still missing were tests of human patients who had undergone surgical commissurotomy. Recall that Gustav Fechner predicted that such an operation would produce two half-brains, each with a separate consciousness, whereas William McDougall was sufficiently impressed by Bruce's (1889-1890) negative evidence based on agenesis cases that he was ready to sacrifice his own corpus callosum for a definitive test.

PARTIAL SECTION OF THE CORPUS CALLOSUM FOR APPROACH TO VENTRICULAR TUMORS: THE WORK OF WALTER E. DANDY

By the 1930s, there was a definitive test, or what was regarded as such by its chief investigator, the distinguished American neurosurgeon Walter E. Dandy. Through a long career at Johns Hopkins, Dandy was said to have done more to advance neurosurgical techniques than any other pioneer in this speciality (Walker, 1970, p. 549). Writing in the journal *Archives of Surgery*, Dandy (1936) described the effects of partially sectioning the corpus callosum in approaching posterior third-ventricle tumors in three patients, a 10-year-old boy, a 15-year-old boy, and a 28-year-old woman (among a total of 10 patients under 37 years of age). Finding that "No symptoms follow its division," he concluded, "This simple experiment at once disposes of the extravagant claims to function of the corpus callosum" (p. 40).

Given the controversy swirling around the callosal hypothesis, Dandy's unqualified judgment seems precipitous, particularly because he did not mention which "extravagent claims" he had in mind and did not mention, much less critically review, any previous clinical or experimental studies (the only citations are to his own surgical work). His assessment of the patients' postoperative behavior also drew heavily on accounts of their gross adjustment rather than on formal behavioral tests, so that, at least in retrospect, it is possible that certain potentially significant clues were not followed up. For instance, two and one half years after his operation, the youngest patient, now nearly 13 years old, said that he could "throw a ball accurately but was unable to catch it" (p. 25). This may have been a sign of the sort of long-term motor coordination problems that we now know can occur following commissurotomy (D. Zaidel & Sperry, 1977).

Partial and Complete Section to Arrest Epileptic Seizures: The Work of Akelaitis, Von Wagenen, Herren, and Others

Dandy's dismissal of the "extravagant claims to function of the corpus callosum" hardly closed off further study. Dandy, however, did appear to be vindicated by the far more comprehensive investigations of commissurotomy patients in the 1940s by Andrew Akelaitis, William Van Wagenen, R. Yorke Herren, and their co-workers at the University of Rochester (New York) School of Medicine and Dentistry and at Strong Memorial Hospital. The immediate impetus for these studies had been clinical observations of patients with convulsive seizures who also had different kinds of callosal injuries. In each case, the observations suggested that generalized convulsive seizures became less frequent as the corpus callosum was more and more nearly destroyed. For example, in patients with callosal tumors (nearly all glioblastomas), which develop over a 12- to 15-month period, convulsions were common in earlier stages but much rarer in later stages. In a patient with a long history of seizures, seizure activity ceased following a cerebrovascular accident that interrupted the scar of a former hemorrhage from the anterior cerebral artery (Van Wagenen & Herren, 1940).

It was with these clinical observations in mind that Van Wagenen and Herren (1940) decided to divide the corpus callosum in epileptic patients for whom conventional therapies had failed. The first operation, a partial callosotomy, was performed in 1939 on a 33-year-old man; this was followed by partial or complete callosotomies on nine more individuals.

Van Wagenen and Herren (1940) cited only their own clinical observations as reasons to proceed with this radical procedure, but they would also have been able to muster independent support from animal experiments by Theodore Erickson (1940), first reported at the Montreal Neurological Society in 1938, and the American Psychiatric Association in 1939. Erickson, a neurologist at the Montreal Neurological Institute, presented clear and convincing evidence that section of the corpus callosum in monkeys (*Macacca mulatta*) prevented the spread of the epileptic after-discharge induced by electrical stimulation of the cerebral cortex. The "after-discharge," Erickson (1940) pointed out, was "a faithful experimental counterpart of clinical types of epilepsy" (p. 452). In contrast to earlier studies, this research thus firmly supported the view that the corpus callosum was the central mechanism of generalized seizures. Erickson also offered a reasonable explanation why generalized seizures persisted in Karplus' (1914) prior commissurotomy study of dogs and monkeys.

Based on these and other experimental data, on clinical evidence by Hyndman and Penfield (1937) suggesting that in epileptic patients with callosal agenesis, seizure activity was significantly diminished and non-generalized, and finally on two clinical cases he had personally observed, Erickson (1940) concluded, "I cannot but wonder . . . whether a truly generalized fit occurs in the presence of complete agenesis or surgical section of the corpus callosum in man" (1940, p. 449).[24]

---

[24] Given Hyndman and Penfield's (1937) endorsement of Bykov and Speransky's (1924) demonstration of the effects of commissurotomy on *sensory* transmission, one might expect them to have endorsed Erickson's (1940) prediction about the effects of commissural section on *motor* transmission. Hyndman and Penfield themselves, however, made no comment about the link that Erickson saw in their clinical data between epilepsy and the integrity of the corpus callosum. Perhaps they were less impressed by their own data than Erickson had been. Another consideration is that Penfield himself had proposed that the mechanism of interhemispheric spread of epileptic discharge was "humoral," that is, that it was due to some humoral agent, alpha substance, which is at the same time responsible for the change in blood flow (Penfield, 1938; see also Erickson, 1940, p. 448). Whatever Penfield did or did not think about Erickson's supposition, it was, of course, at Rochester, not Montreal, where the first commissurotomy was performed for the express purpose of relieving epilepsy.

Thus, both Erickson (1940) and Van Wagenen and Herren (1940) had independently arrived at similar positions about the likely effects of commissurotomy for epileptic patients. Their expectations would be largely borne out. For Van Wagenen and Herren's (1940) first epileptic patient and for six of the nine others, the operation did, indeed, succeed in reducing or eliminating generalized seizures. Where the operation did not succeed, Van Wagenen and Herron (1940) suggested that the reason may have been the presence of multiple, bilateral foci. The neurophysiologists Warren S. McCulloch and Hugh Garol (1941) suggested, instead, that the reason may have been that the none of the operations had included the sectioning of the anterior commissure. Their own experimental studies of monkeys showed that the anterior commissure was an additional mechanism for the spread of after-discharge.

The clinical and experimental results, in combination, showed that a motor signal not only was transmitted across the hemispheres by the neocortical commissures, but that the commissures somehow worked to augment the signal. Finally, like Dandy (1936), Akelaitis recognized that the operation also opened the way to the study of hemispheric function through separate testing of each hemisphere. Cognizant of the mixed evidence (the negative reports by Dandy, 1936, and others *vs.* the positive reports by Liepmann, 1905/1908, and Liepmann and Maas, 1907), Akelaitis and his colleagues went on to measure psychological function in their own patients.

The results were encouraging for the patients, but not for the callosal hypothesis because the patients showed few obvious cognitive or perceptual changes, and, with only a few exceptions, none that could be traced exclusively to their callosotomy. Thus, Akelaitis, Risteen, Herren, and Van Wagenen (1942, p. 1007) concluded that "dyspraxia in the subordinate or dominant hand after partial or complete section of the corpus callosum occurs only when damage to the subordinate or dominant hemisphere coexists (see also Akelaitis, 1941a, 1941b; 1943, 1944; Bridgman & Smith, 1945; Parsons, 1940; Smith, 1947; Smith & Akelaitis, 1942). The exceptions just noted, however, were and remain noteworthy. In certain cases, unmistakable "disconnection" effects were seen that, it now seems likely, could be directly attributed to the section of the corpus callosum. Some effects were first noted by Van Wagenen and Herron (1940), for example, a patient who said that the muscles of his left side did not coordinate very well with those of the rest of his body: "For instance, I find myself trying to open a door with the right hand and at the same time trying to push it shut with the left . ." (p. 756). The condition, however, was only temporary. This, presumably, was one of the patients to whom Akelaitis (1944-1945) was referring when he reported that, of 30 patients with callosal section, 2 patients showed "a remarkable type of behavior which has not been described" previously, consisting of "an apparent conflict between the desired act and the actually performed act," and manifested, in both patients, as a "conflict" between the right and left hands (p. 594). Akelaitis called this condition *diagnostic dyspraxia*.

The negative evidence, nonetheless, far outweighed the positive, and so it reinforced previous doubts about the corpus callosum's role in normal cognitive and perceptual functions. The conclusion reached by two researchers who worked with these patients — the physicist Charles S. Bridgman and the psychologist Karl U. Smith — is representative. Having failed to find any marked deficit produced by section of the corpus callosum, including the splenium, on a variety of visual perceptual functions, including binocular perception, visual fusion, and perception of movement, Bridgman and Smith (1945) concluded that the corpus callosum must be excluded as the interhemispheric pathway and that a "prime role" must be proposed for subcortical levels of the central visual system (p. 68). Writing in 1949, McCulloch offered a somewhat more qualified assessment of the state of the evidence. Noting Erickson's (1940) and others' experimental studies with animals, along with Van Wagenen and Herren's (1940) report that, in certain instances, commissurotomy could prevent seizures in epileptic patients from becoming generalized, McCulloch (1949a) concluded that "this multitude of cortico-cortico connections obviously is capable of determining phenomena in *abnormal* situations . . . " (p. 241, emphasis added), but he went on to say that the part played by the corpus callosum "in ordinary activity and in normal behavior remains a mystery" (p. 241). Indeed, the evidence made McCulloch (1949b) wonder whether the structure had any other role: "I have laughingly said that, so far as I can see, it is the only demonstrable function of the corpus callosum, to spread seizures from one side to the other. I still do not know of anything else we can attribute to it safely" (p. 21).

Karl Lashley's Experimental Studies of Animals

The Akelaitis studies, as Joynt (1974) remarked, "coupled with the negative reports of others, almost laid the corpus callosum to rest" (p. 122). Then, the "coup de grace," as Joynt (1974, p. 123) called it, was delivered by the American neuropsychologist Karl Lashley (1950). In unpublished experiments on monkeys that had been trained "in habits which are abolished by destruction of the frontal lobes and which require visual, tactile, and kinesthetic adjustments[25] leaving only the projection fibers for the area" (p. 483), Lashley cut the transcortical fibers of the frontal lobes. In other words, Lashley performed partial commissurotomies, involving the anterior part of the structure. After the operation, however, the animals showed "no disturbance of performance . . . " (p. 483). Lashley called the results "difficult to accept" (p. 483) but noted that they were supported by other lines of evidence, including the commissurotomy studies of Smith (1947) and Akelaitis (1944). Lashley (1950) therefore suggested that the results "point to the conclusion that the associative connexions or memory traces of the conditioned reflex do not extend across the cortex as well-defined arcs or paths. Such arcs are either diffused through all parts of the cortex, pass by relay through lower centres, or do not exist" (p. 484).

---

[25] Lashley (1950) did not identify the kind of task, but, based on his account of "frontal-lobe" tasks used in his other experiments, it was either a complex problem-solving task requiring the opening of a latch box or a task requiring simple sensori-motor associations (what Lashley called a *conditioned-reflex task*).

For Lashley, the Smith (1947) and Akelaitis (1944) studies strengthened a long-held view. Replying to a question following his Hixon Symposium paper on "The problem of serial order in behavior," Lashley (1951) said that "26 years ago," he had "suggested facetiously" that the corpus callosum, along with other long association tracts in the cortex, "might be only skeletal structures, since I could find no function for them" (p. 132).

If McCulloch (1949b) and Lashley (1951) expressed themselves in a jocular vein (in realization, perhaps, of the absurdity that so massive a structure should have no role other than as a conduit for epileptic transmission), the anatomist Joseph Tomasch felt no such reservation. Referring to Akelaitis et al. (1942), Tomasch (1954) said, "They showed very clearly and in accordance with some earlier authors like Dandy, Foerster, Meagher, and Barre [no references cited], . . . that the C.C. [corpus callosum] is hardly connected with psychological function at all" (p. 119; see also Tomasch, 1957).

Other Historical Forces

Given the new evidence, Tomasch's verdict was understandable, if somewhat hyperbolic. What must also be considered is the broader context in which the new evidence could be evaluated. As already noted, Bykov and Speransky's (1924) powerful demonstration seems to have been overlooked, and Dejerine's and Liepmann's work was fast fading from the scene (none of these individuals were cited by Tomasch, 1954, or by Lashley, 1950, 1951, or McCullogh, 1949a, 1949b). The neurologist Norman Geschwind (1974) offered a revealing example of this neglect in the case of Liepmann's work. Even though Liepmann's collaborator, Otto Maas, was still alive in the 1950s, and the work had been confirmed by several investigators, including Goldstein (1908), Geschwind found that those of Goldstein's students whom he had met "were generally unaware" of his contribution. He remarked that this made him realize "not merely of how inaccurate most of the histories of the higher functions were, but also that important confirmed scientific observations could almost be expunged from the knowledge of contemporary scientists" (Geschwind, 1974, p. 19). The reasons, he suggested, are fairly standard: "neglect of work written in a foreign language, neglect of work done by someone in a different field, and excessive reliance on the authority of certain towering individual figures" (p. 19). Political events must also be considered. German neurology and German science generally were blotted out because of the two world wars, Liepmann's work being but one of many causalties. (Soviet science met a similar fate after the beginning of the Cold War.) In addition, as Geschwind (1965a, p. 240) suggested, in the period between the world wars, the criticisms of the "holistically oriented neurologists," such as Henry Head, Pierre Marie, Christian von Monakow, and Goldstein himself, probably contributed to the decline of interest (e.g., Head's 1926 account of apraxia was cursory and, according to Geschwind, 1965, p. 240, "at least in part, incorrect"). Also contributing to the decline were the rise of holistic psychology under the leadership of the Gestaltists and Karl Lashley, and the rapid development of the holistic schools of psychiatry, and the disappearance from the scene of Dejerine and Liepmann themselves. As a result, Geschwind suggested, when papers appeared that reasserted the importance of the corpus callosum, such as those by Foix and Hillemand (1925), Trescher and Ford (1937), and Maspes (1948), they were generally ignored. In this connection, it is noteworthy that one of Dandy's (1936) patients was the one reported by Trescher and Ford (1937) to have hemialexia.

THE 1950S AND AFTER

If, under the circumstances, Tomasch's (1954, 1957) blunt dismissal of the callosal hypothesis was understandable, his timing was unfortunate. During that period at the University of Chicago, Ronald E. Myers and Roger Sperry were finding unmistakable disconnection effects in commissurotomized cats (Myers, 1956; Myers & Sperry, 1953, 1958). In contrast to previous attempts, Myers and Sperry combined the complete sectioning of the corpus callosum with the sectioning (in one experimental condition) of the optic chiasm, thereby ensuring that each eye would be connected to only one hemisphere. The result was remarkable: After being trained to make a visual discrimination with one eye masked, the cats were able to remember, using their second eye, what they had learned with the first eye when only the optic chiasm or the corpus callosum had been sectioned previously, but could not remember the discrimination when both structures had been sectioned. Just as remarkably, with both structures sectioned, the cats could learn, with their second, or untrained eye, just the reverse of what they had learned with the first eye, and evidently with no interference, thereby indicating functional independence of the surgically separated cerebral hemispheres. These initial experiments were amply confirmed by numerous other studies with cats, as well as other species (e.g., Downer, 1958; Schrier & Sperry, 1959; Sperry, Stamm, & Miner, 1956; Trevarthen, 1961). Writing in 1961, Sperry felt confident in saying that, "During the past seven years or so, the old 'riddle' of the corpus callosum has been largely resolved in animal studies in which it has been possible at last to demonstrate definite high-level integrating functions for this structure" (p. 1749).

Following these animal studies there came equally startling clinical and experimental investigations of a new series of some two dozen patients with intractable epilepsy. All had undergone commissurotomy operations by the Los Angeles neurosurgeons Philip J. Vogel and Joseph Bogen (Bogen & Vogel, 1962) in hopes that their seizures could be diminished or eliminated. Afterward, they were studied intensively by Sperry, now at the California Institute of Technology, working in collaboration with Bogen and a host of gifted students. Using a variety of tests of recognition of tachistoscopically-projected stimuli, which allowed the hemispheres to be assessed independently, Sperry and his collaborators obtained results as positive as those of Akelaitis et al. (1942) had been negative (e.g., Gazzaniga, Bogen, & Sperry, 1962; Gordon & Sperry, 1968; Levy, Trevarthen, & Sperry, 1972; Levy-Agresti & Sperry, 1968; Nebes, 1972; Sperry, 1962; D. Zaidel & Sperry, 1977; E. Zaidel, 1975).

In light of the success of these new studies, how was one to explain the largely negative findings reported by Akelaitis and his collaborators? Bogen (1985, p. 304) attributed most of them to two sources. First, when the callosotomy is incomplete, as it was in most of Akelaitis' patients, cross-communication between the hemispheres can be retained even with quite small callosal remnants, especially when the splenium remains intact. In Vogel and Bogen's patients, by contrast, the entire corpus callosum was sectioned, along with the anterior commissure, the hippocampal commissure, and, when it was present, the massa intermedia. Second, in retrospect, Akelaitis' testing methods were largely inappropriate or insensitive for disclosing disconnection effects.

About the same time as the patient testing was underway in California, Norman Geschwind and Edith Kaplan, working in Boston, were making their own contribution to the developing story. Geschwind (1965a, p. 241) recalled how Myers and Sperry's (1953) animal studies had led him and his colleagues in 1961 to re-examine the older clinical literature and to reassess their own patients who had disturbances of higher functions. The result was that Geschwind discovered Dejerine's (1892) paper on alexia without agraphia, which, as he recalled, first made him aware of the occurrence of callosal syndromes in man (Geschwind, 1974, p. 18; see account in Geschwind, 1962). Within a few weeks, Geschwind and his colleague Davis Howes had seen their own first case of alexia without agraphia (Howes, 1962).   Shortly afterward, Kaplan called to Geschwind's attention a patient who showed what proved to be callosal apraxia of the kind described by Liepmann, that is, apraxia following callosal infarct: the patient was unable to carry out commands with his left hand but could imitate and use objects with it. In late 1961, Geschwind and Kaplan presented their findings at the annual research meeting of the Veterans Administration Hospital in Boston and at a meeting of the Boston Society for Neurology and Psychiatry, during which they diagnosed a callosal infarction sparing the splenium. A more extended account of the case was published later (Geschwind & Kaplan, 1962), in which they "were able to point out in a last-minute footnote" that a post-mortem had confirmed their antemortem diagnosis (Geschwind, 1965a, p. 241).

Thus, within a remarkably short time, the scientific world discovered, or rediscovered, the human "split-brain," some of the secrets of "the great cerebral commissure" were revealed, the study of hemispheric communication was given new life, and the work of such seminal figures as Dejerine and Liepmann was revived and introduced to a new generation of neuropsychologists. Finally, in Stockholm in 1981, in recognition of his role as the premier architect of the new scientific era, Roger Sperry was awarded the Nobel Prize in Physiology or Medicine.

CLOSING NOTE

This survey has covered many of the themes and developments in the history of research and theory on hemispheric communication. Although I could not touch on all parts of the record, much less dig deeply into it, what has been included is enough, I hope, to suggest the long and broad sweep of the story as well as some of its twists and turns. The reports that follow present some of the most recent empirical and theoretical developments. These reports document impressive further progress in our understanding of how the corpus callosum works in the promotion of hemispheric communication and what a long way we have come from the time when Nicolaus Steno could write, "Indeed, the corpus callosum is so unknown to us that anyone with the least inclination can say what he pleases about it." At the same time, the new reports show that we continue to struggle with methodological and conceptual issues fundamentally quite similar to those that confronted our predecessors. Having come so far, we more clearly see that we still have far to go.

ACKNOWLEDGMENTS

For help in collecting source material for this work, I thank the librarians of the Reference Department, Science Library, and Document Delivery Service of the Michigan State University Library. I am also grateful to Professors Albert I. Rabin and Michael Peters for help in German translation, and Professor Carl Anderson for Latin translation.

REFERENCES

Adam, C. E., & Tannery, P. (1896-1910). *Oeuvres de Descartes* [Descartes' works]. (Vols. 1-12). Paris: Cerf.

Akelaitis, A. J. (1941a). Psychobiological studies following section of the corpus callosum: A preliminary report. *The American Journal of Psychiatry, 97,* 1147-1157.

Akelaitis, A. J. (1941b). Studies on the corpus callosum: II. The higher visual functions in each homonymous field following complete section of the corpus callosum. *Archives of Neurology and Psychiatry, 45,* 788-796.

Akelaitis, A. J. (1943). Studies on the corpus callosum: VII. Study of language function (tactile and visual lexia and graphia) unilaterally following section of the corpus callosum. *Journal of Neuropathology and Experimental Neurology, 2,* 226-262.

Akelaitis, A. J. (1944). A study of gnosis, praxis and language following section of the corpus callosum and anterior commissure. *Journal of Neurosurgery, 1,* 94-102.

Akelaitis, A. J. (1944-45). Studies on the corpus callosum: IV. Diagnostic dyspraxia in epileptics following partial and complete section of the corpus callosum. *The American Journal of Psychiatry, 101,* 594-599.

Akelaitis, A. J., Risteen, W. A., Herren, R. Y., & Van Wagenen, W. P. (1942). Studies on the corpus callosum: III. A contribution to the study of dyspraxia in epileptics following partial and complete section of the corpus callosum. *Archives of Neurology and Psychiatry, 47,* 971-1008.

Aldini, G. (1804). *Essai théorique et expérimental sur le galvanisme, avec une série d'expériences faites en présence des commissaires de l'Institut national de France* [Theoretical and experimental essay on galvinism, with a series of experiments witnessed by the commissioners of the National Institute of France]. Paris: Fournier.

Alpers, B. J., & Grant, F. C. (1931). The clinical syndrome of the corpus callosum. *Archives of Neurology and Psychiatry, 25*, 67-86.

Anrep, G. V. (1917). Irradiation of conditioned inhibition. *Russian Journal of Physiology, 1*, Nos. 1-2.

Anrep, G. V. (1923). The irradiation of conditioned reflexes. *Proceedings of the Royal Society of London*, Series B, *94*, 404-426.

Armitage, G., & Meagher, R. (1933). Gliomas of the corpus callosum. *Zeitschrift für die gesamte Neurologie und Psychiatrie, 146*, 454-488.

Arnold, F. (1838-1840). *Tabulae anatomicae* [Anatomical tables]. London: Black & Armstrong.

Ayala, G. (1915). Contributo allo studio dei tumori del corpo calloso. [Contribution to the study of tumors of the corpus callosum]. *Rivista di Patologia Nervosa e Mentale, 20*, 449-492.

Babkin, B. P. (1949). *Pavlov: A biography*. Chicago: The University of Chicago Press.

Baker, R. C., & Graves, G. O. (1933). Partial agenesis of the corpus callosum. *Archives of Neurology and Psychiatry, 29*, 1054-1065.

Bastian, H. C. (1898). *A treatise on aphasia and other speech defects*. London: Lewis.

Bean, R. B. (1906). Some racial peculiarities of the Negro brain. *American Journal of Anatomy, 5*, 353-432.

Beevor, C. E. (1891). On the course of the fibres of the cingulum and the posterior parts of the corpus callosum and fornix in the Marmoset monkey. *Philosophical Transactions of the Royal Society of London*, Series B, *182*, 135-199.

Bell, J., & Bell, C. (1827). *The anatomy and physiology of the human body* (Vols. 1-2, with corrections by C. Bell, 5th American ed.) New York: Collins & Co. (reprinted from the 6th London ed. of 1826; revised by J. D. Godman)

Bianchi, G. B. (1749). *Storia del mostro di due corpi* [Story of the monster with two bodies]. Torino: Filippo Antonio.

Bianki, V. L. (1958). Effect of partial division of the corpus callosum in dogs on the differentiation of visual, auditory, and cutaneous stimuli. *Sechenov Physiological Journal of the U.S.S.R., 44*, 660-667. (Original work published 1958 (in Russian) in *Fiziologicheskii zhurnal SSSR imeni I. M. Sechenova, 44* (# 8), 701-708)

Bogen, J. E. (1985). The callosal syndromes. In K. M. Heilman & E. Valenstein (Eds.), *Clinical neuropsychology* (2nd ed., pp. 295-338). New York: Oxford University Press.

Bogen, J. E., & Bogen, G. M. (1969). The other side of the brain: III. The corpus callosum and creativity. *Bulletin of the Los Angeles Neurological Societies, 34*, 191-220.

Bogen, J. E., & Vogel, P. J. (1962). Cerebral commissurotomy in man. Preliminary case report. *Bulletin of the Los Angeles Neurological Societies, 27*, 169-172.

Bonhoeffer, K. (1914). Klinischer und anatomischer Befunde zur Lehre von der Apraxie und der "motorischen Sprachbahn" [Clinical and anatomical findings concerning apraxia and motor speech pathway]. *Monatsschrift für Psychiatrie und Neurologie, 35*, 113-128.

Brazier, M. A. (1984). *A history of neurophysiology in the 17th and 18th centuries.* New York: Raven.

Bridgman, C. S., & Smith, K. U. (1945). Bilateral neural integration in visual perception after section of the corpus callosum. *The Journal of Comparative Neurology, 83*, 57-68.

Bristowe, J. S. (1884). Cases of tumour of the corpus callosum. *Brain, 7,* 315-333.

Broca, P. (1861). Remarques sur le siège de la faculté du langage articulé, suiviés d'une observation d'aphemie (perte de la parole) [Remarks on the site of the faculty of articulate speech, followed by an observation of aphemia (loss of speech)]. *Bulletins de la Société Anatomique de Paris, 6*, 330-357.

Broca, P. (1863). Localisation des fonctions cérébrales. Siège de la faculté du langage articulé [Localization of cerebral functions. Site of the faculty of articulate speech]. *Bulletins de la Société d'Anthropologie de Paris, 4,* 200-204.

Broca, P. (1865). Sur le siège de la faculté du langage articulé [On the site of the faculty of articulate speech]. *Bulletins de la Société d'Anthropologie de Paris, 6,* 377-393.

Brown-Séquard, C. E. (1887). Sur l'existence dans chacun des hémisphères cérébraux de deux séries de fibres capables d'agir sur les deux moitiés du corps, soit pour y produire des mouvements, soit pour déterminer des phénomènes inhibitoires [On the existence in each of the cerebral hemispheres of two series of fibers capable of acting on the two halves of the body, either to produce movements or to produce inhibition]. *Comptes Rendus de la Société de Biologie,* (Series 8, *4*), 261-264.

Bruce, A. (1889-1890). On the absence of the corpus callosum in the human brain, with the description of a new case. *Brain, 12,* 171-190.

Buffon, G. L. LeC., Comte de Buffon (1971). De la nature de l'homme [On the nature of man]. In G. L. LeC. Buffon, *Histoire naturelle* (Vol. 2, *De l'homme*, pp. 3-15). Paris: Vialetay. (Original work published 1750.)

Bykov, K. M., & Speransky, A. D. (1924). Observation upon dogs after section of the corpus callosum. *Collected papers of the physiological laboratories of I. P. Pavlov, 1* (# 1), pp. 47-59. (Also published 1924-1925 in *Zentralblatt für die gesammte Neurologie und Psychiatrie, 39*, 199-211)

Carville, C., & Duret, H. (1875). Sur les fonctions des hémisphères (Histoire, critique et recherches expérimentales) [On the functions of the hemispheres (History, criticism, and experimental studies]. *Archives de Physiologie Normale et Pathologique, 7,* 352-491.

Churchland, P. S. (1986). *Neurophilosophy: Toward a unified science of the mind/brain.* Cambridge, MA: MIT Press.

Clarke, E., & Dewhurst, K. (1972). *An illustrated history of brain function.* Oxford, England: Sandford Publications.

Clarke, E., & O'Malley, C. D. (1968) (Eds., Trans., and Commentators). *The human brain and spinal cord: A historical study illustrated by writings from antiquity to the twentieth century.* Berkeley, CA: University of California Press.

Dandy, W. R. (1936). Operative experience in cases of pineal tumors. *Archives of Surgery, 33,* 19-46.

Dejerine, J. J. (1892). Contribution a l'étude anatamo-pathologique et clinique des différentes variétés de cécité verbale. [Contribution to the anatomical-pathological and clinical study of the different varieties of word blindness]. *Comtes Rendus des Séances de la Société de Biologie, 4,* 61-90.

Dejerine, J. J. (1895). *Anatomie des centres nerveux* [Anatomy of the neuronal centers]. Paris: Rueff.

Dennett, D. C. (1991). *Consciousness explained.* Boston: Little, Brown.

Denny-Brown, D. (Ed.) (1979). *Selected writings of Sir Charles Sherrington.* Oxford, England: Oxford University Press.

Descartes, R. (1988). *The passions of the soul.* Excerpted in *Descartes: Selected philosophical writings* (J. Cottingham, R. Stoolthoff, & D. Murdoch, Trans.). Cambridge, England: Cambridge University Press. (Original work published 1649 as *Les passions de l'ame,* Paris: Chez Henry LeGras)

Descartes, R. (1972). *Treatise on man.* (T. S. Hall, Trans.). Cambridge, MA: Harvard University Press. (Original work published 1664 as *Les traites de l'homme et de la formation du foetus,* Paris: Chez Nicholas Le Gras)

Descourtis, G. (1890). Les deux cerveaux de l'homme [The two brains of man]. *Revue d'hypnologie théorique et pratique, 1,* 97-106.

Douglas-Crawford, D. (1906). A case of absence of the corpus callosum. *Journal of Anatomy and Physiology,* Vol. XL. Third Series, Vol. I, 57-64.

Downer, J. L. deC. (1958). Role of corpus callosum in transfer of training in *Macaca mulatta. Federal Proceedings, 17,* 37.

Eichler, G. (1878). Ein Fall von Balkenmangel im menschlichen Gehirn. [A case of callosal agenesis in the human brain]. *Archiv für Psychiatrie und Nervenkrankeiten, 8* (pt. 2), 355-366.

Elliot, F. A. (1969). The corpus callosum, cingulate gyrus, septum pellucidum, septal area and fornix. In P. J. Vinken & G. W. Bruyn (Eds.), *Handbook of clinical neurology: Localization in clinical neurology* (Vol. 2, pp. 758-777). Amsterdam: North Holland.

Elliotson, J. (1847). On the joint operation of the two halves of the brain: with a notice of Dr. Wigan's work, entitled *The Duality of the Mind, etc. The Zooist, 15*, 209-234.

Erb, W. H. (1885). A case of hemorrhage into the corpus callosum. *The Journal of Nervous and Mental Diseases, 12*, 121. (English abstract of "Ein Fall von Hämorrhagie in das Corpus callosum," in *Virchow's Archiv für pathologische Anatomie und Physiologie und Klinische Medizin*, 1884, *14*, 329-339)

Erickson, T. C. (1940). Spread of the epileptic discharge: An experimental study of the after-discharge induced by electrical stimulation of the cerebral cortex. *Archives of Neurology and Psychiatry, 43*, 429-452.

Espy, W. (1978). *O thou improper, thou uncommon noun*. New York: Clarkson N. Potter, Inc.

Esquirol, J. E. D. (1845). *Mental maladies: A treatise on insanity* (E. K. Hunt, Trans.). Philadelphia: Lea and Blanchard. (Original work published 1838 as *Des maladies mentales, considerées sous les rapports médical, hygiénique et medico-légal*. Paris: J.- B. Ballière et Fils)

Fechner, G. T. (1907). *Elemente der Psychophysik* [Elements of psychophysics]. (Vol. 2). Leipzig: Breitkopf & Hartel. (Original work published 1860)

Ferraro, A. (1970). Giovanni Mingazzini (1859-1929). In W. Haymaker & F. Schiller (Eds.), *The founders of neurology* (2nd ed., pp. 348-351). Springfield, IL: Charles C. Thomas.

Ferrier, D. (1876). *The functions of the brain*. London: Smith, Elder.

Ferrier, D. (1890). The Croonian Lectures on cerebral localisation. Lecture II. *The British Medical Journal, 1*, 1349-1355.

Flechsig, P. (1901). Developmental (myelogenetic) localisation of the cerebral cortex in the human subject. *Lancet, 2*, 1027-1029.

Flourens, M. J. P. (1842). *Recherches expérimentales sur les propriétes et les fonctions du système nerveux dans les animaux vertebrés [Experimental studies on the properties and functions of the nervous system in vertebrates]* (2nd ed.). Paris: J.- B. Ballière et Fils. (Original work published 1824, Paris: Crevot)

Flower, W. H. (1865). On the commissures of the cerebral hemispheres of the Marsupialia and Monotremata as compared with those of the Placental Mammals. *Philosophical Transactions of the Royal Society of London, 155*, 633-651.

Foix, C., & Hillemand, P. (1925). Les syndromes de l'artère cérébrale antérieure [The anterior cerebral artery syndromes]. *Encéphale, 20*, 209-214.

Fontana. F. G. F. (1781). *Traité sur le vénin de la vipère, sur les poisons americans, sur le laurier-cerise et sur quelques autres poisons* [Treatise on the venom of the viper; on the American poisons; and on the cherry laurel and some other vegetable poisons] (Vols. 1-2). Florence, Italy.

Forel, A. H. (1907). *Gesammelte hirnanatomishche Abhandlungen mit einem Aufsatz über die Aufgaben der Neurobiologie* [A collection of essays on the anatomy of the cerebral cortex, with a treatise on the domain of neurobiology]. Munich: E. Reinhardt.

Förster, A. (1861). *Die Missbildungen des Menschen: systematisch dargestellt* [The malformation of man, systematically portrayed] (2nd ed.). Jena: Druck und Verlag von Friedrich Mauke.

Foville, A. L. F. (1844). *Traité complet de l'anatomie de la physiologie et de la pathologie du système nerveux cérébrospinal* [Complete work on the anatomy, physiology, and pathology of the cerebrospinal nervous system]. Paris: Fortin, Masson et Cie.

François-Franck, [no initial], & Pitres, A. (1883a). Recherches expérimentales et critiques sur les convulsions épileptiformes d'origine corticale [Experimental studies and critiques on epileptic convulsions of cortical origin]. *Archives de Physiologie Normale et Pathologique*, Series 2, Vol. 2, 1-40; 117-144.

Fritsch, G., & Hitzig, E. (1870). Uber die elektrische Erregbarkeit des Grosshirns [On the electrical excitability of the cerebrum]. *Archiv für Anatomie und Physiologie*, 300-332. (Reprinted 1960 in English translation in G. von Bonin, Ed. & Trans., *Some papers on the cerebral cortex* (pp. 73-96). Springfield, IL: Charles C. Thomas)

Gall, F. G., & Spurzheim, J. C. (1810-1819). *Anatomie et physiologie du système nerveux en général, et du cerveau en particulier* [Anatomy and physiology of the nervous system in general, and of the brain in particular] (Vols. 1-4 and atlas). Paris: F. Schoell. (Translated excerpts 1968 in E. Clarke & C. D. O'Malley, *The human brain and spinal cord: A historical study illustrated by writings from antiquity to the twentieth century* [pp. 598-602]. Berkeley, CA: University of California Press.

Galvani, L. (1797). *Memorie sulla electricità* [Memoire on electricity]. Bologna: Sassi.

Garrison, H. F. (1929). *An introduction to the history of medicine* (4th ed.). Philadelphia: W. B. Saunders.

Gassendi, P. (1658). *Opera Omnia, in sex tomos divisa* [The complete works, in three tomes] Lugduni.

Gazzaniga, M. S. (1970). *The bisected brain.* New York: Appleton-Century-Crofts.

Gazzaniga, M. S., Bogen, J. E., & Sperry, R. W. (1962). Some functional effects of sectioning the cerebral commissures in man. *Proceedings of the National Academy of Sciences, 48,* 1765-1769.

Geschwind, N. (1962). The anatomy of acquired disorders of reading. In J. Money (Ed.), *Reading disability: Progress and research needs in dyslexia* (pp. 115-129). Baltimore, MD: Johns Hopkins University Press.

Geschwind, N. (1965a). Disconnexion syndromes in animals and man: Part I. *Brain, 88,* 237-294.

Geschwind, N. (1965b). Disconnexion syndromes in animals and man: Part II. *Brain, 88,* 585-644.

Geschwind, N. (1974). *Selected papers on language and the brain.* In R. S. Cohen & M. W. Wartofsky (Eds.), *Boston studies in the philosophy of science* (Vol. 16). Dordrecht-Holland: D. Reidel.

Geschwind, N., & Kaplan, E. F. (1962). A human cerebral deconnection syndrome. *Brain, 90,* 131-148.

Goldstein, K. (1908). Zur Lehre von der motorischen Apraxie [Treatise on motor apraxia]. *Journal für Psychologie und Neurologie, 11,* 169, 270.

Gordon, H., & Sperry, R. W. (1968). Lateralization of olfactory perception in the surgically separated hemispheres of man. *Neuropsychologia, 7,* 111-120.

Gowers, W. R. (1893). *A manual of diseases of the nervous system: Vol. II: Diseases of the brain and cranial nerves. General and functional diseases of the nervous system* (2nd ed.). London: J. & A. Churchill.

Gray, J. A. (1979). *Ivan Pavlov.* New York: The Viking Press.

Hamilton, D. J. (1885). On the corpus callosum in the adult human brain. *The Journal of Anatomy and Physiology, Normal and Pathological, 19,* 385-414 (with plates).

Harrington, A. (1987). *Medicine, mind, and the double brain: A study in nineteenth-century thought.* Princeton, NJ: Princeton University Press.

Harris, L. J. (1983). Henry Holland on the hypothesis of duality of mind. *Behavioral and Brain Sciences, 6,* 732-733.

Harris, L. J. (1985a). "Delicacy of fibres in the brain": Early and recent neuropsychological explanations of sex differences in cognition and temperament. In J. Ghesquiere, R. F. Martin, & F. Newcombe (Eds.), *Human sexual dimorphism: Symposia of the Society for the Study of Human Biology* (Vol. 24, pp. 283-321). London: Taylor & Francis.

Harris, L. J. (1985b). Teaching the right brain: Historical perspective on a contemporary educational fad. In C. T. Best (Ed.), *Hemispheric function and collaboration in the child* (pp. 231-274). New York: Academic Press.

Hartmann, F., Jr., & Trendelenburg, W. (1927). Zur Frage der Bewegungstörungen nach Balkendurchtrennung an der Katze und am Affen. [Inquiry concerning movement disorders following cutting of the corpus callosum in the cat and the ape]. *Zeitschrift fuer die Gesdamte Experimentelle Medizin, 54,* 578.

Head, H. (1926). *Aphasia and kindred disorders of speech.* London: Cambridge University Press.

.Holland, H. (1852). On the brain as a double organ. In H. Holland, *Chapters on mental physiology* (pp. 170-191). London: Longman, Brown, Green & Longmans (Original work published 1839 in H. Holland, *Medical notes and reflections.* London: Haswell, Barrington, and Haswell)

Howes, D. (1962). An approach to the quantitative analysis of word blindness. In J. Money (Ed.), *Reading disability: Progress and research needs in dyslexia* (pp. 131-159). Baltimore, MD: Johns Hopkins University Press.

Hubel, D. H., & Weisel, T. N. (1967). Cortical and callosal connections concerned with the vertical meridian of visual fields in the cat. *Journal of Neurophysiology, 30,* 1561-1573.

Huxley, T. H. (1898). On the relation of man to the lower animals. In T. H. Huxley, *Man's place in nature, and other anthropological essays* (pp. 129-156). New York: D. Appleton and Co.

Hyndman, O. R., & Penfield, W. (1937). Agenesis of the corpus callosum: Its recognition by ventriculography. *Archives of Neurology and Psychiatry, 37*, 1251-1270.

Ireland, W. (1886). *The blot upon the brain: Studies in history and psychology.* New York: G. P. Putnam's Sons.

Ironside, R., & Guttmacher, M. (1929). The corpus callosum and its tumours. *Brain, 52*, 442-483.

Jeeves, M. A. (1986). Callosal agenesis: neuronal and developmental adaptations. In F. Lepore, Mtito, & H. H. Jaspers (Eds.), *Two hemispheres — one brain* (pp. 403-421). New York: Alan Liss.

Jolly, F. (1869). Ein Fall von Mangelhafter Entwicklung des Balkens im menschichen Gehirn [A case of partial development of the corpus callosum in the human brain]. *Zeitschrift für rationelle medicin, 36*, 4-14.

Jones, E. G. (1967). Pattern of cortical and thalamic connections of the somatic sensory cortex. *Nature, 216*, 704-705.

Joynt, R. J. (1974). The corpus callosum: History of thought regarding its function. In M. Kinsbourne & W. L. Smith (Eds.), *Hemispheric disconnection and function* (pp. 117-125). Springfield, IL: Charles C. Thomas.

Kaplan, J. (1980). *Walt Whitman: A life.* New York: Simon & Schuster.

Karplus, J. P. (1914). Experimenteller Beitrag zür Kenntnis der Gehirnvorgänge beim epileptischen Anfalle. [Experimental contribution toward the understanding of brain processes in epileptic attacks]. *Wiener Klinische Wochenschrift, 27*, 645-651.

Kaufmann, E. (1888). Ueber Mangel des Balkens im menschlichen Gehirn [On the absence of the corpus callosum in the human brain]. *Archiv für Psychiatrie und Nervenkrankheiten, 18*, 769-781.

Kennard, M. A., & Watts, J. W. (1934). The effect of section of the corpus callosum on the motor performance of monkeys. *The Journal of Nervous and Mental Diseases, 79*, 159-169.

Kinsbourne, M. (1974). Lateral interactions in the brain. In M. Kinsbourne & W. L. Smith (Eds.), *Hemispheric disconnection and cerebral function* (pp. 239-259). Springfield, IL: Charles C. Thomas.

Knox, D. N. (1875). Description of a case of defective corpus callosum. *The Glasgow Medical Journal* (new series), *7*, 227-237.

Kölliker, R. A. von (1896). *Handbuch der Gewebelehre des Menschen: Band. 2: Nervensysten des Menschen und der Thiere* [Handbook of human histology: Vol. 2: The human nervous system]. Leipzig: Engelmann.

Krasnogorsky, N. I. (1911). *Studies upon central inhibition and upon the localization of the tactile and motor analysers in the cortex of the dog.* Unpublished doctoral dissertation: University of St. Petersburg, St. Petersburg.

Lafora, G. R., & Prados, M y S. (1923). Experimentalversuche über die Funktion des Gehirnbalkens [Experimental studies on the function of the corpus callosum]. *Zeitschrift für die gesamte Neurologie und Psychiatrie, 84,* 617-641.

Lancisi, G. M. (1712). *Dissertatio altera de sede cogitantis animae* [Dissertation concerning the seat of the conscious mind]. (Reprinted 1718 in G. M. Lancisi, *Opera quae hactenus prodierunt omnia* (Vol. 2, pp. 302-318). Geneva: Cramer & Perachon)

Lange, J. (1936). Agnosien und Apraxien [Agnosia and apraxia]. In O. Bumke & O. Foerster (Eds.), *Handbuch der Neurologie* (Vol. 6, pp. 807-960). Berlin: Julius Springer.

Langelaan, J. W. (1908). On the development of the large commissures of the telencephalon in the human brain. *Brain, 31,* 221-241.

La Peyronie, F. (Gigot) de (1741a). Anatomie sur le siège de l'âme dans le cerveau [Anatomy concerning the site of the soul in the brain]. *Histoire de l'Académie Royale des Sciences à Paris,* 39-45.

La Peyronie, F. (Gigot) de (1741b). Observations par lesquelles on de tâche découvrir la partie du cerveau ou l'âme exerce ses fonctions [Observations by which one tries to discover the part of the brain where the soul exercises its functions] *Mémoires de l'Académie Royale des Sciences àParis,* 119-218.

Lashley, K. S. (1950). In search of the engram. In *Symposia of the Society for Experimental Biology: Symposium No. 4: Physiological mechanisms in animal behavior* (pp. 454-482). Cambridge, England: Cambridge University Press (Reprinted 1969 in F. A. Beach, D. O. Hebb, C. T. Morgan, & H. W. Nissen [Eds.], *The neuropsychology of Lashley: Selected papers of K. S. Lashley* (pp. 478-505). New York: McGraw-Hill.

Lashley, K. S. (1951). The problem of serial order in behavior. In L. A. Jeffress (Ed.), *Cerebral mechanisms in behavior: The Hixon Symposium* (pp. 112-146). New York: Hafner Publishing Company.

Lassonde, M., Sauerwin, H., Chicoine, A.-J., & Geoffroy, G. (1991). Absence of disconnexion syndrome in callosal agenesis and early callostomy: Brain reorganization or lack of structural specificity during ontogeny? *Neuropsychologia, 29,* 481-495.

Leuret, F., & Gratiolet, P. (1857). *Anatomie comparée du système nerveux* [Comparative anatomy of the nervous system] (Vol. 2). Paris: J.- B. Ballière et Fils.

Levy, J., Trevarthen, C., & Sperry, R. W. (1972). Perception of chimeric figures following hemispheric disconnection. *Brain, 95,* 61-78.

Levy-Agresti, J., & Sperry, R. W. (1968). Differential perceptual capacities in major and minor hemispheres. In *Proceedings of the National Academy of Sciences of the United States of America, Biological Sciences, 6,* 1151.

Lévy-Valensi, J. (1910). *Le corps calleux (étude anatomique, physiologique, et clinique)* [The corpus callosum (anatomical, physiological and clinical study)]. Paris: G. Steinheil.

Lévy-Valensi, J. (1911). Physiologie du corps calleux [Physiology of the corpus callosum]. *Presse Médicale, 19*, 72-74.

Lewandowsky, M. H. (1907). *Die Funktionen des Zentralnervensystems* [The function of central nervous systems]. Jena: G. Fischer.

Liepmann, H. (1900). Das Krankheitsbild der Apraxia (motorischen Asymbolie) auf Grand eines Falles von einseitiger Apraxie [The clinical manifestation of apraxia (motor asymbolia) as illustrated through a case of unilateral apraxia]. *Monatsschrift für Psychiatrie und Neurologie, 8*, 15-44; 102-132; 182-197.

Liepmann, H. (1907). Ueber die Funktion des Balkens beim Handeln und die Beziehungen von Aphasie und Apraxie zur Intelligenz [On the function of the commissures for action and the relation of aphasia and apraxia to intelligence] *Medizinisch Klinik*, Nos. 25, 26. (Reprinted 1908 in H. Liepmann, *Drei Aufsätze aud dem Apraxiegebeit: neu durchgesehen und mit Zusatzen versehen*, pp. 51-80. Berlin: Von Karger)

Liepmann, H. (1908). Die Linke Hemisphäre und das Handeln [The left hemisphere and action]. Berlin: Von Karger. (Original work published 1905 in *Münchener medizinische Wochenschrift: neu durchgesehen und mit Zusatzen versehen*, 17-50)

Liepmann, H., & Maas, O. (1907). Fall von linksseitiger Agraphie und Apraxie bei rechtsseitiger Lähmung [A case of left-sided agraphia and apraxia associated with right-sided paralysis]. *Journal für Psychologie und Neurologie, 10*, 214-227.

Loeser, J. D., & Alford, E. C. (1968). Clinicopathological correlations in agenesis of the corpus callosum. *Neurology, 18*, 745-756.

Longet, F.-A. (1842). *Anatomie et physiologie du système nerveux de l'homme. I.* [Anatomy and physiology of the nervous system of man] (Vol. 1). Paris: Fortin, Masson.

Lorry, A. C. de (1760). Sur les mouvemens du cerveau. Second mémoire. Sur les mouvemens contre nature de ce viscère, & sur les organes qui sont le principe de son action [On the movements of the brain. Second report. On the unnatural movements of this organ and on the organs that are the source of its action]. *Mémoires de Mathémique et de Physique, presentés à l'Academie Royale des Sciences (Paris), 3*, 344-377.

Lorry, A. C. de (1767). *Mémoires des savants étrangers* [Memoirs of foreign scholars]. In J. Astruc (Ed.), *Mémoires pour servir a l'histoire de la Faculté de médecine de Montpellier: revus & publié par M. Lorry* (Vol. 3). Paris: P. G. Cavelier.

Magendie, F. (1844). *An elementary treatise on human physiology.* New York: Harper & Brothers. (J. Revere, Trans.). (Reprinted, in part, 1978 in D. N. Robinson (Ed.), *Significant contributions to the history of psychology (1750-1920: Series E: Physiological Psychology* (Vol. 4, pp. i -xii, 13-255, 256-533 not included). Washington, D. C.: University Publications of America, Inc. (From the 5th ed. 1838 of *Précis elémentaire de physiologie*)

Magendie, F. (1841). *Leçons sur les fonctions et les maladies du système nerveux, professées au Collège de France* [Lessons on the functions and maladies of the nervous system, taught at the College of France] (Vols. 1-2; C. James, Ed.) Paris: Lacaplain.

Malinverni, S. G. (1875). Absence de corps calleux, de septum lucidum et de la circonvolution du corps calleux dans un cerveau [Absence of the corpus callosum, the septum lucidum, and the convolution of the corpus callosum in a brain]. *Gazette Médicale de Paris* (Series # 4), *4*, 33-34. (Original work published 1874 as "Cervello di uomo mancante del corpo calloso, del setto lucido, grande circonvolutione cerebrale, cella integrità della funzione intellectuali," *Giornalle delle R. Accademia di Medicina di Torino: Giornale delle scienze mediche*)

Mall, F. P. (1909). On several anatomical characters of the human brain, said to vary according to race and sex, with especial reference to the weight of the frontal lobe. *American Journal of Anatomy, 9,* 1-32.

Malpighi, M. (1665). Letter from M. Malpighi to Dr. Carlo Francassati of Pisa in November 1664 (Original work published 1664 as "De cerebro epistola," pp. 1-46 in *Tetras anatomicarum epistolarum de lingua et cerebro*). Bologna: Benati. (Translated excerpts 1968 in E. Clarke & C. D. O'Malley, *The human brain and spinal cord: A historical study illustrated by writings from antiquity to the twentieth century* [pp. 580-581]. Berkeley, CA: University of California Press)

Maspes, P. E. (1948). Le syndrome expérimental chez l'homme de la section du splénium du corps calleux alexie visuelle pure hémianopsique [The experimental syndrome in man of the section of the splenium of the corpus callosum: visual alexia, pure hemianopia]. *Revue Neurologique* (Paris), *80,* 100-113.

McCulloch, W. S. (1949a). Cortico-cortical connections. In P. Bucy (Ed.), *The precentral motor cortex* (2nd ed, pp. 211-242). Urbana, IL: The University of Illinois Press.

McCulloch, W. S. (1949b). Mechanisms for the spread of epileptic activation of the brain. *Electroencephalography and clinical neurophysiology, 1,* 19-24.

McCulloch, W. S., & Garol, H. W. (1941). Cortical origin and distribution of corpus callosum and anterior commissure in the monkey (*Macaca mulatta*). *Journal of Neurophysiology, 4,* 555-563.

McDougall, W. (1918). *Body and mind: A history and a defense of animism* (4th Ed.). London: Methuen & Co. Ltd. (Original work published 1911)

Meyer, A., & Hierons, R. (1962). Observations on the history of the "Circle of Willis." *Medical History, 6,* 119-130.

Meyer, A., & Hierons, R. (1965a). On Thomas Willis's concepts of neurophysiology. Part I. *Medical History, 9,* 1-15.

Meyer, A., & Hierons, R. (1965b). On Thomas Willis's concepts of neurophysiology. Part II. *Medical History, 9,* 143-155.

Meynert, T. (1872). The brain of mammals. (H. Powers, Trans.) In S. Stricker (Ed.), *Manual of human and comparative histology*, Vol. II (pp. 367-537). London: The New Sydenham Society. (Original work published 1872 as "Von Gehirne der Säugethiere" in S. Stricker, Ed., *Handbuch der Lehre von dem Geweben des Menschen und der Thiere*, Chapter 31. Leipzig: W. Engelmann.)

Mihalkovics, V. G. (1877). *Entwicklungsgeschichte des Gehirns* [Development of the brain]. Leipzig: W. Engelmann.

Mingazzini, G. (1922). *Der Balkan: Eine anatomische, physio-pathologische und klinische Studie* [The corpus callosum: An anatomical, pathophysiological, and clinical study]. Berlin: Julius Springer.

Mingazzini, G. (1926). Uber die Beziehungen den Balken und den lentikularen Fasern und der innern Kapsel [On the relationship between the corpus callosum, the lenticular fibers, and the internal capsule]. *Deutsche Zeitschrift für Nervenheilkunde, 94,* 168-198.

Monakow, C. von (1914). *Die Lokalisation im Grosshirn* [Localization in the brain]. Wiesbaden: J. F. Bergmann.

Mott, F. W. (1890). Report on bilaterally associated movements, and on the functional relations of the corpus callosum to the motor cortex. *British Medical Journal, 1,* 1124-1125.

Mott, F. W., & Schaefer, E. A. (1890). On movements resulting from faradic excitation of the corpus callosum in monkeys. *Brain, 13,* 174-177.

Muratoff, W. (1893). Secondäre Degeneration nach Durchschneidung des Balkens [Secondary degeneration following bisection of the corpus callosum]. *Neurologie Centralblatt Neurologisches, 12,* 714-729.

Myers, R. E. (1956). Function of corpus callosum in interocular transfer. *Brain, 79,* 358.

Myers, R. E. (1965). The neocortical commissures and interhemispheric transmission of information. In E. G. Ettlinger (Ed.), *Functions of the corpus callosum: Vol. 20. Ciba Foundation Study Group* (pp. 1-17). Boston: Little, Brown.

Myers, R. E., & Sperry, R. W. (1953). Interocular transfer of a visual form discrimination habit in cats after section of the optic chiasma and corpus callosum [Abstract]. *The Anatomical Record, 115,* 351-352.

Myers, R. E., & Sperry, R. W. (1958). Interhemispheric communication through the corpus callosum. Mnemonic carry-over between the hemispheres. *Archives of Neurology and Psychiatry, 80,* 298-303.

Nebes, R. (1972). Dominance of the minor hemisphere in commissurotomized man on a test of figural unification. *Brain, 95,* 633-638.

Neuburger, M. (1981). *The historical development of experimental brain and spinal cord physiology before Flourens.* (E. Clarke, Ed. & Trans., with additional material by E. Clarke). Baltimore, MD: Johns Hopkins University Press. (Original work published 1897 as *Die historische Entwicklung der experimentellen Gehirn- und Rückenmarksphysiologie vor Flourens.* Stuttgart: Ferdinand Enke Verlag)

Nielson, J. M. (1963). The myelogenetic studies of Paul Flechsig. *Bulletin of the Los Angeles Neurological Societies, 28,* 127-134.

Owen, R. (1837). On the structure of the brain in Marsupial animals. *Philosophical Transactions of the Royal Society of London, 127,* 87-96.

Paget, J. (1846). An account of a case in which the corpus callosum, fornix, and septum lucidum, were imperfectly formed. *Medico-Chirurgical Transactions, 34,* 55-73.

Parsons, F. H. (1940). Psychological tests of patients one year after section of corpus callosum [Abstract]. *Psychological Bulletin, 37,* 498.

Pavlov, I. P. (1927). *Conditioned reflexes: An investigation of the physiological activity of the cerebral cortex.* (G. V. Anrep, Ed. & Trans.). Oxford, England: Oxford University Press. (Reprinted 1960 in New York: Dover Publications)

Pavlov, I. P. (1928). *Lectures on conditioned reflexes: Twenty-five years of objective study of the higher nervous activity (behaviour) of animals.* (W. H. Gantt, Trans.) New York: International Publishers Co.

Penfield, W. (1938). The circulation of the epileptic brain. In *The circulation of the brain and spinal cord: A symposium on blood supply* (pp. 605-637). The Proceedings of the Association for Research in Nervous and Mental Disease (meeting of Dec. 27-28, New York), *18,* Baltimore: Williams and Wilkins.

Plater [also Platter], F. (1614). *Observationum in hominis affectibus plerisque corpori & animo, functionem lesione, dolore, ali'ave molestia & vitio incommodantibus libri tres* [Three books of observations on the generally affected problems for the body and the mind of man, whether caused by lesion, by pain, or by some other difficulty or fault]. Basileä: Ludovici König.

Puccetti, R. (1981). The case for mental duality: Evidence from split brain data and other considerations. *Behavioral and Brain Sciences, 4,* 93-123.

Ramón y Cajal, S. (1909-1911/1960). Considérations anatomique et physiologique sur le cerveau [Anatomical and physiological considerations about the brain]. In G. von Bonin (Trans. and Ed.), *Some papers on the cerebral cortex* (pp. 251-282). Springfield, IL: Charles C. Thomas. (From French trans. by L. Azoulay, 1909-1911, of S. Ramón y Cajal, *Histologie du système nerveux de l'homme et des vertébrés,* Vols. 1-2. Paris: Maloine)

Ransom, W. B. (1895). On tumours of the corpus callosum, with an account of a case. *Brain, 18,* 531-550.

Reil, J. C. (1809). *Das Balken-System oder die Balken-Organisation im grossen Gehirn* [The commissural system or the commissural organization of the forebrain]. *Archiv Physiologie Halle, 9,* 172-195. (Translated excerpts 1968 in E. Clarke & C. D. O'Malley, *The human brain and spinal cord: A historical study illustrated by writings from antiquity to the twentieth century* [pp. 593-598]. Berkeley, CA: University of California Press)

Reil, J. C. (1812). Mangel des mittleren und freien Theils des Balkans im Menschengehirn [Absence of the middle and free part of the corpus callosum in the human brain]. *Archiv für die Physiologie, 11*, 341-344.

Rush, B. (1981). *Memoirs of the American Philosophical Society: Vol. 144. Benjamin Rush's lectures on the mind.* (Edited, annotated, and introduced by E. T. Carlson, J. L. Wollock, & P. S. Noel). Philadelphia: American Philosophical Society.

Schrier, A. M., & Sperry, R. W. (1959). Visuomotor integration in split-brained cats. *Science, 129*, 1275-1276.

Seletzky, W., & Gilula, J. (1929). Zur Frage der Funktionen des Balkens bei Tieren [On the question of the function of the corpus callosum in animals] *Archiv für Psychiatrie und Nervenkrankheiten, 86*, 57-73.

Sherrington, C. S. (1889). On nerve-tracts degenerating secondarily to lesions of the cerebral cortex. *The Journal of Physiology, 10*, 429-432.

Singer, C. (1956). *Galen on anatomical procedures.* London: Oxford University Press.

Singer, C. (1952). *Vesalius on the human brain (being a translation of a section of his Fabrica of 1543).* (Introduction, translation of text, translation of description of figures, notes to the translation and figures by C. Singer). London, New York: Oxford University Press.

Smith, K. W. (1947). Bilateral integrative action of the cerebral cortex in man in verbal association and sensori-motor coordination. *Journal of Experimental Psychology, 37*, 367-376.

Smith, K. W., & Akelaitis, A. J. (1942). Studies on the corpus callosum: I. Laterality in behavior and bilateral motor organization in man before and after section of the corpus callosum. *Archives of Neurology and Psychiatry, 47*, 519-543.

Sperry, R. W. (1961). Cerebral organization and behavior. *Science, 133*, 1749-1757.

Sperry, R. W. (1962). Some aspects of interhemispheric integration. In V. B. Mountcastle (Ed.), *Interhemispheric relations and cerebral dominance* (pp. 43-49). Baltimore, MD: Johns Hopkins University Press.

Sperry, R. W. (1969). A modified concept of consciousness. *Psychological Review, 76*, 532-536.

Sperry, R. W. (1983). *Science and moral priority: merging mind, brain, and human values.* New York: Columbia University Press.

Sperry, R. W., Stamm, J. S., & Miner, N. (1956). Relearning tests for intero/cular transfer following division of optic chiasma and corpus callosum in cats. *Journal of Comparative and Physiological Psychology, 49*, 529-533.

Spiegel, E. (1931). The central mechanism of generalized epileptic fits. *The American Journal of Psychiatry, 10*, 595-609.

Spitzka, E. A. (1908). A study of the brains of six eminent scientists and scholars belonging to the American Anthrometric Society, together with a description of the skull of Professor E. D. Cope. *Transactions of the American Philosophical Society, 21* (New Series), 175-308.

Steno, N. (1965). *Nicolaus Steno's lecture on the anatomy of the brain.* (A. J. Pollock, Trans.) Copenhagen: Nyt Nordisk Forlag. Arnold Busck (Original work published 1669 as *Discours de Monsieur Stenon sur l'anatomie du cerveau.* Paris: Robert de Ninville)

Symington, J. (1892). The cerebral commissures in the Marsupialia and Monotremata. *The Journal of Anatomy and Physiology, 27,* 69-84.

Tomasch, J. (1954). Size, distribution, and number of fibres in the human corpus callosum. *The Anatomical Record, 119,* 119-135.

Tomasch, J. (1957). A quantitative analysis of the human anterior commissure. *Acta Anatomica, 30,* 902-906.

Trescher, J. H., & Ford, F. R. (1937). Colloid cyst of the third ventricle: Report of a case: Operative removal with section of posterior half of corpus callosum. *Archives of Neurology and Psychiatry, 37,* 959-973.

Trevarthen, C. B. (1961). *Studies on visual learning in split-brain monkeys.* Unpublished doctoral dissertation. California Institute of Technology, Pasadena.

Turner, W. (1878). A human cerebrum imperfectly divided into two hemispheres. *The Journal of Anatomy and Physiology, 12,* 241-253.

Valentin, G. G. (1841). *Ueber dis Thätigkeit des Balkens* [On the action of the corpus callosum]. In G. G. Valentin (Ed.), *Repertorium für Anatomie und Physiologie* (Vol. 6).

Van Valkenburg, C. T. (1913). Experimental and pathologico-anatomical researches on the corpus callosum. *Brain, 36,* 119-165.

Van Wagenen, W. P., & Herren, R. Y. (1940). Surgical division of commissural pathways in the corpus callosum: Relation to spread of an epileptic attack. *Archives of Neurology and Psychiatry, 44,* 740-759.

Vesalius, A. (1543). *De humani corporis fabrica libra septum* [On the fabric of the body]. Basel: Ex officino Joannis Oporini. (Translated excerpts 1968 in E. Clarke & C. D. O'Malley, *The human brain and spinal cord: A historical study illustrated by writings from antiquity to the twentieth century* [pp. 578-580]. Berkeley, CA: University of California Press)

Vicq d'Azyr, F. (1784). Recherches sur la structure du cerveau, du cervelet, de la moelle elongée, de la moelle épinière; et sur l'origine des nerfs de l'homme et des animaux [On the structure of the brain, the cerebellum, the medulla oblongata, the spinal marrow; and on the origin of the nerves of man and of animals]. *Histoire de l'Académie royale des Sciences, 1781,* 495-622. (Translated excerpts 1968 in E. Clarke & C. D. O'Malley, *The human brain and spinal cord: A historical study illustrated by writings from antiquity to the twentieth century* [pp. 591-594]. Berkeley, CA: University of California Press)

Voris, H. C., & Adson, A. W. (1935). Tumors of the corpus callosum: A pathologic and clinical study. *Archives of Neurology and Psychiatry, 34,* 965-972.

Voris, H. C., Adson, A. W., & Moersch, F. P. (1935). Tumors of the frontal lobe: Clinical observations in a series verified microscopically. *The Journal of the American Medical Association, 104,* 93-99.

Voris, H. C., Kernohan, J. W., & Adson, A. W. (1935). Tumors of the frontal lobe: An anatomic and pathologic study. *Archives of Neurology and Psychiatry, 34,* 605-617.

Wada, J. (1951). An experimental study on the neural mechanism of the spread of epileptic impulse. *Folia Psychiatrica et Neurologica Japonica, 4,* 289-301.

Walker, A. E. (1970). Walter Dandy (1886-1946). In W. Haymaker & F. Schiller (Eds.), *The founders of neurology* (2nd ed., pp. 549-552). Springfield, IL: Charles C. Thomas.

Wallace, I., & Wallace, A. (1978). *The two.* New York: Simon & Schuster.

Wepfer, J. J. (1658). *Observationes anatomicae, ex cadaveribus eorum, quos sustulit apoplexia, cum exercitatione de eius loco affecto* [Anatomical observations drawn from the cadavers of those who have died from apoplexy, with additional observations concerning the location of its effect]. Schaffhausen: J. C. Suter.

Wernicke, K. (1874). *Der Aphasische Symptomencomplex. Eine Psychologische Studie auf Anatomischer Basis* [The aphasia symptomcomplex: A psychological study on an anatomical basis]. Breslau: M. Cohn und Weigart. (Reprinted 1977 in *Wernicke's works on aphasia: A source book and review* [G. E. Eggert, Trans. and Commentator; pp. 91-144]. The Hague, Netherlands: Mouton)

Wigan, A. L. (1844a). *A new view of insanity: The duality of the mind.* London: Longman, Brown, Green & Longmans.

Wigan, A. L. (1844b). The duality of the mind, proved by the structure, functions, and diseases of the brain. *The Lancet, 1,* 39-41.

Willis, T. (1965). *The anatomy of the brain and nerves* (Vols. 1-2; facsimile of the 1681 English translation by S. Pordage [W. Feindel, Ed.]. Montreal: McGill University Press. (Original work published 1664 as *Cerebri anatome: cui accessit nervorum descriptio et usis.* London: Martyn & Allestry)

Woolley, H. T. (1910). A review of the recent literature on the psychology of sex. *Psychological Bulletin, 7,* 335-342.

Zaidel, D., & Sperry, R. W. (1977). Long-term motor coordination problems following cerebral commissurotomy in man. *Neuropsychologia, 15,* 193-204.

Zaidel, E. (1975). A technique for presenting lateralized visual input with prolonged exposure. *Vision Research, 15,* 283-289.

Zangwill, O. L. (1974). Consciousness and the cerebral hemispheres. In S. Dimond & J. G. Beaumont (Eds.), *Hemispheric function in the human brain* (pp. 264-278). New York: Wiley.

Zinn, J. G. (1749). *Experimenta quaedam circa corpus callosum, cerebellum, duram meningem, in vivis animalibus instituta* [Some experiments concerning the corpus callosum, cerebellum, and dura mater, conducted in living animals]. (Reprinted 1751 in A. von Haller, *Disputationum anatomicarum selectarum* [Vol. 7, pp. 421-469]. Göttingen: A. Vandenhoeck)

2 Neuroanatomical Bases of Hemispheric Functional Specialization in the Human Brain: Possible Developmental Factors[1]

Sandra F. Witelson
McMaster University

FUNCTIONAL ASYMMETRY: NATURE AND ONTOGENY

Hemispheric functional specialization or functional asymmetry is a well-established characteristic of functional organization in the human brain. In essence, the right and left hemispheres have different roles in mediating various behaviors and higher mental processes. Tasks involving speech production, phonemic discrimination; comprehension of oral and written language; the ability to write; performance of voluntary finger, limb, and oral movements; and the perception of sequences of stimuli are more dependent on left- than right-hemisphere functioning in most people. In contrast, tasks involving the perception of two- and three-dimensional visual or tactual shapes, spatial position and orientation of stimuli, the perception of faces and colors, mental rotation of three-dimensional shapes, the ability to direct attention to both lateral sensory fields, the perception of musical chords and melodies, aspects of the perception of emotional stimuli and prosodic features of speech, and the abilities to dress oneself and to construct block models are more dependent on the right hemisphere. In the past decade, numerous books have summarized these findings based on the study of brain-damaged people with unilateral lesions, people who have undergone commissurotomy, and neurologically intact people who were tested with various behavioral and perceptual tests involving right- and left-sided input or output (e.g., Beaton, 1985; Boller & Grafman, 1988-1990; Bradshaw & Nettleton, 1983; Bryden, 1982; Corballis, 1983; H. Damasio & A. Damasio, 1990; Geschwind & Galaburda, 1984; Hannay, 1986; Heilman & Valenstein, 1985; Hellige, 1983; Kolb & Whishaw, 1990; Molfese & Segalowitz, 1988; Ottoson, 1987).

However, several key issues related to hemispheric specialization remain unresolved. First, the lists of tests that are more dependent on one hemisphere or the other are continually expanding. There is no demonstration, however, of what specific cognitive functions are common to each set of skills and are indicative of the type or types of processing that each hemisphere is specialized for. The numerous dimensions postulated for hemispheric differences, such as verbal versus

---

[1] A slightly modified and updated version of a chapter in Kostovic, I., Knezevic, S., Wisniewski, H.M., & Spilich, C.J. (1992) (Eds.), *Neurodevelopment, Aging, and Cognition* [pp. 112-137]. Boston: Birkhäuser (with permission of Birkhäuser Press).

nonverbal or analytic versus synthetic, are merely inferred hypotheses derived from the numerous tasks studied, of what the essential functional characteristics of the hemispheres are. Moreover, it has been shown that it is not only the nature of the task stimuli, but also the strategy or process the subject uses to perform the task, that determines which hemisphere is dominant in processing for that task. Currently, a widely used working hypothesis is that the left hemisphere is specialized for analytic, sequential, time-dependent functions, and the right hemisphere is specialized for synthetic, spatial perceptual functions (e.g., Bradshaw & Nettleton, 1983).

A second issue concerns whether the specialization is based on a greater contribution or a better, more efficient contribution: that is, whether the functional difference is quantitative or qualitative. A third issue is whether the functional differences between the hemispheres are absolute or relative. Finally, recent work has underlined the existence of multiple functional asymmetries, with some degree of dissociation even among cognitive functions usually related and lateralized to the same hemisphere. For example, although most right-handers have both speech production and manual motoric control represented in the left hemisphere, the majority of left-handers, who must have at least some right-hemisphere involvement in the motoric system, still have speech production represented mainly in the left hemisphere (Rasmussen & Milner, 1977). A small minority of right-handers may have speech production or other typically left-sided functions mediated by the right hemisphere (e.g., Fischer, Alexander, Gabriel, Gould, & Milione, 1991).

This last issue of dissociation among subsets of functional asymmetries leads to consideration of individual differences in hemispheric specialization. This relates to two dimensions, direction and degree. There is a species-typical pattern in the direction of functional asymmetry. The large majority of people, about 80% (approximately 90% of right-handers, who constitute about 90% of the population), have the pattern described previously. The pattern of "analytic" and "synthetic" functions may be reversed for at least some components of these two main types of processing in a small minority of the population (e.g., 15% of left-handers who have speech represented mainly in the right hemisphere; Rasmussen & Milner, 1977). Whether such left-handers have "synthetic" functions represented mainly in the left hemisphere is not known. Statistical analysis of verbal and spatial deficits following unilateral brain damage in large groups of right- and left-handers suggests that there is considerable independence in the lateralization of verbal and spatial skills; that is, lateralization of one set of skills does not necessarily predict lateralization of the other set of skills (Bryden, Hécaen, & de Agostini, 1983).

In addition to these directional differences, there is evidence that the degree of functional asymmetry between the two hemispheres may be less in some people than in others. For example, as a group, left-handers show less marked functional asymmetry (or greater bihemispheric representation of functions). This is evidenced in studies of brain-damaged patients by a greater prevalence of aphasic deficits following right-sided lesions in left-handers compared to right-handers

(Hécaen, de Agostini, & Monzon-Montes, 1981), and in neurologically intact individuals by a smaller right-left difference in perceptual tests of auditory or visual perception (Bryden, 1982).

Sex differences in the degree of lateralization have also been noted. In studies of groups of neurologically intact children (e.g., Witelson, 1976) and adults (e.g., Levy & Reid, 1978), performance on tests of right-left perception indicate less marked asymmetry for both verbal and spatial skills. Studies with brain-damaged people have indicated sex differences in the prevalence and possibly duration of aphasia and other deficits associated with right- or left-sided damage (e.g., McGlone, 1980, 1986). Other studies have indicated that some sex differences in functional organization are neither in degree nor direction, but in intrahemispheric organization (e.g., Hécaen et al., 1981; Kimura & Harshman, 1984). For example, Kimura and Harshman (1984) have suggested that women have a more focused representation of speech and praxis (motor programming) functions in the left anterior regions, compared to men, who have representation in both anterior and posterior regions of the left hemisphere.

Some clinical groups show variation in patterns of functional asymmetry. For example, children with developmental dyslexia show less asymmetry on tasks of spatial perception (e.g., Hynd & Cohen, 1983; Witelson, 1977a); individuals with chromosomal abnormalities, such as Turner and Klinefelter syndromes show different patterns of asymmetry on tasks of verbal and nonverbal perception compared to matched control groups (Netley & Rovet, 1988); and homosexual men and women show a greater prevalence of non-right-handedness (Lindesay, 1987; McCormick, Witelson, & Kingstone, 1990) and less asymmetry on perceptual tasks involving auditory linguistic stimuli (McCormick & Witelson, 1992).

The ontogenetic course of hemispheric specialization is a controversial issue. Is it present in children or in neonates and, if so, does functional asymmetry change in magnitude with age? Early in the history of developmental neuropsychology, it was generally accepted that hemispheric specialization developed during childhood (e.g., Lenneberg, 1967). This position was consistent with the few data available at the time. The phenomenon of functional plasticity, that is, recovery of function lost subsequent to brain damage, was well documented, particularly following brain insult early in development. This was taken to mean that hemispheric specialization was not yet established. Moreover, the generally accepted conception that hemispheric specialization was based on speech and language functions was considered as further evidence that hemispheric specialization could not exist in preverbal children. The empirical results of studies with brain-damaged and neurologically intact children done in the past few decades indicate that hemispheric specialization is, indeed, present within the first few months of life. These results have been reviewed elsewhere (e.g., Hiscock, 1988; Molfese & Segalowitz, 1988; Witelson, 1977b, 1985b, 1987b; Witelson & Swallow, 1988). Moreover, the demonstration of functional asymmetry in nonhuman primates supports the idea that it is not verbal or hand-usage functions, per se, but processes, such as analytic perception, that are the essence of left-hemisphere functioning (e.g., Hamilton & Vermeire, 1988) and that functional asymmetry may well exist from the start.

In the case of children, the clearest results are from studies with neurologically intact groups, because such results indicate what the organization of the brain is at the time of testing. These results demonstrate asymmetry not only in children and infants, but in neonates. For example, 4-day-old neonates showed evidence of functional asymmetry on tests of dichotic (simultaneous right and left auditory stimulation) discrimination as evidenced by response involving a sucking procedure (Bertoncini et al., 1989).

Studies of the performance of brain-damaged children provide less clear evidence regarding functional asymmetry, because such results are frequently confounded with the effects of neural plasticity. Psychological testing is often assessed months after the initial insult, and, consequently, the observed performance reflects both hemispheric specialization and the functional consequences of neural plasticity. These are two aspects of brain functioning that have been shown to coexist (Witelson, 1987b). These two aspects of brain functioning are further complicated by the fact that not all mental functions follow the long-held *Kennard principle*: that lesions sustained early in life lead to fewer deficits than do later lesions (Kennard, 1942). This may hold for specific functions, such as sensory or motor skills studied experimentally in animals or for speech production in children, but it does not hold for more general intellectual functions, such as concept formation or problem solving (Witelson, 1987a). Figure 2.1 presents schematically the different courses of recovery (or functional plasticity) depending on the nature of the cognitive skills in question, with recovery decreasing for specific skills as age of insult increases (Fig. 2.1c), and recovery increasing for general skills as age of insult increases (Fig. 2.1d). This operates on a brain that is already functionally asymmetric, in a pattern that remains invariant over development (Fig. 2.1a), but in which the extent of cognition that becomes lateralized increases over time (Fig. 2.1b).

There is no evidence of greater bihemispheric representation of cognitive functions earlier compared to later in development, which suggests that the magnitude of asymmetry does not change. However, this is difficult to assess unequivocally, because baseline performance changes with age, and measurement issues become complex (see Hiscock, 1988). It is also possible that the intrahemispheric organization for the representation of cognitive functions changes with age (see, e.g., Brown & Jaffe, 1975), although the extent of hemispheric specialization does not.

Two facts concerning functional asymmetry suggest that there is a genetic contribution to some neural substrate for the maturation of this aspect of organization of the human brain. First, there is a population bias in the direction of the pattern of functional asymmetry in people across cultures and generations, and second, this same pattern is present in neonatal life. Elucidation of the origins and mechanisms of functional asymmetry may be aided by recent neuroanatomical studies that are beginning to reveal what the neuroanatomical substrates of functional asymmetry may be.

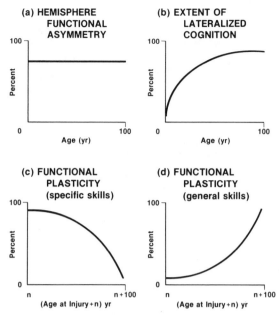

FIG 2.1. Theoretical scheme of hemispheric specialization and plasticity over time. (a) Degree of hemispheric specialization over time in which the slope of the curve is zero. (b) Extent of cognitive skill having lateralized brain representation over time: an epiphenomenon of cognitive development in a brain having invariant hemispheric specialization. The decreasing positive slope represents the more rapid rate of cognitive development earlier in life. (c) Degree of functional plasticity for *specific* skills *n* years after brain damage; the hypothesized increasing negative slope represents the slower rate of decrease in plasticity early in life. (d) Degree of functional plasticity for *general* skills *n* years after damage; the hypothesized increasing positive slope represents the relatively greater impact of early brain damage. (Adapted from Witelson, 1987b)

NEUROANATOMICAL ASYMMETRY

Neuroanatomical asymmetry in the human brain has been noted and studied since the mid-19th century. Little attention was paid to anatomical asymmetry as a possible basis of functional asymmetry, however, until a few decades ago. Since then, numerous studies have revealed reliable right-left morphological differences. Moreover, some of these have been found to correlate with neuropsychological measures of functional asymmetry. The anatomical asymmetries and the relationships between anatomical and functional asymmetries are reviewed in detail elsewhere (Witelson & Kigar, 1988b). For example, numerous measures of gross anatomical asymmetry are reported for weights, volumes, and lengths of the hemispheres and for torque of the occipital lobes. These are of small magnitude and are somewhat unreliable. In contrast, marked and very reliable differences have been found, particularly in the parieto-temporal region, as measured by the morphology and length of the Sylvian fissure and the extent of the parietal operculum. The posterior region of the superior surface of the superior temporal gyrus, termed the planum temporale, has been studied most extensively. Figure

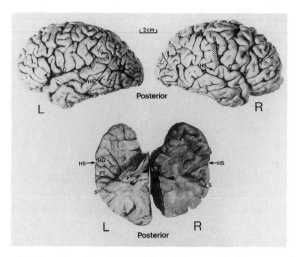

FIG. 2.2. Views of the lateral surface of the two hemispheres and of the exposed superior surface of each temporal lobe of a human adult, showing the typical asymmetries of a more extended, horizontal extent of the Sylvian fissure on the left side and a larger planum temporale on the left side. Note that in the left hemisphere two rami appear as possible ends of the Sylvian fissure. Examination from only the lateral aspect could not reveal the actual end of the fissure. Note, also, that the anterior end of the right temporal block is positioned with an upward tilt so that the planum is photographed in a horizontal plane. (S, posterior end of the Sylvian fissure; C, inferior tip of the central sulcus; HS, Heschl sulcus; HG, Heschl gyrus; PT, planum temporale; dotted lines indicate the posterior boundary of the planum; hatched lines indicate the lateral edge of the planum: adapted from Witelson, 1987a)

2.2 shows the right and left hemispheres of an adult brain, revealing the longer posterior portion of the Sylvian fissure on the left side compared to the more anterior and sharply angulated upturn of the posterior ramus on the right side, and the larger posterior parietal operculum and the larger planum temporale in the left than the right hemisphere. In a recent report, components of the Sylvian fissure were examined in a sample of 67 postmortem brain specimens. Only the postcentral horizontal segment was larger (approximately twofold) on the left side than the right. The posterior vertical segment was comparably greater on the right side (Witelson & Kigar, 1992b). Similar results have been found for the anatomy of the planum temporale (Witelson & Kigar, 1991). The involvement of the cortical areas in the parieto-temporal region mediating cognitive functions that are lateralized in the brain are well documented (H. Damasio & A. Damasio, 1990).

Several studies have assessed neuroanatomical asymmetries in the frontal opercular regions (pars opercularis and pars triangularis) involved in the lateralization of speech production. In general, there is a tendency for the cortical extent in the left region to be greater than that in the right, but it is not statistically significant. In a recent study, in which the factors of hand preference and sex were considered, right-left asymmetry was observed in the areal extent of the inferior frontal gyri (Witelson & Kigar, 1992a).

Of the few studies that have addressed asymmetry in the histology of cortical regions, some indication of differences in the *extent* of a particular cytoarchitectonic area has been noted. Little work has addressed the issue of quantitative microscopic right-left differences within a cytoarchitectonic area (Witelson & Kigar, 1988b).

The prominent parieto-temporal asymmetries are present early in life. For example, the planum temporale is reliably larger on the left side in neonates (e.g., Wada, Clarke, & Hamm, 1975; Witelson & Pallie, 1973). Asymmetry in the development of Heschl's sulcus (the transverse sulcus, see Fig. 2.2), which delineates the planum temporale from Heschl's gyrus, occurs by about the 31st (gestational) week, when Heschl's sulcus appears on the right side. This is about 2 weeks earlier than its appearance on the left side in the majority of cases (Chi, Dooling, & Gilles, 1977). Other asymmetries have been described as occurring even earlier. Fontes (1944) indicated that the course of the Sylvian fissure is more horizontal (in relation to the brain's anterior-posterior axis) on the left side than on the right in most cases that showed asymmetry in a series of 39 human fetal brains ranging in age from 16 to 40 weeks. LeMay and Culebras (1972) observed that the posterior end of the Sylvian fissure was lower on the left side than on the right side in all 10 of the fetal brains they studied. Figure 2.3 presents this asymmetry in a 16-week-old fetus.

Neuroanatomical Asymmetry as a Basis of Functional Asymmetry

Although it is tempting to assume that neuroanatomical asymmetries are a basis for functional asymmetries, and this has been done frequently in the literature, it is only recently that evidence for such a relationship has emerged. Handedness was found to be associated with asymmetry in the inferred size of the parietal operculum (Hochberg & LeMay, 1975; LeMay & Culebras, 1972) and with asymmetry in the size of the planum temporale (Steinmetz, Volkmann, Jäncke, & Freund, 1991); and speech lateralization was found to be associated with asymmetry in the parietal operculum (Ratcliff, Dila, Taylor, & Milner, 1980) and in temporal lobe morphology (Strauss, LaPointe, Wada, Gaddes, & Kosaka, 1985); but an equal number of studies failed to find similar associations (see Witelson & Kigar, 1988b). All of these findings were based on measures from various in vivo imaging techniques. More recently, a study based on postmortem brain specimens reported variation in Sylvian fissure morphology with handedness, but the difference was not simply in degree of asymmetry, but in a feature involving both

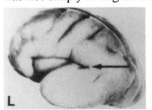 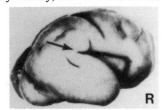

FIG 2.3. Views of the lateral surface of the left and right cerebral hemispheres of a 16-week-old human fetus, showing that the posterior end of the Sylvian fissure, indicated by the arrow, is lower in the left hemisphere. (Adapted from LeMay & Culebras, 1972)

hemispheres (Witelson & Kigar, 1992b).

CALLOSAL ANATOMY AND FUNCTIONAL ASYMMETRY

Since the early 1980s, work in my laboratory has been directed at studying relationships between variation in several gross neuroanatomical and histological measures derived from the study of postmortem brains, and variation in neuropsychological measures of functional asymmetry in cognitively normal people. One focus has been on the corpus callosum. This structure is the main interhemispheric commissure connecting the neocortex of the right and left hemispheres. It was hypothesized that the gross anatomy of the corpus callosum might differ between right- and left-handers because left-handers as a group differ from right-handers in the pattern and magnitude of their functional asymmetry. Although the majority of studies with brain-damaged people have defined handedness predominantly by the hand used for writing, the model of handedness proposed by Annett (1985) was used in the studies in my laboratory. Annett's model suggests that people with consistent right-hand (CRH) preference comprise a genetically different group than those showing mixed- or left-hand preference, that is, nonCRH preference. Specifically, the working hypothesis was that the less marked functional asymmetry or greater bihemispheric representation of cognitive functions in nonCRH compared to CRH may be associated with a larger corpus callosum, which would allow for more interhemispheric communication.

Anatomical measurements were made from postmortem study of brain specimens. Many current magnetic resonance imaging (MRI) systems do not have sufficient resolution capabilities to measure the size of some of the regions that vary among people. The approach of the research involves prospectively testing seriously ill cancer patients. Although the patients have metastases, they are tested when they feel well and are ambulatory. The patients agree to participate in this research involving neuropsychological testing and an autopsy in the event of death. The details of our method are presented elsewhere (Witelson & McCulloch, 1991).

A larger total area of the midsagittal section of the corpus callosum was found in nonCRH individuals than in CRH, based on a sample of 42 cases (Witelson, 1985a). This was found for the anterior and posterior halves of the corpus callosum, but not for the region of the splenium. It was suggested that the association of callosal area with handedness indicates that variation in callosal size is an anatomical substrate of variation in functional asymmetry.

To test this hypothesis further, we considered whether those regions of the corpus callosum that house axons from cortical regions predominantly involved in asymmetrical representation of cognitive functions would differ more between right-handers and non-right-handers. The posterior region of the body of the callosum, the isthmus, includes axons from parieto-temporal regions that are involved in the asymmetrical representation of many verbal, spatial, emotional, and attentional skills (see Fig. 2.4, region 6). In an expanded group of 50 cases (Witelson, 1989), it was found that the posterior half of the body of the callosum

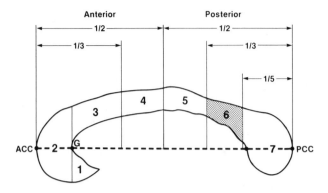

FIG 2.4. Diagram of the midsagittal view of the corpus callosum of the human adult, divided into seven subdivisions, numbered 1 to 7. ACC-PCC, defined by the anteriormost and posteriormost points of the callosum, was used as the linear axis to subdivide the callosum into anterior and posterior halves; anterior, middle, and posterior thirds; and the posterior one fifth (region 7), which is roughly congruent with the splenium. The line perpendicular to the axis at point G, the anteriormost point on the inner convexity of the anterior callosum, was used to define the anteriormost divisions of the callosum, roughly congruent with the genu (region 2) and the rostrum (region 1). Regions 3 and 4 constitute the anterior body of the callosum; regions 5 and 6, the posterior body. The region of interest here, the isthmus (region 6, stippled area), was defined as the posterior one third of the corpus callosum minus the posterior one fifth. The isthmus is 2/15 of the total area of the callosum, situated just anterior to the more posterior splenial region. (Adapted from Witelson, 1989)

was greater in nonCRH individuals than in CRH, particularly in the isthmus. The extremities, the splenium, and genu, were not larger in nonCRH. Also noteworthy is the finding that the anterior body of the corpus callosum, which houses the motor and premotor interhemispheric fibers, did not differ between CRH and nonCRH. This result suggests that it is not the motoric aspect of handedness per se that is related to callosal anatomy, but rather handedness as it reflects variation in asymmetrical representation of praxic or linguistic skills. With this larger group and the further regional division of the corpus callosum, sex differences in structure-function relationships and in callosal morphology were also noted. These are discussed in a later section.

Subsequent to the group of 50 cases, the brain specimens of 7 more men were studied. Using discriminant functions derived from analysis of the previous group of 15 men in the sample of 50 cases (Witelson, 1989), hand-preference category was predicted correctly using isthmal area in 6 of the 7 male cases. In addition, the correlation between isthmal area and a hand-preference score (min/max = -12 to +12) was $r = -0.67$ ($n = 21$, $p < .01$), indicating a strong relationship between anatomy of the isthmus of the corpus callosum and handedness in men (Witelson & Goldsmith, 1991). Subsequent studies using MRI and the CRH-nonCRH classification system have also found increased left-handedness to be associated with larger callosal areas (Denenberg, Kertesz, & Cowell, 1991; Habib et al., 1991; Steinmetz et al., 1992, but see Witelson, 1992).

AXON LOSS AS A DEVELOPMENTAL FACTOR IN ASYMMETRY

The size of the corpus callosum varies with a behavioral index of functional asymmetry, at least in men. A larger corpus callosum could indicate a greater total number of axons. A larger callosal area could also, of course, reflect other histological features, such as thicker axons, thicker myelin, or more myelinated versus nonmyelinated fibers. There is extensive evidence that axon loss occurs as part of the regressive phase of brain development in prenatal and early postnatal periods (Cowan, Fawcett, O'Leary, & Stanfield, 1984). In this neurobiological context, it could be suggested that the larger corpus callosum in nonCRH is due, at least in part, to less axon loss (Witelson, 1985a, 1989). There is very little information on the histology of the human corpus callosum, even without regard to possible associations with behavior. The few reports available have used light microscopy (Luttenberg, 1965; Tomasch, 1954), which could miss the smaller nonmyelinated fibers that have been demonstrated to exist in the monkey corpus callosum (LaMantia & Rakic, 1990b). Luttenberg (1965) did report smaller densities of axons in the corpus callosum at maturity than in early life, but he did not report total numbers of axons.

Considerable recent experimental work on nonhuman species has addressed the developmental course of change in callosal axon number or in callosal connectivity patterns. Both types of studies indicate that few, if any, axons cross the midline after birth, and that there is extensive early loss of axons. For example, with quantitative analysis, there is evidence in cat brain (Koppel & Innocenti, 1983) and in monkey (LaMantia & Rakic, 1990a) that the total number of fibers is greater soon after birth than at maturity, indicating that, as in other fiber tracts, there is a loss of exuberant axons, which develop during embryonic stages of brain development.

Loss of early developed axons is also indicated by the demonstration that specific connectivity patterns of callosal axons develop early in life through the loss of connections that were present at an earlier stage. The timing of the emergence of the adult patterns varies across sensory modalities and species. For example, in lower mammals, such as the rat and the cat, the mature pattern of discontinuous distribution of callosal connections is finalized during the early postnatal months (e.g., Innocenti & Caminiti, 1980; Ivy & Killackey, 1981). In contrast, in monkeys, the adult patterns of callosal connectivity emerge before birth. For example, they are present in the primary and secondary somatosensory cortex 1 month before birth (Killackey & Chalupa, 1986), and in the secondary visual cortex (area 18) within the last prenatal month (Dehay, Kennedy, Bullier, & Berland, 1988).

However, these findings do not indicate that environmental factors have no influence on anatomical development. With environmental conditions typical for the species, a particular pattern develops; but with altered sensory input, callosal connectivity is affected. For example, with reduction in peripheral stimulation by prenatal removal of the eyes in the monkey on embryonic (E) day 77, area 18 increases in size relative to area 17, and also develops so that more neurons have callosal projections in these animals than in normal animals (Dehay, Horsburgh, Berland, Killackey, & Kennedy, 1989).

These experimental results support the hypothesis that, to the extent that variation in human callosal anatomy reflects differences in axon number, the variation may be due to a difference in the extent of axon loss, and not to a difference in the number of axons produced postnatally. These results also suggest that axon loss in the human brain may occur completely or mainly in the prenatal period. In this model, axon loss would occur in both males and females, resulting in the variation of callosal size and shape. However, in men, the loss may be related to functional asymmetry. It was hypothesized that the majority of men have a relatively smaller corpus callosum, which is related to relatively greater axon loss, and they eventually manifest with CRH preference, the typical pattern of functional asymmetry, and with the pattern of cognitive skills associated with right-handedness. The minority of men have a relatively larger corpus callosum, which is related to less axon loss and they manifest with nonCRH preference, and with atypical patterns of functional asymmetry (Witelson, 1985a, 1989). Figure 2.5 presents this hypothesis schematically.

Time Course of Axon Loss

The corpus callosum is visibly present as early as 10 E weeks in the human brain (e.g., Rakic & Yakovlev, 1968). The size of the midsagittal section of the corpus callosum increases most rapidly in prenatal development. By approximately the end of the middle trimester (26 E weeks), the corpus callosum has more than doubled in size. It then doubles again by birth, and again by about 2 years, when it reaches minimal adult values. Figure 2.6 presents a summary of the results of studies charting the growth of the corpus callosum in the human brain from conception to maturity (Witelson & Kigar, 1988b).

Axons may be lost due to death of the parent neuron or by loss of one collateral of a neuron (Purves & Lichtman, 1985). Neuron death may be associated with the development of synapses and the competition for connections. The first synapses in neocortex in the human brain appear by 23 E weeks (Molliver, Kostovic, & van der Loos, 1973). Thus, some callosal axons could die consequent to neuron death as early as 23 E weeks. On the basis of the timing of the emergence of adult patterns of callosal connectivity in the monkey, callosal axon loss may be essentially complete by 30-35 E weeks in human development. These results suggest a window from about 25 to 35 E weeks when most axon loss may occur in humans. Consistent with this proposed time frame of axon loss is Luttenberg's (1965) report that the density of axons in the human corpus callosum starts to decrease beginning at 30 E weeks.

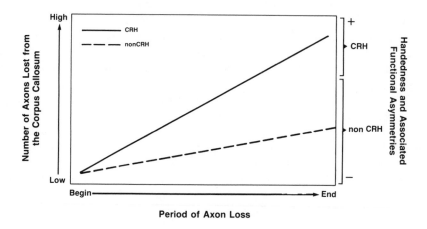

FIG 2.5. A schematic diagram of the proposed relationship between the extent of axon loss in the corpus callosum and the pattern of handedness and associated functional asymmetries as a function of early developmental age in men. The abscissa represents the prenatal and early postnatal periods during which axons are lost. The left ordinate indicates the number of callosal axons lost. The greater the axon loss, the smaller the corpus callosum in the adult. The right ordinate represents the direction and magnitude of functional asymmetries (e.g., preference for use of the right hand or representation of linguistic functions in the left hemisphere), with + representing typical, and − atypical asymmetry. The solid line shows the hypothetical developmental course of axon loss in consistent-right-handers (CRH). In the case of hand preference, up to a certain point of axon loss, people manifest as nonCRH, beyond that, they manifest as CRH, as indicated on the right ordinate. The point above which CRH is manifested was chosen such that it is at 2/3 the range of the left ordinate, to represent the greater range of callosal size in nonCRH than in CRH (see Figure 3, in Witelson & Goldsmith, 1991). The dashed line represents the developmental course for nonCRH. (Adapted from Witelson & Nowakowski, 1991)

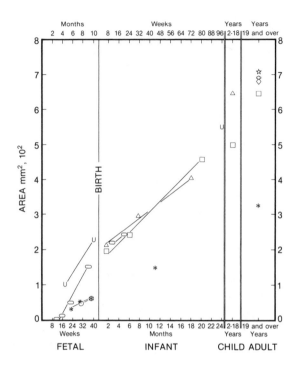

FIG 2.6. Summary of studies measuring total midsagittal area of the human corpus callosum to show its growth over development. Most data points are mean values; a few are scores for individual cases. The location of scale marks on the x-axis for fetal and infant age intervals corresponds to exactly the same time interval (8 weeks or 2 months). Data points of different studies are indicated by different symbols. Note that callosal area increases rapidly in prenatal life, doubling with the last trimester, and doubling again by a postnatal age of 2 years, by which time it is quite close to adult minimal values. (Adapted from Witelson & Kigar, 1988a)

Symbols

□   Bean (1906)
△   Bell & Variend (1985)
U   Clarke, Kraftsik, Innocenti, and van der Loos (1986)
○   de Lacoste, Holloway, and Woodward (1986)
☆   de Lacoste-Utamsing & Holloway (1982)
◇   Holloway & de Lacoste (1986)
⊖   Luttenberg (1965)
*   Rakic & Yakovlev (1968)
⇔   Witelson (1985a)

Prematurity and Axon Loss

Many retrospective and prospective studies of the cognitive consequences of prematurity indicate that among its many behavioral sequelae is an increase in the prevalence of left-handedness. A recent report is relevant to the present hypothesis of an association between loss of callosal axons and functional asymmetry. The effects of prematurity were studied directly as a function of birthweight and indirectly as a function of gestational age (O'Callaghan et al., 1987). A group of very premature infants (birthweight less than 1000 g and gestational age at birth of about 26 weeks) had a 50% prevalence of left-handedness. This was significantly higher than for prematurely born infants with birthweight greater than 1000 g and higher than for full-term infants, and if a definition of nonCRH were to be used, the proportion of left-handers to right-handers would likely be even greater in the 26-E-week group of infants. The intensive and varied stimulation that neonates necessarily receive compared to the stimulation they received in utero could result in a different progressive course of synaptogenesis and regressive course of neuron death and axon loss. Thus, birth at 26 E weeks could interfere with the typical course of axon loss, resulting in the observed left-handedness and a larger corpus callosum. This issue has been elaborated elsewhere (Witelson & Nowakowski, 1991). A recent report of thumb-sucking in utero observed via ultrasound investigation reported a preference for sucking the thumb of the right hand. Inspection of the Results table there indicates a tendency for a decreasing proportion of left thumb-sucking in the sample as gestational age advanced from 15 weeks to term (Hepper, Shahidullah, & White, 1990). These results are consistent with the hypothesis presented here.

Clearly, it is not yet known whether the corpus callosum is, in fact, larger in very prematurely born infants but this is a testable hypothesis. An association between prematurity and atypical neuroanatomical development was demonstrated in monkeys who showed atypical synaptogenesis subsequent to their birth 3 weeks preterm (approximately day E 146; Bourgeois, Jastreboff, & Rakic, 1989). Callosal anatomy was not considered in this report, but the monkeys in this study were probably not sufficiently premature for callosal anatomy to be affected. In summary, I suggest that in human development under normal conditions there is variation in rate or extent of axon loss and that, at least in men, individuals with less axon loss manifest as non-right-handers, with cognitive characteristics associated with left handedness. Under atypical conditions there may be an altered course of the typical progression, and this also results in less axon loss, subsequent non-right-handedness, and possible cognitive correlates.

CALLOSAL INHIBITION OR EXCITATION IN HEMISPHERIC SPECIALIZATION

The concept of interhemispheric inhibition via callosal activity was a widely held notion used to account for the apparent increase in hemispheric specialization with chronological development (e.g., Moscovitch, 1977), which is more likely to be a manifestation of the decrease in functional plasticity (see Fig. 2.1). Callosal inhibition was also proposed as a mechanism for the active suppression of secondary systems in the minor hemisphere, for example, of a secondary language system in the right hemisphere (Levy, 1985). This model is different from the one I proposed (Witelson, 1987b), in which functional asymmetry is present and constant from birth and recovery of function depends on the recruitment or realization of alternate systems given conditions of sufficient impetus, such as brain damage, and not on the release of inhibited secondary systems present from the start.

In a model involving callosal inhibition of secondary systems, right-handers, having greater lateralization of functions, would be expected to have more callosal interconnections (although inhibitory), and a larger corpus callosum. This prediction is not consistent with the present anatomical results.

An alternate hypothesis is that the atypical pattern of relatively less or differently organized functional asymmetry in left-handers is associated with greater callosal excitation for greater interhemispheric communication. This model is consistent with the empirical result of a larger corpus callosum in non-right-handers. Two sets of data regarding hemispheric specialization support the excitation hypothesis. Greater bihemispheric representation could be of two patterns: a "twinned" situation, in which each hemisphere has independent representation of a particular function; or a "shared" situation in which regions of the two hemispheres provide a combined substrate for a function. The data support the latter pattern. Results of speech representation on the basis of intracarotid amytal testing reveal that bilateral representation of speech is associated with some disruption of speech with injections of either side (Milner, 1974), which indicates that neither side is sufficient alone. A twinned situation would be supported by the observation of a lack of speech disruption with injections to either hemisphere, which does not occur. Similarly, the higher incidence of transient aphasia in left-handers than right-handers (Hécaen et al., 1981) is compatible with a shared type of representation. It would seem that a shared pattern of lateralization of related functions would require greater facilitation between hemispheres.

The second aspect supporting the callosal excitation model concerns the possibly greater dissociation of lateralization of related functions among left-handers than among right-handers. In most right-handers, there is a strong association between the hemispheric representations of language and praxic functions. In contrast, in some left-handers, it appears that the right hemisphere plays the major role in motor learning and praxis, even when the left hemisphere is the major hemisphere for speech and language functions (Heilman, Coyle, Gonyea, & Geschwind, 1973). The fact that the majority of left-handers have predominant language representation in the left hemisphere, but are still left-handed, indicates that at least some part of the network of motor programming is represented in the non-language hemisphere. There is little study of apraxia following right- and left-sided lesions in large groups of left-handers, which would help clarify this issue. Greater interhemispheric communication may be needed for the execution of written language with such a dissociated neural organization for language perception and praxis. The question remains as to what advantages led to the development and continuation of such an apparently inefficient neural network in which information must cross the midline at some level for the manual output of linguistic information represented in the other hemisphere.

Some right-handers also show a dissociation between the hemispheric representations of language and praxis. Some right-handers with left-hemisphere damage do not become apraxic (Heilman & Rothi, 1985). The proportion of right-handers who do not show aphasia with left-sided lesions is not known. Numerous "exceptional" cases of such "crossed" aphasia that is, right-handers who suffer aphasia following right-hemisphere damage have been documented (e.g., Fischer et al., 1991). The existence of such cases is consistent with the report of a minority (about 5% to 10%) of right-handers who show right-hemisphere speech with amytal testing (Rasmussen & Milner, 1977). Such right-handers would also seem to require greater interhemispheric excitation or facilitation. The prediction follows that these right-handers may have a larger corpus callosum than those with typical lateralization. Such "crossed dextrals" may be the right-handers who are not genotypically CRH, but in whom random or environmental factors led to a right-hand bias (Annett, 1985).

CALLOSAL ANATOMY AND NEUROANATOMICAL ASYMMETRY

Some association exists between the various hemispheric neuroanatomical asymmetries and measures of functional asymmetry. Some of these results were summarized in a previous section and are reviewed in detail elsewhere (Witelson & Kigar, 1988b). It follows that callosal anatomy and neuroanatomical asymmetry may be related. Such studies remain to be done.

The question may be raised whether one type of anatomical variation — callosal or hemispheric asymmetry — drives the other. In this context, I note that some anatomical asymmetries have been investigated early in ontogenetic development. In infants, asymmetry has been demonstrated between the size of the planum temporale on the right and left sides (e.g., Wada et al., 1975; Witelson & Pallie, 1973). Asymmetry in the planum temporale has been demonstrated as early as 31 E weeks (Chi et al., 1977). The earliest gross anatomical asymmetry noted is in Sylvian fissure morphology. By 16 E weeks, the posterior end of the right Sylvian fissure appears higher than that of the left (see Fig. 2.3), the same pattern of asymmetry noted in adults (Witelson & Kigar, 1988b). This asymmetry is probably genetically determined and could result from any one of several factors, such as asymmetric cell proliferation, cell migration, cell differentiation or some other histological factor. It is likely that regressive events in neural development have not yet started at this point. This suggests that both the early rapid phase of development of callosal fibers and the variation in axon loss postulated to be associated with functional asymmetries occur in an already asymmetric brain. The axon loss may be symmetric, resulting in an asymmetric brain, or the axon loss may be asymmetric, exaggerating the asymmetric base (see Witelson & Nowakowski,

1991). A symmetric brain may result from symmetric loss on a symmetric base or asymmetric loss counteracting the asymmetric base. If, in future studies, a correlation is found between measures of anatomic asymmetry and callosal anatomy, it would suggest that there may be some common factor leading to both, or that the pruning of callosal fibers is determined, to some degree, by asymmetry in hemispheric anatomy.

A SEX FACTOR IN STRUCTURE-FUNCTION RELATIONSHIPS

The relationship of callosal anatomy to hand preference is different in males and females. In men, hand preference can be predicted by callosal size (Witelson & Goldsmith, 1991). In women, no relationship has been observed. This is so even though the variation in callosal anatomy is as great in women as it is in men. Callosal anatomy may prove to be correlated with other behavioral or cognitive measures in women, which may or may not also be found in men, but the finding remains that the anatomical basis of handedness shows a sex difference. Similar results were found for Sylvian fissure anatomy. In men, the morphology of the Sylvian fissure differed between CRH and nonCRH groups. In women, CRH and nonCRH did not differ in Sylvian fissure morphology (Witelson & Kigar, 1992b).

Such sex differences in structure-function relationships are not the same as differences in absolute size per se, such as the findings of a larger isthmus or possibly larger splenium in women compared to men (see reviews in Clarke, Kraftsik, van der Loos, & Innocenti 1989; Witelson, 1989).

What appears to be the most marked difference between men and women is not in anatomy nor in anatomic asymmetry per se, but in the relationship of anatomy to functional asymmetry. Such results require some factor to account for the sex difference. Some sex-related biological factor must differentially and specifically influence neuroanatomical variation in relation to functional asymmetry in males versus females. The most direct evidence for the operation of such a factor is the observation of right-left differences in the level of androgen receptors in frontal and temporal association neocortex in the male fetal monkey brain, but of no consistent pattern in the distribution of those receptors in females (Sholl & Kim, 1990). These results are strikingly analogous to the sex differences in human neuroanatomy observed in my laboratory. The sex difference in the distribution of androgen receptors could conceivably allow the presence of early sex hormones to affect brain development differentially: to affect asymmetry in males, and not in females. The key here is the asymmetric localization of the receptors, at least in males. It is difficult to conceptualize how variation only in the level of sex hormones throughout a system could lead to anatomic asymmetry.

A TWO-FACTOR GENETIC AND HORMONAL MODEL OF FUNCTIONAL ASYMMETRY

There may be two factors leading to brain anatomy as a substrate of functional asymmetry. One is genetic, leading to typical asymmetry in the human brain, whether male or female. I postulate this because the same basic anatomic asymmetry is present in both sexes. Therefore, it is unlikely that any factor that is different in males and females, such as early levels of sex steroids, produces the basic pattern of anatomic asymmetry. The second factor is sex-related, either a genetic factor acting relatively directly, or a sex hormonal factor, acting on the neuroanatomically asymmetric brain and differentially influencing the relation of anatomy to function in males versus females. The isthmus region of the corpus callosum varies with handedness in men, but does not in women (Witelson & Goldsmith, 1991). This suggests that the cortical regions connecting through the isthmus have different functions in males and females. There also is some evidence that the pattern or degree of anatomical asymmetry per se minimally differs between males and females (e.g., Wada et al., 1975; Witelson & Kigar, 1992b). This could be due to the operation of the sex-related factor. Such a two-factor model would allow for a typical neuroanatomical substrate in both sexes but a different relationship of the anatomy to at least some aspects of functional asymmetry. It would also be consistent with sex differences in the pattern of functional asymmetries (e.g., Beaton, 1985) and the sex differences in patterns of cognitive skills that are asymmetrically represented in the hemispheres (e.g., Hyde & Linn, 1988; Linn & Petersen, 1985).

The observation of neuroanatomical asymmetry in higher apes (e.g., LeMay, Billig, & Geschwind, 1982) suggests that functional asymmetry in these species may also exist. The required neuropsychological studies are difficult to do. The observation of a consistent pattern of functional asymmetry within species of lower apes, even if less marked (e.g., for auditory perception, H. E. Heffner & R. S. Heffner, 1986; for visual perception, Hamilton & Vermeire, 1988), suggests some neuroanatomical asymmetry may also be present. These results could be related to the operation of a genetic factor. The operation of an additional sex-related factor might be operative in nonhuman animals, too, but it would be less visible if it were operating on a much less asymmetric substrate to begin with.

Other difficult long-standing questions remain. Why is there neuro-anatomical asymmetry? Why is neuroanatomical asymmetry in a consistent direction? Why does neuroanatomical asymmetry occur in the particular direction it does? What advantages accrue from the typical right-left organization of the human brain, and what, if any, advantages may be associated with atypical brain organization?

ACKNOWLEDGMENTS

This research was supported by contract NS62344 and Grant NS18954 from the U.S. National Institutes of Health, and Grant MA-10610 from the Medical Research Council of Canada.

REFERENCES

Annett, M. (1985) *Left, right, hand and brain: The right shift theory*, Hillsdale, N.J.: Lawrence Erlbaum Associates.

Bean, R.B. (1906). Some racial peculiarities of the Negro brain. *American Journal of Anatomy, 5*, 353-432.

Beaton, A. (1985). *Left side, right side: A review of laterality research*. London: Batsford.

Bell, A.D., & Variend, S. (1985). Failure to demonstrate sexual dimorphism of the corpus callosum in childhood. *Journal of Anatomy, 143*, 143-147.

Bertoncini, J., Morais, J., Bijeljac-Babic, R., McAdams, S., Peretz, I., & Mehler, J. (1989). Dichotic perception and laterality in neonates. *Brain & Language, 37*, 591-605.

Boller, F., & Grafman, J. (Eds.). (1988-1989). *Handbook of Neuropsychology*, (Vols. 1-4). New York: Elsevier Science.

Bourgeois, J.-P., Jastreboff, P.J., & Rakic, P. (1989). Synaptogenesis in visual cortex of normal and preterm monkeys: Evidence for intrinsic regulation of synaptic over-production. *Proceedings of the National Academy of Sciences, 86*, 4297-4301.

Bradshaw, J.L., & Nettleton, N.C. (1983). *Human cerebral asymmetry*. Englewood Cliffs, N.J.: Prentice-Hall.

Brown, W., & Jaffe, J. (1975). Hypothesis on cerebral dominance. *Neuropsychologia, 13*, 107-110.

Bryden, M.P. (1982). *Laterality, functional asymmetry in the intact brain*. Toronto: Academic Press, 1982.

Bryden, M.P., Hécaen, H., & de Agostini, M. (1983). Patterns of cerebral organization. *Brain & Language, 20*, 249-262.

Chi, J.G., Dooling, E.C., & Gilles, F.H. (1977). Gyral development of the human brain. *Annals of Neurology, 1*, 86-93.

Clarke, S., Kraftsik, R., Innocenti, G., & van der Loos, H. (1986). Sexual dimorphism and development of the human corpus callosum.[Abstract]. *Neuroscience Letters, 26*, S 299.

Clarke, S., Kraftsik, R., Van der Loos, H., & Innocenti, G. (1989). Forms and measures of adult and developing human corpus callosum: Is there sexual dimorphism? *Journal of Comparative Neurology, 280*, 213-230.

Corballis, M.C. (1983).. *Human laterality*. New York: Academic Press.

Cowan, W.M., Fawcett, J.W., O'Leary, D.D.M., & Stanfield, B.B. (1984). Regressive events in neurogenesis. *Science, 225*, 1258-1265.

Damasio, H., & Damasio, A. *Lesion analysis in neuropsychology*. Oxford: Oxford University Press.

Dehay, C., Horsburgh, G., Berland, M., Killackey, H., & Kennedy, H. (1989). Maturation and connectivity of the visual cortex in monkey is altered by prenatal removal of retinal input. *Nature, 337*, 265-267.

Dehay, C., Kennedy, H., Bullier, J., & Berland, M. (1988). Absence of interhemispheric connections of area 17 during development in the monkey. *Nature, 331*, 348-350.

de Lacoste, M.C., Holloway, R.L., & Woodward, D.J. (1986). Sex differences in the fetal human corpus callosum. *Human Neurobiology, 5*, 93-96.

de Lacoste-Utamsing, C., & Holloway, R.L. (1982). Sexual dimorphism in the human corpus callosum. *Science, 216*, 1431-1432.

Denenberg, V.H., Kertesz, A., & Cowell, P.E. (1991). A factor analysis of the human's corpus callosum. *Brain Research, 548*, 126-132.

Fischer, R.S., Alexander, M.P., Gabriel, C., Gould, E., & Milione, J. (1991). Reversed lateralization of cognitive functions in right handers. *Brain, 114*, 245-261.

Fontes, V. (1944). *Morfologia do cortex cerebral*. [Morphology of the cerebral cortex]. Lisbon.

Geschwind, N., & Galaburda, A.M. (Eds) (1984). *Cerebral dominance, the biological foundations*. Cambridge, MA: Harvard University Press.

Habib, M., Gayraud, D., Oliva, A., Regis, J., Salamon, G., & Khalil, R. (1991). Effects of handedness and sex on the morphology of the corpus callosum: A study with brain magnetic resonance imaging. *Brain and Cognition, 16*, 41-61.

Hamilton, C.R., & Vermeire, B.A. (1988). Complementary hemispheric specialization in monkeys. *Science, 242*, 1691-1694.

Hannay, H.J. (Ed) (1986). *Experimental techniques in human neuropsychology*. New York: Oxford University Press.

Hécaen, H., de Agostini, M., & Monzon-Montes, A. (1981). Cerebral organization in left-handers. *Brain & Language, 12*, 261- 284.

Heffner, H.E., & Heffner, R.S. (1986). Effect of unilateral and bilateral auditory cortex lesions on the discrimination of vocalizations by Japanese macaques. *Journal of Neurophysiology, 56*, 683-701.

Heilman, K.M., Coyle, J.M., Gonyea, E.F., & Geschwind, N. (1973). Apraxia and agraphia in a left hander. *Brain, 96*, 21-28.

Heilman, K.M., & Rothi, L.J.G. (1985). Apraxia. In K.M. Heilman & E. Valenstein (Eds). *Clinical neuropsychology* (2nd ed., pp. 131-150). New York: Oxford University Press.

Heilman, KM, & Valenstein, E. (Eds.). (1985). *Clinical neuropsychology*, (2nd ed.). New York: Oxford University Press.

Hellige, J.B. (Ed). (1983). *Cerebral hemisphere asymmetry. Method, theory, and application.* New York: Praeger.

Hepper, P.G., Shahidullah, S., & White, R. (1990). Origins of fetal handedness. *Nature, 347*, 431.

Hiscock, M. (1988). Behavioral asymmetries in normal children. In D.L. Molfese & S.J. Segalowitz (Eds.) *Brain lateralization in children*. (pp. 85-169). New York: Guilford Press.

Hochberg, F.H., & LeMay, M. (1975). Arteriographic correlates of handedness. *Neurology, 25*, 218-222.

Holloway, R.L., & de Lacoste, M.C. (1986). Sexual dimorphism in the human corpus callosum: An extension and replication study. *Human Neurobiology, 5*, 87-91.

Hyde, J.S., & Linn, M.C. (1988). Gender differences in verbal ability: A meta-analysis. *Psychological Bulletin, 102*, 53-69.

Hynd, G.W., & Cohen, M. (1983). *Dyslexia: Neuropsychological theory, research and clinical differentiation.* Toronto: Grune & Stratton.

Innocenti, G.M., & Caminiti, R. (1980). Postnatal shaping of callosal connections from sensory areas. *Experimental Brain Research, 38*, 381-394.

Ivy, G.O., & Killackey, H.P. (1983). The ontogeny of the distribution of callosal projection neurons in the rat parietal cortex. *Journal of Comparative Neurology, 195*, 389-389.

Kennard, M.A. (1942) Cortical reorganization of motor function: Studies on series of monkeys of various ages from infancy to maturity. *Archives of Neurology and Psychiatry, 48*, 227-240.

Killackey, H.P., & Chalupa, L.M. (1986). Ontogenetic change in the distribution of callosal projection neurons in the postcentral gyrus of the fetal rhesus monkey, *Journal of Comparative Neurology, 244*, 331-348.

Kimura, D., & Harshman, R.A. (1984). Sex differences in brain organization for verbal and non-verbal functions. *Progress in Brain Research, 61*, 423-441.

Kolb, B., & Whishaw, I.Q. (1990). *Fundamentals of human neuropsychology.* (3rd ed.) New York: W.H. Freeman.

Koppel, H., & Innocenti, G.M. (1983). Is there a genuine exuberancy of callosal projections in development? A quantitative electron microscopic study in the cat. *Neuroscience Letters, 41*, 33-40.

LaMantia, A.-S, & Rakic, P. (1990a) Axon overproduction and elimination in the corpus callosum of the developing rhesus monkey. *Journal of Neuroscience, 10*, 2156-2175.

LaMantia, A.-S., & Rakic, P. (1990b) Cytological and quantitative characteristics of four cerebral commissures in the Rhesus monkey. *Journal of Comparative Neurology, 291*, 520-537.

LeMay, M., Billig, M.S., & Geschwind, N. (1982). Asymmetries of the brains and skulls of nonhuman primates. In E. Armstrong, & D. Falk (Eds.) *Primate brain evolution.* (pp. 263-277). New York: Plenum Press.

LeMay, M., & Culebras, A. (1972). Human brain-morphologic differences in the hemispheres demonstrable by carotid arteriography. *New England Journal of Medicine, 287*, 168-170.

Lenneberg, E.H. (1967). *Biological foundations of language.* New York: Wiley.

Levy, J. (1985). Interhemispheric collaboration: Single-mindedness in the asymmetric brain. In C. Best (Ed.), *Hemispheric function and collaboration in the child.* (pp. 11-31). New York: Academic Press.

Levy, J., & Reid, M. (1978). Variations in cerebral organization as a function of handedness, hand posture in writing, and sex. *Journal of Experimental Psychology: General, 107*, 119-144.

Lindesay, J. (1987). Laterality shift in homosexual men. *Neuropsychologia, 25,* 965-969.

Linn, M.C., & Petersen, A.C. (1985). Emergence and characterization of sex differences in spatial ability: A meta-analysis. *Child Development, 56,* 1479-1498.

Luttenberg, J. (1965). Contribution to the fetal ontogenesis of the corpus callosum in man. II. *Folia Morphologica, 13,* 136-144.

McCormick, C.M., & Witelson, S.F. (1992). *Functional cerebral asymmetry and sexual orientation in men and women.* Manuscript submitted for publication.

McCormick, C.M., Witelson, S.F., & Kingstone, E. (1990). Left-handedness in homosexual men and women: Neuroendocrine implications. *Psychoneuroendocrinology, 15,* 69-76.

McGlone, J. (1980). Sex differences in human brain asymmetry: a critical survey. *The Behavioral and Brain Sciences, 3,* 215-263.

McGlone, J. (1986). The neuropsychology of sex differences in human brain organization. In G Goldstein & RE Tarter (Eds.) *Advances in clinical neuropsychology.* (Vol. 3). New York: Plenum Press.

Milner, B. (1974). Hemispheric specialization: Scope and limits. In F.O. Schmitt & F.G. Worden (Eds.) *The neurosciences: Third study program.* (pp. 75-89). Cambridge, MA: MIT Press.

Molfese, D.L., & Segalowitz, S.J. (Eds.) (1988). *Brain lateralization in children. Developmental implications.* New York: Guilford Press.

Molliver, M.E., Kostovic, I., & Van der Loos, H. (1973). The development of synapses in cerebral cortex of the human fetus. *Brain Research, 50,* 402-407.

Moscovitch, M. (1977). The developmental lateralization of language functions and its relation to cognitive and linguistic development: A review and some theoretical speculations. In S.J. Segalowitz & F.A. Gruber (Eds.), *Language development and neurological theory.* (pp. 193-211). New York: Academic Press.

Netley, C., & Rovet, J. (1988). The development of cognition and personality in X aneuploids and other subject groups. In D.L. Molfese & S.J. Segalowitz (Eds.), *Brain lateralization in children: Developmental implications* (pp. 401-416). New York: Guilford Press.

O'Callaghan, M.J., Tudehope, D.I., Dugdale, A.E., Mohay, H., Burns, Y., & Cook, F. (1987). Handedness in children with birthweights below 1000 g. *Lancet, 1,* 1155.

Ottoson, D. (Ed.) (1987). *Duality and unity of the brain.* London, England: MacMillan Press.

Purves, D., & Lichtman, J.W. (1985). *Principles of neural development.* Sunderland, MA: Sinauer, Associates.

Rakic, P., & Yakovlev, P.I. (1968). Development of the corpus callosum and cavum septi in man. *Journal of Comparative Neurology, 132,* 45-72.

Rasmussen, T., & Milner, B. (1977). The role of early left-brain injury in determining lateralization of cerebral speech functions. *Annals of the New York Academy of Sciences, 299,* 328-354.

Ratcliff, G., Dila, C., Taylor, L., & Milner, B. (1980). The morphological asymmetry of the hemispheres and cerebral dominance for speech: A possible relationship. *Brain & Language, 11,* 87-98.

Sholl, S.A., & Kim, K.L. (1990) Androgen receptors are differentially distributed between right and left cerebral hemispheres of the fetal male rhesus monkey. *Brain Research, 516,* 122-126.

Steinmetz, H., Volkmann, J., Jäncke, L., & Freund, H.J. (1991). Anatomical left-right asymmetry of language-related temporal cortex is different in left- and right-handers. *Annals of Neurology, 29,* 315-319.

Steinmetz, H., Jäncke, L., Kleinschmidt, A., Schlaug, G., Volkmann, J., & Huang, Y. (1992). Sex but not hand difference in the isthmus of the corpus callosum. *Neurology, 42,* 749-752.

Strauss, E., LaPointe, J.S., Wada, J.A., Gaddes, W., & Kosaka, B. (1985). Language dominance: Correlation of radiological and functional data. *Neuropsychologia, 23,* 415-420.

Tomasch, J. (1954). Size, distribution, and number of fibres in the human corpus callosum. *Anatomical Record, 119,* 119-135.

Wada, J.A., Clark, R., & Hamm, A. (1975). Cerebral hemispheric asymmetry in humans. Cortical speech zones in 100 adults and 100 infant brains. *Archives of Neurology, 32,* 239-246.

Witelson, S.F. (1976). Sex and the single hemisphere: Right hemisphere specialization for spatial processing. *Science, 193,* 425-427.

Witelson, S.F. (1977a). Developmental dyslexia: Two right hemispheres and none left. *Science, 195,* 309-311.

Witelson, S.F. (1977b). Early hemisphere specialization and interhemisphere plasticity: An empirical and theoretical review. In S.J. Segalowitz & F.A. Gruber (Eds.) *Language development and neurological theory.* (pp. 213-287). New York: Academic Press.

Witelson, S.F. (1985a). The brain connection: The corpus callosum is larger in left handers. *Science, 229,* 665-668.

Witelson, S.F. (1985b). On hemisphere specialization and cerebral plasticity from birth: Part II. In C. Best (Ed.), *Hemispheric function and collaboration in the child.* (pp. 33-85). New York: Academic Press.

Witelson, S.F. (1987a). Brain asymmetry, functional aspects. In G. Adelman (Ed.) *Encyclopedia of neuroscience.* (pp. 152-156). Cambridge, MA: Birkhauser Boston.

Witelson, S.F. (1987b). Neurobiological aspects of language in children. *Child Development, 58,* 653-688.

Witelson, S.F. (1989). Hand and sex differences in the isthmus and genu of the human corpus callosum: A postmortem morphological study. *Brain, 112,* 799-835.

Witelson, S.F. (1992). Cognitive neuroanatomy: A new era. Editorial. *Neurology, 42*, 709-713.

Witelson, S.F., & Goldsmith, C.H. (1991). The relationship of hand preference to anatomy of the corpus callosum in men. *Brain Research, 545*, 175-182.

Witelson, S.F., & Kigar, D.L. (1988a). Anatomical development of the human corpus callosum: Implications for individual differences and cognition. In D.L. Molfese & S.J. Segalowitz (Eds.), *Developmental implications of brain lateralization.* (pp. 35-57). New York: Guilford Press.

Witelson, S.F., & Kigar, D.L. (1988b). Asymmetry in brain function follows asymmetry in anatomical form: Gross, microscopic, postmortem and imaging studies. In F. Boller & J. Grafman (Eds.), *Handbook of neuropsychology.* (Vol. 1, pp. 111-142). Amsterdam: Elsevier Science.

Witelson, S.F., & Kigar, D.L. (1991). Anatomy of the planum temporale in relation to side, handedness and sex. *Society for Neuroscience Abstracts, 17*, 414.3.

Witelson, S.F., & Kigar, D.L. (1992a). Broca's region: Anatomical and functional asymmetries. *Society for Neuroscience Abstracts, 18.* 144.2

Witelson, S.F., & Kigar, D.L. (1992b). Sylvian fissure morphology and asymmetry in men and women: Bilateral differences in relation to handedness in men. *Journal of Comparative Neurology, 323*, 326-340.

Witelson, S.F., & McCulloch, P.B. (1991) Method for pre- and post-mortem measurement to study structure-function relations: A normal human brain collection. *Schizophrenia Bulletin, 17*, 583-591.

Witelson, S.F., & Nowakowski, R.S. (1991). Left out axons make men right: A hypothesis for the origin of handedness and functional asymmetry. Commentary. *Neuropsychologia, 29*, 327-333.

Witelson, S.F., & Pallie, W. (1973). Left hemisphere specialization for language in the newborn: Anatomical evidence of asymmetry. *Brain, 96*, 641-646.

Witelson, S.F., & Swallow, J.A. (1988). Neuropsychological study of the development of spatial cognition. In J. Stiles-Davis, M.Kritchevsky & U. Bellugi (Eds.), *Spatial cognition: Brain bases and development.* (pp. 373-409). Hillsdale, NJ: Lawrence Erlbaum.

3 Sex Differences in Interhemispheric Relations for Language

Eran Zaidel
University of California at Los Angeles

Francisco Aboitiz
University of Chile

Jeffrey Clarke
University of North Texas

David Kaiser
University of California at Los Angeles

Rana Matteson
Northwestern University

VIEWS OF LATERAL SEX DIFFERENCES

The two human cerebral hemispheres can be conceptualized as two independent and parallel information-processing systems, each fairly complete but specialized for different higher cognitive functions. The corpus callosum can be further conceptualized as a set of multiple and overlapping channels for communication and control, defined by the number, type, and destination of fibers in different regions of the callosum. In this view, both hemispheric competencies and regional callosal connectivities differ across individuals (Zaidel, Clarke, & Suyenobu, 1990). Individual differences in behavioral laterality effects can reflect differences in hemispheric competence only or in callosal connectivity also, depending on whether the lateralized tasks do not (direct access) or do (callosal relay, interhemispheric interaction) require interhemispheric exchange, respectively. Both types of tasks need to be sampled systematically before general conclusions about group differences in interhemispheric relations can be reached. That has not yet been done in the study of sex differences and is the purpose of this chapter. In particular, we ask whether there are consistent sex differences in hemispheric competencies for word recognition and in the connectivity of callosal channels that interconnect cortical word processing modules in the two hemispheres.

In an influential review based on both clinical and normal data, McGlone (1980) concluded that "verbal asymmetries suggesting left hemisphere dominance appear to be more common and more marked in male than in female adult right-handers across several dichotic listening and tachistoscopic studies" (p. 226) and that "the male brain may be more asymmetrically organized than the female brain, both for verbal and nonverbal functions" (p. 215). This review, however, fails to consider the distinction between direct access and callosal relay and has also been challenged on both its clinical and normal evidence (e.g., Fairweather, 1982; M. Hiscock, C.K. Hiscock, & Kalil, 1990; M. Hiscock, C.K. Hiscock, & Inch, 1991). The available evidence to date can be classified one of four ways.

Interhemispheric: Females Have Greater Callosal Connectivity Than Males. For example, Witelson (1989) found that the isthmus of the corpus callosum of the female brain at postmortem (when normalized for total callosal area) is larger than that of the male brain, and argued that this reflects better connectivity of the anatomically specialized language cortex and, consequently, reduced laterality effects in such lateralized tasks as dichotic listening to stop consonant-vowel (CV) syllables. In principle, this account applies only to callosal relay tasks; then, the reduced laterality effect could reflect some combination of greater callosal connectivity and/or smaller left hemisphere (LH) specialization or competence. In the specific case of dichotic listening to CV syllables, increased connectivity would translate into increased left ear (LE) scores and, if channel capacity is limited, into a consequent decrease in right-ear (RE) scores, due to competition. Lesser specialization, on the other hand, would result in a primary reduction of the RE score, or perhaps a reduction of both ear scores (Zaidel, Clarke, & Suyenobu, 1990). This kind of analysis is described further on.

Intrahemispheric: Females and Males Have Different Language Organization in the Two Hemispheres. This has two aspects: First, females have greater language competence in the right hemisphere than males, especially for lexical processes (McGlone, 1980). Consequently, females as a group should have weaker right visual field advantages (RVFAs) or right-ear advantages (REAs) and a higher proportion of females than males should show no visual field advantages or even left visual-field advantages (LVFAs) or left-ear advantages (LEAs) in linguistic tasks (Bryden, 1989). Second, females have a more focal organization of language functions within the left hemisphere (Kimura, 1989). Thus, basic speech and motor control is said to be more focally represented in the anterior (frontal) left hemisphere in females and is more diffusely represented across anterior and posterior (temporal) regions in males. Now, because dichotic listening and hemifield tachistoscopic experiments sample asymmetries in the posterior cortex, close to primary auditory and visual areas, males might tend to show artifactually stronger laterality effects, because intrahemispheric relay effects would not dilute interhemispheric relay effects or hemispheric competence differences (cf. Kimura and Durnford , 1974).

Strategic: ***Females Use Verbal (LH) Strategies to Perform Spatial Tasks.*** This results in reduced LVFAs relative to males (e.g., Inglis & Lawson, 1982). Because it is unlikely that females use spatial (right hemisphere; RH) strategies to perform linguistic tasks, this explains the alleged sex differences in REAs or LEAs for linguistic stimuli. More generally, females may exhibit a more dynamic deployment of available resources resulting in more frequent shifts of dominance for direct access tasks. Along these lines, Boles (1984) argued that sex differences in behavioral laterality effects are more likely to occur for speeded (e.g., suprathreshold lexical decision and naming) tasks which are sensitive to strategy shifts and, thus, are more likely to show up in latency than in accuracy measures. He found no evidence for sex differences in threshold word recognition experiments that use accuracy as a dependent variable. We address this issue in a meta-analysis of some 30 laterality experiments further on.

The view that females show more dynamic, or strategically mediated, lateralized behavior than males, is also consistent with the observation that they are more likely to show systematic shifts of laterality effects with experience. Thus, Boles (1984) reviewed evidence that females show increasing RVFAs (or LEAs) as tests progress whereas males do not. This qualifies the observation (Goldberg & Costa, 1981; Zaidel, 1979) that all subjects show such a shift. Wexler and Lipman (1988) even found that while females show increasing lateralization across test halves in a dichotic CV-syllable experiment, males showed a decreasing REA across test halves. Boles himself found no evidence for an interaction of sex with test half on threshold word recognition experiments recording accuracy (1984). We will address this issue further on by comparing the effect of test half on the laterality effects of males and females in lexical decision and naming tasks in which both accuracy and latency are recorded.

Mediated: ***Sex Differences in Laterality are Mediated by Some Other Trait Variables.*** Candidate variables have variously included handedness (Harshman, Hampson, & Berenbaum, 1983), familial handedness (McKeever, Seitz, Hoff, Marinor, & Dielhl, 1983), cognitive style (Pizzamiglio & Zoccolotti, 1981), reasoning ability (Harshman & Hampson, 1987), age at puberty (Vrbancic & Bryden, 1989), and levels of circulating hormones (Hampson, 1990). We review the evidence briefly. Harshman and Hampson (1987) analyzed dichotic ear advantages with verbal stimuli in three large samples and found that sex interacted with handedness in opposite directions in high reasoning and in low reasoning subjects (as determined by the ETS Inference Test, the ETS Nonsense Syllogisms, or a modified Raven's Progressive Matrices). Thus, only high-reasoning right-handed males showed a greater REA for dichotic syllables than females, whereas only low reasoning left-handed males showed a greater REA than females.

It should be noted that there is a higher incidence of left handedness in males (12%) than in females (8%). McKeever et al. (1983) reported males without a familial history of left-handedness to be more lateralized than comparable females, whereas the reverse was true for subjects with a familial history of sinistrality.

Cognitive style affects laterality: Field-independent individuals show greater RVFAs and REAs than field-dependent individuals (Pizzamiglio & Zoccolotti, 1981). Females are often observed to be more field dependent than males, but these sex differences, though reliable, are small (Hyde, 1981 cited in Matteson, 1991). Still, one wonders whether some of the observed sex differences in linguistic laterality effects are actually due to cognitive style and, if so, whether cognitive style affects relative hemispheric competence, callosal connectivity, or both.

Finally, Vrbancic and Bryden (1989) found that early maturing females showed greater laterality effects than did later maturing females, whereas early maturing males showed smaller laterality effects than did later maturing ones. Futhermore, recent studies reported by Hampson (1990) suggest that low levels of estrogen depress LH function in females: The dichotic REA is low during menstruation and high at the midluteal phase, when both estrogen and progesterone are high. In this chapter we address, among others, the effects of handedness, cognitive style, and reasoning ability on anatomical and functional sex differences in laterality.

Galaburda, Rosen and Sherman (1990) argued that intrahemispheric and interhemispheric connectivities are inversely correlated and that both are related to anatomical and functional asymmetries. Thus, they purported to account for both intrahemispheric and interhemispheric sex differences in language organization. Specifically, greater asymmetry was said to be associated with decreased callosal connectivity and with a decrease in the size of the nondominant hemisphere, as well as with increased intrahemispheric connectivity. The authors proceeded to hypothesize that males (and left-handers) have more symmetric brains, stronger interhemispheric connectivity and weaker intrahemispheric connectivity than females, so that they rely on bilateral language modules, whereas females rely more on LH modules. They accounted for the smaller linguistic laterality effects in females by the facts that (a) the female system, including the right hemisphere, is more efficient; (b) the female right hemisphere is less connected and hence less dependent on both callosal information and the left hemisphere; and (c) in females, the processing of left visual field (LVF) stimuli can be monitored more effectively using other well-connected modules in the right hemisphere. Suffice to say that this unusual account seems to presuppose that there is better language competence in the right hemisphere of females than of males, that hemifield tachistoscopic testing operates largely by direct access, and that efficient linguistic processing in males is always dependent on interhemispheric exchange. Thus, this account blurs the distinction between direct access and callosal relay tasks. Further on, we will report on anatomical and anatomical-behavioral studies that address the Galaburda et al. hypothesis concerning the relation of anatomical and functional asymmetry to anatomical and functional callosal connectivity, focusing on sex differences.

Direct Access and Callosal Relay Tasks

Behavioral laterality effects can reflect differences in hemispheric competencies, differences in callosal connectivity, or both.   If the task is one exclusively specialized, say, in the left hemisphere, then stimuli presented initially to the left visual field will have to be relayed through the corpus callosum from the right hemisphere to the left hemisphere prior to processing.   Then, the behavioral laterality effect, or the RVFA, reflects the costs of the callosal relay. Relay may be slower for later stages of processing, when the relayed information is more abstract and is mediated by smaller diameter callosal fibers (Aboitiz, 1991; Aboitiz, 1992a). Because in callosal relay tasks one hemisphere processes all stimuli, we do not expect significant Visual Field (VF) × Y interactions for experimental variables Y, that require specialized processing in one hemisphere (Zaidel, Clarke, & Suyenobu, 1990).

The corpus callosum is conceptualized as a set of separate, if overlapping, channels characterized by the number of fibers of particular sizes that interconnect specialized areas of cortex.   Callosal connectivity for specific channels may be sensitive to trait variables (e.g., handedness or sex) or to state variables (e.g., anxiety or the effects of psychoactive drugs).

If the lateralized behavioral task is one that can be processed in either hemisphere, at least up to a certain level, then the behavioral laterality effect reflects, at least in part, relative differences in hemispheric competence. These can also be affected by trait and state variables, such as the degree of hemispheric arousal (Levy, Heller, Banich, & Burton, 1983) or experience (Goldberg & Costa, 1981). In these tasks, each hemisphere processes input projected to it in a direct access fashion. If the two hemispheres differ in their processing style, we would expect significant VF × Y interactions for experimental variables Y, processed differently in the two hemispheres.   This kind of interaction *processing dissociation* is the one usually adduced for inferring independent hemispheric processing or direct access (Zaidel, Clarke, and Suyenobu, 1990).

Of course, matters may be complicated if hemispheric competence is itself affected by callosal connectivity, as in cross-callosal inhibition. This would require us to distinguish callosal channels that serve to relay sensory, motor, or more abstract information from those that serve to relay control signals, such as facilitation or inhibition.   The distinction is best made by joint behavioral and anatomical analysis.

Many other criteria can be used to distinguish direct access tasks from callosal relay tasks (Zaidel, 1983, 1986). Using several of them it has been shown that both direct access and callosal relay tasks exist. Thus, we have demonstrated that the identification of dichotic nonsense CV syllables is done through callosal relay, exclusively specialized in the left hemisphere (Zaidel, 1983).   On the other hand, lexical decision regarding concrete nouns and orthographically regular nonwords is done through direct access, as is a lateralized primed version of the same task using word association as the priming relation (Zaidel, 1983; Zaidel, Clarke, & Subyenobu, 1990).

Thus, lateral sex differences in the primed lexical decision task a priori reflect sex differences in hemispheric competence. This task is used in several experiments described further (Sections I, IV, and VI). In turn, lateral sex differences in the dichotic listening task can reflect differences in both hemispheric competencies and callosal relay. This task is also used in some of the experiments we describe below.

I. AN OVERVIEW OF 31 LINGUISTIC HEMIFIELD TACHISTOSCOPIC EXPERIMENTS

We have examined some thirty experiments on hemispheric specialization for word recognition carried out in our laboratory between 1988 and 1993. Most of these experiments used equal (or approximately equal) numbers of male and female undergraduate psychology students as subjects. This cannot be considered a random sample, of either subjects or tasks. All of the experiments investigated some lexical variable, 4 had partly overlapping stimulus lists; and most, but not all, were run on IBM-PC compatibles. Thus, we may expect greater uniformity of sex differences in laterality effects here than in a random sample in the literature.

Previous reviews have been mixed. Fairweather (1982) reviewed numerous studies circa 1980 and concluded that there were no consistent sex differences in laterality. Bryden (1989) provided a "modest and incomplete summary" and found 10 studies showing sex differences with verbal material. Of those, 8 showed greater laterality effects in males, and 2 showed greater laterality effects in females. Bryden observed that, although this is not a significant effect, it is at least a trend in the direction of indicating greater lateralization in males. He further noted that many studies that have reported no sex differences have used small samples and insufficient power to detect them. M. Hiscock et al. (1991) surveyed the entire contents of six neuropsychological journals. Of 516 hemifield tachistoscopic experiments, only 216 provided information about sex differences in adults and only 24 of those (10%) revealed significant Sex $\times$ VF interactions. Of these 24, 17 showed greater hemispheric specialization in males. The authors noted that this number did not differ significantly from chance. Twenty-five more experiments (13%) showed a significant interaction of Sex $\times$ VF, and another experimental variable.

The observation that males show greater lateralization than females is ambiguous. Statistically, some experiments yield a significant overall Sex $\times$ VF interaction. Such an interaction could reflect a greater VF difference in males (Fig. 3.1a), a greater VF difference in females (Fig. 3.1b), or an opposite pattern of hemispheric specialization in males and females (e.g., Fig. 3.1c). Our data show only variants of pattern 3.1a.

Other experiments yield a significant interaction of Sex $\times$ Y $\times$ VF, where Y is an independent experimental variable. Here, Y is typically a psycholinguistic parameter with two levels, say Y_1 and Y_2, such as wordness (word, nonword), word concreteness (concrete, abstract), or Word frequency (high, low) in a lexical decision task. Such a three-way interaction could reflect a stronger two-way

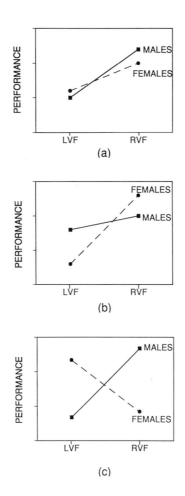

FIG. 3.1. Some possible patterns of Sex × Visual Field interactions. * = significant effect or interaction.

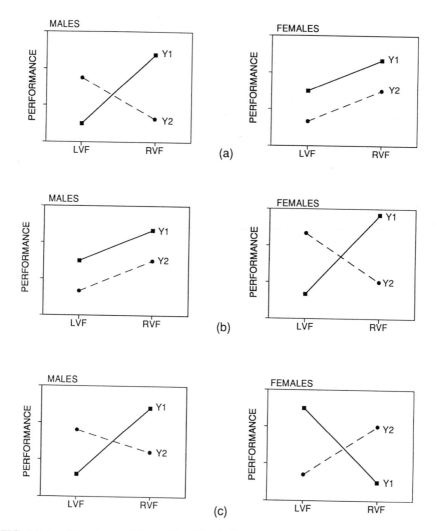

FIG. 3.2. Possible patterns of Sex × Y × Visual Field interactions for an experimental variable Y with two levels Y_1 and Y_2.

interaction of $Y \times VF$ in males, where Y_1 or Y_2 shows a greater VF differentiation in males than in females (Fig. 3.2a). Alternatively, there could be the converse pattern of lateralization, with a stronger interaction of $Y \times VF$ in females (Fig. 3.2b), or there could be an opposite pattern of specialization in males and females (Fig. 3.2c). Our data show mostly variants of pattern 3.2a and one example each of variants of patterns 3.2b and 3.2c.

It should be noted that the same experiment may reveal a significant Sex $\times$ VF interaction with, say, males more lateralized than females, and yet a significant three-way Sex $\times$ Y $\times$ VF interaction with only females showing a significant Y $\times$ VF two-way interaction (Fig. 3.2b, and example further on).

We now review, briefly, each of seven experiments that revealed significant Sex $\times$ Y $\times$ VF interaction for some independent variable, Y. None of these experiments showed significant Sex $\times$ VF interactions.

Effect of Medium of Presentation on Lateral Sex Differences in Lexical Decision

The experiments of Copeland, David, and Zaidel (1993) compared the laterality effects observed in three different presentation modes of the same stimulus materials: a back projection slide tachistoscope, a standard computer video presentation in amber on black background, and a reverse video presentation in black on amber background to eliminate screen persistence. The slide stimuli in the projector tachistoscope were in Helvetica Medium 24 uppercase Letraset typeface, and the computer fonts were designed to imitate it using custom-made dot matrix font design software developed by Steve Hunt in our lab. Stimuli included 68 words high in concreteness, imageability, and familiarity; and 68 orthographically regular and pronounceable nonwords, matched for length (4, 5, or 6 letters long). Word/nonword responses were signalled unimanually by pressing forward or backward a two-position switch placed at midline. Stimuli were flashed for 40 msec to one visual hemifield so that their innermost edge was 2° off a fixation mark.

Only the standard computer presentation revealed a lateral sex difference. There was a significant Sex $\times$ Wordness (W) $\times$ VF interaction in accuracy, with only males showing a significant classic W $\times$ VF interaction. Males showed a significant RVFA for words and a significant word advantage in the right visual field (RVF). Figure 3.3 suggests that the sex difference is due to a selectively high score for words by females in the LVF. This pattern supports the hypothesis of greater lateralization (i.e., lateral differentiation) in males in the second sense of the introduction (Sex $\times$ Y $\times$ VF), and it may be due to greater language competence in the right hemisphere of females than of males.

It is noteworthy that all conditions showed the expected overall RVFA on both dependent measures, and all except latency in the standard computer condition showed the classic W $\times$ VF interaction (Copeland et al., 1993). In the computer condition, the latency data failed to reveal a RVFA or a significant W $\times$ VF interaction in either males or females. This was also true of the accuracy data for females. Thus, early perceptual factors (medium of presentation) affect later psycholinguistic effects (W × VF interactions) so that these stages of processing are not pairwise modular. Perhaps, females are especially susceptible to such mutual influences across processing stages because they failed to show the classic W × VF interaction with computer presentation in either latency or accuracy.

Effect of Font on Lateral Sex Differences in Lexical Decision

Measso & Zaidel (unpublished data) studied the effect of font type on the RVFA and on the W × VF interaction in Lexical Decision. They ran three experiments, using the same stimulus list, presented on an Amdek 310-A monitor controlled by an IBM-XT-compatible personal computer. The experiments were run using a software package developed in our lab, which includes a custom-made program for designing an arbitrary dot matrix font. Each experiment included uppercase and lowercase letters as a between-subjects variable. The first experiment employed the standard IBM uppercase and lowercase fonts. The second experiment employed a font designed to reproduce the Helvetica Medium 24 Letraset. The third experiment employed the font of the second experiment, but with proportional spacing.

Stimuli consisted of 60 concrete, imageable, and familiar words and 60 pronounceable and orthographically regular nonwords. Stimulus strings were presented horizontally 2° off fixation at the nearest edge for 80 msec and varied in length from 4 to 6 letters. Word/nonword responses were signalled unimanually in counterbalanced blocks. Sixteen UCLA undergraduate students, eight males and eight females, participated in each experiment. All were right-handed native English speakers with no left-handed first-degree relatives.

Independent within-subject variables included wordness (words, nonwords), string length (4, 5, 6 letters), and visual field (left, right). Independent between-subject variables included case (upper, lower) and sex (male, female). Dependent variables were accuracy and latency. There were no Sex × T × VF or Sex × Y × VF interactions in the first (IBM) or third ("Helvetica Medium," proportional) experiments. The second experiment, with the computer-designed reproduction of Helvetica Medium yielded a nonsignificant latency interaction of Sex × Wordness × VF with $F(1,12)=4.3$ $p= .058$ (Fig. 3.4). Neither males nor females showed a W × VF interaction. Males exhibited a significant word advantage in the LVF, and females exhibited a significant word advantage in the RVF. This is a complementary pattern of specialization, suggesting a surprising parallel between language organization in the right hemisphere of males and the left hemisphere of females.

Concreteness of Nouns and Verbs

This lateralized lexical decision task (Eviatar, Menn & Zaidel, 1990) manipulated the concreteness of nouns and the "activity" status of verbs. Action verbs (e.g., throw) have strong multisensory associations while quiet verbs (e.g., choose) do

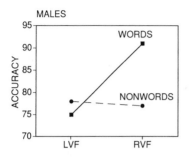 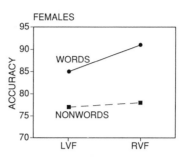

FIG. 3.3. Sex × Wordness × Visual Field interaction for accuracy of lexical decision in the computer condition (Copeland, et al., 1993)

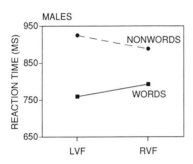 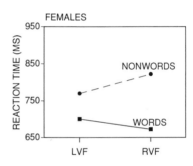

FIG. 3.4. Sex × Wordness × Visual Field interaction for latency of lexical decision in the Font experiment (Measso & Zaidel, 1990).

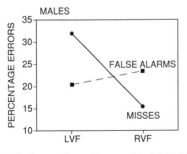 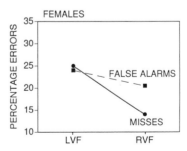

FIG. 3.5. Sex × Error Type × Visual Field interaction for lexical decision in Eviatar et al. (1990).

not. The stimulus set included 72 words and 72 nonwords. The words included -
=18 concrete nouns, 18 abstract nouns, 18 action verbs, and 18 quiet verbs, all
matched for frequency. Nonwords were matched with words for length in letters
and phonemes, and for distributions of initial and final consonants and vowels.
Stimuli were presented for 80 msec using a slide projection tachistoscope with a
back projection screen. The slides had black lettering on a white background.
Subjects included 21 female and 11 male right-handed undergraduate students at
UCLA.

An analysis of variance (ANOVA) for unequal groups on the accuracy
scores included sex as a between-subjects factor and word class (concrete nouns,
abstract nouns, action verbs, quiet verbs) and VF as within-subject factors. There
was an overall RVFA, concrete nouns were more accurate than abstract nouns in
both VFs, and there was no effect of verb activity.

An ANOVA on the types of errors made in each field, with sex as a
between-subjects factor and with VF and error type (misses or false alarms) as
within-subject factors, revealed a significant Sex $\times$ VF $\times$ Error Type interaction
($p<.05$, Fig. 3.3; Eviatar et al., 1990). Both sexes showed significant VF $\times$ Error
Type interactions, but males had significantly more misses than false alarms in the
LVF. Thus, both males and females tended to have a "yes" bias in the RVF,
whereas only males had a "no" bias in the LVF. Figure 3.5 shows that the error
rate for nonwords (false alarms) does not differ between males and females or
between VFs. However, for words (misses), males made more errors in the LVF
than did females. This is consistent with the hypothesis of better language
competence in the RH of females than of males. For females, both VFs show a
pattern similar to that of the male RVF.

Separate analyses of accuracy, sensitivity (d') and latency scores for nouns
all showed a RVFA and a concreteness effect. Latency also yielded an almost-
significant Sex $\times$ Concreteness (C) $\times$ VF interaction ($p = .053$; Fig. 3.6). Here,
males showed a RVFA only for abstract nouns, and a concreteness effect only in
the LVF. Females, on the other hand, showed a RVFA only for concrete nouns,
and a concreteness effect only in the RVF. This pattern was not observed for
accuracy, where both males and females showed a similar RVFA for concrete and
for abstract nouns and a similar concreteness advantage in both VFs. This
suggests that males and females can use complementary resource assignments and
operate at different points on the speed-accuracy tradeoff function. Males appear
to demonstrate a speed-accuracy tradeoff in processing concrete nouns in the
RVF, whereas females appear to demonstrate a speed-accuracy tradeoff in
processing abstract nouns in the LVF.

Separate analyses of accuracy, d' and latency scores for verbs all showed a
RVFA, but no effect of verb activity. For d' there was also a significant interaction
of Sex $\times$ Verb Type $\times$ VF (p = .027) (Fig. 3.7a). Both sexes showed a pattern
consistent with a Verb Type $\times$ VF interaction, but in opposite directions. This
pattern for sensitivity contrasts with the pattern for latency (Fig. 3.7b), where
neither males' nor females' scores were consistent with a Verb Type $\times$ VF

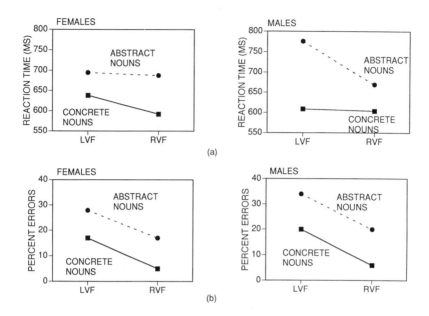

FIG. 3.6. Sex × Noun Concreteness × Visual Field interactions in (a) latency and (b) accuracy of lexical decision in Eviatar, Menn & Zaidel (1990).

interaction. The pattern for accuracy resembles the pattern for sensitivity (Fig. 3.7c). Thus, here again, males and females appear to operate at different points on the speed-accuracy tradeoff function: Males show a tradeoff in the RVF, whereas females show it in the LVF.

In sum, these data suggest that males and females sometimes adopt different hemispheric strategies, deploying resources differently, in performing lateralized tasks. The presence of such strategic differences may not be apparent from consideration of either accuracy or latency alone, but may emerge from plotting speed-accuracy tradeoff functions and from the signal detection measures of sensitivity and bias (Eviatar et al., 1990).

Error Correction of Lateralized Lexical Decision

This experiment (Rayman, Taylor & Zaidel, unpublished data) was designed to test asymmetries in error correction of lateralized lexical decision in an attempt to confirm and extend earlier findings (Stein, 1987; Zaidel, 1987). A 96-stimulus subset of the original 128-item lateralized lexical decision test used in the experiments of Copeland et al. (1993) and Measso and Zaidel (1990) was used here. Forty-eight words and 48 orthographically regular nonwords of variable lengths (3, 4, and 5 letters long) were flashed for 80 msec on an Amdek monitor controlled by an IBM-AT compatible microcomputer. In an attempt to manipulate

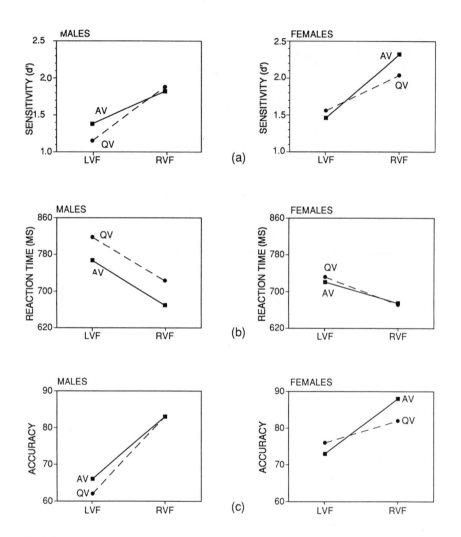

FIG. 3.7. Sex × Verb Concreteness × Visual Field interactions in (a) sensitivity (*d*'), (b) latency, and (c) accuracy (percentage correct responses) of lexical decision in Eviatar et al. (1990).

error rate, stimuli were followed at variable delays (50, 100, 200, 300, 400, and 500 msec) by a 400 msec window delimited by beeps, in which the subject had to respond. Subjects were instructed to correct themselves manually if they thought they had made an error in their initial manual response.

Initial responses showed a significant Sex × W × VF interaction ($p = .006$) with a significant W × VF interaction in males ($p = .005$), but not in females ($p = .294$; Fig. 3.8). Both sexes showed a RVFA (males, $p = .003$; females, $p = .035$). Males showed an advantage of words over nonwords ($p = .001$), but females did not. The males did, however, show a RVFA for words and not for nonwords, whereas the females showed a RVFA for nonwords and not for words. Further, in males there was a significant word advantage in the RVF but not in the LVF, and in females there was no significant word advantage in either VF. In this weak sense, the females exhibited in both hemispheres the pattern of the male right hemisphere.

Response changes showed a significant interaction between sex and accuracy of initial responses. Males corrected a greater proportion of their incorrect responses (44.45%; $p < .01$) than did females (31.61%), but both males (7.5%) and females (5.2%) changed about the same proportion of initially correct responses ($p < .5$). There was no interaction involving sex and VF in either response changes or error corrections.

In sum, there were no sex differences in laterality of monitoring operations, but, rather, only in hemispheric lexical access strategies.

Lexical Decision in Bilinguals

Alexandrov (1989) wrote an honors undergraduate thesis in psychology at UCLA on the effect of bilingualism on lateralized lexical decision in English. In addition to wordness (W; words, nonwords) and visual field of presentation (VF; left, right), Alexandrov's independent within-subject variables included part of speech (nouns, function words), noun concreteness (high, low), noun frequency (high, low) and string length (3, 5, 7 letters). Between-subjects variables included language status (L; monolingual, bilingual), and sex (male, female). The stimulus list consisted of 60 English words and 60 pronounceable and orthographically legal English nonwords. Stimuli were randomized and counterbalanced for visual field and order of presentation across subjects. Strings were presented horizontally on an IBM-AT compatible computer with a monochrome monitor so that the inner edge occurred 2° off fixation and word/nonword responses were made unimanually, with response hand counterbalanced across blocks.

Subjects were all right-handed with no left-handed immediate relatives. The monolingual subjects included 18 native English speakers (7 males, 11 females) who were UCLA undergraduates. The bilingual subjects included 24 students (13 males, 11 females) who acquired English between ages 2 and 15 years ($M=9$), ranging in age from 15 to 25. Languages of origin varied from Spanish, French, and German to Mandarin and Korean. A preliminary ANOVA with language family as a between-subjects variable (Indo-European, Oriental) disclosed no main effects or interactions with any of the experimental variables, so all bilingual subjects were subsequently included in one experimental group.

There were no main effects of Sex nor significant Sex × VF interactions, but there was a significant Sex × L × VF interaction in latency and a significant Sex × L × W × VF interaction in accuracy (Alexander & Zaidel, unpublished data). The Sex × L × VF interaction revealed a significant L × VF interaction in males, but not in females (Fig. 3.9a). There was a lateral sex difference in the bilingual but not in the monolingual subjects, and of the bilinguals, only the males showed a (right) VFA (Fig. 3.9b). This pattern, then shows greater lateralization in males, in the senses of both overall VFA and lateral differentiation.

The interaction of Sex × L × W × VF in accuracy reveals the classic W × VF accuracy interaction in both male and female monolingual subjects (Fig. 3.10a). Among the bilingual subjects, the classic W × VF interaction occurred for neither males nor females (Fig. 3.10b). This is consistent with the view that bilinguals are less lateralized than monolinguals. However, males showed a significant L × W × VF interaction (Fig. 3.10c), whereas females did not (Fig. 3.10d). Thus, male accuracy on words revealed an interaction of L × VF, such that monolinguals were lateralized and bilinguals were not, and there was a significant difference between monolinguals and bilinguals only in the RVF (Fig. 3.10c). Male accuracy on nonwords also revealed an interaction of L × VF, but here, the monolinguals were not lateralized: the bilinguals were, and there was a significant difference between the monolinguals and the bilinguals only in the LVF (Fig. 3.10d). Females showed no significant differences or interactions (Fig. 3.10d). Here, then, males were more lateralized laterally differentiated than females, in the second sense described in the introduction. Male monolinguals and bilinguals exhibited a complementary pattern of hemispheric specialization (for words and nonwords).

In sum, the data of this experiment support the hypothesis of greater language lateralization in males. The male data do not support assertions of greater lateralization in monolinguals. In fact, their latency data show greater lateralization (RVFA) in bilinguals, and their accuracy data show a complementary pattern as a function of language status, with bilinguals more lateralized for nonwords (RVFA) and monolinguals more lateralized (RVFA) for words (Fig. 3.10c). In this experiment, lateral sex differences were all second order in the sense that they interacted with another individual difference, namely, language background.

Lexical Decision and Naming in Farsi and in English

Melamed, a native of Iran, wrote an undergraduate honors thesis in psychology at UCLA, reopening the issue of differential laterality effects in hemifield tachistoscopic tests with linguistic stimuli as a function of direction of reading and writing. Much of it is presented in Melamed and Zaidel (1993). A selective role for the right hemisphere in reading print from right to left would be predicted by the fact that during reading fixation, most attention is directed to letters ahead of fixation, that is, to letters in the LVF in right-to-left languages, such as Farsi, and

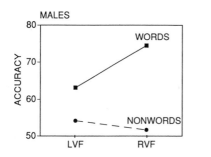
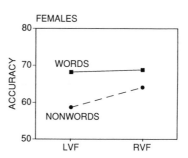

FIG. 3.8. Sex × Wordness × Visual Field interactions in accuracy in lexical decision with error correction (Rayman, Taylor, & Zaidel, unpublished).

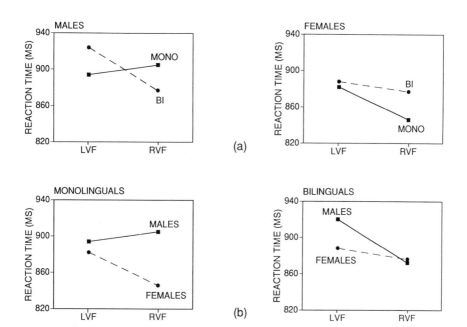

FIG. 3.9. Sex × Language Status × Visual Field interaction for latency of lexical decision in monolinguals and bilinguals (Alexandrov, 1991).

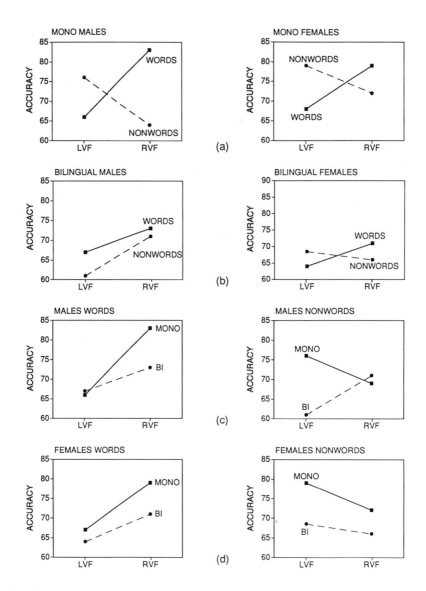

FIG. 3.10. Sex × Wordness × Language Status × Visual Field interactions for accuracy of lexical decision in monolinguals and bilinguals (Alexandrov, 1991).

to letters in the RVF in left-to-right languages, such as English. Melamed further attempted to determine whether the right hemisphere plays a greater role in postlexical access semantic processing or in early lexical access, by comparing the laterality effects in lexical decision and in naming of the same stimuli in native speakers and readers of Farsi and English. Melamed's stimuli were not only translation equivalents in the two languages, but were also matched for word frequency and string length; in addition, word concreteness was controlled for by the inclusion of only highly concrete nouns.

Melamed ran four experiments: lexical decision and naming in Farsi and in English. In each experiment, independent within-subject variables included visual field of stimulus presentation (VF; left, right), and wordness (W; word, nonword). Sex was an independent between-subjects variable. Latency and accuracy were the dependent variables (Melamed & Zaidel, 1993).

Both lexical decision tasks but neither naming task showed lateral sex differences. English lexical decision revealed a significant Sex × VF interaction in accuracy (Fig. 3.11a). Both males and females showed significant RVFAs, but females were also superior in the LVF. This supports the hypothesis of greater lateralization in males and of greater RH-language competence in females.

Farsi lexical decision also revealed a significant Sex × VF interaction in accuracy (Fig. 3.11c). There was a RVFA in males but not in females, and females were superior in the LVF. Together, the two experiments support the hypothesis of greater language lateralization in males and show that this may be associated with greater RH-language competence in females.

An ANOVA on lexical decision accuracy data in the two languages did not reveal a Sex × Language × VF interaction, so there is no basis for discussing lateral sex differences as a function of reading direction. An overall ANOVA on the accuracy data in all four experiments revealed a significant Sex × Task × VF interaction ($p = .025$). There was a significant Sex × VF interaction in lexical decision, but not in naming (Fig. 3.11e, 3.11f). This implicates the sex differences in late lexical semantic processing stages, after lexical access.

Conclusion

The overview of 31 lateralized lexical experiments from our lab leaves the question of sex differences elusive. The majority of the experiments revealed no sex differences in laterality. Four experiments (13%) showed significant or near-significant Sex × VF interactions (3 in accuracy, 1 in latency) and 14 experiments showed significant or near- significant Sex × Y × VF interactions (9 in accuracy, 5 in latency). Thirty-one experiments and 2 dependent variables provide 31 × 2 × .05 = 4 opportunities to obtain significant Sex × VF interactions by chance at the p=.05 level. Counting all the independent variables in all the experiments (73), and 2 dependent variables, we get 73 × 2 × .05=7.3 (or 8) opportunities to obtain significant Sex × Y × VF interactions by chance at the .05 level (14 at the .095, to account for trends). Using the binomial approximation $(z=(x-\mu)/(npq)^{1/2}$,

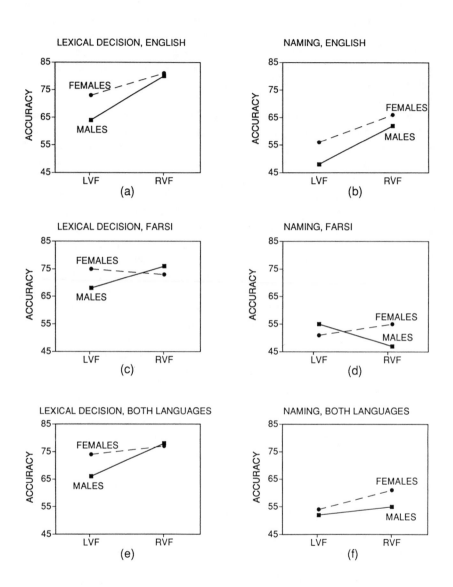

FIG. 3.11. Lateral sex differences in accuracy of lexical decision and of naming in Farsi and in English (Melamed & Zaidel, 1993).

n=146, p=.05, q=.95, μ=8) at z=1.96 or the .05 level, we find that at least 14 experiments must show significant interactions to significantly exceed chance (21 when including trends). Thus, the incidence of neither Sex × VF nor Sex × Y × VF interactions is significantly greater than would be expected by chance. A similar result was obtained by M. Hiscock et al. (1991) on the basis of a much more heterogeneous sample of experiments, and in our lab on a more homogeneous sample of experiments by Kaiser (discussed further on).

Of the 31 hemifield tachistoscopic experiments that were surveyed, 26 involved lexical decision and 29 involved lexical stimuli. Because most of these experiments provide evidence for direct access, they can inform us about the psycholinguistic structure of the RH lexicon in females. Of the 26 lexical decision experiments, 5 showed significant or nearly significant Sex × Wordness × VF interactions. Three of the interactions occurred in accuracy and 2 in latency. Four showed a pattern of W × VF interaction in males but not in females, and females tend to show the male RVF pattern in both the LVF and the RVF. One experiment (Mwasso & Zaidel, 1990), however, showed a complementary pattern in males and females, with a significant word latency advantage in the LVF of males, but in the RVF of females. Other lexical variables (e.g., concreteness, verb activity, bilingualism) similarly tended to show greater VF differentiation (interaction with VF and differences within each VF) in males, but some experiments showed greater VF differentiation in females (e.g., Wordness in bilinguals), and others showed a complementary pattern in males and females (e.g., noun Concreteness). Thus, the data are complex and do not yield a simple generalization.

Other factors, including task (lexical decision vs. naming) and dependent measure (accuracy vs. latency) were also not effective in accounting for systematic sex differences in laterality (see further on).

II. SEX DIFFERENCES IN THE DUAL ROUTE MODEL OF WORD RECOGNITION: A META-ANALYSIS OF LEXICAL DECISION VERSUS NAMING

Kaiser and Zaidel (unpublished data) carried out 10 lateralized tachistoscopic experiments studying the effects of orthographic, semantic, and phonological variables on word recognition in the two visual fields. For 8 of the 10 experiments, we used word lists developed by Seymour (1986) to apply the dual-route model of word recognition to congenitally dyslexic children. Each experiment included 10 male and 10 female subjects. Each list was run between subjects as two separate experiments, once as a lexical decision task and once as a naming task, and each test was run in two counter-balanced blocks, with the response hand changing across blocks so that the effect of practice could be included as an independent within-subject variable.

In this meta-analysis, we also address three more specific hypotheses about sex differences in lateralized tachistoscopic linguistic tests. The first is that males are more lateralized in word recognition experiments with nonverbal responses, whereas females are more lateralized in experiments that involve language production, such as naming (Healey, Waldstein, & Goodglass, 1983). The second is that accuracy measures are less sensitive than reaction time in finding visual field differences as a function of sex. In this view, lateral sex differences occur only in speeded tasks, but not in ones where accuracy is emphasized and so, is presumably due to sex differences in arousal, motivation, or strategy (Boles, 1984). The third hypothesis is that practice interacts with sex and laterality, such that females show increasing asymmetry across the length of the session, whereas males do not (Boles, 1984; J.M. Clarke, 1990). This would probably reflect differences in strategy shifts with increased experience.

All 10 of Kaiser and Zaidel's (unpublished data) experiments manipulated the word status (words, nonwords) of the stimuli. Experiments 1-5 were lexical decision tasks. Experiments 6-10 were naming tasks using the same stimuli. Experiments 1 and 6 manipulated semantic variables, including word concreteness, word frequency, and part of speech; Experiments 2 and 7 manipulated a phonological variable, the homophony of the nonwords to real words; Experiments 3 and 8 manipulated both a phonological and a semantic variable: the phonological regularity of the words and word frequency. Experiments 4 and 9 manipulated the consistency (consistent, inconsistent) of the phonological environment of the nonwords (regular or irregular); and Experiments 5 and 10 manipulated the orthographic environment (high or low frequency) of nonwords and of (low-frequency) words.

All stimuli were presented on an Amdek 310A monochrome monitor controlled by an IBM-AT compatible personal computer. Letter strings appeared as amber-colored characters against a dark background and were flashed for 80 msec horizontally to one visual hemifield, with the near edge 2° off fixation and the far edge up to 6° from fixation. In the lexical decision experiments, subjects responded by pressing one of two keys on the keyboard with either the index or the middle finger. Response hand was switched midway through the experiment. In the naming experiments, responses were recorded by a voice-activated relay.

Only experiments showing significant Sex $\times$ VF or Sex $\times$ Y $\times$ VF interactions (where Y was the independent experimental variable) are discussed here. First, we discuss interactions involving Sex and VF; we then discuss interactions involving Sex, test half, and VF.

Interactions Involving Sex and Visual Hemifield

Lexical Decision

Pseudohomophones. This experiment manipulated the nonlexical variable of pseudohomophony (P) and the lexical variable of wordness (W). There was no overall sex difference, but there was a significant Sex $\times$ VF interaction in latency ($p = .0242$). The interaction was due to a LVFA in males ($p = .016$), but no VFA in females (Fig. 3.12). Thus, males were more lateralized than females but, unexpectedly, showed a LVFA rather than a RVFA.

Word Regularity. This experiment manipulated the nonlexical variable of phonological regularity (R) of the words and the lexical variables of word frequency (F) and wordness (W). Because regularity effects are often observed in low-frequency words only, separate analyses for Sex $\times$ Y $\times$ VF were included for regularity effects in high frequency words and in low frequency words. There was no overall effect of Sex nor a significant Sex $\times$ VF interaction, but there was a trend toward a significant Sex $\times$ F $\times$ VF interaction in accuracy ($p = .08$). This was due to a significant F $\times$ VF interaction in males ($p = .012$) but not in females (Fig. 3.13). In males, there was a RVFA for high frequency words ($p = .042$), but no VFA for low-frequency words, and there was an advantage for high- over low-frequency words in the RVF ($p = .0004$). In females, there was also a RVFA for high frequency words and a trend toward an advantage for high- over low-frequency words in both the RVF ($p = .065$) and the LVF ($p = .074$). Thus, males showed a greater hemispheric differentiation in the sense of exhibiting different laterality effects for the two levels of the independent variable. Females appear to resemble the male RVF pattern in both their visual fields, consistent with the hypothesis of bilateral language representation.

Phonological Environment of Nonwords. This experiment manipulated the consistency of the phonological environment of the nonword stimuli and the regularity of the predominant pronunciation, both nonlexical route variables, as well as the wordness of the stimuli. There was no overall sex difference, but there was a Sex $\times$ VF interaction in accuracy ($p = .0156$). Males showed a significant RVFA ($p = .007$), but females did not (Fig. 3.14). This is consistent with males being more lateralized. There were no Sex $\times$ Y $\times$ VF interactions for Y = consistency, regularity, or wordness.

Orthographic Environment of Words and Nonwords. This experiment manipulated the orthographic environment (E; or combined frequency of lexical neighbors) of words and of nonwords, as well as stimulus wordness (W). There was no overall sex difference, but there was a weak trend toward a significant Sex $\times$ VF interaction in latency ($p = .0951$). This time, females showed a significant RVFA ($p = .012$), but males did not (Fig. 3.15a).

There was also a trend toward a significant Sex $\times$ W $\times$ VF interaction in latency ($p = .0561$), with only females showing a significant W $\times$ VF interaction ($p = .02$; Fig. 3.15b). Females showed a significant RVFA for words ($p = .003$) and a significant advantage for words over nonwords in the RVF ($p = .00002$). Males showed no VFA for either words or nonwords, but word advantages in both the RVF ($p = .00002$) and the LVF ($p = .001$). Thus, in this case, females were more lateralized and showed greater hemispheric differentiation than males. Here, both hemispheres of the males resembled the LH pattern of females.

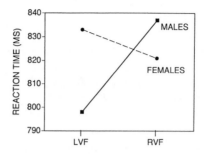

FIG. 3.12. Sex × Visual Field interaction for latency in the Pseudohomophone lexical decision experiment.

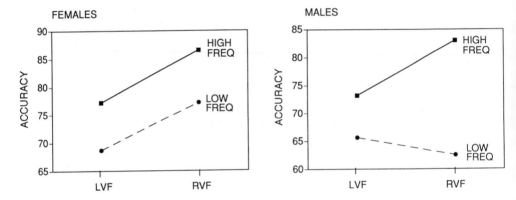

FIG. 3.13 Sex × Word Frequency × Visual Field interaction for accuracy in the Word Regularity Lexical Decision experiment.

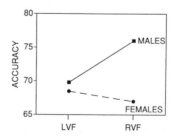

FIG. 3.14 Sex × Visual Field interaction for accuracy in the Phonological Environment Lexical Decision experiment.

Naming

Word Regularity. There was no main effect of Sex and the Sex × VF interaction was not significant. There was a Sex × R × VF interaction in latency for low-frequency words. Only females showed a significant R x VF interaction (p = .0145; Fig. 3.16). In females, the irregular words showed a significant RVFA (p = .007), and there was an advantage for regular words in the LVF (p = .014). Again, females showed a greater hemispheric differentiation than males. Surprisingly, the effect of word regularity, a phonological or nonlexical route variable, was only significant in the right hemisphere of the females!

Phonological Environment of Nonwords. There was no main effect of Sex and the Sex × VF interaction was not significant, but there was a trend toward a significant Sex × nonword Consistency (Cons) × VF interaction in accuracy (p = .068). This was due to a significant Cons × VF interaction only in females (p = .018; Fig. 3.17). In females, there was a RVFA for inconsistent nonwords (p = .005) and there was an advantage for inconsistent nonwords in the RVF (p = .053). In males, there was only a trend for a RVFA for consistent nonwords (p = .076). Thus, in this case females showed a greater hemispheric differentiation than males. If anything, the pattern in both hemispheres of males resembles that of the left hemisphere of females. Again, the advantage for inconsistent words in the RVF of females is surprising.

Orthographic Environment. There was an overall latency advantage in females (p = .046) but the Sex × VF interaction was not significant (Fig. 3.18), nor were any of the Sex × Y × VF interactions significant for any independent variable, Y.

Summary

Kaiser and Zaidel's 10 experiments revealed two significant Sex × VF interactions and one that was nearly significant, all in lexical decision. With 20 statistical tests involved, we would expect .05 × 20 = 1 to be significant by chance at the .05 probability level or .095 × 20 = 1.9 (i.e., 2) by chance at the .095 level, which corresponds to a weak trend. At the .05 level, we would require at least 3 tests to show Sex × VF interactions in order to exceed chance using the normal approximation. In turn, at the .095 level, we would require at least 5 tests to show Sex × VF interactions in order to exceed chance using the normal approximation. Thus, this rough statistical test suggests that in neither case do our results exceed what would be expected by chance, and there is no support for the hypothesis that there is a sex difference in degree of lateralization.

The patterns in the three experiments that do show interactions diverge. Two show greater lateralization is males, and one shows a trend toward greater lateralization in females.

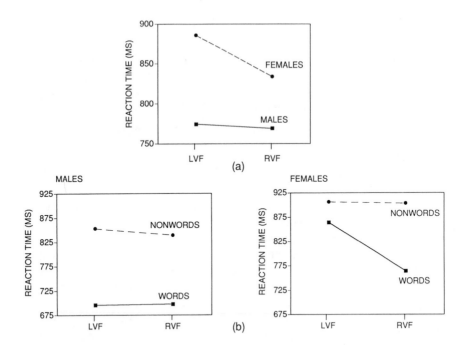

FIG. 3.15 Lateral sex differences for latency in the Orthographic Environment Lexical Decision experiment: (a) Sex × Visual Field interaction. (b) Sex × Wordness × Visual Field interaction.

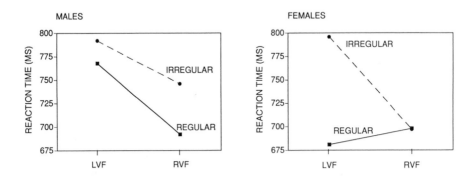

FIG. 3.16 Sex × Word Regularity × Visual Field interaction for latency to low frequency words in the Word Regularity Naming experiment.

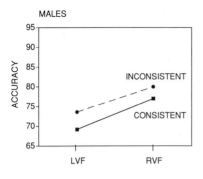
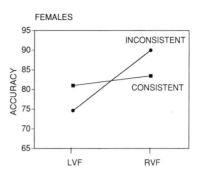

FIG. 3.17 Sex × Consistency of Nonword Environment × Visual Field interaction for accuracy in the Phonological Environment of Nonwords Naming experiment.

Kaiser's experiments also revealed one significant Sex × Y × VF interaction and three trends toward significance on such interactions. The 10 experiments involved 19 independent variables, each included in two tasks (lexical decision and naming) and analyzed with two dependent variables (accuracy and latency), for a total of 19 × 2 × 2 = 76 statistical tests. Of these, we would expect .05 × 76 = 3.8 (i.e., 4) to be significant by chance at the .05 probability level. Thus, our results do not exceed what we would expect by chance and, using this rough normal approximation, there is no support for the hypothesis that the males and females differ in the degree of their hemispheric differentiation.

Again, the patterns in those experiments that show significant or near-significant sex differences in differentiation diverge. One (accuracy in lexical decision for frequency in word regularity) showed greater differentiation in males, and three (latency in lexical decision in wordness in orthographic environment; latency in naming for low-frequency words in word regularity; and accuracy in naming for consistency of nonword phonological environment) showed greater differentiation in females. Clearly, the significant effects are not limited to particular experimental variables, tasks, or dependent variables. Moreover,

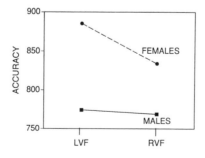

FIG. 3.18 Sex × Visual Field interaction for accuracy in the Orthographic Environment Naming experiment.

although the variable wordness occurred in 10 statistical tests, it was involved in only one trend toward a significant Sex × W × VF interaction.

Meta-Analyses

By way of a more formal evaluation of the significance of the Sex × VF and Sex × Y × VF interactions, we use Stouffer's method of meta-analysis (Rosenthal, 1978). Suppose that N interactions are tested and that the one-tailed significance level of the i th interaction is p_i. Let z_i be the z-score corresponding to p_i in the normal distribution table. Then let a combined $z' = (\Sigma\, z_p)/_n 1/2$. The significance of z' is found in a standard normal table and provides a combined one-tailed probability level.

Table 3.1 shows that the Sex × VF meta-analysis combining accuracy and latency statistical tests in lexical decision yields a significant effect ($z' = 1.8088$, $p = .0351$), although neither dependent variable alone reaches significance. The naming task does not yield a significant effect for either dependent variable alone or for the two in combination. The combined meta-analysis for the two tasks is not significant.

Table 3.2 shows that the meta-analyses of the Sex × Y × VF interactions were not significant for either dependent variable in either task or in the two tasks combined. Thus, there is evidence for a sex difference in degree of lateralization in lexical decision, but no evidence for a sex difference in degree of hemispheric differentiation in either task (see Table 3.5 further on).

Interactions Involving Sex, Test Half, and Visual Field

We assert here that experience or test half changes the degree of hemispheric differentiation in an experiment if there is a significant Test Half (TH) × Y × VF interaction for an independent variable, Y, and if, in addition, Y × VF is significant for one half and not for the other. Thus, if Y × VF is significant for the first half but not for the second, the degree of differentiation can be said to decrease with experience. Of course TH × Y × VF may be significant even though Y × VF is not significant for either half, or, conversely, even though Y × VF is significant for both halves. In those cases, adopt a less formal rule that the half that exhibits more differences in laterality effects across variables is more differentiated. These differences in laterality effects can be a VFA for Y_1 but not for Y_2, or Y_1 greater than Y_2 in one VF but not in the other. We may also wish to adopt the liberal convention that if one half of the experiment shows a significant Y × VF interaction when the other does not, then there is a change in hemispheric differentiation with experience even though TH × Y × VF is not, itself, significant. Finally, we consider adopting the informal rule of comparing counts of simple laterality effects in the two halves, even when the TH × Y × VF interaction is not significant. We tally changes of differences in laterality effects with experience using both the formal and the informal (or liberal) rules.

Table 3.1. Meta-analysis of Sex × Visual Field Interactions for Kaiser & Zaidel's 10 Experiments (unpublished data).

| | Lexical Decision | | | | Naming | | | |
| | Accuracy | | RT | | Accuracy | | RT | |
Experiment	p	z	p	z	p	z	p	z
Concrete	.6061	-.27	.4450	.140	.2925	.55	.1152	.120
Homophony	.2153	.79	.0242*	1.970	.3251	.45	.5817	-.210
Regularity	.5956	-.24	.9520	-.166	.4640	.09	.6139	-.290
Phonogical Environment	.0156*	2.16	.1933	.870	.9733	-1.93	.6795	-.470
Orthographic Environment	.2570	.65	.0950*	1.310	.5436	-.11	.9910	-2.370

$p < .05$, ** $p < .10$

Statistics for the Meta-analysis

| | Lexical Decision | | | Naming | | | Combined | | |
	Accuracy	RT	Both	Accuracy	RT	Both	Accuracy	RT	Both
n	5	5	10	5	5	10	10	10	20
Σz_p	3.09	2.63	5.72	-.95	-2.14	-3.09	2.14	.49	2.63
z'	1.382	1.176	1.81	-.425	-.96	-.987	.068	.15	.59
p	ns	ns	.0351*	ns	ns	ns	ns	ns	ns

* $p < .05$

TABLE 3.2. Meta-analysis of Sex × Y × Visual Field Interactions for all Independent Variables Y in Kaiser and Zaidel's (unpublished) 10 experiments.

Experiment		Lexical Decision				Naming			
		Accuracy		RT		Accuracy		RT	
		z	p	z	p	z	p	z	p
Concreteness	C	-.87	.807	-1.00	.8410	.73	.232	-.76	.776
	H.Fq C	.25	.402	-.86	.8050	.30	.383	1.27	.1018
	L.Fq C	.77	.2198	-1.47	.9295	.48	.317	.83	.204
	F	.60	.275	1.14	.1276	.67	.251	-.05	.5199
	PS	-1.25	.895	-.32	.6260	-1.95	.974	.05	.480
	W	.38	.352	.89	.1860	1.09	.137	-.64	.739
Homophony	P	.39	.3499	-.68	.9508	-2.57	.9949	1.23	.1103
	W	-1.17	.8789	.16	.4350	-.60	.7262	-1.07	.8575
Regularity	R	-.10	.5410	-1.88	.9702	.01	.4950	1.08	.1397
	H.Fq R	-.83	.7963	-1.35	.9112	.28	.3914	-.33	.6284
	L.Fq R	-.45	.3272	-1.77	.9611	.73	.2317	1.78	.0375*
	F	1.40	.080*	-.17	.5673	-2.08	.9814	-.54	.7047
	W	.60	.2729	-.25	.5985	-.05	.5206	-1.52	.9355
Phonological Environment	W̄R	-2.18	.9854	.13	.4492	-.04	.5155	.08	.4662
	W̄C	.26	.3961	-2.07	.9807	1.49	.068*	1.18	.1199
	W	.89	.1854	-.35	.6360	.19	.4257	.24	.4046
Orthographic Environment	W̄₊E	.08	.4662	-1.83	.9665	-1.46	.9277	-1.20	.8854
	W̄E	.68	.2743	-.86	.8048	-2.32	.9898	-1.67	.9524
	W	.60	.2757	1.59	.056*	1.23	.1090	.75	.2255

Statistics for the meta-analysis.

	Lexical Decision			Naming			Combined		
	Accuracy	RT	Both	Accuracy	RT	Both	Accuracy	RT	Both
n	19	19	38	19	19	38	38	38	72
Sz_p	.05	-10.95	-10.9	-3.87	.71	-.316	-3.82	-10.24	-14.06
z'	.011	-2.5121	-1.768	-.888	.1629	-5.126	-6.197	-1.66	-1.613
p	ns	ns	ns	ns	ns	ns	ns	ns	ns

C = concreteness, H.Fq = high frequency words, F = frequency, PS = part-of-speech, W = wordness,
R = regularity of words, W˜ = nonwords, E = orthographic environment.

Lexical Decision

Concreteness. Recall that this experiment manipulated lexical variables, including frequency, concreteness (C; abstract, concrete) and part of speech (content words, function words), as well as length and wordness. The three-way interaction Sex × TH × VF was not significant, nor were any Sex × TH × Y × VF interactions for any independent variable, Y, but there was a significant Sex × TH × C × VF interaction for latencies to high-frequency words. This was due to a weak trend for a significant TH × C × VF interaction in males ($p = .086$), but not in females (Fig. 3.19). The males had a significant C × VF interaction in the second half of the test ($p = .014$), but not in the first half. In the second half, there was a (high-frequency) concreteness advantage in the LVF ($p = .006$) and a weak trend ($p = .09$) toward a significant RVFA for abstract (high-frequency) nouns. Thus, in this case males showed increased lateral differentiation with experience, whereas females demonstrated no change.

Pseudohomophones. This experiment manipulated the nonlexical variable of pseudohomophony of nonwords, as well as length and wordness. There was a trend for a significant Sex × TH × VF interaction in latency ($p = .065$). This was due to a significant LVFA in the second half in males ($p = .013$), but a RVFA in the second half for females (Fig. 3.20). Thus, in this experiment, there was a trend for a decreasing RVFA (increasing LVFA) in males, but an increasing RVFA in females, as a function of experience.

Phonological Regularity of Words. This experiment manipulated the nonlexical variable of grapheme-phoneme regularity of the words, as well as the lexical variables of wordness, word frequency, and word length.
There was no Sex × TH × VF interaction, but there was a weak trend toward a significant Sex × TH × Frequency (F) × VF interaction in accuracy ($p = .091$; Fig. 3.21). The TH × F × VF interaction was not significant for either sex, but the first half showed a significant F × VF interaction ($p = .023$) and a significant high-frequency advantage in the RVF ($p = .001$) in males, as contrasted with only a significant high-frequency advantage in the LVF ($p = .014$) in females. Using the strict criterion that an effect of experience on laterality must be indicated by a significant TH × Y × VF interaction, we found that neither males nor females exhibit a change of laterality effects with experience. However, using the less stringent and less formal criteria, both males and females showed a significant laterality interaction in the first half, but none in the second half. In that sense, we may say that experience serves to reduce lateral differentiation in both males and females.

Phonological Environment of Nonwords. This experiment manipulated the nonlexical variable of phonological environment of the nonwords. The word environment of the nonword can be pronounced consistently or inconsistently (Cons) and the predominant pronunciation can be regular or irregular (R). In

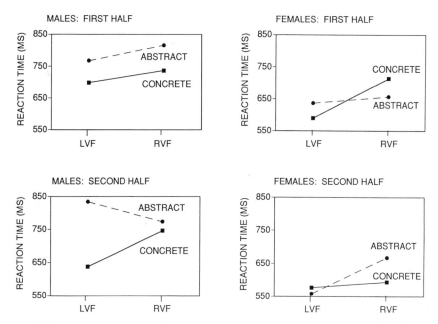

FIG. 3.19. Sex × (high-frequency word) Concreteness × Test Half × Visual Field interaction for latency in the Concreteness Lexical Decision experiment.

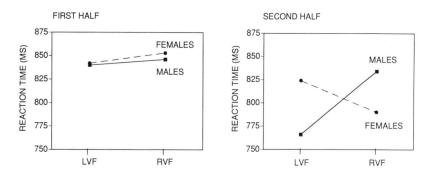

FIG. 3.20. Sex × Test Half × Visual Field interaction for latency in the Pseudohomophones Lexical Decision experiment.

addition, the experiment manipulated the lexical variables of wordness, word frequency and length.

There was a trend toward a significant Sex × TH × VF interaction in latency ($p = .06$). There was no TH × VF interaction in males but there was a significant one in females ($p = .013$; Fig. 3.22). In males there were trends toward RVFAs in both halves (first, $p = .077$; second, $p = .087$), whereas in females there was a significant RVFA in the first half, which changed into an insignificant LVFA in the second half. In this case, then, males showed unchanged laterality, and females showed decreased laterality (i.e., a decrease in the RVFA) with experience.

There was also a significant Sex × TH × R (of predominant nonword environment) × VF interaction in latency ($p = .012$). The TH × R × VF interaction was not significant in males, but it was significant in females ($p = .006$) (Fig. 3.23). The R × VF interaction was significant in both halves for the females (both $p = .04$). Thus, by our formal criteria, neither sex showed a change in lateral differentiation with experience. If we adopt the informal rule, however, we note a significant R × VF interaction in the first half ($p = .04$) but not in the second half for males, suggesting a decrease of lateral differentiation with experience. In the case of females, too, adopting the more liberal convention yields only a trend toward a RVFA for nonwords with a predominantly regular environment ($p = .076$), whereas the second half exhibits the opposite trend toward a LVFA, for such nonwords ($p = .063$), as well as an advantage of regular over irregular nonwords ($p = .03$). This suggests an increase in lateral differentiation with experience. In this case, then, males showed decreased lateral differentiation with experience and females showed increased lateral differentiation with experience.

Orthographic Environment. This experiment manipulated the lexical variable of Orthographic Environment of low frequency words and of nonwords, as well as the lexical variables of wordness and word length. Orthographic environment (E) estimates the mean frequency (high or low) of all the orthographic neighbors of the stimulus (i.e., words that share the end spelling). There was no Sex × TH × VF interaction, but there was a significant Sex × TH × E × VF interaction in accuracy. There were weak trends toward significant TH × E × VF interactions for both males ($p = .0956$) and females ($p = .0962$) (Fig. 3.24). In males, the E × VF interaction was not significant in either half, so that formally they showed no change of lateral differentiation with experience. There was, however, one significant laterality effect in the second half: a RVFA for high-frequency environment words ($p = .022$), but none in the first half. Thus, by the liberal convention we may say that males showed a slight increase of lateral differentiation with experience.

In females, the E × VF interaction was not significant in the first half, but was significant in the second half ($p = .0028$). No laterality effects occurred in the first half, whereas in the second half there was a RVFA for words with a low-frequency environment ($p = .025$) and an advantage for low-frequency environment over high-frequency environment words in the RVF ($p = .0047$).

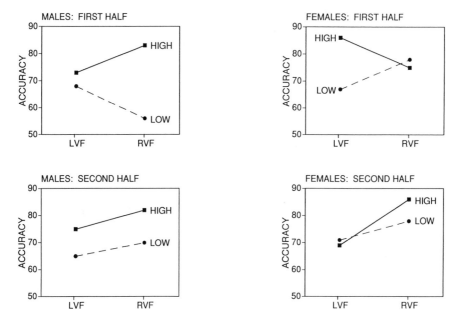

FIG. 3.21. Sex × Test Half × Word Frequency × Visual Field interaction for accuracy in the Phonological (Word) Regularity Lexical Decision experiment.

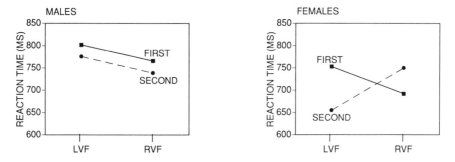

FIG. 3.22. Sex × Test Half × Visual Field interaction for latency in the Phonological Nonword Environment Lexical Decision experiment.

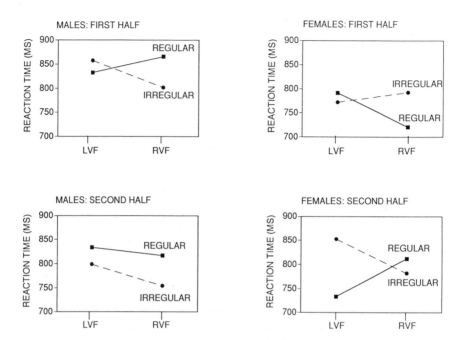

FIG. 3.23. Sex × Test Half × Regularity of predominant Nonword Environment × Visual Field for latency in the Phonological Environment Lexical Decision experiment.

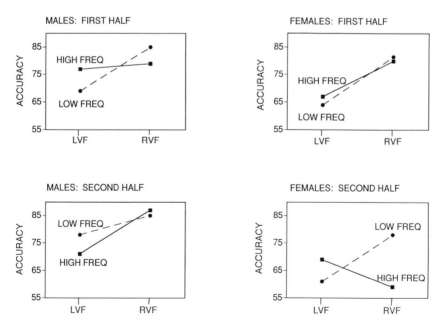

FIG. 3.24. Sex × Test Half × Orthographic Environment of low frequency Words × Visual Field interaction for accuracy in the Orthographic Environment Lexical Decision experiment.

Thus, here females showed an increase of lateral differentiation with experience.

Naming

Concreteness. There was no Sex $\times$ H $\times$ VF interaction and, thus, no sex differences in degree of lateralization as a function of experience. There was a significant Sex $\times$ TH $\times$ W $\times$ VF interaction in accuracy ($p = .007$). This was due to a shift from a significant W $\times$ VF interaction in the first half ($p = .033$) to a nonsignificant interaction in the second half in males, as contrasted with a shift in the opposite direction from an insignificant W $\times$ VF interaction in the first half to a significant interaction in the second half ($p = .008$) in females (Fig. 3.25).

As Fig. 3.25 shows, in the first half, males had a word advantage in both VFs, but also a RVFA for words only. In the second half, males also had a word advantage in both VFs but showed, in addition, a RVFA for both words and nonwords. Thus, males showed decreased hemispheric differentiation, but a pattern actually consistent with increased overall lateralization as a function of experience. Females exhibited word advantages in both VFs and no VFA for either words or nonwords in the first half. In the second half, they exhibited word advantages in both VFs, but also showed a RVFA for words only. Thus, females showed increased hemispheric differentiation, as well as a pattern consistent with increased overall hemispheric lateralization, as a function of experience.

Pseudohomophones. There was no Sex $\times$ TH $\times$ VF interaction. There was a significant Sex $\times$ TH $\times$ Pseudohomophony (P) $\times$ VF interaction in accuracy ($p = .017$). This was due to a significant TH $\times$ P $\times$ VF interaction in males ($p = .043$) but not in females (Fig. 3.26). However, the P $\times$ VF interaction was not significant in either test half in either sex. For males, there was a RVFA for nonhomophones ($p = .0031$) and an advantage for homophones in the LVF ($p = .007$) in the first half. In the second half, there was only a trend toward a significant advantage for homophones in the RVF ($p = .062$). Thus, males appeared to show decreased hemispheric differentiation with experience, as well as a pattern consistent with decreased overall lateralization.

For females, there was a RVFA for homophones ($p = .02$), and a trend toward a significant homophone advantage in the RVF ($p = .08$) in the first half. In the second half, there was a RVFA for nonhomophones ($p = .01$) and significant advantages for homophones in both the LVF ($p = .01$) and the RVF ($p = .039$). Thus, females appeared to exhibit stable overall lateralization, as well as a similar degree of (complementary) hemispheric differentiation as a function of experience.

Regularity. The Sex $\times$ TH $\times$ VF interaction was not significant, and neither were the Sex $\times$ TH $\times$ Y $\times$ VF with Y= word regularity, word frequency, word length or wordness. However, an analysis of Sex $\times$ TH $\times$ Regularity $\times$ VF for high-frequency words was significant for latency ($p = .046$). There was a weak trend toward a significant TH $\times$ R $\times$ VF interaction in males ($p = .09$), but not in females. There was no R $\times$ VF interaction for either half in either sex (Fig. 3.27).

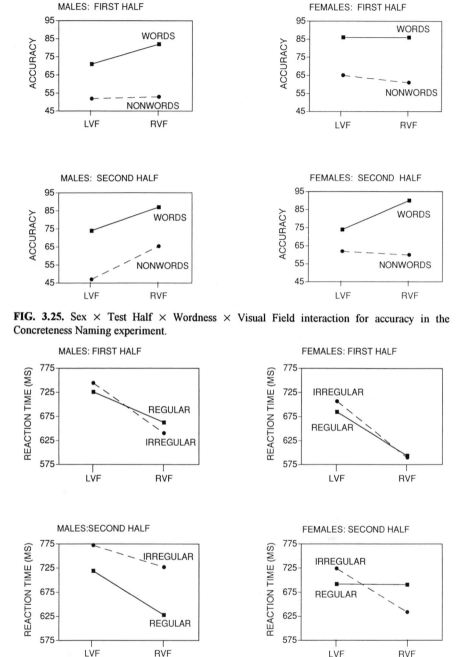

FIG. 3.25. Sex × Test Half × Wordness × Visual Field interaction for accuracy in the Concreteness Naming experiment.

FIG. 3.26. Sex × Test Half × Pseudohomophony × Visual Field interaction for accuracy in the Pseudohomophones Naming experiment. P+ = pseudohomophone, P⁻ = not a pseudohomophone.

In males, the first half yielded a RVFA for irregular words ($p = .005$), and the second half yielded an advantage for regular words in the RVF ($p = .05$). Adopting the liberal convention, we may say that males showed unchanged or reduced overall lateralization and unchanged differentiation with experience, because there was a RVFA for irregular words, but not for regular words, in the first half, whereas in the second half there was no VFA. There was, however, an advantage for regular (high-frequency) words in the RVF in the second half and none in the first half.

In females, there was RVFA for irregular words ($p = .0024$) and a trend toward a RVFA for regular words ($p = .074$) in the first half. In the second half, there was a RVFA for irregular words only ($p = .043$). Thus, adopting the liberal convention, females may be said to show decreased overall lateralization and increased hemispheric differentiation with experience.

Phonological Environment of Nonwords. There was no Sex × TH × VF interaction. There was a Sex × TH × R × VF interaction in accuracy. The TH × R × VF interaction was significant in males ($p = .0002$) and showed a weak trend in females ($p = .093$; Fig. 3.28). In males, both halves showed significant R × VF interactions (first half: $p = .0025$; second half: $p = .018$), but, they were in opposite directions. The first half exhibited a RVFA for nonwords with irregular environments ($p = .005$) and an advantage for nonwords with regular over irregular environments in the LVF ($p = .005$). The second half, on the other hand, exhibited a RVFA for nonwords with regular environments ($p = .008$) and an advantage for nonwords with regular over irregular environments in the RVF ($p = .009$). Thus, males showed unchanged overall lateralization, as well as a similar (if opposite) degree of hemispheric differentiation as a function of experience.

In females, neither half showed a significant R × VF interaction. In the first half, there was a RVFA for nonwords with regular environments ($p = .047$) and an advantage for nonwords with regular over irregular environments in the RVF ($p = .022$). In the second half, on the other hand, there was a RVFA for irregular environments ($p = .034$) and a weak trend toward a significant advantage for regular environments in the LVF ($p = .08$). Thus, females also showed unchanged overall lateralization, as well as a similar (if opposite) degree of hemispheric differentiation as a function of experience. Interestingly, the pattern of R × VF scores of females in the first half resembles, in part, that of males in the second half, and the female pattern in the second half resembles, in part, that of males in the first half. The sexes appear to use some complementary or opposite shifts of strategy as a function of experience, and these shifts are not captured by overall measures of degree of hemispheric lateralization or differentiation.

Summary

Kaiser's 10 experiments, with two dependent variables each, revealed two nearly significant Sex × TH × Visual Field interactions. Because 20 statistical

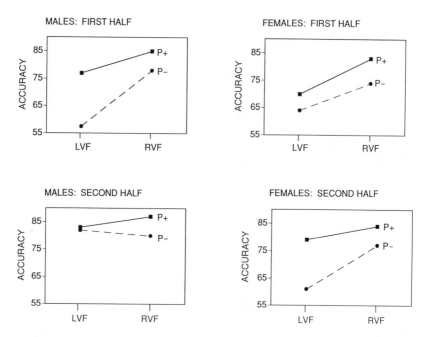

FIG. 3.27. Sex × Test Half × Regularity of high frequency words × Visual Field interaction for latency in the Word Regularity Naming experiment.

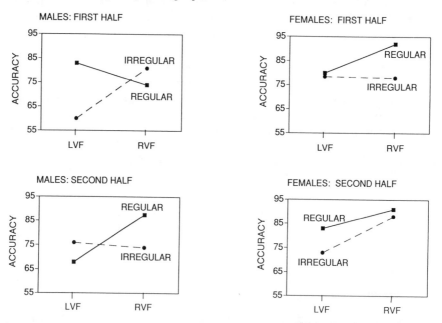

FIG. 3.28. Sex × Test Half × Regularity of Nonword Environment × Visual Field interaction for accuracy in the Phonological Nonword Environment Naming Experiment.

tests were involved, we would expect $.05 \times 20 = 1$ to be significant by chance at the .05 probability level, or $.065 \times 20 = 1.3$ (i.e., 2) by chance at the .065 level, which corresponds to the trends obtained. At that level, we would require at least 3.4 (i.e., 4) experiments to show Sex $\times$ TH $\times$ VF interactions with $p<.065$ in order to claim significant differences from chance at the .05 level using the normal approximation to the binomial guessing distribution, $z = 1.96 = (x - 1.3)/(20 \times .065 \times .935)^{1/2}$. Thus, this rough test provides no support for the hypothesis that laterality shifts with experience mask sex differences.

The two experiments that do reveal sex-dependent laterality shifts show divergent patterns. One (RT for lexical decision on pseudohomophones) showed no significant shifts (interactions) in either sex but a change from no VFA in the first half to a LVFA in the second half in males, together with a pattern of an increased RVFA in females. This pattern is consistent with the hypothesis that males show a decreased RVFA and females show an increased RVFA with experience. However, the other experiment (RT for lexical decision on phonological environment of nonwords) showed no laterality shift in males and a shift from a significant RVFA to a non-significant LVFA in females. This is not consistent with the hypothesis.

Kaiser's 10 experiments involved 19 independent variables (Y), each included in two tasks (lexical decision, naming) and analyzed with two dependent variables, for a total of 76 statistical tests of Sex $\times$ TH $\times$ Y $\times$ VF interactions. Of these, we would expect $.05 \times 76 = 3.8$ (i.e., 4) to be significant by chance at the .05 probability level, or $.09 \times 76 = 6.9$ (i.e., 7) at the .913 probability level, accounting for weak trends. In turn, to exceed chance at the .05 confidence level, we would need 7.5 (or 8) significant interactions, and to exceed chance at the .091 confidence level, we would need 11.8 (or 12) significant interactions. In fact, we found 7 significant interactions (9, including trends), neither of which qualifies as exceeding chance.

Those 8 experiments that did reveal significant or nearly significant Sex $\times$ TH $\times$ Y $\times$ VF interactions showed diverse patterns of sex differences in shifts of hemispheric differentiation with experience. Using the formal criteria of shifts, we find that of 8 experiments, males showed no shift in 6, increased differentiation in 1, and decreased differentiation in 1. Of the same 8 experiments, females showed no shift in 6 and increased differentiation in 2. Again, the hypothesis of sex differences in the effects of experience is not supported.

Using the informal rule and the liberal convention, we find that of those 8 experiments that revealed interactions, males showed no shift in 2, increased differentiation in 2 and decreased differentiation in 4. Females, by comparison, showed no shift in 3 experiments, increased differentiation in 4, and decreased differentiation in 1. Thus, there is slight support for the hypothesis that females tend to show increased differentiation and males tend to show decreased differentiation with experience.

Meta-Analysis

Again, we used the Stouffer method of meta-analysis (Rosenthal, 1978). Recall that there the z-score, z_p, corresponding to the one-tailed significance (p) level of each of the n interactions is found, and a combined $z' = (\sum z_p)/_n1/2$ is computed. The significance of z' is determined from a standard normal table yielding an overall one-tailed probability level.

Table 3.3 shows that the 5 Sex $\times$ TH $\times$ VF interactions do not yield a significant overall effect in either accuracy or latency for either lexical decision or naming. Neither do the 20 interactions involving both tasks and both dependent variables ($z' = -.5121$).

Table 3.4 shows that the Lexical Decision tasks do not yield a significant overall Sex $\times$ H $\times$ Y $\times$ VF effect in accuracy ($z' = .7227$), in latency ($z' = .3671$), or in the two combined ($z' = .7706$). On the other hand, the naming tasks do yield a significant overall effect for accuracy ($z' = 2.9296$, $p = .0018$), and for accuracy and latency combined ($z' = 2.1738$, $p = .015$), but not for latency alone ($z' = .1445$). The combined effect for both tasks is significant for accuracy ($z' = 2.58$, $p = .005$), but not for latency ($z' = .36$) and the combined overall effect is significant as well ($z' = 2.0819$, $p = .0188$). Thus, sex does affect the interaction of lexical and nonlexical variables with experience and field of presentation, although the effects are sporadic and they do not take the direction of the effect into account.

Conclusion

Kaiser's experiments are relatively homogenous in materials and methods, yet they show the same sporadic and inconsistent sex differences in laterality and in lateral differentiation that we observed in the more heterogenous collection of experiments surveyed earlier. In particular, no dual-route variable showed a strong and consistent sex difference in lateral differentiation. This suggests that the lability in sex differences is due to more general variables, potentially ranging from strategy dictated by task difficulty to individual differences in arousal asymmetries or levels of fluctuating hormones.

As Table 3.5 shows, the hypothesis that males are relatively more lateralized in lexical decision than naming received some meta-analytic support, in the sense that lexical decision was more likely than naming to show sex differences in lateralization, and that males were somewhat more likely to be lateralized than females. The hypothesis that latency is more sensitive to lateral sex differences than accuracy was not supported. If anything, accuracy was more sensitive than latency to sex differences in lateral differentiation. Finally, the hypothesis that females become selectively more lateralized with experience was not supported. There was a significant sex difference in lateral differentiation as a function of experience (in naming accuracy), but it was not consistently in the predicted direction.

TABLE 3.3. Meta-analysis of Sex × TH × VF Interactions for all Kaiser's 10 Experiments.

| | Lexical Decision | | | | Naming | | | |
| | Accuracy | | RT | | Accuracy | | RT | |
	p	z	p	z	p	z	p	z
Concreteness	.1109	1.22	.8687	-1.12	.1833	.90	.8629	-.94
Homophony	.5851	-.22	.0652*	1.51	.2921	.06	.4978	.01
Regularity	.4814	.05	.7481	-.67	.5883	-.23	.5911	-.23
Phonological Environment	.5412	-.10	.0611*	1.54	.3797	.25	.8958	-1.26
Orthographic Environment	.7779	-.76	.2973	.53	.9760	-1.98	.8021	-.85

* $p < .10$

Statistics for the Meta-analysis.

| | Lexical Decision | | | Naming | | | Combined | | |
	Accuracy	RT	Both	Accuracy	RT	Both	Accuracy	RT	Both
n	5	5	10	5	5	10	10	10	20
S_{zp}	.19	1.79	1.98	-1.0	-3.27	-4.27	-.81	-1.48	-2.29
z'_p	.088	.8005	.6261	-.4472	-1.4624	-1.35	-2.561	-.468	-.5121
p	ns	ns	ns	ns	ns	ns	ns	ns	ns

TABLE 3.4. A Meta-analysis of the Sex × Test Half × Y × Visual Field Interactions for all the Independent Variables Y in Kaiser's Experiment.

Experiment		Lexical Decision				Naming			
		Accuracy		RT		Accuracy		RT	
		p	z	p	z	p	z	p	z
Concreteness	C	.976	-.198	.3049	.51	.3371	.42	.351	.38
	H.Fq C	.7179	-.58	.0410*	1.74	.2696	.61	.583	-.21
	L.Fq C	.748	-.67	.799	-.84	.900	-1.28	.1556	1.01
	F	.5596	-.15	.1418	1.04	.379	.31	.586	-.22
	PS	.4976	.01	.220	.77	.774	-.75	.688	-.49
	W	.1256	1.15	.540	-.10	.007*	2.46	.8676	-1.12
Homophony	P	.7767	-.76	.9359	-1.52	.0174*	2.11	.9085	-1.34
	W	.3256	.45	.2575	.65	.2178	.78	.4595	.10
Regularity	R	.3543	.37	.9677	-1.85	.089*	1.34	.6633	-.42
	H.Fq R	.1087	1.23	.7367	-.63	.2488	.68	.0458*	1.69
	L.Fq R	.7005	-.52	.5309	-.08	.1246	1.15	.1754	.93
	F	.091*	1.33	.2404	.71	.3176	.47	.1946	.86
	W	.3619	.35	.4691	.35	.8171	-.90	.6713	-.44
Phonological Environment	$\overline{W}$ R	.3081	.50	.0116*	2.27	.0003*	3.4	.2226	.76
	$\overline{W}$ C	.2710	.61	.4983	0	.1736	.94	.5311	-.08
	W	.5314	-.08	.5166	-.04	.1007	1.28	.3002	.52
Orthographic Environment	$\overline{W}_+$E	.7460	-.66	.6615	-.39	.2472	.68	.7661	-.73
	$\overline{W}$ E	.0230*	2.0	.1400	1.08	.8278	-.33	.5440	-.11
	W	.2841	.57	.9640	-1.80	.7270	-.60	.6763	-.46

Statistics for Meta-analysis.

	Lexical Decision			Naming			Combined		
	Acc	RT	Both	Acc	RT	Both	Acc	RT	Both
n	19	19	38	19	19	38	38	38	76
ΣZ_p	3.15	1.6	4.75	12.77	.63	13.4	15.92	2.23	18.15
Z	.7227	.3671	.7706	2.93	.1445	2.17	2.58	.36	2.08
p	ns	ns	ns	*.0018	ns	*.015	*.005	ns	*.0188

TABLE 3.5. Summary of Meta-analyses of Kaiser's Experiments.

	Lexical Decision			Naming			Combined		
	Acc	RT	Both	Acc	RT	Both	Acc	RT	Both
Sex × VF	-	-	+	-	-	-	-	-	-
Sex × Y × VF	-	-	-	-	-	-	-	-	-
Sex × H × VF	-	-	-	-	-	-	-	-	-
Sex × H × Y × VF	-	-	-	+	-	+	+	-	+

III. THE POSTMORTEM ANATOMY STUDY

In this section, we discuss sex differences in the sizes of the left and right plana temporale and their asymmetry; in the sizes of different parts of the corpus callosum; in the fiber composition of these parts; and in the relationships among these asymmetries, the callosal morphometry, and the callosal morphology (Aboitiz, Scheibel, & Zaidel, 1992). The first question is whether gross callosal morphology reflects callosal microstructure, in terms of number and types of fibers in different parts of the corpus callosum. The second question is whether couplings between anatomical asymmetries in language areas and callosal macrostructure (by partition of a cross-section of the callosal area) is duplicated in parallel couplings between anatomical asymmetries and callosal microstructure.

Of course, sexual dimorphism in cortical and callosal anatomy may have only an indirect, or even no, functional significance, but at least one model (Galaburda et al., 1990) posits an anatomical asymmetry underlying functional asymmetry, which is itself related to an ontogenetic perinatal process of elimination of callosal fibers (Geschwind & Galaburda, 1985a, 1985b, 1985c; Innocenti, 1986). This predicts an inverse relationship between degree of anatomical asymmetry and callosal size. In particular, Galaburda, Corsiglia, Rosen, & Sherman (1987) stated that the asymmetry is due to variations in the size of the smaller hemisphere. All of those predictions were put to a direct test by Francisco Aboitiz, a recent graduate of the Neuroscience Program at UCLA, as part of his doctoral dissertation under the supervision of Arnold Scheibel and Eran Zaidel.

Methods

Aboitiz obtained 40 brains, 20 male and 20 female, of people aged 25 to 60 years old, who died of non-neurological causes. The mean age for males was 48.5 years (SD = 11.47; range: 32-66) and the mean age for females was 45.1 years (SD = 14.1; range: 22-68). Brains were extracted from the skulls within 12 hours of death and were immersed in 20% buffered formalin for 7 days. They were then sectioned midsagittally and photographed medially and laterally. The planum temporale was exposed and photographed using the procedures of Geschwind and Levitsky (1968). The Sylvian fissure on each side was measured from the posterior end of Heschl's gyrus to the end of the superior branch (see Figs. 3.29, 3.30) using a computerized digitizing system. The midsagittal area of the corpus callosum was obtained from pictures of the medial surface of the brain and partitioned into five regions according to the scheme of Witelson (1989), using a computer algorithm implemented by Steve Hunt in our laboratory. Measures were corrected for overall brain size or for corpus callosum size only if they correlated positively with those variables.

The callosal pieces extracted were embedded in paraffin and sectioned at 5 µm intervals in the sagittal plane. Alternate sections were stained with the Loyez (for myelin) and the Holmes (for neurofibrils) silver methods under light microscopy. Fibers were counted in 54 × 54 µm fields in 11 positions distributed

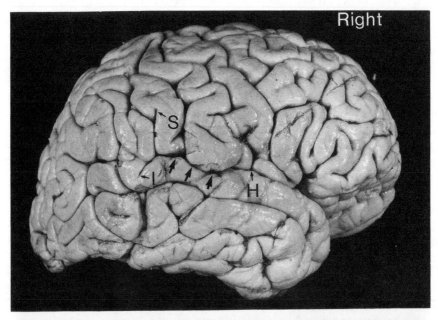

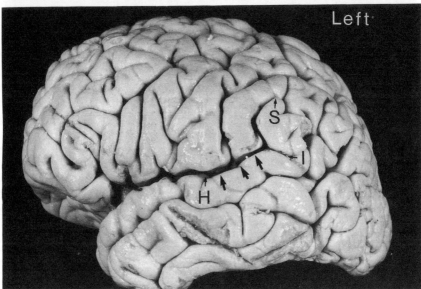

FIG. 3.29. Lateral views of the two cerebral hemispheres. Pictures of this surface were made perpendicular to the plane formed by the medial surface. The figures show the Sylvian fissure (big arrows), its superior (S) and inferior (I) branches and the location of the posterior border of Heschl's first gyrus (H). The curved distance between H and S was called SF. Bar = 2 cm.

along the length of the callosum (Fig. 3.31). The Holmes stain permitted counting fibers larger than .4 μm in diameter, and the Loyez stain permitted counting myelinated fibers larger than 1 μm, larger than 3 μm and larger than 5 μm. Measured diameters are estimated to shrink by 65% after the tissue is fixed and embedded in paraffin.

The fixed callosum was divided into three equal portions according to straight length (genu, midbody and isthmus + splenium). The genu and midbody were further divided into three equal portions according to straight length (G1, G2, and G3, and B1, B2, and B3). The third portion was divided into the isthmus (the area between the anterior 2/3 and the posterior 1/5) and the splenium (the posterior 1/5). The splenium was subdivided into three equal portions according to maximal length (S1, S2, and S3). The area of each of the segments was determined using a computerized planimeter. For determining the total number of fibers, a shrinkage factor had to be applied to the observed fiber densities, which were found to be the same for all specimens (a factor of 0.65×). Fiber counts were made in each of the dots indicated in the figure. With the exception of the isthmus, where two loci were counted, each of the subdivisions had only one counting locus, situated in the middle of the segment. Under the microscope, fibers were counted in three different areas at each locus (a counting area was defined by a reticle inserted in the microscope ocular; see Fig. 3.31 top). In each of these areas, two counts were always made, and the correlations between the pairs were high ($r > .9$). The standard deviations among the three different counting areas in each locus were usually below 5% of the mean.

Differences in density between B1 and B3, and between B3 and S2 were significant for all fiber types ($F(1,18) = 14.0$, $p < 0.01$), except for the difference between B1 and B3 in fibers larger than 1 μm ($F(1,18) = 0.73$, $p < 0.05$). Differences between S2 and S3 were significant in all cases ($F(1,18) = 4.6$, $p < 0.05$).

Results and Discussion

Planum Temporale. The size of the planum is represented here by the size of the Sylvian fissure. Planum temporale area estimations correlated .93 and .96 with Sylvian fissure length on the left and right sides, respectively. Although the mean length was larger on the left than on the right, this difference was not statistically significant (cf. Galaburda et. al., 1987). Similarly, although males' measurements were, on the average, slightly larger than females', this difference was not significant either, nor was there an interaction of sex with Sylvian fissure asymmetry (Table 3.6). Among both males and females 13 subjects in each group had larger left fissures and 7 subjects had larger right fissures. Sylvian fissure length did not depend on brain weight in either males or females, nor did Sylvian fissure asymmetry (L - R) depend on total Sylvian fissure length (L + R). Finally, in both males and females, the Sylvian fissure asymmetry, regardless of its direction, correlated with the size of the right hemisphere rather than with the size of the left hemisphere, but the correlations did not differ significantly from each

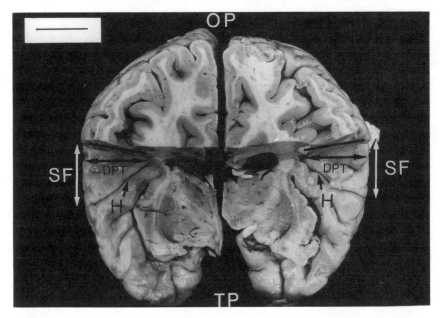

FIG. 3.30. Exposed surface of the superior temporal lobe. It shows the planum temporale, which is the triangle-shaped structure located between the posterior border of Heschl's first gyrus (H) and the posterior end of the Sylvian fissure (black bar). The distance DPT inside the planum is also shown. SF = Sylvian fissure (posterior and superior aspect); OP = occipital pole; TP = temporal pole. Bar = 2 cm.

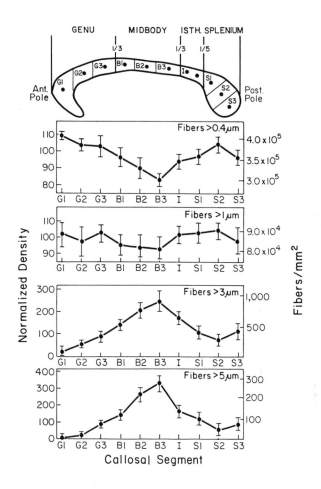

FIG. 3.31. Morphology of the human corpus callosum. Top: Partition of the corpus callosum used for this study. Bottom: Fiber densities in different regions of the corpus callosum (normalized values) for each class of fibers studied under light microscopy. Note that the two loci for counting fibers in the isthmus were averaged. H = Holmes stain; L = Loyez stain.

other (Table 3.7). This pattern contrasts with that proposed by Galaburda et al. (1987), who suggested that the smaller side determines the size of the asymmetry.

Corpus Callosum. Males had nonsignificantly larger overall corpus callosums (about 6%), especially at the genu (not significant) and at the isthmus (about 13%, significant), but these differences disappeared when measures were corrected for brain weight. When callosal measurements were corrected for total callosal size, no significant sex differences emerged (Table 3.8). Males, but not females, showed a significant correlation between brain weight and the sizes of the genu (positive) and the splenium (negative; Table 3.9).

Sylvian Fissure and Callosal Regions. When the size of the Sylvian fissure was correlated with the size of callosal regions normalized for total callosal area, only males exhibited a negative correlation of the right fissure with the posterior midbody, as well as a negative correlation of the left fissure with the anterior midbody (Table 3.10). The sex difference in the anterior midbody is statistically significant. Again, males showed a selective coupling between peri-Sylvian language areas and callosal structure.

The anterior midbody of the corpus callosum may include fibers from Broca's area (Pandya & Seltzer, 1986). Perhaps, in males growth in the left peri-Sylvian language-gifted cortex involves increased ipsilateral projections to more anterior language regions. If long ipsilateral projections compete with contralateral projections for synaptic targets (Galaburda et al., 1990), then increased ipsilateral projection may be associated with decreased commissural connections for these anterior areas, resulting in smaller midbody areas in the callosum.

Although the male left Sylvian fissure has a stronger negative correlation with the anterior midbody of the callosum, the male right Sylvian fissure has a stronger negative correlation with the posterior midbody. Perhaps the male right peri-Sylvian area differs from the left by projecting ipsilaterally to more posterior cortex, resulting in fewer commissural connections through the posterior midbody.

If greater connectivity of the left peri-Sylvian language cortex with the anterior LH cortex reflects more diffuse language organization in the left hemisphere of males, then our data are consistent with Kimura's (1989) concept of more focal anterior language representation in the female brain.

Sylvian Fissure Asymmetry and Regional Size of the Callosum. The absolute value of the Sylvian fissure asymmetry had a significant negative correlation with the size of the isthmus (either absolute or as a percentage of the total corpus callosum) in males, but not in females. Because the isthmus contains fibers that interconnect peri-Sylvian regions in the two hemispheres (de Lacoste, Kirkpatrick, & Ross, 1985; Pandya & Seltzer, 1986), this morphometric result would suggest that males may have a selective inverse relationship between anatomical-functional language lateralization and the interhemispheric connectivity of language-gifted cortex.

TABLE 3.6. Measures of the Sylvian Fissure in Males and Females.

Subjects		M (mm)	S.D.
Females	Left	44.4	(10.9)
	Right	41.3	(13.5)
Males	Left	48.3	(10.5)
	Right	44.5	(8.8)

TABLE 3.7. Correlations (r) Between Sylvian Fissure (SF) Asymmetry and the Size of the Left and Right Sylvian Fissures.

Asymmetry	n	Left SF	Right SF
Left > Right	26	.32	-.41*
Right > Left	14	.54*	-.68**

* $p < .05$
** $p < .01$

TABLE 3.8. Midsagittal Areas of Regions of the Corpus Callosum (in mm^2), M (SD).

			Total CC	Genu	midbody		Isthmus	Splenium
					Anterior	Posterior		
Females	Area	M (SD)	616 (81)	264 (40)	76 (11)	62 (10)	52 (10)	165 (28)
	% Total	M (SD)	-	43 (2)	12 (1)	10 (1)	8 (1)	27 (2)
Males	Area	M (SD)	659 (87)	289 (43)	78 (13)	62 (11)	60 (14)	170 (26)
	% Total	M (SD)	-	44 (3)	12 (1)	9 (1)	9 (2)	26 (3)

TABLE 3.9. Correlations Between Callosal Regions and Brain Weight.

	Total CC	Genu		Splenium	
		Absolute	% Total	Absolute	% Total
Females	.08	.19	.33	-.04	-.2
Males	.31	.52*	.49*	.05	-.45*

TABLE 3.10. Correlations Between the Lengths of the Left and Right Sylvian Fissures and Areas of Selected Regions of the Corpus Callosum.

		Genu	Anterior Midbody	Posterior Midbody
Females (n=20)	Left SF	.12	.02	-.21
	Right SF	.07	.0	-.31
Males (n=20)	Left SF	-.09	-.5*	-.22
	Right SF	.41*	-.17	-.34

Correlations Between the Length of the Sylvian Fissure and Selected Normalized Regions of the Corpus Callosum.

		% Genu	Mid-body	
			% Anterior	% Posterior
Females (n=20)	Left SF	.22	-.03	-.29
	Right SF	.34	.24	-.27
Males (n=20)	Left SF	.18	-.62**	-.07
	Right SF	.52**	-.44**	-.59**

* $p < .05$
** $p < .01$

Fiber Counts. The Loyez counts (larger than 1 μm, mean density 8.7 × 10^4 fibers per mm^2, $SD = 1.8 \times 10^4$) were about 20% of the Holmes counts (larger than .4 μm, mean density 3.7 × 10^5 per mm^2, $SD = 2.8 \times 10^4$). Fibers larger than 3 μm (mean density of 383, $SD = 187$) and fibers larger than 5 μm (mean density of 81, $SD = 45$) represented about .1% and .02% of the Holmes counts, respectively. There were no statistically significant sex differences in either total or regional fiber counts. Fiber density in the Holmes stain decreased from the genu to the posterior midbody, increasing again when entering the splenium (Fig. 3.31). A similar, but less pronounced, pattern was observed in the Loyez stain (Fig. 3.31).

Fiber Counts and Callosal Area. Males showed significant correlations between regional fiber counts and areas for the total Holmes and Loyez counts, but not for fibers greater than 3 μm and 5 μm. Females showed a slightly different pattern, with significant correlations between regional Holmes counts and areas, but Loyez counts correlated with areas only in the isthmus and the splenium. Moreover, unlike males', females' counts of fibers larger than 3 μm and 5 μm did correlate with the midbody area, and number of fibers larger than 5 μm correlated with the area of the isthmus. These sex differences were statistically significant.

Sylvian Fissure Asymmetries and Regional Fiber Counts. There were significant negative correlations between Sylvian fissure asymmetries and Holmes ($r = -.67$) and Loyez ($r = -.8$) counts in the isthmus of males but not of females ($r = -.34$ and $r = -.04$, respectively), paralleling the morphometric sex differences. The sex difference in Holmes counts was statistically significant. Although it showed no morphological sex difference, the anterior splenium showed a significant negative correlation between Sylvian fissure asymmetry and Holmes counts in females ($r = -.74$), but not in males ($r = -.45$).

Conclusion

The findings are summarized in Table 3.11. We found no first-order sex differences in either anatomical asymmetries or regional callosal sizes and fiber counts, but we did find second-order sex differences in the relationship between anatomically asymmetric cortex and regional callosal size and counts. Perhaps, sexual dimorphism for higher cortical functions is established at a relatively late stage of embryogenesis, while the absolute dimensions of anatomical structures are already determined but when their relative internal organization is still plastic. By analogy, it may follow that individual differences in higher cognitive functions reflect relatively late reciprocal rearrangements of neural structures.

Our results showed no sex differences in Sylvian fissure size. On the one hand, our data contrast with Geschwind and Galaburda (1985a, 1985b, 1985c) and with Galaburda et al. (1990), who believed that females should show greater

TABLE 3.11.   Summary of Sex Differences in Planum Temporale, Corpus Callosum Morphometry and Morphology, and Their Interrelationships. SF=Sylvian Fissure, CC=Corpus Callosum, Morphom=Corpus Callosum Morphometry, Morphol=Corpus Callosum Morphology.

| | Main Effects of Gender | | | |
	Size of SF	Asymmetry of SF	Morphometry of CC	Morphology of CC
Sex difference:	-	-	-	-

| | Interactions Involving Gender | | | | |
	Morphom vs. Morphol	Size of SF vs. Morphom	Size of SF vs. Morphol	Asymm of SF vs. Morphom	Asymm of SF vs. Morphol
Male	+	+	+	+	+
Female	+	-	-	-	-
Difference	+[1]	+[3]	+[5]	+[6]	+[7]
Significance	+[2]	+[4]	-	-	+[8]

[1] In males, CC morphometry and morphology correlate for Holmes and Loyez counts, but not for fibers larger than 3 or 5 mm. In females, (a) CC morphometry and morphology correlate for Holmes counts, (b) CC morphometry and morphology correlate for Loyez counts only in the isthmus and splenium, (c) CC morphometry and morphology correlate for fibers larger than 3 and 5 μm in the midbody and in the isthmus.

[2] The sex differences are significant for counts larger than 3 and 5 μm in the midbody, and for fibers larger than 5 μm in the isthmus.

[3] In males only, L SF correlates negatively with anterior midbody of the CC, R SF correlates negatively with posterior midbody of the CC.

[4] Correlations of left SF, right SF and L+R SF with the normalized area of the anterior midbody are significant in males, nonsignificant in females and the sex differences are significant.

[5] Correlations of size of L+R SF and Holmes and Loyez counts in the anterior midbody of the CC are significant in males, nonsignificant in females, and the sex differences are not significant.

[6] In males only, the absolute value of SF asymmetry correlates negatively with the size of the isthmus.

[7] In males, SF asymmetry correlates negatively with Holmes and Loyez counts in the isthmus, In females, SF asymmetry correlates negatively with Holmes counts in the anterior splenium.

[8] Correlation of SF asymmetry with Loyez counts in the isthmus is significant in males, nonsignificant in females, and the sex difference is statistically significant.

asymmetries. On the other hand, our data contrast with Wada, Clarke, & Hamm (1975) and McGlone (1980), who believed that males show greater asymmetries.

We found no sex differences in overall callosal size corrected for brain weight, supporting previous data (e.g., J. M. Clarke, 1990; Witelson, 1989). Unlike Witelson (1989), J. M. Clarke (1990), and Steinmetz et al. (1992), however, in this material we found no sex differences in the size of the normalized isthmus (see Section V below). The discrepancy with the data of J. M. Clarke, obtained in the our own lab, is especially telling and may be due to (a) different methodologies (i.e., postmortem vs. MRI) and/or (b) different populations (i.e., older general hospital admissions in Santiago, Chile vs. younger graduate students at UCLA). Most likely, however, the sex difference in the size of the isthmus interacts with handedness, so that mixed-handed males have a larger isthmus than right-handed males, but this is not the case for females (J. M. Clarke & Zaidel, in press). This sometimes does and sometimes does not result in sex differences in the isthmus of consistent right-handers.

Most dramatically, we found a negative correlation between Sylvian fissure asymmetry and isthmus size in males but not in females. The correlation in males was even stronger between Sylvian fissure asymmetry and number of isthmus fibers greater than 1 µm, but not greater that 3 µm or 5 µm. A smaller isthmus may reflect a lower density of small diameter fibers (La Mantia & Rakic, 1990b) as a result of selective synaptic elimination during embryogenesis (Rosen, Sherman, & Galaburda, 1989). Perhaps, more asymmetric cortex contains fewer homotopic connections and leads to more extensive perinatal terminal retraction (Innocenti, 1986). This may result in greater interhemispheric cognitive (rather than sensory) independence and possibly greater intrahemispheric cognitive connectivity in males (cf. Galaburda et al., 1990). Similarly, inverse relations between Sylvian fissure length and the size of both the genu and the size of the midbody of the corpus callosum were observed in males only, confirming a closer coupling between anatomical-functional (language) asymmetry and callosal connectivity in males than in females.

It should be recalled that the posterior parietal and temporal regions tend to interconnect through the posterior midbody, the isthmus, and the anterior splenium. It is generally believed that association areas tend to be connected with small- and mid-diameter axons (smaller than 2 µm), whereas larger axons tend to connect primary and secondary visual and somatosensory cortices (Aboitiz, Zaidel, & Scheibel, 1989; La Mantia & Rakic, 1990b), presumably in order to effect quick sensory integration across the midline. Jerison (1991) reported no major species differences in the distribution of callosal axons with thin diameters, but an increase in the density and diameter of large axons with increasing brain size, presumably in order to interconnect faster those regions that are farther apart in larger brains.

It is likely that the density peak of large diameter fibers in the posterior midbody represents commissural connections of primary and secondary auditory areas, but these densities show no sex difference and no relation to anatomical asymmetries. On the other hand, there was a sex difference in the relation of anatomical asymmetries and counts of small-diameter fibers, which presumably mediate the transfer of higher cognitive information. In particular, language areas seem to interconnect more anteriorly in males (isthmus) than in females (anterior splenium). This suggests a different topographical mapping of the peri-Sylvian areas in the callosum in the two sexes.

It is noteworthy that callosal channels that interconnect asymmetric areas of language cortex show a correlation between the number of "association" fibers and the area of particular callosal regions, so that gross morphological studies (done, e.g., with MRI) hold promise for further research on the anatomical basis of hemispheric asymmetry.

We now see that the isthmus contains at least two overlapping channels, one presumably for sensory interconnection mediated by large-diameter fibers and showing no relationship between size and fiber count, and the other presumably for higher level communication between areas of asymmetric cortex, mediated by smaller diameter fibers and showing a positive relationship between size and fiber count. This helps explain the lack of correlation between isthmus size and LE score in dichotic listening (large fibers), but the significant correlation between isthmus size and the laterality effect in a lexical decision task found by J. M. Clarke (1990, and see Section IV).

IV. SEX DIFFERENCES IN CALLOSAL MORPHOMETRY, BEHAVIORAL LATERALITY, AND COGNITION, AND THEIR INTERRELATIONS

In his doctoral dissertation, J. M. Clarke (1990) analyzed individual differences in regional callosal morphometry as imaged by midsagittal MRIs and related them to differences in laterality on a direct access lexical decision task and a callosal relay dichotic listening task, as well as to tests of visual perception, verbal production, memory, attention, and problem solving. It is commonly reported that males tend to perform better than females on visuospatial tasks, whereas females outperform males on verbal tasks (e.g., Wittig & Petersen, 1979). It has also been found sometimes that the isthmus of the corpus callosum is larger in females than in males (e.g., Witelson, 1989). Since the isthmus is believed to interconnect functionally specialized temporal-parietal cortex, its size variation with sex may be related to sex differences in laterality, especially auditory, linguistic, and visuo-perceptual.

Animal studies showed that sex differences in the size of the corpus callosum in the rat reflect differences in both the number and type of callosal fibers (Juraska & Kopcik, 1988). At first glance, we may expect size correlates of callosal connectivity to affect behavioral laterality effects in callosal relay tasks that require sensory transfer or in complex tasks that require interhemispheric integration but not in direct access tasks. However, Aboitiz's discovery (described earlier, Section III) suggests that only cognitive, and not sensory, connectivity is reflected in the size of the callosum, because a larger callosal area includes more small-diameter, but not large-diameter, fibers.

Methods

Sixty UCLA graduate students participated in this experiment, half males and half females, half right-handed and half left-handed. Each had a midsagittal MRI from a .3 tesla FONAR Beta 3000 machine (TR=500 msec, TE=28 msec, 5 mm to 7 mm thickness) in the Radiology Department at UCLA, with the collaboration of Dr. Robert Lufkin. The outline of the corpus callosum was digitized and its cross section area partitioned by a computer algorithm into five linear segments (Fig. 3.32) following Witelson (1989). In addition to the five area measures, three linear measures were determined (Fig. 3.33b).

Each subject was administered four behavioral laterality tests designed to tap hemispheric specialization and callosal transfer in touch, vision, and audition, including both linguistic and nonlinguistic material. These tests included unimanual lexical decision of lateralized tachistoscopic concrete nouns and orthographically regular nonwords and verbal identification of dichotically presented CV syllables. There was also a nonverbal shape discrimination task within and between the visual hemifields and a roughness discrimination task within and between the hands.

The cognitive profile measures were designed to tap different basic cognitive components and different cortical regions. They included tests of handedness, visual perception, verbal production, memory, and frontal lobe functions (Table 3.12). Of special interest are the Space Relations subtest of the Differential Aptitude Test and the ETS Hidden Patterns test (cognitive style), which tend to show male superiority, and the Stroop Test, which taps automatic lexical semantic interference. The question is whether the corpus callosum has a role in mediating such inhibition. In addition, because Clarke did not use a measure of reading ability, we subsequently administered to 20 UCLA undergraduates the Davis Reading Test (college level) and the lateralized lexical decision test in order to correlate them.

The laterality indices used were either L - R or Bryden and Sprott's (1981) lambda, which corrects for overall accuracy.

Results and Discussions

Callosal morphometry. The mean midsagittal cerebral area was 11% larger in males than in females (102.7 cm^2 vs. 92.5 cm^2 ; Clarke & Zaidel, in press). There was a significant sex difference in absolute minimum body width ($F(1,56)$=6.4, p = .01) which was larger in females (4.6 mm) than in males (4.0 mm). Minimum body width normalized for total callosal size showed a sex difference ($F(1,56)$=9.1, $p < .01$)) and was larger in females (17.7%) than in males (15.02%). The relative isthmus area was also larger in females (8.7%) than in males (7.98%; $F(1,56)$ = 4.8, p = .032). These findings, like others, fail to replicate the original claim by de Lacoste and Holloway (1982) that splenial measures are larger in females. Our findings are generally consistent with Byne,

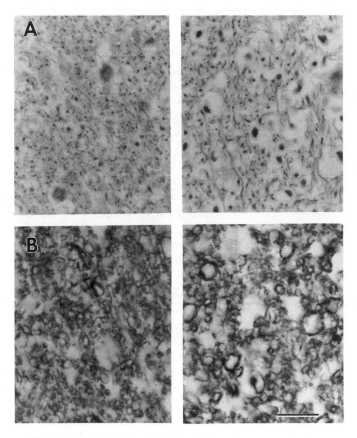

FIG. 3.32. Photomicrographics of the anterior midbody (left) and posterior midbody (right). (A) Holmes stain and (B) Loyez stain. bar=10 μm.

Bleier, and Houston (1988, using MRI), and Witelson (1989, on postmortems), and with Steinmetz et al. (1982, using MRI; but see Habib et al., 1991).

Our data did not show any handedness differences in callosum measures, nor any significant Sex × Handedness interactions. However, when consistent right-handers were compared with mixed-handers (all of whom were left-hand dominant for writing), but excluding consistent left-handers, there was a significant Sex × Handedness interaction in the size of the normalized isthmus (Fig. 3.34). No such interaction occurred for consistent right- and left-handers. This replicates the Sex × Handedness interaction but not the handedness data of Witelson (1989) or of Habib et al. (1991). It is interesting that callosal organization of consistent right- and left-handers is more similar than is that of consistent right- and mixed-handers. The Sex × Handedness interaction in isthmus size for consistent right-handers versus mixed-handers is a more general finding than is the sex difference for consistent right-handers.

Cognitive Profile. There were no significant effects of Sex, nor were there any significant interactions of Sex or Handedness in any of the 14 cognitive measures, including Spatial Relations, Hidden Patterns, and Tower of Hanoi. This is probably due to the highly selected sample of graduate students who participated in this experiment.

Behavioral Laterality. The lateralized lexical decision task with associative priming disclosed a main effect of visual field of prime, but an advantage for RVF targets in accuracy, and the usual Wordness × VF interaction (RVFA for words only, word advantage in the LVF only); there were no effects or interactions due to Sex (Fig. 3.25). Analysis of word responses again showed a RVFA, an advantage for associated pairs (priming) and, for right-handers, significant priming only in the LVF (Fig. 3.36)! None of these effects interacted with Sex.

Hiscock and MacKay (1985a, 1985b) and Hiscock and Hiscock (1988) reviewed the literature and found no consistent sex differences in REA in dichotic listening to CV syllables. The dichotic listening task was analyzed for effects of sex, handedness, ear, and test half (TH) and disclosed a REA, a Handedness × Ear interaction (higher RE scores in right-handers), and a Sex × TH × Ear interaction (Fig. 3.37). Here, the interaction of Ear × TH was significant for females, but not for males. In principle, the increased REA with experience in females (cf. Wexler & Lipman, 1988) could be due to decreased callosal connectivity or increased ipsilateral suppression, but then we would expect the change in the LE rather than the RE score to be significant. Instead, the observed pattern suggests an increase in LH activation across test halves. It should be recalled that all of these subjects were UCLA graduate students who have high reasoning ability and tend to be field independent. Harshman et al. (1983) suggested that sex differences in both cognitive abilities and laterality effects are more likely to occur in subjects with lower, rather than higher, reasoning ability, and there is evidence that field-

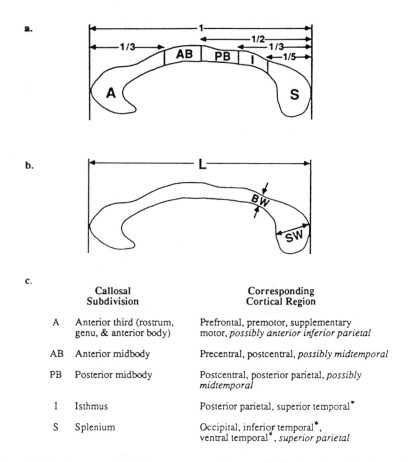

a.

b.

c.

	Callosal Subdivision	Corresponding Cortical Region
A	Anterior third (rostrum, genu, & anterior body)	Prefrontal, premotor, supplementary motor, *possibly anterior inferior parietal*
AB	Anterior midbody	Precentral, postcentral, *possibly midtemporal*
PB	Posterior midbody	Postcentral, posterior parietal, *possibly midtemporal*
I	Isthmus	Posterior parietal, superior temporal*
S	Splenium	Occipital, inferior temporal*, ventral temporal*, *superior parietal*

FIG. 3.33. Morphometry of the human corpus callosum. (a) Horizontal partitioning method adapted from Witelson (1989) for dividing the corpus callosum into the following subregions: A = anterior-third, AB = anterior midbody, PB = posterior midbody, I = isthmus, and S = splenium. (b) Linear measures of the corpus callosum: L = total anterior-to-posterior callosum length, SW = maximum splenial width, and BW = minimum body width. (c) Putative topographic relationships between five callosum subdivisions and corresponding cortical regions, based on findings from the rhesus monkey (Pandya & Seltzer, 1986) and human (de Lacoste et al., 1985). Italicized cortical regions represent potentially positive findings in the human that were not found in the rhesus monkey. * = positive findings in the rhesus monkey that were not found in the human case studied by Degos et al. (1987). After J. M. Clarke (1990).

independent subjects are more lateralized than field-dependent ones (Pizzamiglio & Zoccolotti, 1981, and see Section V).

Although there was no overall Sex × Handedness interaction in the REA, this interaction was significant ($p = .033$) when consistent left-handers were excluded (Fig. 3.38). Thus, whereas there was a sex difference for consistent right-handers in the size of the isthmus, there is a sex difference for mixed-handers in the REA. Put differently, the difference between the REAs of consistent right-handed and mixed-handed females is significant, whereas the difference between the sizes of the isthmus in consistent right-handed and mixed-handed males is significant.

J. M. Clarke's (1990) battery of cognitive tasks included the ETS Hidden Patterns test, which measures field independence, and the Tower of Hanoi, which can be taken to measure reasoning ability. In order to determine the effects of cognitive style and reasoning ability on sex differences in the RVFA and the REA, Clarke correlated the behavioral laterality effects with the cognitive scores in males and in females separately. Neither the RVFA in the primed lexical decision nor the REA in the dichotic listening task correlated with either the Hidden Patterns or the Tower of Hanoi for males or females (Table 3.12). Thus, it would appear that the sample variability in cognitive style and reasoning ability does not mask sex differences in laterality.

The absence of an overall sex difference in the REA shows that the morphometric sex difference in the isthmus of the callosum does not reflect better cross-callosal auditory connectivity (Witelson, 1989), which would have resulted in smaller REAs in females. This is consistent with the anatomical data of Aboitiz (1991), who showed that isthmus morphometry is related to higher order rather than sensorimotor connectivity (see earlier discussion in Section III).

Callosal Morphometry Versus Cognitive Tests. A principal components analysis of the 14 cognitive tests disclosed five interpretable factors (Table 3.13). No significant correlation was found between any factor and any callosal region, absolute or normalized.

Callosal Morphometry Versus Behavioral Laterality. Correlations between anatomy and priming in lexical decision were computed separately for within-hemisphere conditions (prime-target in same VF: LL, RR) and between-hemispheres conditions (LR, RL). No significant correlations were found overall. However, when each sex group was analyzed separately, the size of the normalized isthmus correlated negatively with the RVFA (lambda) for associated pairs in males ($r = -.518$, $p < .01$), but positively in females ($r = .377$, $p < .05$; Fig. 3.39). The correlations were even stronger in females for the normalized minimum body width (MBW), a measure that was, itself, significantly larger in females (see earlier discussions). Thus, the correlation of normalized MBW with lambda for associated pairs in males was $r = -.481$, $p < .01$ (for associated pairs in the LVF, the correlation was $r = .111$ and for associated pairs in the RVF it was $r = -.162$). The correlation of normalized MBW with lambda for associated pairs in females

TABLE 3.12. Pearson's r correlation coefficient between behavioral laterality effects (RVFA in Primed Lexical Decision, and REA in Dichotic Listening to nonsense CV syllables) and cognitive tests measuring cognitive style and reasoning in males and in females.

| | Hidden patterns (Cognitive style) | | Tower of Hanoi (Reasoning) | |
	Males (n=30)	Females (n=30)	Males (n=24)	Females (n=24)
RVFA	-.236	.333	-.176	-.126
REA	.339	.014	.201	-.048

Table 3.13. Cognitive profile tests.

I. Handedness
    Handedness Inventory Score
    Purdue Pegboard (Lafayette Instruments Co.)
    Grip Strength

II. Visual Perception
    Hidden Patterns test (Educational Testing Service)
    Gestalt Completion test (Educational Testing Service)
    Space Relations subtest of the Differential Aptitude Test (Form V) (The Psychological Corporation)

III. Verbal Production
    Thing Categories test (Educational Testing Service)
    Expressional Fluency (Sheridan Psychological Services)
    Verbal Fluency / FAS test

IV. Memory
    Rey Auditory Verbal Learning Test (RAVLT)
    Continuous Visual Memory Test (CVMT) (Psychological Assessment Resources Inc.)

V. Frontal Lobe Functions
    Stroop test
    Trail Making test
    Computerized Tower of Hanoi Problem (Perceptronics, Inc.)

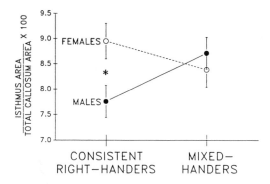

FIG. 3.34. Isthmus size, normalized for total callosal area, as a function of sex and handedness, excluding consistent left handers.

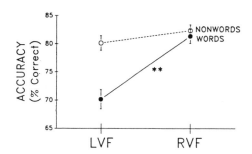

FIG. 3.35. Mean accuracies and standard errors for 60 subjects on the Primed Lexical Decision task for words or nonwords presented in the LVF or RVF.

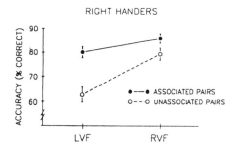

FIG. 3.36. Mean accuracies and standard errors for left- (n=30) and right-handed (n=30) subjects for Lexical Decision to associated and unassociated prime-target pairs when the target appeared in the LVF and in the RVF.

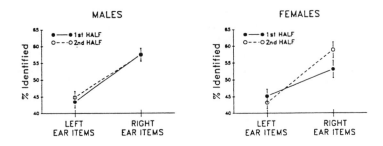

FIG. 3.37. Mean accuracies and standard errors for identifying CV consonant-vowel syllables presented to the left and right ears, for males (*n*=28) and females (*n*=30) for the first and second half of the Dichotic Listening task.

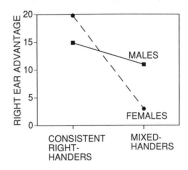

FIG. 3.38. Right ear advantage as a function of Sex and Handedness, excluding consistent left handers.

was $r = .474$, $p < .01$ ($r = -.234$ for associated LVF pairs, $r = .133$ for associated RVF pairs). The correlations of normalized MBW with lambda for unassociated pairs was not significant ($r = .151$ in males, $r = .047$ in females). However, these positive correlations in females were due to one subject with an outlying laterality index (3 SDs from the mean). When that subject was excluded, none of the correlations in females were significant, although the difference between the correlation coefficients in males and females was significant.

These results are surprising. They occurred in a direct access task and were not associated with interhemispheric transfer. Rather, they appear to reflect a structural basis for channel-specific inhibitory interhemispheric effects that are sex-dependent: In males, a larger callosum is associated with worse performance in the RVF.

It is important that the significant behavioral-anatomical correlations between the RVFA and regional callosum size occurred for associated targets, which did not show a large overall RVFA (p < .01), whereas there were no significant behavioral-anatomical correlations between the RVFA and regional callosum size for unassociated targets, which did show a large significant RVFA (p < .01; Figs. 3.35, 3.36). Because the associated targets were probably processed independently in each hemisphere (i.e., by direct access) the significant correlation with callosal size appears to reflect cross-callosal inhibition or facilitation or, alternatively, a structural basis for the competencies of the two cerebral hemispheres, rather than the efficacy of callosal relay of sensory information.

In the dichotic listening task, there were no significant correlations between any callosal measure and the LE score. There was, however, a significant negative correlation between the area of the anterior third of the callosum and the RE score ($r(58) = -.35$, $p < .01$; J. M. Clarke, Lufkin, & Zaidel, 1993). There were no sex differences in this effect, which implicates inhibitory right-to-left hemisphere cross-callosal influences on the specialized phonetic processor in the left hemisphere. In males, most of the correlations between the REA and callosal morphometry (total callosum, anterior 1/3, anterior midbody, isthmus, and splenium) were significant, whereas in females none of these negative correlations reached significance. Nevertheless, none of the differences in correlations between the sexes were significant (all z's < 1.3). The phonetic inhibition in dichotic listening involves different channels than those used in the semantic inhibition observed in lexical decision, and the two inhibitory effects are independent of each other across individuals.

Behavioral Laterality Versus Cognitive Tests. Dichotic listening scores were not correlated with any cognitive measure, with the exception of a positive correlation between the REA and degree of right-handedness as determined by questionnaire. There was no interaction of sex with ear scores or with any cognitive performance.

In the primed lexical decision task, there was a significant correlation between performance on the unassociated targets and speed of completing the Stroop test, especially in the between-field condition (LR, RL; $r = .5$, $p < .01$) and

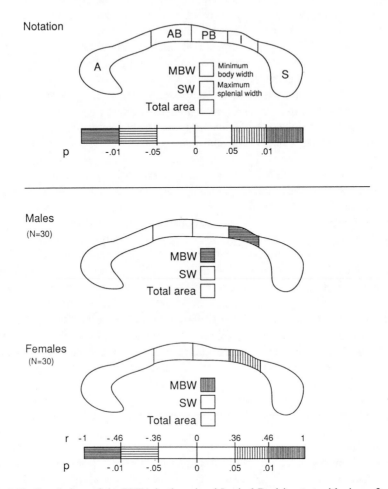

FIG. 3.39. Correlations of the RVFA in the primed Lexical Decision test with sizes of callosal regions for males and for females.

the LVF ($r = .4, p < .01$). Both tasks presumably share automatic lexical semantic interference. Indeed, performance on the associated between-field targets in the lexical decision task correlated significantly with memory in the Rey Auditory Verbal Learning Task ($r = .39, p < .01$). This implicates interhemispheric interaction in memory for words (cf. D. W. Zaidel, 1990). Both of these results were similar in males and females.

Although there were no sex differences in either the behavioral laterality effects or the cognitive tests, there was a sex difference in the relationship between them (Table 3.14). In males ($n = 24$), there was a significant negative correlation between the RVFA and speed of performance on the Stroop test ($r = -.466, p < .05, z(p) = -.5049$) but in females ($n = 24$) there was no significant relationship ($r = .181, ns: z(p) = .183$). This difference in correlations is significant ($z' = 2.23, p < .01$). In females, there was a significant positive correlation between the RVFA and performance on the Continuous Visual Memory Test ($r = .44, p < .05, z(p) = .4722$) but in males there was none ($r = -.403, p < .05, z(p) = -.4272$). This difference between the correlations is also significant ($z'=2.9, p<.01$). Table 3.15 shows even stronger sex differences in correlations between the absolute values of the RVFA in lexical decision or the REA in dichotic listening and cognitive test performances. Here, again, the sex differences are second order effects.

To find out how competence for lexical decision in either VF is related to reading ability, we administered the same primed lexical decision task as well as the college level form of the Davis Reading Test (F.B. Davis & C.C. Davis,1957), to 33 UCLA undergraduate students (21 males and 12 females; Zaidel, Taylor, & Clarke, 1990). The overall pattern of results on the lexical decision task replicated that of J. M. Clarke (cf. Fig. 3.35, 3.36), showing a significant RVFA, a significant advantage of associated over unassociated pairs, and a significant Association × VF interaction (Fig. 3.40a). Furthermore, there was a significant correlation of speed of reading comprehension (scaled scores) with accuracy on associated targets ($r = .41, p < .05$), but not on unassociated targets ($r = .07$). Within the associated targets, the correlation was significant for RVF targets ($r = .40, p < .05$), but not for LVF targets ($r = .24$). In contrast to speed, level of reading comprehension did not correlate with any of the lateralized decision scores.

The replication of the primed lexical decision task showed no Sex × Target VF interaction, $F(1,31) = 1.75, p = .192$, but a weak trend toward a Sex × Association ×Target VF interaction, $F(1,31) = 3, p = .089$. Females showed a stronger Association × Target VF interaction (Fig. 3.39b), but only males showed a significant correlation of reading comprehension with lateralized performance (i.e., with associated targets), particularly in the RVF. Thus, the effect of callosal size on reading, as assessed by lateralized lexical decision, is restricted to males. Even here, it is relatively small and is limited to RVF performance. Of course, it is possible that other lateralized tasks will show a greater correlation with reading competence or that lateralized lexical decision, including performance in the LVF, will show a greater correlation with other reading tests.

Interhemispheric Versus Intrahemispheric Relations. J. M. Clark's data can speak to the issue of whether sex differences selectively involve differences in hemispheric competence or in callosal relay. All four of Clarke's behavioral laterality tests included intrahemispheric and interhemispheric components, and those components are separable. In the dichotic listening test, LE stimuli require callosal transfer; in the primed lexical decision, primes and targets in opposite hemifields require callosal transfer; in the Nonsense Shape Discrimination test, comparisons across the hemifields require callosal transfer; and in the Roughness Discrimination test, comparisons across the hands require callosal transfer. Specifically, a sex difference in the LE but not in the RE score in the dichotic listening task would suggest a difference in callosal connectivity for auditory signals, but a sex difference in the bilateral conditions of the shape, texture, and primed lexical decision tasks could involve both callosal exchange and hemispheric competence. Thus, sex differences in the unilateral conditions alone would suggest differences in hemispheric competencies, but sex differences in the bilateral conditions alone would not necessarily suggest differences in interhemispheric communication (provided the hemispheric competence components in the two conditions are not the same). Further, sex differences may occur in either the behavioral laterality effects themselves (first order) or in the relations of the behavioral laterality effects to cognition or to anatomy (second order).

There was much evidence from lateralized performance, from the relation of lateralized performance to anatomy, and from the relation of lateralized performance to cognition that the intrahemispheric and interhemispheric components are distinct. First, there was a difference in response bias between the interhemispheric and intrahemispheric conditions of the nonverbal visual and tactile tests (J. M. Clarke, 1990). Second, only the intrahemispheric conditions of these tests correlated with callosal anatomy. Third, the intrahemispheric and interhemispheric components of both tests (as well as of the primed lexical decision test) correlated with different cognitive factors. Thus, the intrahemispheric, but not interhemispheric, component of the shape matching task correlated with the continuous visual memory test: and the interhemispheric, but not intrahemispheric, component of the tactile matching task correlated with manual dominance in grip strength. However, there were no sex differences in either the interhemispheric or intrahemispheric conditions of the nonverbal tests, or in their correlations with anatomy or with cognition, and sex did not interact with the inter-intra factor or with any interaction involving this factor. Thus, the data from the two nonverbal tests do not determine the issue of whether sex differences selectively involve hemispheric competence or interhemispheric exchange.

The dichotic listening and primed lexical decision tests showed sex differences in the correlations of both interhemispheric and intrahemispheric components with cognitive tests (Table 3.16). In dichotic listening, there was a (second-order) sex difference (in the laterality-cognition correlations) for the left ear (Stroop) as well as for the right ear (Hidden Patterns). This suggests sex differences in hemispheric competencies (RE) as well as in callosal connectivity (LE). In primed lexical decision, there were sex differences in the correlations of the intrahemispheric LL, RR, and Uni (= LL + RR) conditions with Hidden Patterns, suggesting differences in hemispheric competence (both left and right). Thus, on the basis of these data we would predict (second-order) sex differences in both hemispheric competencies and callosal exchange.

Conclusions

J.M. Clarke's (1990) dissertation showed that sexual dimorphism in callosal morphometry can occur in the absence of sex differences in behavioral laterality effects in tasks that are presumed to tap the sexually dimorphic regions of the corpus callosum. Although the isthmus was found to be larger in females and it is believed to interconnect auditory cortex and language-gifted cortex, there was no overall sex difference in the REA in the dichotic listening task, which is exclusively specialized to the left hemisphere and requires cross-callosal relay of the LE signal from the right hemisphere to the left hemisphere. Indeed, the REA did not correlate at all with isthmus size but rather with the size of the anterior callosum. Thus, the sex difference in isthmus size is not related to a sex difference in interhemispheric auditory transfer.

The lateralized lexical decision task presumably engages independent word recognition modules in the two hemispheres that also interconnect through the isthmus of the corpus callosum. From the findings of Aboitiz et al. (1992a, 1992b) we now know that sexual dimorphism in the gross morphometry of the isthmus of the corpus callosum is related to the number of small-diameter fibers that interconnect association cortex in language-specialized cortex. We may therefore expect that a sexual dimorphism in the isthmus should be related to a sex difference in hemispheric competencies for lexical decision. Although there was no sex difference in the RVFA, there was a sex difference in the relation of the RVFA (for associated targets) to isthmus size. Indeed, the fact that females had a larger isthmus plus the fact that a larger isthmus is related to a larger RVFA for associated targets in females but a smaller RVFA for associated targets in males suggest that males have a greater RVFA for associated targets than do females with equal isthmus size. Again, this sex difference is second order: It does not occur in either anatomy or lateralized behavior, but rather in the relationship between the two.

There was also a second-order Sex × Handedness interaction for isthmus size and a second-order Sex × Handedness interaction for REA in dichotic listening, when consistent left-handers were excluded and only consistent right-handers and mixed-handers were considered. However, the sex difference in anatomy was significant for consistent right-handers, whereas the sex differences in behavioral laterality effect was significant for mixed-handers. Thus, even those second-order sex differences in anatomy and behavioral laterality appear to be independent of each other.

If both the REA in dichotic listening and the RVFA in lateralized Primed Lexical Decision reflect components of callosal inhibition, it is noteworthy that such inhibition (a) sometimes originates in the specialized hemisphere and

TABLE 3.14. Sex differences in Pearson's r correlations between absolute values of the laterality effects and cognitive test performances. RVFA=Right Visual hemiField Advantage in primed lexical decision. REA=Right Ear Advantage in dichotic listening. N=24 males, 24 females. For r=.404, p=.05; for r=.515, p=.01. Rey=Rey Auditory Verbal Learning Test, CVMT=Continuous Visual Memory Test, Stroop=speed performance on the Stroop test.

		Rey	CVMT	Stroop
RVFA	Male	.219	-.352	-.46*
	Female	-.015	.604*	.089
	Sex difference	-	+	+
REA	Male	-.428*	-.185	-.113
	Female	.206	-.115	.183
	Sex difference	+	-	-

* $p < .05$
** $p < .01$

TABLE 3.15. Sex Differences in Correlations of Lateralized Scores with Cognitive Tests.

			Dichotic Listening		Primed Lexical Decision			
		n	Inter LE	Intra RE	Intra LL	Intra RR	Intra Uni	Inter Bi
Rey	Males	24	-.477*	-.034	.157	.237	.225	.349
AVLT	Females	24	-.165	.284	.139	.256	.209	.259
	Sex Diff		-	-	-	-	-	-
Stroop	Males	24	.455*	.331	.465*	.093	.337	.410*
	Females	24	-.065	-.054	.195	.241	.238	.474*
	Sex Diff		+	-	-	-	-	-
Hidden	Males	30	.142	.551**	.397*	.373*	.464**	.317
Patterns	Females	30	-.026	0.0	-.001	.117	.060	.177
	Sex Diff		-	+	+	~+	+	-

Note. LE=left ear, LL=left visual field prime and left visual field target, Uni = LL+RR, Bi = LR+RL

*$p < .05$
**$p < .01$

TABLE 3.16. Summary of Sex Differences in (a) Callosum Anatomy, Behavioral Laterality and Cognition, and in (b) their Intercorrelations. X=Inapplicable. DL = Dichotic Listening Task, LD = Primed Lexical Decision Task.

(a)

	Callosum anatomy	Laterality effect		Cognition
		DL	LD	
Overall effect	X	+	+	X
Effect of Sex	+	~	-	-

(b)

	Callosum vs. laterality		Callosum vs. cogition	Laterality vs. cognition	
	DL	LD		DL	LD
Significant Correlation	+	+	-	-	+
Effect of Sex	-	+	-	-	+

sometimes in the unspecialized hemisphere, (b) varies from task to task, and (c) may involve different callosal channels. Consequently, these presumed dynamic inhibitory callosal channels cannot be the mechanism that implements the hemispheric arousal effects of Levy et al. (1983), which were said to be stable across tasks in a given individual.

An alternative interpretation of the anatomical-behavioral correlations appeals to structurally based differences in hemispheric competencies associated with changes in callosal size during development. According to this interpretation, an anatomical asymmetry in some cortical region and its associated functional asymmetry are negatively correlated with (i.e., associated with lesser) callosal connectivity for the part of the callosum that interconnects areas of the cortical region. In the case of the primed lexical decision task in males, this region may be the left planum temporale, which interconnects with the right planum through the isthmus. Note that the finding of a negative correlation between the RVFA for associated pairs in lexical decision and the size of the isthmus in males but not in females, parallels the findings of Aboitiz (discussed in Section III). He also found a negative correlation between planum temporale asymmetry and the number of small-diameter fibers in the isthmus of males but not of females. In the case of the dichotic listening task, the specialized region may be the left posterior frontal cortex, which may interconnect with the right posterior frontal cortex through the anterior callosum.

It should be noted that the hypothesis that the laterality effect is inversely proportional to the size of the associated callosal channel applies strictly to direct access tasks. In the case of a callosal relay task, such as the dichotic listening test used here, both ear signals are processed in the left hemisphere and so both (or perhaps, neither), rather than their difference, should show a negative correlation with the size of the anterior callosum.

Of course, a significant behavioral-anatomical correlation need not involve a sex difference, as is evident for dichotic listening. More generally, sex differences in callosal anatomy, in behavioral laterality effects, and in cognition can all be independent of each other (Table 3.16).

V. THE EFFECT OF COGNITIVE STYLE ON SEX DIFFERENCES IN INTERHEMISPHERIC RELATIONS

Sex and cognitive style are related in the general population. Males tend to be more field independent and better able to separate figure from ground, whereas females tend to be more field dependent (Witkin & Goodenough, 1981). Moreover, field-independent subjects are more lateralized than field-dependent subjects (Pizzamiglio & Zoccolotti, 1981). Most studies of sex differences in laterality do not control for cognitive style and this may account for some of the variability in the data. This experiment was designed to separate the effects of sex and cognitive style on laterality, by explicitly including field-dependent and -independent male and female subjects, and assessing the effect of each factor on (a) hemispheric competence and (b) interhemispheric exchange.

Methods

Subjects included 12 field-dependent males, 15 field-independent males, 12 field-dependent females, and 9 field-independent females. All were right-handed native speakers of English. Cognitive style classification was based on speed and accuracy of performance on Witkin's Group Embedded Figures test (Witkin et al., 1971). The scores of 95 other subjects were submitted to a principal components analysis, and the factor scores generated from the extracted first principal component were scaled as z-scores and used to categorize the subjects in this experiment. Field-dependent subjects had positive scores, and were both slow and inaccurate. Field-independent subjects had negative scores, and were fast and accurate. Seven subjects (4 males, 3 females) with factor scores between -.2 and +.2 were excluded because they were relatively fast and inaccurate or slow and accurate. Additional field-dependent males were recruited so that this group would be adequately represented.

Lateralized targets included 128 three- to six-letter long strings, consisting of 64 orthographically regular nonwords and 64 concrete, imageable, and frequent nouns. Half of the target words were preceded by associatively related lateralized primes and half by unrelated primes. Primes were flashed randomly to one visual hemifield for 150 msec and, following a 500 msec interstimulus interval, targets were flashed randomly to one visual hemifield for 80 msec. Stimuli were presented by an IBM-AT PC on an AMDEK-310A monitor with yellow letters on a dark background and appeared 2° off fixation at the inner edge. Subjects were instructed to ignore the prime and to indicate unimanually on a two-choice button whether the target was a word or a nonword (lexical decision).

Results and Discussion

Laterality. An ANOVA was performed with sex (male, female) and cognitive style (dependent, independent) as between-subjects factors, and with prime-target visual field congruence (congruent: LL, RR; incongruent: LR, RL), target wordness (word, nonword), target VF (RVF, LVF), and priming condition for word targets (related, unrelated), as within-subject factors.

There was an overall RVFA in both accuracy and latency. The Sex $\times$ VF interaction was not significant in either accuracy or latency ($F < 1$) (Fig. 3.41a), but the Style $\times$ VF interaction was significant in latency ($F(1,44) = 7.0, p = .011$) and almost significant in accuracy ($F(1,44) = 3.1, p = .079$; Fig. 3.40b). Males and females showed similar RVFAs, but there were significant RVFAs for field-independent and not for field-dependent subjects. The Sex $\times$ Style $\times$ VF interactions were not significant. Thus, cognitive style rather than sex is associated with greater laterality (LH superiority) in this direct access linguistic task.

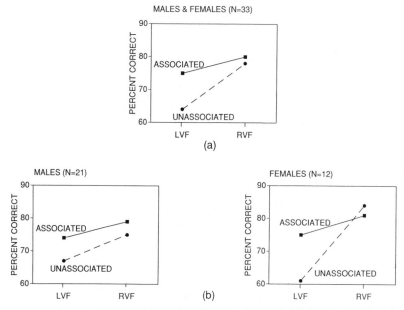

FIG. 3.40. Pearson *r* correlation coefficients between scaled speed of comprehension scores in the Davis Reading Test and lateralized performances in the Primed Lexical Decision test.

Effect of Congruence on Laterality. The Sex × Congruence × VF interaction was not significant ($F < 1$) but the Style × Congruence × VF interaction in latency was significant ($F(1,44) = 4.3$, $p = .043$; Fig. 3.42). Here, there was no Style × VF interaction for congruent pairs but the Style × VF interaction was significant for incongruent pairs $F(1,44) = 11.2$, $p = .002$. This was due to a RVFA for independent subjects ($p < .001$), but not for dependent subjects. Thus, cognitive style was associated with greater lateral differentiation in the interhemispheric rather than the intrahemispheric conditions.

Effect of Congruence on Laterality of Priming. The Style × Congruence × Priming × VF latency interaction was not significant, $F < 1$ (Fig. 3.43), but the Sex × Congruence × Priming × VF latency interaction was significant, $F(1,42) = 14.4$, $p < .001$ (Fig. 3.44). Here, females showed similar priming in the two visual hemifields for both congruent and incongruent pairs, whereas in males, there was a significant Congruence × Priming × VF interaction, $F(1,42) = 25.3$, $p < .001$, with a RVFA in priming for congruent pairs, $F(1,42) = 13.1$, $p = .001$, and a LVFA in priming for incongruent pairs $F(1,42) = 4.8$, $p = .032$ (Fig. 3.44). Thus, males had greater priming when the prime was presented to the RVF (RR, RL). There was a significant Sex × Priming × VF interaction for congruent pairs ($F(1,42) = 9.5$, $p = .004$), but not for incongruent pairs. Here, the congruent pairs disclosed a sex difference in priming in the LVF ($F(1,42) = 13.8$, p < .001), but not

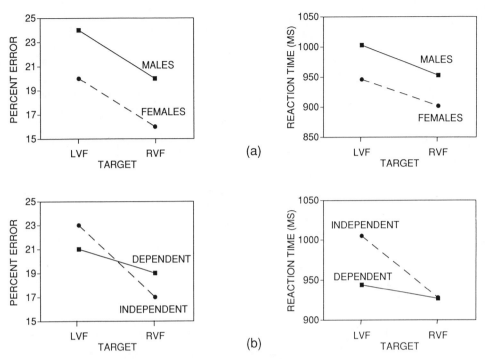

FIG. 3.41. Sex and Cognitive Style effects in Primed Lexical Decision (Matteson, 1991). (a) There were no significant Sex × Visual Field interactions in either latency or accuracy; (b) significant Cognitive Style × Visual Field interactions.

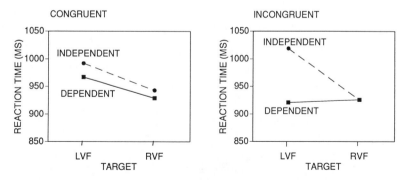

FIG. 3.42. Cognitive Style × Congruence × Visual field interactions for latency in the Primed Lexical Decision experiment.

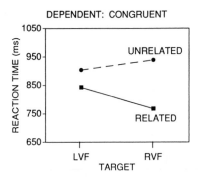
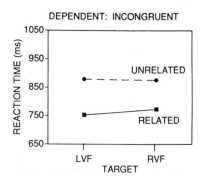
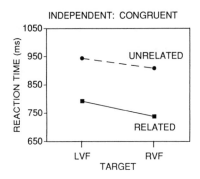
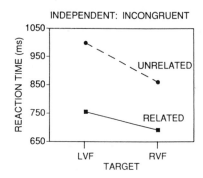

FIG. 3.43. Laterality of priming for within-field (congruent) and between-hemifields (incongruent) priming as a function of Cognitive Style.

in the RVF ($F(1,42) = 1.8, p = .179$). Thus, the sex difference in priming occurred in the *intra*hemispheric rather than *inter*hemispheric condition, and is consistent with weaker language competence in the male than in the female right hemisphere (LL condition).

Conclusion

Matteson (1991) concluded that sex and cognitive style contribute independently to laterality effects in primed lexical decision. Cognitive style selectively affects performance asymmetries in the interhemispheric conditions, whereas sex selectively affects performance asymmetries in the intrahemispheric conditions, especially in the right hemisphere. It should be noted that the effects of cognitive style on laterality were not uniform across tasks. Matteson (1991) showed that field-independent subjects were more lateralized than field-dependent subjects in the lexical decision task, less lateralized in a figural identification task, and equally lateralized in mental image transformation tasks.

Thus, future studies on sex differences in interhemispheric relations need to control not only "interactive" factors, such as handedness, but also "independent" factors, such as cognitive style, which may be confounded with sex in the general population.

It should be recalled that J. M. Clarke did find sex differences in the interhemispheric component of the dichotic listening task (Table 3.15). Thus, sex differences are not restricted to intrahemispheric relations and can extend to callosal functions.

GENERAL CONCLUSIONS

The Laterality Index

What does a significant behavioral laterality effect, such as a RVFA or a REA, mean?
1. If the task is processed independently in each hemisphere, in a direct access fashion, then a VF advantage means, first, that one hemisphere has greater competence for the task.
2. If the task is exclusively specialized in one hemisphere, then a VF advantage reflects callosal relay.
3. If the task requires interhemispheric integration, then a VF advantage could reflect both contributions from differences in hemispheric competence as well as from callosal exchange at various stages of information processing.
4. If the task is done best by independent parallel early information processing in the two hemispheres, so that dividing the stimuli bilaterally in the two visual hemifields is more effective than presenting them in the same VF (input segregation), then the VF advantage in the bilateral condition could reflect the degree of hemispheric "isolation," or *callosal flexibility*.
5. If the task calls for two different operations, and assigning a different process to

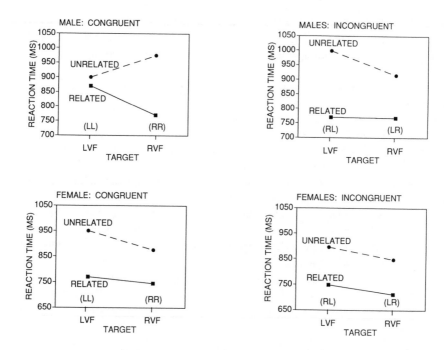

FIG. 3.44. Laterality of priming for within-hemisfield (congruent) and between-hemifield (incongruent) priming as a function of Sex.

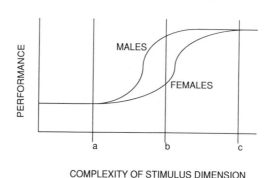

COMPLEXITY OF STIMULUS DIMENSION

FIG. 3.45. A theoretical function illustrating putative sex differences in performance-resource functions. Sampling the function at a low level of stimulus complexity, a, or at a high level of complexity, c, reveals no sex difference in performance, but sampling the function at an intermediate level of complexity, b, reveals a male advantage.

each VF works better than combining both operations in both VFs (task segregation), then the VF advantage in the one field-one operation condition could reflect a more effective segregation of hemispheric resources, or hemispheric *shielding* (Merola & Liederman, 1985).

6. There may also be a contribution to the VF advantage from interhemispheric inhibition that is specific to particular tasks and particular callosal channels (see Section IV).

7. Finally, the VF advantage may be modulated by stable individual differences in arousal asymmetries (Levy et al., 1983).

Is there evidence for a sex difference in any of those components? In the following summary, + following a component heading means that sex differences were found for that component, and - means that no sex differences have been found for that component.

Hemispheric Competence (+).   We have already discussed the sporadic, but persistent, evidence for sex differences in hemispheric specialization and differentiation for lexical variables in word recognition (Section II).   Although males tend to show greater lateralization or lateral differentiation, this is not universal, and occasionally, females are both more lateralized and more laterally differentiated.   Sometimes, males and females show complementary laterality patterns.

We have shown that those occasional sex differences in hemispheric competence are not more likely to occur for one dependent measure than another and are not affected by experience, but they are more likely to occur for lexical decision than for naming (Table 3.5).   This suggests that these sex differences involve relatively late, semantic stages of word recognition, occurring after lexical access.   Sex differences in hemispheric differentiation, on the other hand, are affected by experience, and they are more likely to occur in naming than in lexical decision, and in accuracy rather than in latency.

Why are sex differences in hemispheric competence or hemispheric differentiation so labile, sometimes even with the same lexical variables?   Probably because those sex differences reflect dynamic, strategic changes in resource allocation and vary with task demands.   For example, males and females may have different performance-resource functions for various stimulus dimensions (J. M. Rayman, personal communication, January, 1991; and see Fig. 3.45). Alternatively, sex differences may be affected by other, uncontrolled, state variables, such as hormonal circadian or diurnal rhythms, or trait variables, such as cognitive style (Section V) or regional cerebral arousal (see further on).

Callosal relay (+).   From Section IV, we have no evidence for first-order sex differences in callosal relay, but we do have evidence for second-order sex differences in the callosal relay of the LE signal in the dichotic listening task.

Callosal exchange (-).   From Sections IV and V, we have no evidence for either first- or second-order sex differences in callosal integration in the visual and tactile nonverbal matching tests or in the primed lexical decision task. Section V suggested that there are cognitive style differences in callosal exchange in the primed lexical decision task and that sex differences are restricted to the intrahemispheric component of the task.

Callosal isolation **(-).** J. M. Clarke (1990) found a "bilaterality advantage" of interhemispheric matching over intrahemispheric matching of "same" pairs in the nonverbal visual and tactile tasks. But there were no sex differences in this effect (J. M. Clarke & Zaidel, in press). Banich and Belger (1991) failed to find sex differences in the bilaterality advantage in a letter-name matching task. Thus, there is, as yet, no evidence for sex differences in hemispheric isolation that would permit more effective parallel processing.

Callosal shielding **(-).** Merola & Liederman (1985) found an "independence advantage" in segregating two letter-matching processes (straight vs. mirror image) to the separate hemispheres over requiring the subject to apply both processes to stimuli in each VF, but they found no sex differences in the independence advantage, although they did find other effects of sex.

Callosal inhibition **(+).** In Section IV, we presented evidence consistent with sex differences in cross-callosal inhibition in the primed lexical decision task, but not in the dichotic listening task.

Hemispheric arousal **(-).** Kim, Levine, and Kertesz (1990) found no evidence for sex differences in hemispheric arousal, but it may be that the concept of hemispheric-wide arousal as a trait variable is too broad, that specific modules within the hemispheres may be selectively "aroused" in some individuals, and that this pattern may be subject to sex differences.

The Four Views

How do our data bear on the four views mentioned in the introduction, concerning sex differences in interhemispheric language relations?

Interhemispheric. Summarizing the previous section, we see some evidence of second-order sex differences in callosal relay and in callosal inhibitions, but not in callosal exchange, isolation, or shielding.

However, we observed no first-order sex differences in callosal relay. We did observe sex differences in callosal morphometry in MRI (size of the isthmus, Section IV), but, counter to speculations in the literature, they were not associated with auditory callosal relay, presumably because callosal morphometry is not correlated with large, sensorimotor fiber morphology (Section III). Furthermore, postmortem analysis failed to replicate the morphometric, or to find a morphologic, sex difference in the normalized isthmus (Section III). Instead, the postmortem study found a second-order sex difference in the relation of anatomical hemispheric asymmetry to callosal morphology. Unfortunately, the causal and functional significance of the correlation remains unclear. It does suggest that the general relationship of hemispheric specialization to callosal function may be different in males than in females. Perhaps, asymmetric planum temporale cortex is specialized for somewhat different functions in males and in females and is consequently interconnected by somewhat different callosal pathways (isthmus in males, anterior splenium in females).

There is also suggestive evidence, from correlations between Sylvian fissure asymmetry and callosal morphometry, that hemispheric specialization is more closely connected to callosal function in males than in females. This may, in turn, be associated with an opposite sex difference in intrahemispheric connectivity (Section IV).

Intrahemispheric. Again summarizing the earlier section, we found significant, if infrequent and variable, first-order sex differences in hemispheric lexical competence (Sex × VF) and second order sex differences in hemispheric differentiation as a function of experience and lexical variables Y (Sex × TH × Y × VF). Some, but not all, of the experiments reviewed in Sections I and II were consistent with the hypothesis that females have a more bilateral representation of language, in the sense that their LVF performance showes a pattern similar to that of the male RVF.

Are sex differences in behavioral laterality effects more or less likely to occur in naming than in lexical decision? Healey, Waldstein, and Goodglass (1983) suggested that females may be as lateralized as males in expressive language tasks, or even more so. On the other hand, as argued early on, if LH speech functions are more focally and anteriorly represented in females (Kimura, 1991), then their intrahemispheric performance on lateralized visual and auditory tasks that engage speech mechanisms may be slowed down, minimizing the effects of callosal relay and reducing the RVFA or REA. In fact, the meta-analyses in Section II showed that Sex × VF interactions are less likely to occur in naming than in lexical decision (see Table 3.5), supporting the conjecture suggested by Kimura's findings. On the other hand, Sex × TH × Y × VF interactions are more likely to occur in naming than in lexical decision (see Table 3.5), arguing against the conjecture suggested by Kimura's findings. Similarly, the opposite prediction from Healey et al. (1983) receives mixed support and, therefore, is not confirmed either.

The arousal hypothesis of Kim et al. (1990) also focuses on individual differences in intrahemispheric contributions to behavioral laterality effects. Is there a sex difference in arousal asymmetry, which may account for sex differences in behavioral laterality effects? Kim et al. (1990) looked for sex differences in arousal asymmetries, but failed to find any. Of course, if arousal is module-specific, then it is still possible that there are sex differences in arousal for some modules not yet indexed by the standard measures (the Chair test and the Faces test, Kim et al., 1990).

Strategic. The frequent shift in sex differences in behavioral laterality or lateral differentiation as a function of small changes in task parameters are best explained as strategic shifts in response to changing task demands and resource assignment, but such strategic shifts may well be mediated by structural sex differences in intrahemispheric or interhemispheric relations.

The specific hypothesis that females are more likely than males to show consistent increased laterality with experience was not corroborated (Section II, Table 3.5, but see Section IV). However, whereas there were no sex differences in lateral differentiation (Sex × Y × VF), there were significant sex differences in shifts of lateral differentiation with experience (Sex × TH × Y × VF) in Kaiser's naming experiments (Table 3.5).

Mediated. J. M. Clarke (1990) who studied both right- and left-handed males and females, did find a modified Sex × Handedness interaction in callosal morphometry (isthmus size) and in behavioral laterality effects, but not in cognition or the intercorrelations of anatomy, laterality, and cognition (Section IV).

Clarke analyzed the effect of cognitive style (Hidden Figures) and reasoning ability (Tower of Hanoi) on sex differences in the RVFA in primed lexical decision and in the REA in dichotic listening but found no significant correlations (Section IV). Matteson analyzed the effect of cognitive style on sex differences in the RVFA in primed lexical decision more systematically by studying both field-dependent and field-independent males and females. She found no interactions, but did find independent behavioral laterality effects of sex (on intrahemispheric relations).

In sum, we have evidence for some behavioral sex differences in interhemispheric as well as intrahemispheric relations, and we have interpreted many of them as strategic. We found evidence for behavioral sex differences mediated by a form of handedness, but not by cognitive style or reasoning ability.

Where is the Causality in Second Order Relationships Involving Sex and Laterality?

Interactions Involving Sex × VF and Sex × TH × VF. Of the 31 experiments reviewed in Section I, four showed Sex × VF interactions and 14 showed Sex × Y × VF interactions. Similarly, the meta-analysis for naming accuracy in Section II showed a significant overall Sex × TH × Y × VF effect but not a Sex × TH × VF effect. What does it mean for there to be a Sex × Y × VF interaction, but not a Sex × VF interaction? Because the interaction is symmetric relative to Sex and Y, it gives us no causal information about whether sex "causes" the interaction of Y × VF, or whether Y "causes" the interaction of Sex × VF. In principle, larger population studies could provide a causal analysis by comparing the variances of the two variables.

Interrelationships Between Anatomy, Behavioral Laterality, and Cognition. Table 3.17 summarizes J. M. Clarke's (1990) findings on sex differences in callosal morphometry, behavioral laterality effects and cognition, and in their intercorrelations (cf. Table 3.1b). In Section IV, we concluded that sex differences in each of the three domains (callosal morphometry, lateralized behavior, and cognition) can be independent of each other, in the sense that a sex difference in one of them need not involve a sex difference in another. One problem with generalizing from these data is that new measures in each of the three domains may reveal different patterns from the ones we observed. And, as usual, one should address not only the presence of a statistically significant effect, but also its size and relative importance. All of the significant correlations obtained by Clarke were below .6.

The picture may be somewhat less indeterminate in Aboitiz's experiments on sex differences in the relationships among Sylvian fissure asymmetries, callosal morphology, and callosal morphometry. Here, fiber counts and planum temporale asymmetries are probably reliable estimates of stable structural features of the brain, even if their functional significance is not yet fully known. The sex differences here are pervasive, starting with the relationship of callosal morphometry to morphology, continuing with the relationship of size of asymmetry in the specialized language area to callosal morphometry, and extending to the relationship of asymmetry of specialized language area to callosal morphology (and function?). Those are all structural differences with rich potential functional significance for differences in both lateralization and cognition.

TABLE 3.17. Sex differences in the relationships between behavioral laterality, callosal anatomy in the relevant regions, and cognition in any of the tests (+ = a significant sex difference). A+ = associated pairs, A- = unassociated pairs.

	Laterality Effect	CC^1	CC^1 vs. Laterality	Laterality vs. Cognition[2].
Lexical decision	-	+[1]	+[1]	+[2]
A-	+	+[1]	-	-
A+	-	+[1]	+[1]	-
Dichotic listening	+	-	-	-
Shape discrimination	-	-	-	-
Texture discrimination	-	-	-	-

[1] Isthmus

[2] Reading

ACKNOWLEDGMENTS

This work was supported by NIH grant NS 20187 and by an HIMH grant RSA MH00179.

REFERENCES

Aboitiz, F.D. (1991). *Quantitative morphology and histology of the human corpus callosum and its relation to brain lateralization* Unpublished doctoral dissertation, University of California at Los Angeles.

Aboitiz, F., Scheibel, A.B., Fisher, R.S., & Zaidel, E. (1992a). Fiber composition of the human corpus callosum. *Brain Research, 598*, 143-153.

Aboitiz, F., Scheibel, A.B., Fisher, R.S., & Zaidel, E. (1992b). Individual differences in brain asymmetries and fiber composition in the human corpus callosum. *Brain Research, 598*, 154-161.

Aboitiz, F., Scheibel, A., & Zaidel, E. (1992). Morphometry of the Sylvian fissure and corpus callosum with emphasis on sex differences. *Brain, 115*, 1521-1541.

Aboitiz, F.D., Zaidel, E., & Scheibel, A.B. (1989). Variability in fiber composition in different regions of the corpus callosum in humans. *The Anatomical Record, 223*, 6A.

Alexandrov, M. (1989). *Linguistic hemispheric lateralization in bilingual subjects: An examination of relative hemispheric specialization.* Unpublished undergraduate honors thesis, University of California at Los Angeles.

Banich, M.T., & Belger, A. (1991). Interhemispheric interaction: How do the hemispheres divide and conquer a task? *Cortex, 26*, 77-94.

Boles, D.B. (1984). Sex in lateralized tachistoscopic word recognition. *Brain and Language, 23*, 307-317.

Bryden, M.P. (1988). An overview of the dichotic listening procedure and its relation to cerebral organization. In K. Hugdahl (Ed.), *Handbook of dichotic listening: Theory, methods and research*, (pp. 1-43). Chichester: Wiley.

Bryden, M.P. (1989, March). *Sex differences in cerebral organization: Real or imagined?* Paper presented at the 10th Annual Conference of the New York Academy of Sciences, New York.

Bryden, M.P., & Sprott, D.A. (1981). Statistical determination of degree of laterality. *Neuropsychologia, 19*, 571-581.

Byne, W., Bleier, R., & Houston, L. (1988). Variations in human corpus callosum do not predict gender: A study using MRI. *Behavioral Neuroscience, 102*, 222-227.

Clarke, J.M. (1990). *Interhemispheric functions in humans: Relationships between anatomical measures of the corpus callosum, behavioral laterality effects, and cognitive profiles.* Unpublished doctoral dissertation, University of California at Los Angeles.

Clarke, J.M., Lufkin, R.B., & Zaidel, E. (1993). Corpus callosum morphometry and dichotic performance: Individual differences in functional interhemispheric inhibition? *Neuropsychologia, 31,* 547-557.

Clarke, J.M., & Zaidel, E. (in press). *Anatomical-behavioral relationships: Corpus callosum morphometry and hemispheric specialization. Behavioral Brain Research.*

Copeland, S., David, A.S., & Zaidel, E. (1993). *Effects of mode of stimulus presentation on laterality effects in lexical decision.* Manuscript submitted for publication.

Davis, F.B., & Davis, C.C. (1957). *Davis Reading Test.* New York: The Psychological Corporation.

de Lacoste, M.C., & Holloway, R.L. (1982). Sexual dimorphism in the human corpus callosum. *Science, 216,* 1431-1432.

de Lacoste, M.C., Kirkpatrick, J.B., & Ross, E.D. (1985). Topography of the human corpus callosum. *Journal of Neuropathology and Experimental Neurology, 44,* 578-591.

Degos, J.D., Gray, F., Louarn, F., Ansquer, J.C., Poirier, J., & Barbizet, J. (1987). Posterior callosal infarction: Clinicopathological correlations. *Brain, 110,* 1155-1171.

Eviatar, Z., & Zaidel, E. (1991). The effects of word length and emotionality on hemispheric contribution to lexical decision. *Neuropsychologia, 29,* 415-428.

Eviatar, Z., Menn, L., & Zaidel, E. (1990). Concreteness: Nouns, verbs and hemispheres. *Cortex, 26,* 611-624.

Fairweather, H. (1982). Sex differences: Little reason for females to play midfield. In J.G. Beaumont (Ed.), *Divided visual field studies of cerebral organization.* (pp. 147-194). New York: Academic Press.

Galaburda, A.L., Rosen, G.D., & Sherman, G.F. (1990). Individual variability in cortical organization: Its relationship to brain laterality and implications to function. *Neuropsychologia, 28,* 529-546.

Galaburda, A.M., Corsiglia, J., Rosen, G.D., & Sherman, G.F. (1987). Planum temporale asymmetry: Reappraisal since Geschwind and Levitsky. *Neuropsychologia, 25,* 853-868.

Geschwind, N., & Galaburda, A.M. (1985a). Cerebral Lateralization: Biological mechanisms, associations and pathology: I. *Archives of Neurology, 42,* 428-459.

Geschwind, N., & Galaburda, A.M. (1985b). Cerebral lateralization: Biological mechanisms, associations and pathology: II. *Archives of Neurology, 42,* 521-552.

Geschwind, N., & Galaburda, A.M. (1985c). Cerebral lateralization: Biological mechanisms, associations and pathology: III. *Archives of Neurology, 42,* 632-654.

Geschwind, N., & Levitsky, W. (1968). Human brain: Left-right asymmetries in temporal speech regions. *Science, 161,* 186-187.

Goldberg, E., & Costa, L.D. (1981). Hemispheric differences in relationship to the acquisition and use of descriptive systems. *Brain and Language, 14,* 144-173.

Habib, M., Gayraud, D., Oliva, A., Regis, J., Salamon, G., & Khalil, R. (1991). Effects of handedness and sex on the morphology of the corpus callosum: A study with magnetic resonance imaging, *Brain and Cognition, 16,* 41-61.

Hampson, E. (1990).   Estrogen-related variations in human spatial and anticulatory-motor skills. *Psychoneuroendocrinology, 15,* 97-111.

Harshman, R.A., & Hampson, E. (1987).   Normal variation in human brain organization: Relation to handedness, sex and cognitive abilities.   In D. Ottoson (Ed.), *Duality and unity of the brain* (pp. 83-99). Hampshire: Macmillan.

Harshman, R.A., Hampson, E., & Berenbaum, S.A. (1983).   Individual differences in cognitive abilities and brain organization: Part I.   Sex and handedness differences in ability. *Canadian Journal of Psychology, 37,* 144-192.

Healey, J.M., Waldstein, S., & Goodglass, H. (1983). *Lateralization of receptive and expressive language functions in normal males and females: Methodological considerations.*   Paper presented at the American Psychological Association Convention, Anaheim, CA.

Healey, J.M., Waldstein, S., & Goodglass, H. (1985).   Sex differences in the lateralization of language discrimination versus language production. *Neuropsychologia, 23,* 777-789.

Hiscock, M., Hiscock, C.K., & Inch, R. (1991).   Is there a sex difference in visual laterality?   [Abstract]. *Journal of Clinical and Experimental Neuropsychology, 13,* 37.

Hiscock, M., & Hiscock, C.K. (1988).   An anomalous sex difference in auditory laterality [Note]. *Cortex, 24,* 595-599.

Hiscock, M., & MacKay, M. (1985a).   Neuropsychological approaches to the study of individual differences.   In C.R. Reynolds & V.L. Willson (Eds.), *Methodological and statistical advances in the study of individual differences* (pp. 117-176). New York: Plenum Press.

Hiscock, M., & MacKay, M. (1985b).   The sex difference in dichotic listening: Multiple negative findings. *Neuropsychologia, 3,* 441-444.

Hiscock, M., Hiscock, C.K., & Kalil, K.M. (1990).   Is there a sex difference in auditory laterality?   [Abstract]. *Journal of Clinical and Experimental Neuropsychology, 12,* 43.

Hyde, J. S. (1981). How large are cognitive gender differences? *American Psychologist, 36,* 892-901.

Inglis, J., & Lawson, J.S. (1982). A meta-analysis of sex differences in the effects of unilateral brain damage on intelligence test results. *Canadian Journal of Psychology, 36,* 670-683.

Innocenti, G.M. (1986).   General organization of callosal connections in the cerebral cortex.   In E.G. Jones & A. Peters (Eds.), *Cerebral Cortex* (Vol. 5, pp. 291-354). New York: Plenum Press.

Jerison, H.J. (1991). *Brain size and the evolution of mind.* Fifty-Ninth James Arthur Lecture on the Evolution of the Human Brain. New York: American Museum of Natural History.

Juraska, J.M., & Kopcik, J.R. (1988). Sex and environmental influences on the size and ultrastructure of the rat corpus callosum, *Brain Research, 450,* 1-8.

Kim, H., Levine, S.C., & Kertesz, S. (1990). Are variations among subjects in lateral asymmetry real individual differences or random error in measurement: Putting variability in its place. *Brain and Cognition, 14,* 220-242.

Kimura, D. (1989). Sex differences and human brain organization. In G. Adelman (Ed.), *Encyclopedia of Neuroscience* (pp. 1084-1085). Boston: Birkhauser.

Kimura, D. (1991). *Sex differences in cognitive function vary with the season.* (Research Bulletin, No. 697). London, Ontario: The University of Western Ontario Department of Psychology.

Kimura, D., & Durnford, M. (1974). Normal studies on the function of the right hemisphere in vision. In S.J. Dimond & J.G. Beaumont (Eds.), *Hemisphere function in the human brain* (pp. 25-47). London: Elek Science.

Kimura, D., & Harshman, R.A. (1984). Sex differences in brain organization for verbal and non-verbal functions. In G.J. de Vries, J.P.C. de Bruin, H.B.M. Uylings, & M.A. Corner (Eds.), *Progress in brain research: Vol. 61. Sex differences in the brain: relation between structure and function* (pp. 423-441). Amsterdam: Elsevier.

La Mantia, A.S., & Rakic, P. (1990b). Cytological and quantitative characteristics of four cerebral commissures in the Rhesus monkey. *Journal of Comparative Neurology, 291,* 520-537.

La Mantia, A.S., & Rakic, P. (1990a). Axon overproduction and elimination in the corpus callosum of the developing Rhesus monkey. *The Journal of Neuroscience, 10,* 2156-2175.

Levy, J., Heller, W., Banich, M.T., & Burton, L.A. (1983). Are variations among right-handed individuals in perceptual asymmetries caused by characteristic arousal differences between hemispheres? *Journal of Experimental Psychology: Human Perception and Performance, 9,* 329-359.

Matteson, R.L. (1991). *Individual differences in interhemispheric relations.* Unpublished doctoral dissertation, University of California at Los Angeles.

McGlone, J. (1980). Sex differences in human brain organization: A critical survey. *Behavioral and Brain Sciences, 3,* 215-227.

McKeever, W.F., Seitz, K.S., Hoff, A.L., Marino, M.F., & Diehl, J.A. (1983). Interacting sex and familial sinistrality characteristics influence both language lateralization and spatial ability in right handers. *Neuropsychologia, 21,* 661-668.

Measso, G., & Zaidel, E. (1990). Effect of response programming on hemispheric differences in lexical decision. *Neuropsychologia, 28,* 635-646.

Melamed, F., & Zaidel, E. (1993). Language and task effects on lateralized word recognition. *Brain & Language, 45*, 70-85.

Merola, J.L., & Liederman, J. (1985). Developmental changes in hemispheric independence. *Child Development, 56*, 1184-1194.

Pandya, D.N., & Seltzer, B. (1986). The topography of commissural fibers. In F. Lepore, M. Ptito, & H.H. Jasper (Eds.), *Two hemispheres-One brain: Functions of the corpus callosum* (pp. 47-73). New York: Alan R. Liss.

Pizzamiglio, L., & Zoccolotti, F. (1981). Sex and cognitive style influence on visual hemifield superiority for face and letter recognition. *Cortex, 17*, 215-226.

Rayman, J., & Zaidel, E. (1991). Rhyming and the right hemisphere. *Brain and Language, 40*, 89-105.

Robertson, L.C., Lamb, M.R., & Zaidel, E. (1993). Interhemispheric relations in processing hierarchical patterns: Evidence from normal and commissurotomized subjects. *Neuropsychology, 7*, 325-342.

Robinson, T.E., Becker, J.B., Camp, D.M., & Mansour, A. (1985). Variation in the pattern of behavioral and brain asymmetries due to sex differences. In S. D. Glick (Ed.), *Cerebral lateralization in non-human species* (pp. 185-231). New York: Academic Press.

Rosen, G.D., Galaburda, A.M., & Sherman G.F. (1990). The ontogeny of anatomic asymmetry: constraints derived from basic mechanisms. In A.B. Scheibel and A.F. Wechsler (Eds.), *Neurobiology of higher cognitive function* (pp. 215-238). New York: Guilford Press.

Rosen, G.D., Sherman G.F., & Galaburda, A.M. (1989). Interhemispheric connections differ between symmetrical and asymmetrical brain regions. *Neuroscience, 33*, 525-533.

Rosenthal, R. (1970). Combined results of independent studies. *Psychological Bulletin, 85*, 185-193.

Seymour, P.H.K. (1986). *Cognitive analysis of dyslexia*. New York: Routledge & Kegan Paul.

Stein, R. (1987). *Hemispheric monitoring in lexical decision*. Unpublished undergraduate honors thesis, University of California at Los Angeles.

Steinmetz, H., Jancke, L., Kleinschmidt, A., Schlaug, G., Volkmann, J., & Huang, Y. (1992). Sex but no hand difference in the isthmus of the corpus callosum. *Neurology, 42*, 749-752.

Vrbancic, M.I., & Bryden, M.P. (1989). Rate of maturation, cognitive ability, handedness, and cerebral asymmetry. *Canadian Psychologist, 30*, 455.

Wada, J., Clarke, R., & Hamm, A. (1975). Cerebral hemispheric asymmetry in humans. *Archives of Neurology, 32*, 239-246.

Wexler, B.E., & Lipman, A.J. (1988). Sex differences and change over time in perceptual asymmetry. *Neuropsychologia, 26*, 943-946.

Witelson, S.F. (1989). Handedness and sex differences in the isthmus and genu of the corpus callosum in humans. *Brain, 112*, 799-835.

Witelson, S.F., & Kigar, D.L. (1988). Asymmetry in brain function follows asymmetry in anatomical form: Gross, microscopic, postmortem and imaging studies. In F. Boller & J. Grafman (Eds.), *Handbook of neuropsychology* (Vol. 1, pp. 111-142). New York: Elsevier.

Witkin, H.A., & Goodenough, D.R. (1981). *Cognitive style: Essence and origins.*New York: International Universities Press.

Witkin, H.A., Oltman, P.K., Raskin, E., & Karp, S.A. (1971). *A manual for the Embedded Figures Test.* Palo Alto: Consulting Psychologists Press.

Wittig, M., & Petersen, A.C. (1979). *Sex-related differences in cognitive functioning: Developmental issues.* New York: Academic Press.

Zaidel, D.W. (1990). Memory and spatial cognition following commissurotomy. In F. Boller & J. Grafman (Eds.), *Handbook of neuropsychology* (Vol. 4, pp. 151-166). New York: Elsevier.

Zaidel, E. (1979). On measuring hemispheric specialization in man. In B. Rybak (Ed.), *Advanced technobiology: Proceedings of the Nato-Asi* (pp. 365-403). Alphen aan den Rijn: Sijthoff & Noordhoff.

Zaidel, E. (1983). Disconnection syndrome as a model for laterality effects in the normal brain. In J. Hellige (Ed.), *Cerebral hemisphere asymmetry: Method, theory and application* (pp. 95-151). New York: Praeger.

Zaidel, E. (1986). Callosal dynamics and right hemisphere language. In F. Lepore, M. Ptito, & H.H. Jasper (Eds.), *Two hemispheres-One brain: Functions of the corpus callosum* (pp. 435-459). New York: Alan R. Liss.

Zaidel, E., (1987). Hemispheric monitoring. In D. Ottoson (Ed.), *Duality and unity of the brain* (pp. 247-281). London: Macmillan Press.

Zaidel, E., Clarke, J., & Suyenobu, B. (1990). Hemispheric independence: A paradigm case for cognitive neuroscience. In A.B. Scheibel & A.F. Wechsler (Eds.), *Neurobiology of higher cognitive function* (pp. 297-362). New York: Guilford Press.

Zaidel, E., Spence, S., & Kasher, A. (1993). *The right hemisphere communication battery: performance following cerebral commissurotomy and hemispherectomy.* Unpublished manuscript, Department of Psychology, University of California at Los Angeles.

Zaidel, E., Taylor, K., & Clarke, J. (1990). Reading correlates of lateralized primed lexical decision [Abstract]. *Journal of Clinical & Experimental Neuropsychology, 12,* 411-412.

4 Does The Corpus Callosum Play a Role in the Activation and Suppression of Ambiguous Word Meanings?

Christine Chiarello
Syracuse University

The corpus callosum is the most prominent fiber tract in the human brain, yet our knowledge of its functional significance, despite decades of intense scrutiny (e.g., Lepore, Ptito, & Jasper, 1986), is minimal. Recent anatomical studies document a remarkable degree of structural heterogeneity (Demeter, Ringo, & Doty, 1988; Lamantia & Rakic, 1990). The corpus callosum is composed of a number of distinct areas, differing not only in the cortical areas they interconnect, but also in their axonal composition (Lamantia & Rakic, 1990). For example, callosal areas interconnecting association cortex are populated primarily by axons with very small diameters, many of which are unmyelinated, whereas those areas interconnecting primary visual and somatosensory cortices contain very large axons, most of which are myelinated. Thus, there is a tremendous range of conduction velocities for axons within the corpus callosum. If function follows form, then there are a variety of callosal functions, and thus many different ways in which the two hemispheres can interact. To date, the majority of laterality researchers have focused on two plausible roles for the corpus callosum: (a) to transfer information across hemispheres (e.g., Moscovitch, 1986) and (b) to inhibit processing in the opposite hemisphere (e.g., Moscovitch, 1976). In this chapter I explore yet another conceptualization of corpus callosum functioning, first suggested by Norman Cook (1986) in his book *The Brain Code*.

The basic notion is that this cerebral commissure acts to produce complementary sets of information in each hemisphere, rather than duplicate sets of information, as implied by the standard view of the corpus callosum as a conduit for interhemispheric information transfer (Cook, 1986). I have found this to be an attractive theory because, at least at a certain level of abstraction, it seemed very consistent with the semantic priming data my colleagues and I have been collecting in my laboratory since the mid-1980s.

I begin by reviewing the basic premises of Cook's theory and then describe how some of our previous semantic priming data are consistent with it. Next I discuss an empirical test of this theory that we are currently conducting. This test builds on some recent findings about the activation and suppression of ambiguous word meanings (Simpson & Kellas, 1990). These findings suggest that when one encounters an ambiguous word, such as *bank*, used with one of its meanings, let's say *bank-teller*, then for a period of at least several seconds the other meaning of *bank*, as in *bank-river*, is inhibited or suppressed. The research I present here considers the possibility that this *typical* pattern of activation and inhibition of ambiguous meanings is reversed when ambiguous words are repeated across, rather than within, visual fields. If this can be shown, it would provide rather dramatic evidence that, at least in some situations, the corpus callosum enables complementary information to be maintained in each hemisphere.

THE HOMOTOPIC INHIBITION THEORY

The first premise of Cook's (1986) theory is that the corpus callosum primarily interconnects homologous areas of each hemisphere. There is certainly a great deal of anatomical evidence for this. Cook argued that the cortical column is the basic unit of information processing within each hemisphere, and that the corpus callosum serves to interconnect homologous columns across the hemispheres. He further assumed that the information represented in these homologous areas is very similar in each hemisphere. Thus, there may be no real asymmetry in the kind of information potentially available to each hemisphere.

How can one account for the fact that the hemispheres appear to function as if there were asymmetries in the kinds of information available to each? This brings us to the second major premise, that the corpus callosum is primarily inhibitory, but in a very precise and nondiffuse manner. That is, when a given cortical area is active in one hemisphere, the corpus callosum will provide inhibitory input to the homologous area of the opposite hemisphere. Thus, even if comparable information is represented in each hemisphere, at any moment in time the action of the corpus callosum would ensure that whatever information is highly accessible in one hemisphere will be highly inaccessible in the other.

Let us consider an abstract example of how this might work. Assume that a given column in one hemisphere, shown on the left in Fig. 4.1, becomes activated. The homotopic inhibition theory states that this column will send inhibitory input to surrounding columns in that hemisphere, via lateral inhibition. Further, callosal inhibition will be sent to the homotopic area in the opposite hemisphere, shown on the right. Of course, this will serve to disinhibit its

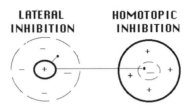

LATERAL INHIBITION   HOMOTOPIC INHIBITION

FIG 4.1. Schematic representation of activation and inhibition of cortical areas in each hemisphere, based on the homotopic inhibition theory of callosal function (Cook, 1986). Heavy circles and + indicate activated columns, dashed circles and - indicate inhibited columns. If a cortical column in one hemisphere (shown as the center area on the left) becomes activated, it will inhibit (a) surrounding columns in that same hemisphere, and (b) the homologous column in the opposite hemisphere (shown on the right), thereby disinhibiting the surrounding columns.

own surrounding columns. So, via these two mechanisms, lateral inhibition within a hemisphere, and homotopic inhibition across hemispheres, one could derive complementary patterns of activation in each hemisphere.

This view contrasts with the more standard view of the cerebral commissures. We have come to assume that whatever information is provided to a single hemisphere will be duplicated in the opposite hemisphere via callosal transfer, and thus that the corpus callosum acts to reduce rather than promote asymmetrical functioning. In the homotopic inhibition theory, however, the corpus callosum actually induces asymmetrical functioning, which is an intriguing conjecture about the role of the cerebral commissures in information processing.

I initially found this view appealing because, in my laboratory, we have identified some conditions in which word meanings appear to be activated in the right hemisphere (RH), but not in the left hemisphere (LH), (Chiarello, 1985; Chiarello, Burgess, Richards, & Pollock, 1990; Chiarello & Richards, 1992). This seems counterintuitive if the LH is dominant for language processing, as we generally assume. But the homotopic inhibition theory suggested another possibility. Perhaps certain meanings are highly accessible to the right hemisphere as a consequence of their being suppressed or inhibited within the language-dominant LH.

Let me take a brief detour, then, to describe some of this data. I stress that these initial experiments were not designed to test the homotopic inhibition theory. Rather, they lay the groundwork for our current studies which are moving in that direction.

SEMANTIC PRIMING ACROSS THE HEMISPHERES

My major interest is in understanding hemisphere differences in meaning accessibility during visual word recognition (see Chiarello, 1991, for review). I have been using semantic priming paradigms to address these issues. When a word to be recognized has been preceded by a semantically related word prime, its processing is facilitated, as measured by faster response times, as compared to recognition of the same word when preceded by an unrelated prime. Under appropriate experimental conditions, this facilitation or priming can be attributed to automatic meaning activation within a semantic network (Neely, 1991), and I only discuss these sorts of experiments here[1]. One question I've been trying to address is this: When we see a word, what meanings become activated in the left, and in the right, cerebral hemispheres?

In a recent study (Chiarello et al., 1990), we compared priming for words, such as *arm-leg* which were strongly related via both category membership and association, to words that were less strongly related sharing only category membership such as *arm-nose*. Note that words that are not associated also tend

---

[1] In these experiments a low proportion of related trials was used, comparable results were obtained in lexical decision and word pronunciation tasks, and there was no slowing of responses on unrelated, as compared to neutral, trials. Thus, there is converging evidence that the observed priming reflects automatic meaning activation processes.

to share fewer semantic features than do the associated category members. In our study we were able to rule out association as a variable contributing to our results, and so, attribute any priming differences to variations in the amount of semantic feature overlap. Prime and target stimuli were presented to either left or right visual fields in both lexical decision and pronunciation tasks.

Figure 4.2 displays our results, plotting the amount of priming obtained. For the most closely related stimuli, the category associates, we obtained equivalent priming in the two visual field (VFs). However, for the less related stimuli, we obtained priming only for words presented to the left visual field (LVF)/RH. We have recently replicated this result with a new set of stimuli (Chiarello & Richards, 1992). These findings, along with others, suggested to us that the RH may be involved in the activation of rather distantly related meanings, whereas the LH activates only a smaller set of very closely related meanings. Note one additional aspect of these findings. It appears that in the LVF, there is actually greater priming for words with less semantic overlap than there is for words with much greater semantic similarity. So, another way to interpret these results is to argue that the RH increments just those related meanings that are not at all facilitated in the LH, for example, *arm-nose*.

It now seemed possible that the priming seen in each hemisphere might be somehow yoked to the processing typically performed by the opposite hemisphere. This led me to wonder whether there were some situations in which complementary sets of meanings would be accessible in each hemisphere and to attempt to reinterpret these data within the homotopic inhibition theory (Chiarello, 1990). I argued then that priming in the LH involved activating only highly related meanings, with inhibition of distantly related meanings, as shown on the left in Fig. 4.3.

Homotopic callosal inhibition would then tend to inhibit the closely related meanings in the RH (shown on the right in Fig. 4.3), which would then disinhibit the more distantly related meanings within the RH, resulting in the complementary pattern shown here.

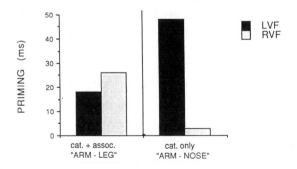

FIG 4.2. Priming ($RT_{unrelated} - RT_{related}$) for categorical associates and nonassociated category members in each visual field.

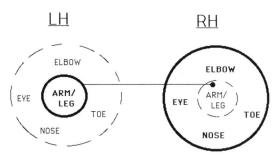

FIG. 4.3. Schematic representation of activated and inhibited meanings in each hemisphere. Activated meanings are indicated by heavy circles and bold type, inhibited meanings by dashed circles and standard type.

This was not, however, a terribly convincing explanation of our priming results. First, the priming data described here were obtained when both prime and target stimuli were presented to the same VF, where one could plausibly argue that the priming had little or nothing to do with interhemispheric relations. Second, we never actually obtained the predicted inhibition effects. At best, priming was reduced or absent in those conditions in which we should have observed inhibition. For example, if the activation of certain meanings in the LH implied the inhibition of those same meanings in the RH, then they should have been much less accessible than completely unrelated meanings in the RH, hence, a negative priming effect, which was certainly not obtained. Finally, my entire explanation was premised on certain assumptions about how meanings were represented in memory. The explanation proferred above presumes that lateral inhibition exists between strongly and distantly related category members. Although somewhat plausible (see Martindale, 1981, 1991, for related suggestions), there was no independently justified reason to make this assumption.

At this point a wiser person might have dropped the whole idea that the corpus callosum has anything to do with the activation and suppression of word meanings. However, the notion of complementary patterns of activation and suppression in the two hemispheres still made sense, so I began searching for a better way to test this using semantic priming paradigms. An ideal paradigm would be one in which both positive and negative priming are expected to occur under specifiable conditions, and where one could also make some reasonable assumptions about how the relevant meanings are actually represented in memory. If such a paradigm existed, it would be relatively easy to include an interhemispheric condition to test the homotopic inhibition theory in a much more rigorous fashion.

Fortunately, Greg Simpson and his colleagues (Simpson & Kellas, 1988, 1990; Simpson & Kang, 1994) had just begun reporting some priming results with ambiguous words that fit the bill exactly. Many, if not most, of the words we encounter have more than one meaning, yet, when reading a passage or listening to speech we are generally only aware of a single meaning, the one that is contextually appropriate. For example, when I just used the phrase "fit the bill," the sense of *bill* as a duck's bill probably did not occur to you. However, a number of priming experiments have indicated that, very early in the comprehension process, all meanings of a word are activated in memory (Simpson & Burgess, 1985; Swinney, 1979). So how is it that these multiple meanings do not interfere with our ability to construct a single, unified meaning representation? It has been assumed by many psycholinguists that the irrelevant meanings are quickly suppressed (e.g., Gernsbacher, 1990), so that we only become aware of a single interpretation. What Simpson has been able to do is to demonstrate this suppression effect experimentally, using the standard single-word priming paradigm.

In these experiments, the primes are always ambiguous words (i.e., homographs) with at least two mutually inconsistent meanings, such as *bank*. Each prime word is shown twice in the experiment. On the first presentation, the target word is related to one of these meanings, for example *bank-money*. The subject is to pronounce the target as quickly as possible. Some time later in the experiment, this same prime is shown again with a new target word. Again, the subject pronounces the target. Sometimes the new target is related to the previously shown meaning, *bank-teller*. Sometimes, the new target is related to the other meaning, *bank-river*. There are also completely unrelated target words, to provide a base line from which we can compute the effect of priming. We are mainly concerned with which meanings are primed on this second presentation.

When the second presentation retained the same meaning as the first, Simpson found a small, positive priming effect. However, when the second presentation instantiated the alternate meaning, negative priming occurred. That is, under these circumstances, it took longer to pronounce *river* when it was preceded by *bank*, than when it was preceded by a completely unrelated word. So, here we have evidence for a true inhibition effect. When we encounter an ambiguous word with one meaning this appears to produce an inhibition of the alternate meanings. Simpson showed that this inhibition persists for lags of up to 12 intervening trials, and he also showed that the effects are the same, regardless of whether the dominant or subordinate meaning is shown first.

I saw that this paradigm could be modified to provide a very powerful test of the homotopic inhibition theory. We have an experimental situation in which both facilitory and inhibitory priming effects can be observed. These data support a model of memory in which alternate meanings of a single word, although activated initially, eventually are mutually inhibitory. Some studies that are ongoing in my laboratory have modified Simpson's procedures slightly to examine the pattern of meaning activation and inhibition both within and across hemispheres.

In our experiments, we vary the VF in which the target words are presented. First, the ambiguous prime, for example *bank*, is shown centrally for 130 msec and is immediately replaced by a pattern mask. At the same time that the mask appears, the target is shown for 120 msec in either the right or the left visual field. Thus, the prime-target stimulus onset asynchrony is 130 msec. The subject is asked to pronounce the target (i.e., *save*). Next, there are either one or six intervening trials. Then the same prime reappears as before, and is followed by a new target, which is either related to the same meaning as the original target (*teller*), is related to the alternate (i.e., different) meaning (*river*), or is unrelated (*sport*). In the intrahemispheric (within-field) condition, the first and second presentation targets appear in the same VF; in the interhemispheric (cross-field) condition, the second presentation target is presented in the VF opposite to that of the first prime presentation. In these experiments, then, we focused on the priming observed on the second presentation of an ambiguous prime, depending on whether (a) the target for this second presentation has the same meaning or a different meaning from the initial target, and (b) the first and second presentation targets appear in the same or opposite VFs.

Before making firm predictions about the cross-hemispheric conditions, we must consider how ambiguous word meanings are activated and/or inhibited within each hemisphere. I outline our within- and cross-field predictions separately for those trials in which disambiguation is initiated in the left, and in the right, hemisphere.   Figures 4.4 and 4.5 depict the predictions suggested by the homotopic inhibition theory. In these figures the words shown above in the shadow type represent the first homograph-target presentation, and those below, the resulting facilitation or inhibition that is expected for the meanings that might be shown on the second presentation.

Left-Hemisphere Initiated Processing

Our predictions for the LH within-field conditions are straightforward. Here, we expect to obtain the same results as Simpson, namely positive priming when the second target is consistent with the meaning of the first presentation, and negative priming or inhibition when the meaning of the second target is different. This is because we view LH semantic processing as rapidly settling on one interpretation of a word and suppressing any alternate meanings (Chiarello, 1991). Thus, when the first presentation (e.g., *bank-money*) is shown to the LH, we expect contextually-relevant financial meanings to remain activated (i.e., the meanings consistent with the first presentation target).   In contrast, the contextually irrelevant earth formation meanings should be inhibited in the LH (see Fig. 4.4).

Now consider what the homotopic inhibition theory would predict about the cross-hemisphere conditions, when the first presentation is shown to the LH, and the second to the RH. This theory argues that the within-hemisphere pattern will be reversed, with the irrelevant meaning being activated and the contextually appropriate meaning being inhibited. Thus, if the second presentation was to the opposite VF (i.e., RH), we would expect positive priming for *bank-river* which is the new meaning, and negative priming for *bank-teller*, the previously instantiated meaning.

Contrasting the within-field and cross-field conditions in Fig. 4.4, we see that the homotopic inhibition theory predicts complementary patterns in the two hemispheres: Meanings that are facilitated in the LH are suppressed in the RH, and vice versa. In contrast, the callosal duplication view would predict that one

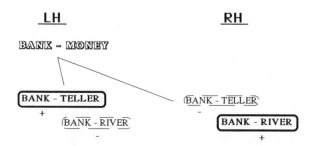

FIG 4.4. Pattern of meaning activation and inhibition in each hemisphere, hypothesized by the homotopic inhibition theory, when the first presentation of an ambiguous prime and related target is presented to the RVF/LH. Activation is indicated by heavy ellipses and +, inhibition by dashed ellipses and - .

should see similar patterns of priming in the within-field and cross-field conditions.

Right-Hemisphere Initiated Processing

Consider, now, the predictions for trials in which the first presentation of the target is to the RH. If semantic processing for words input to the RH is similar to that of words input to the LH, RH within-field trials should evidence the same pattern of facilitation and inhibition as just described for the within-field LH conditions. But, on the basis of our other semantic priming research, I have previously argued that semantic processing in the RH operates nonselectively (Chiarello, 1991). That is, a wider set of meanings is initially activated in the RH, and this multiple activation is maintained, in contrast to the more focal meaning selection which we posit for the LH. This view would predict that both meanings of the ambiguous word would be primed on the second presentation. Thus, regardless of the meaning shown on the first presentation, we would expect to see positive priming for both meanings on the second presentation for the within-field RH conditions (see Fig. 4.5).

The homotopic inhibition theory makes a very interesting and counterintuitive prediction about what we should observe if the second presentation is to the opposite VF (i.e., LH), (cross-field conditions). Here, we would expect both meanings to be suppressed with no positive priming for either

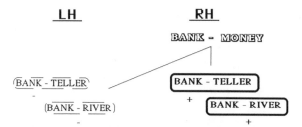

FIG 4.5. Pattern of meaning activation and inhibition in each hemisphere, hypothesized by the homotopic inhibition theory, when the first presentation of an ambiguous prime and related target is presented to the LVF/RH. Activation is indicated by heavy ellipses and +, inhibition by dashed ellipses and - .

meaning. Now if we put these two patterns together, the complementary nature of the meaning activation in the hemispheres becomes clear (see Fig. 4.5). Again the callosal duplication view would certainly not predict this result, but rather would posit a replication of the RH activation in the cross-field LH condition.

RESULTS AND DISCUSSION

We can now examine the extent to which our results conform to the predictions just outlined. Consider, first, the results of the within-field priming conditions. Table 4.1 (upper panel) diplays this data for the second presentation of the ambiguous prime, when second presentation targets instantiated the same or different meanings of the homograph.[2] In the RVF, there was normal priming of same meanings, but a complete loss of priming when target meanings varied. Thus, there is some evidence for suppression of irrelevant meanings within the LH. We do not actually see negative priming here as Simpson did, but we certainly did see priming altered in the predicted direction. This is consistent with our view of LH semantic processing: Once one meaning of an ambiguous word is instantiated, the other, irrelevant, meanings are suppressed, at least to the point of not being strongly activated by the ambiguous word. In contrast, there was no significant effect of same versus different contexts for LVF trials. If anything, it appears that the greatest priming is obtained when a different meaning occurs on the second presentation. Thus, there is little evidence that the RH discards inappropriate or irrelevant meanings. Overall, the intrahemispheric priming data suggest that ambiguity is resolved in a unique manner within each hemisphere.

We can now consider whether these activation patterns are reversed (Cook, 1986) or duplicated (Moscovitch, 1986) when second presentation targets

TABLE 4.1. Priming, in Msec ($RT_{unrelated}$-$RT_{related}$) for the Second Presentation of an Ambiguous Prime When the Meaning is the Same or Different From That of the First Presentation. The First (P_1) and Second (P_2) Presentations Were Displayed in the Same Visual Field (Within-Hemisphere Condition) or in Opposite Visual Fields (Cross-Hemisphere Condition).

P_1VF-P_2VF	Within-Hemisphere Condition ($n = 64$)	
	SAME	DIFFERENT
RVF-RVF	+24	+ 3
LVF-LVF	- 4	+13

P_1VF-P_2VF	Cross-Hemisphere Condition ($n = 16$)	
	SAME	DIFFERENT
RVF-LVF	+33	+ 9
LVF-RVF	- 9	+16

---

[2] The data displayed in Table 4.1 represent those trials in which a single trial intervened between first and second homograph prime presentation, since evidence for meaning suppression was maximal in this condition.

are shown to the opposite VF. This research is ongoing, but we currently have some cross-field data from 16 subjects (see Table 4.1, lower panel). Although these data are preliminary, they clearly resemble the within-field data when first presentation VF is the same. There is no evidence for the opposite within- and cross-field activation patterns predicted by the homotopic inhibition theory (Cook, 1986), and outlined in Figs. 4.4 and 4.5. Rather, the current results are consistent with the callosal duplication view. They imply that whatever within-hemisphere meaning suppression occurs as a consequence of the first presentation prime-target processing is shared with the opposite hemisphere. That is, ambiguity is resolved differently depending on which hemisphere receives the disambiguating information (i.e., the first presentation target), but the outcome of these hemisphere-specific processes appears to be equally available to either hemisphere.

Homotopic callosal inhibition was proposed as a mechanism to account for complementary hemispheric processing. It is interesting that we obtained some evidence for complementary patterns of meaning activation across hemispheres, even though the current data do not support the view that the corpus callosum produces these patterns. In the within-hemisphere condition, same, but not different, meanings were primed in the RVF, whereas there was a trend in the opposite direction for LVF trials. (Note a similar pattern for the corresponding cross-hemisphere conditions.) In other words, the contextually appropriate (same) meanings may only be available in the LH, whereas the irrelevant (different) meanings may only be maintained in the RH. If subsequent data confirm these findings, this would suggest that the RH functions to maintain just those meanings that the LH has suppressed.

One might ask of what value it would be to have meanings activated in a complementary fashion in the two hemispheres. Consider this example. It is probably safe to assume that the LH is the primary system used in language comprehension, with the RH playing a subsidiary role. If it is the case that the LH rapidly selects the most contextually appropriate meaning of an ambiguous word and inhibits alternate meanings, then how are we to recover from semantic garden paths, such as "The accountant had no luck at all at this bank, so he decided to try fishing from the other side"? The initially discarded earth formation meaning of *bank* would have been inhibited and highly inaccessible in the LH at the time of the second clause. However, if such meanings were maintained in a high state of accessibility in the RH, detection of a semantic anomaly could be rapidly repaired by simply accessing the RH system, rather than by somehow undoing the inhibition in the LH. Given the pervasiveness of ambiguity in language at all levels, a system that provided both the rapid suppression of irrelevant meanings, as well as a mechanism to instantiate those same meanings if they suddenly became relevant, would be very advantageous.

We are now exploring the idea that the apparent complementarity results from a RH inability to successful complete disambiguation processes that it may initiate (Chiarello, Richards, & Maxfield, 1992). In any case, hemispheric complementarity may arise for a variety of reasons, and its presence need not imply that the corpus callosum is required for it to originate.

It is too early to answer definitively the question posed in the title of this chapter. Although there is some evidence that activation and suppression of ambiguous word meanings occurs in a complementary fashion across hemispheres, our current data do not implicate commissural function as an explanatory mechanism. But even if subsequent research confirms the findings reported here, it would be premature to completely abandon homotopic inhibition as a candidate mechanism for some corpus callosum functions. Laterality research was said to have come of age once investigators gave up the idea that a single processing dichotomy could "explain" every left-right hemisphere difference. Given the anatomical heterogeneity of the corpus callosum, it seems equally unwise to suggest that a single callosal function will characterize all aspects of interhemispheric interaction. I believe the research described here demonstrates that the homotopic inhibition view is testable and worth considering further, as we attempt to uncover the operating characteristics of the human cerebral commissures.

ACKNOWLEDGMENTS

This research was supported by NIMH grant MH43868. Lorie Richards, Lisa Maxfield, and Kim Cannon assisted in the collection and analysis of the data reported here.

REFERENCES

Chiarello, C. (1985). Hemisphere dynamics in lexical access: Automatic and controlled priming. *Brain and Language, 26,* 146-172.

Chiarello, C. (1990, May). *Semantic priming in neuropsychological research: Theoretical issues and evidence from visual half-field studies.* Paper presented at the first annual meeting of TENNET, Montreal, Quebec.

Chiarello, C. (1991). Interpretation of word meanings by the cerebral hemispheres: One is not enough. In P. Schwanenflugel (Ed.), *The psychology of word meanings* (pp. 251-278). Hillsdale, N.J.: Lawrence Erlbaum Associates.

Chiarello, C., Burgess, C., Richards, L., & Pollock, A. (1990). Semantic and associative priming in the cerebral hemispheres: Some words do, some words don't...Sometimes, some places. *Brain and Language, 38,* 75-104.

Chiarello, C., & Richards, L. (1992). Another look at categorical priming in the cerebral hemispheres. *Neuropsychologia, 30,* 381-392.

Chiarello, C., Richards, L., & Maxfield, L. (1992, Nov.). *Reversal of meaning suppression effects for ambiguous words: Time course and laterality effects.* Paper presented at the 33rd Psychonomic Society, St. Louis, MO.

Cook, N.D. (1986). *The brain code: Mechanisms of information transfer and the role of the corpus callosum.* London: Methuen.

Demeter, S., Ringo, J.L., & Doty, R.W. (1988). Morphometric analysis of the human corpus callosum and anterior commissure. *Human Neurobiology,* *6,* 219-226.

Gernsbacher, M.A. (1990). *Language comprehension as structure building.* Hillsdale, NJ: Lawrence Erlbaum Associates.

Lamantia, A.-S., & Rakic, P. (1990). Cytological and quantitative characteristics of four cerebral commissures in the rhesus monkey. *The Journal of Comparative Neurology, 291,* 520-537.

Lepore, F., Ptito, M., & Jasper, H.H. (Eds.). (1986). *Two hemispheres-one brain: Functions of the corpus callosum.* New York: Alan R. Liss.

Martindale, C. (1981). *Cognition and consciousness.* Homewood: Dorsey Press.

Martindale, C. (1991). *Cognitive psychology: A neural-network approach.* Pacific Grove, CA: Brooks/Cole.

Moscovitch, M. (1976). On the representation of language in the right hemisphere of right-handed people. *Brain and Language, 3,* 47-71.

Moscovitch, M. (1986). Hemispheric specialization, interhemispheric codes and transmission times: Inferences from studies of visual masking of lateralized stimuli in normal people. In F. Lepore, M. Ptito, & H.H. Jasper (Eds.), *Two hemispheres-one brain: Functions of the corpus callosum* (pp. 483-510). New York: Alan R. Liss.

Neeley, J. H. (1991). Semantic priming effects in visual word recognition: A selective review of current findings and theories. In D. Besner & G. W. Humphreys (Eds.), *Basic Processes in Reading: Visual word recognition* (pp. 264-336). Hillsdale, NJ: Lawrence Erlbaum Associates.

Simpson, G.B., & Burgess, C. (1985). Activation and selection processes in the recognition of ambiguous words. *Journal of Experimental Psychology: Human Perception and Performance, 11,* 28-39.

Simpson, G.B., & Kang, H. (1994). Inhibitory processes in the recognition of homograph meanings. In D. Dagenbach & T.H. Carr (Eds.), *Inhibitory processes in attention, memory, and language* (pp. 359-381). New York: Academic Press.

Simpson, G.B., & Kellas, G. (1988). *Repetition priming of homograph meanings.* Paper presented at 29th Annual Meeting, Psychonomics Society, Chicago, IL.

Simpson, G.B., & Kellas, G. (1990). Dynamic contextual processes and lexical access. In D.S. Gorfein (Ed.), *Resolving semantic ambiguity* (pp. 40-56). New York: Springer-Verlag.

Swinney, D.A. (1979). Lexical access during sentence comprehension: (Re)consideration of context effects. *Journal of Verbal Learning and Verbal Behavior, 18,* 645-659.

5 Visualizing the Working Cerebral Hemispheres

Justine Sergent
Montreal Neurological Institute

The problem of the functional asymmetry of the brain lies at the core of human neuropsychology, which could be defined as "the study of the relationships between mental functions and cerebral structures" (Hécaen, 1972, p. 12). This problem can be formulated in a straightforward manner. On the one hand, the brain is composed of two hemispheres that are essentially identical with respect to their morphology, organization, and physiological properties: these two hemispheres are linked to a common stem and are connected to one another through a rich bundle of commissural fibers. On the other hand, the two hemispheres do not sustain the same mental functions: Damage in a particular location of one hemisphere does not result in the same deficit as that produced by damage in the homotopic area of the other hemisphere. For instance, destruction of the left inferior parietal lobule produces agraphia and acalculia, whereas damage to the right inferior parietal lobule results in neglect of the left side of the body and space and does not affect writing or mathematical computations.

This constitutes a paradoxical phenomenon that has no equivalent in nature. Indeed, both logic and experience lead us to believe that two symmetrical structures, made of the same tissue and having the same anatomical organization, should possess the same properties and functions, as is the case of the eyes, lungs, kidneys, or ears. This is not so for the brain, and the structural similarity of its two main components is not accompanied by functional equivalence. It should therefore come as no surprise that only in the second half of the 19th century, after overcoming philosophical and religious beliefs and scientific resistance, did the idea of functional asymmetry of the brain become accepted as an indisputable fact (Broca, 1861). No one would now think of casting doubt on the overwhelming evidence accumulated since then. The understanding and specification of the respective roles of the cerebral hemispheres in the control of cognition and behavior are inescapable considerations in any account of the functional organization of the brain.

The study of the cerebral lateralization of functions has mainly focused on the specialization of the hemispheres for processing information, with the purpose of describing the psychological functions at which each excelled and was superior to the other, and of identifying the contribution of each hemisphere to the realization of specific functions. This has given rise to a catalogue of competencies and processing styles that are said to uniquely characterize each hemisphere and that are summarized through the use of labels conceived to describe these abilities in terms of single bipolar principles. Although this approach may have been a necessary step in the understanding of the phenomenon, its limitations are now obvious. Several factors have led to casting the study of cerebral lateralization in a more global and comprehensive framework that takes into account the fact that the two hemispheres are part of a highly connected and integrated central nervous system and that their operations must be understood as contributing to a whole system devoted to the production of adapted and unified behavior.

Two central themes have now become integral to the study of functional cerebral lateralization. One is the aforementioned realization that each hemisphere should not be treated as a single entity, but as a component of a system that cannot be understood as being the mere sum of its components. Knowing what a cerebral hemisphere is capable of doing alone (as in split-brain, hemispherectomized, or unilaterally brain-damaged patients, or in normal subjects presented with unilateral information) is not directly relevant to understanding how this hemisphere operates when working in conjunction with the other hemisphere in an intact brain (Sergent, 1990b). Indeed, it is well established that any cognitive function engages the participation of both cerebral hemispheres. What is of interest is not so much which hemisphere is better in carrying out a particular function, but how the two hemispheres coordinate their respective operations in the realization of this function. The second theme derives from computational models of mental functions that have emphasized the decomposition of a given function into subprocesses. This suggests that mental functions should not be considered as made of unitary processes (e.g., reading, writing, face recognition), but a series of operations, organized in specific ways (e.g., serially, hierarchically, in parallel), each representing a specific contribution to the processes underlying the realization of a given function. As a result, hemispheric specialization can no longer be studied in terms of unitary processes, and experiments must be designed in such a way that the respective contribution of the hemispheres to the various operations inherent in the realization of a given task, and their level of competence, can be identified and specified. Few studies so far have been designed along these lines. Although this does not invalidate findings from experiments relying on older conceptions, much remains to be done to understand the cooperation of the cerebral hemispheres in the production of behavior.

One of the main assets of research in cerebral lateralization is the wide variety of sources of relevant information. Even if this variety sometimes complicates things because each technique and population has its own limitations and yields results that do not necessarily tap the same level of processing and may thus appear inconsistent, it offers the advantage of providing converging information about specific questions. The interpretations of the results of each technique and population may, thus, be constrained by one another, allowing a better understanding of the mechanisms underlying the patterns of performance and the way they come to the fore, depending on the particulars of each approach.

This chapter reports on how a new technique, positron emission tomography (PET) measurement of cerebral blood flow (CBF), may provide additional information on questions of functional cerebral asymmetry. They are examined through the study of face recognition, with examples provided of how different approaches to the problem of hemisphere asymmetry may constrain one another in the interpretation of findings that could, at first glance, appear contradictory.

FACE RECOGNITION

The human face has always been an object of fascination, as illustrated by the many writings elicited in ancient Egypt, Greece, and Rome. These writings were essentially concerned with issues related to aesthetics and character, and few authors addressed problems of face perception and recognition prior to the 19th century. This presumably reflects the common belief that there is nothing special about recognizing faces, which is regarded as a natural activity, a belief still shared by the philosopher John Searle (1984), who suggested that recognizing faces "is as simple and automatic as making footprints in the sand" (p. 52). The literature bearing on the neuropsychology of face recognition is relatively recent, but there are some isolated mentions of this issue in several ancient writings. For instance, one of the first texts to describe a man with a selective deficit in face recognition was written by the Roman historian Pliny the Younger (62-113 C.E.) some 2,000 years ago. He reported that a soldier who had suffered a closed head injury had become unable to recognize his relatives and his friends, but seemed to have no other impairment and could live a normal life. In the neurological literature, the first case of agnosia for faces was described by Quagliano and Borelli in 1867, and these authors pointed out that the deficit resulted from a bilateral lesion. It was almost a century later, in 1966, that De Renzi and Spinnler published the first systematic group study of face recognition by brain-damaged patients, and they found that a right posterior lesion resulted in impaired performance, especially in patients with visual field defects. The first published lateral tachistoscopic study of face processing in normals was written by Rizzolatti, Umiltà, and Berlucchi in 1970, and, interestingly enough, they found no performance difference between left and right visual field presentations in a reaction-time experiment. Then, Marzi and Berlucchi (1977) conducted the first tachistoscopic study of face identification in normal subjects, which indicated better performance after presentation in the right visual field which projects to the left hemisphere.

Some Problems Inherent in Studying Hemisphere Asymmetry in Face Processing

At the outset, these pioneering studies showed that, with respect to hemispheric specialization for face processing, there was no clear-cut pattern: Every possible outcome was reported. In the very large number of studies that followed, considerable variation in the findings still prevailed, but there was some consistency in at least three types of results.

At present, some 146 cases of prosopagnosia have been reported in the literature and, although not all have been thoroughly described, the location of the brain damage was indicated in all of them.   Considering only right-handed individuals, there is not one whose lesion was restricted to the left hemisphere, and the damaged cortical areas were either bilateral or located in the right hemisphere. This seems to indicate that, with respect to the identification of faces, the left hemisphere is not sufficient to sustain, on its own, the realization of this function. An exception to this suggestion would be the finding that commissurotomized patients can identify faces projected to the left hemisphere (Levy, Trevarthen, & Sperry, 1972; Sergent, 1990a). The reason for this discrepancy may be related to the testing technique used, which is discussed further on.

Another consistent finding in the study of unilaterally brain-damaged patients is the systematically lower performance of right- compared to left-hemisphere damaged patients in the recognition of faces, when access to memorized representations of faces is required. This is not the case with face perception, and there are examples (e.g., Hamsher, Levin, & Benton, 1979) of equally impaired left- and right-posterior brain-damaged patients on the Benton (1983) test which uses simultaneously presented target and test faces of unfamiliar individuals.

The third consistent finding is related to the previous one and comes from studies of normal subjects, using lateral tachistoscopic presentation.   When accuracy is the dependent variable, in recognition experiments designed so that many errors are to be committed, the pattern of visual field asymmetry typically favors the left visual field, and this is always the case when stimulus presentation is bilateral.

On the other hand, data bearing on other aspects of face processing are rather equivocal. This is specifically true of most of the studies that have examined the perception of faces in discrimination or categorization tasks. For instance, Benton (1980) has reported that prosopagnosic patients, who are totally unable to recognize people they know by inspection of their faces, can perform as well as normals on his test of face perception. Clearly, face perception and face recognition are two distinct processes, whose performance is dissociable, and the deficit that affects prosopagnosic patients is one of recognition, even if a large proportion of them are also impaired in purely perceptual face tasks. There is also evidence that discrimination tasks using schematic faces can produce a right visual field advantage in normals.   For instance, Patterson and Bradshaw (1975) used faces made of a large circle with small circles, and plus, minus, and equal signs as facial features, and found a right visual field advantage for discriminating faces that differed from one another by only one feature. The question, however, is whether these stimuli elicit the type of processing that would normally underlie the perception and recognition of faces.   When I used such stimuli with a prosopagnosic patient (R.M., described further on), and asked him to describe what he saw, he was unable to derive from such stimuli a facial representation. When asked to describe specifically what he saw, he responded that they were arithmetic symbols embedded in a circle.   Even when the schematic faces were drawn in such a way as to express different emotions, he could not see any expression of emotion in these drawings.   Yet, this patient, who had a right occipito-temporal lesion from a ruptured aneurism with no sign of left-hemisphere damage, was able to discriminate faces from other objects; he could also identify 172 out of 210 cars, providing for each the name of the manufacturer, the name of the model, and the year of its fabrication. He obviously had to rely on small details to discriminate and recognize all of those cars, so his inability to recognize a schematic drawing as a face had nothing to do with a general perceptual impairment as such. Thus, the suggestion that the left hemisphere is superior to the right in dealing with schematic faces may not be well founded, as this patient had an intact left hemisphere.

Similarly, the capacity to distinguish male and female faces, as investigated in tachistoscopic studies with normal subjects, has been found to be equally well performed after projection in the right or the left visual field, yet R.M. complained that he often mistook men for women and vice versa, which he found quite embarrassing (Sergent and Signoret, 1992b). He, therefore, usually waited for others to speak in order to know whether they should be addressed as "Mister" or "Madam." When he was presented with the faces of men and women I had used in previous experiments, he had little difficulty telling them apart with respect to their gender, but when their hair was no longer a discriminative clue, he responded at chance levels, suggesting that he was unable to rely on facial configuration to determine the gender of the faces (Sergent & Signoret, 1992a). Clearly, the faces I had used earlier to determine the respective competence of the cerebral hemispheres at male-female categorization lent themselves to an easy decision on the basis of features independent of facial configuration. This is not to say that the variations in patterns of visual field asymmetry I had found in these tasks as a function of manipulation of various procedural variables were invalid: it is simply that they had little relevance to the problem of face perception as such.

Another problem regarding inferences about the respective competence of the cerebral hemispheres at processing faces has been the use of unfamiliar faces, yet, as early as 1967, Warrington and James had reported finding that, even though right-brain damaged patients were defective at recognizing both unknown and known faces, the deficits on these two categories of faces resulted from damage to different areas of the brain, and performance on these two tasks was not correlated. In addition, as noted earlier, prosopagnosic patients are not necessarily impaired at processing unfamiliar faces. Nonetheless, I am one of many who have drawn on the results of lateral tachistoscopic studies with unfamiliar faces to make suggestions about the cerebral organization of processing structures underlying the identification of faces.

All of these considerations suggest that neuropsychological research on face perception and recognition had, for a long time, proceeded without a clear theoretical framework capable of making the relevant distinctions among the various operations to which faces lend themselves, of guiding the empirical investigations, and of providing the right questions to ask. Consequently, there was much confusion which resulted from efforts to disentangle and identify the relevance of very diverse findings. A significant step forward was accomplished with the development of cognitive models of face recognition (e.g., Bruce &

Young, 1986) that put order and logic into the field and offered a clear rationale for the design of experimental inquiries into face recognition and its neurobiological substrates.

Face Processing in Prosopagnosic Patients

Prosopagnosia is a rare, neurologically based deficit characterized by the inability to experience a feeling of familiarity on viewing faces of known individuals, and, therefore, an inability to identify those faces. It occurs in the absence of severe intellectual, perceptual, and memory impairments. Although associated deficits may be detected in these patients, none is more dramatic than the failure to identify faces of known persons, including those of relatives and even oneself. One of the main difficulties in understanding the underlying nature of this deficit comes from the diversity of impairments displayed by these patients. Although the functional deficit is the same across patients, it may result from a breakdown at different stages in the succession of operations that must be performed from the initial perception of a face to its recognition. This can be illustrated by examining four prosopagnosic patients.

A specification of the decomposition of the operations inherent in the perception and recognition of faces provides a useful framework for examining the various steps that must be implemented for a face to be identified. Faces lend themselves to a variety of operations corresponding to the extraction of different types of information about an individual. Figure 5.1 presents some of the steps leading to the recognition of a face. This figure is adapted from the model suggested by Bruce and Young (1986). It should not be regarded as a theoretical model of face recognition, but only as a schematic functional description of some of the operations by which faces acquire meaning and can eventually be identified. The first step indicated here is that of structural encoding, which is the end product of visual sensory processing of the incoming information and broadly corresponds to Marr's (1982) "two and a half" description. From such a description, a series of operations can be performed to access information on the basis of the visual properties of the face, irrespective of its identity (cf. Sergent, 1989). The ability of the patients to perform such operations may provide some indications about the functional level of their deficits.

Looking at the performance of the prosopagnosic patients shown in Table 5.1, one patient, R.M., was unable to extract from the physical attributes of the face the information related to its gender, (as was P.M.), its age, and its emotion. In fact, R.M. was defective at all aspects of face processing, including matching two identical views of the same face presented simultaneously in front of him. Another patient, P.C., performed above chance, but was nonetheless impaired compared to controls, whereas the performance of the fourth patient, P.V., was not significantly different from that of controls. What these findings suggest is that not only is prosopagnosia a selective deficit, but there exists a good deal of

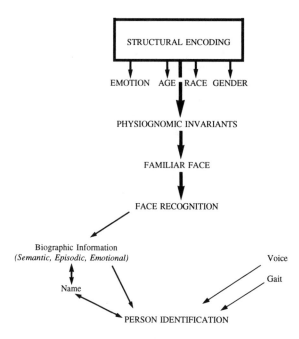

FIG. 5.1. Schematic description of some of the steps leading from face perception to identification.

selectivity even within the prosopagnosic disturbance. In other words, prosopagnosia is not a homogeneous impairment. In addition, the perceptual deficit that results from a breakdown of the structural encoding stage and that characterizes R.M.'s prosopagnosia is specific to the processing of faces and does not necessarily extend to the discrimination and recognition of other categories of objects. For instance, as noted earlier, R.M., who collected miniature cars as a

TABLE 5.1. Performance of Prosopagnosic and Control Subjects on Face and Object Processing Tasks

	Patients				
Task	P.C	P.M.	P.V.	R.M.	Controls (range)
WAIS Verbal	114	108	102	103	
Memory Quotient	109	111	98	112	
Object recognition (canonical)	52/54	54/54	52/54	52/54	50-54
Object recognition (non-canonical)	24/54	18/54	---	23/54	45-54
Gender categorization	38/50	31/50*	43/50	18/50*	43-50
Age estimation	17/20	16/20	17/20	4/20*	16-20
Face emotion	12/24	8/24*	18/24	6/24*	18-24
Physiognomic Invariance	14/24	4/24*	17/24	2/24*	16-24
Face recognition	7/100	4/100	2/100	0/100	94-100

*Performance not different from chance

hobby and owned old cars, was quite adept at identifying cars (Sergent & Signoret, 1992b).

A next step in the processing of a face indicated in Fig. 5.1 consists of extracting the invariant physiognomic attributes that uniquely describe that face. This does not involve the recognition of the face as such, only the ability, for instance, to determine whether two different views of the same face are of the same individual or of two different individuals. For example, the patients were tested on a series of matching tasks, in which faces taken from different viewpoints, or at different ages, were presented, and the patients had to put together the faces of the same individuals. Such tasks cannot be performed by simply comparing the visual information contained in the faces. It requires perceptual operations by which the facial features that are unique to a face are extracted. The results are shown in Table 5.1 (as Physiognomic Invariant) and indicate that two patients, R.M. and P.M., performed at chance, whereas patients P.C. and P.V. achieved above-chance matching. Although R.H.'s deficit lies at the structural encoding level, P.M.'s deficit reflects an inability to derive the configuration that is unique to a face. A next step shown in Fig. 5.1 consists in determining whether a face is familiar or not, which requires that some contact be made between the perceived face and the representation of that face in memory. This is the level at which all prosopagnosics are defective, and the other two patients, P.C. and P.V., performed at chance when deciding whether a face was familiar or not. As the diversity in the patterns of deficits displayed by these four patients suggests, the prosopagnosic disturbance may result from a breakdown at different levels of processing, and the deficits associated with this disturbance vary among patients.

Face Processing Examined by Positron Emission Tomography

These different patterns of disruption across patients reflect different underlying breakdowns, and suggest that the different stages that compose the face recognition system may be selectively disabled and must therefore be represented in different locations in the cerebral structures. There are, however, several difficulties in inferring the actual anatomical locus of the various stages that compose face recognition from the performance of prosopagnosic patients, because their lesions generally invade large cerebral territories and may even affect, functionally, adjacent cortical regions that are structurally intact.

Recent advances in brain-imaging techniques for measuring blood flow within cerebral structures have made possible the visualization of the neuronal substrates of cognitive abilities in normal subjects (Fox, Mintun, Reiman, & Raichle, 1988; Mintun, Fox, & Raichle, 1989). Such techniques provide the opportunity to infer the neuroanatomy of a given function without interference from the dynamic effects of a cortical lesion on the functioning of the whole brain. The subject is injected with a radioactive material that binds to a physiologically active compound. This serves as a blood-flow tracer by detecting, through a tomograph, the gamma rays that are emitted following the decay of positrons.

Much progress has been achieved in the study of cognition by the use of ^{15}O, whose half life is very short and thus allows one to obtain repeated measures on the same subject (Raichle, Martin, Herscovitch, Mintun, & Marklam, 1983). Posner and his colleagues (e.g., Posner, Petersen, Fox, & Raichle, 1988; Petersen et al., 1989) have developed a technique using several complementary tasks that differ from one another in one or a few cognitive operations, thereby "isolating" the cerebral areas specifically activated by these operations.

This basic procedure was used to examine the neural substrates of face and object processing in normal subjects with the ^{15}O water-bolus technique. In addition, a magnetic resonance (MRI) scan of each subject's brain was obtained, so that we could perform a mapping of the physiological activation measured in the PET study on the actual cerebral structures of the subjects, following the method developed by Evans and his colleagues (Evans, Marrett, Collins, & Peters, 1989).

Six tasks were run consecutively, in a different order for each subject, with three control and three experimental tasks (Sergent, Ohta, & MacDonald, 1992). The control tasks consisted of passive fixation of the lit screen, a passive viewing of unfamiliar faces, and a two-choice reaction-time task requiring the subjects to discriminate sine wave gratings of varying spatial frequencies as a function of their vertical or horizontal orientation. The experimental tasks were an object categorization task, using common objects, either living or nonliving; a gender categorization task, in which the subjects had to decide whether each face was that of a man or a woman, using faces that could not be easily categorized based solely on hair; and a face identity task requiring the occupational categorization of famous faces, a task that requires recognition of the face. The subjects responded with the right index or middle finger by pressing one of two buttons of the computer mouse which lay on their abdomen. The three experimental tasks, as well as the grating discrimination task, were exactly the same for normal subjects, in terms of procedure, monitor apparatus, and stimuli, as those carried out on the prosopagnosic patients, such that the neural substrates of the operations involved in these tasks can be compared in normal and neurological subjects. The main foci of activation in the normal subjects' brains are shown in Fig. 5.2; the radiological data of the patients are presented in Fig. 5.3.

In the experimental tasks and the gratings task, there was strong activation of the sensorimotor area of the left hemisphere, corresponding to the representation of the right hand, which was used to make the two-choice response. This is illustrated for the grating condition (b in Fig. 5.2). In the figure, the foci of activation obtained from the PET study are superimposed on the MRI of the subjects' brain, in the latero-dorsal region of the left frontal and parietal lobes. Although the passive viewing of faces was intended as a control task, it did not result in significantly different activation from that of the grating condition. Compared to the passive fixation condition, both the passive face viewing and the grating discrimination tasks produced significant activation of areas 17 and 18 in the occipital cortex and resulted in greater involvement of the lingual gyrus in the right hemisphere than in the left (Fig. 5.2, Gratings a). Comparing the passive fixation and the gender categorization task, cerebral activation was significantly observed in the ventro-medial region of the right hemisphere and involved the lingual gyrus and the posterior part of the fusiform gyrus. In this and the following PET images, the sequence of slices from top-left to bottom-right corresponds to moving from ventral cerebral regions toward dorsal regions. As can be seen for the gender categorization task (Fig. 5.2, Face Gender), there was bilateral activation at the level of the striate cortex, but much of the processing underlying this task took place within the lingual gyrus of the right hemisphere, with no corresponding activation of the left hemisphere beyond area 18.

We now compare this pattern of activation in normal subjects performing the gender categorization with the radiological data from the two prosopagnosic patients, P.M. and R.M., whose disturbance included the categorization of faces into male and female (see Table 5.1). In the case of P.M. (Fig. 5.3), the entire right occipital cortex and posterior ventral temporal cortex were ablated in 1972, and she has been prosopagnosic since then. Her lesion affects the cerebral structures that were activated during the PET study in the normal subjects. Similarly, in the case of R.M., whose impairment encompasses all operations on faces, the lesion also affects the ventro-medial area of the right occipital and posterior temporal cortex at the level of the fusiform gyrus, but it extends

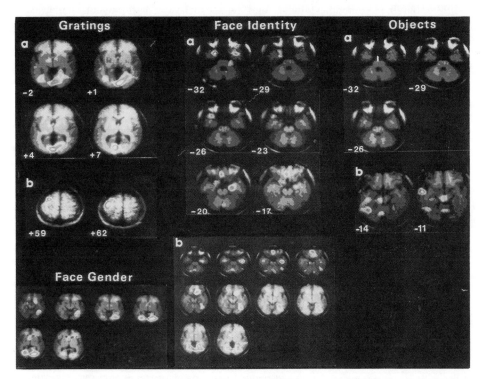

FIG. 5.2. Foci of activation, derived by subtraction of PET measures of CBF, superimposed on magnetic resonance images of the subjects' brains, in the grating, gender, face identity, and object categorization tasks.

somewhat more anteriorly than the damage of P.M. (Fig. 5.2). In both patients, the lesion invades those areas activated in normal subjects during the gender-categorization task. By contrast, the MRI of P.C., one of the two patients who were able to (a) tell men from women, (b) perform the extraction of physiognomic invariants, and (c) match different views of the same face indicates a more anterior lesion in the white matter surrounding the fusiform gyrus without affecting the cortex of this gyrus. Patient P.C., although impaired, performed above chance at tasks that required him to extract physiognomic invariants. This suggests that his functional deficit reflects an inability to activate the semantic information of the faces from their percept. Therefore, the processes underlying the reactivation of pertinent memories must take place in cerebral areas anterior to the fusiform gyrus.

This was confirmed in the PET study when we looked at the pattern of activation associated with the face identification task. As shown in Fig. 5.2 (Face Identity b), the same pattern of activation found in the gender discrimination task is apparent in the posterior region of the right hemisphere during the face identity task. However, there is now activation located more anteriorly, specifically in the right parahippocampal gyrus; no such activation can be detected on the left side. There are two additional findings worth noting with respect to the activation associated with the face identity task. One concerns the activation of the orbital region of the frontal cortex. This activation was also present during the object recognition task and may, therefore, not be specific to the processing of faces as such, but the actual operations served by this region in the processing of faces cannot be identified at this point. The other finding is the activation of the left fusiform gyrus, which was not involved in the face gender categorization task and which must, therefore, participate in the processing of face identity. However, this area was also activated during the object recognition task, which again suggests that its participation may not be specific to the processing of faces and may reflect the more general visual analysis of complex objects.

The top image of the face identity condition (Fig. 5.2) presents the results of the subtraction of the gender categorization from the face identity task. It suggests several foci of activation specifically associated with the processing of face identity. Clearly apparent here is the activation of the right parahippocampal gyrus, as already mentioned, but there is also activation in the most anterior parts of the temporal lobes of both hemispheres. As a comparison, the computerized tomography (CT) scan of patient P.V. (Fig. 5.3), whose deficit involved only the recognition of familiar faces but did not markedly affect any other aspect of face processing, indicates a lesion that had destroyed the anterior half of her right temporal lobe, as well as the pole of the left temporal lobe, as a result of encephalitis. This pattern of brain damage concurs with the pattern of activation observed in the normal subjects during the face identity task. The type of prosopagnosia that characterizes patient P.V.'s disturbance is therefore different from the essentially perceptual impairment discussed earlier with respect to R.M. and P.M., and suggests an inability to evoke the pertinent stored information about an individual without which a face cannot become meaningful and be identified (cf.

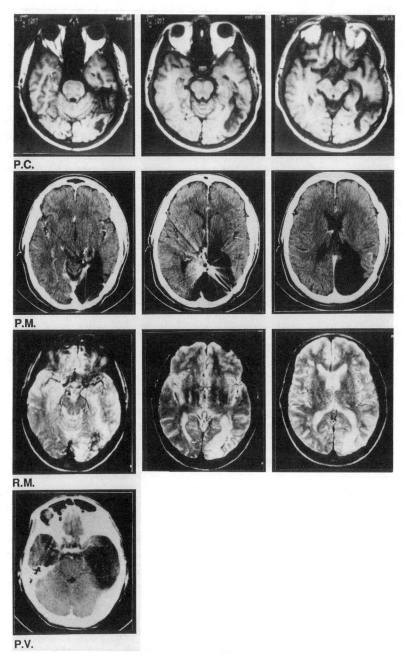

FIG. 5.3. Radiological data of four prosopagnosic patients.

Ellis, Young, & Critchley, 1989). In contrast, the object categorization task resulted in no activation of the anterior temporal cortex when compared to the grating discrimination condition (see Fig. 5.2). In fact, this task did not result in any significant activation of the cerebral structures in the right hemisphere that were specifically involved in the processing of faces. At a functional level, this means that one does not need to access specific information related to the particular instance of an object to recognize it, consistent with the different processing requirements made by the recognition of faces and objects. Instead, the categorization of objects resulted in significant activation of the lateral occipito-temporal cortex and the fusiform gyrus of the left hemisphere, as well as in the activation of the left temporal area 21 in the middle temporal gyrus. The activation of the posterior left hemisphere is consistent with the evidence suggesting that this area plays a crucial role in the processing of the semantics of visual objects; its disruption results in visual agnosia of the associative type (A. Damasio, H. Damasio, Tranel, & Brandt, 1991; Kertesz, 1979; McCarthy & Warrington, 1990). Thus, not only do the recognition of faces and the recognition of objects make different processing demands, but their respective representations are not inscribed in the same areas of the brain.

The present findings may help us to understand the anatomical and functional architecture underlying the processing of faces and its dissociation from the processing of objects. The recognition of faces requires the involvement of the ventral areas of the right hemisphere and, as shown by the PET and radiological data from the patients, the right hemisphere appears to be both necessary and sufficient to sustain face recognition. Three cortical areas seem to be essential to this function, and they subserve specific operations. The right lingual and fusiform gyri perform the perceptual operations by which the physiognomic invariants are extracted and the uniqueness of the face is accessed. The right parahippocampal gyrus, but not the hippocampus itself, seems to play a crucial role in the reactivation of stored facial information by the afferent stimulus. The anterior temporal lobes of both hemispheres seem to contain the biographical information which must be reactivated for a given face to become meaningful and thus be identified. None of these areas was specifically activated in the object recognition task, which relied, instead, on structures in the posterior left hemisphere. This is consistent with the frequently observed dissociation between visual agnosia and prosopagnosia. In fact, these two deficits are associated only in patients with bilateral damage. When the lesion responsible for prosopagnosia is restricted to the right hemisphere or does not involve the posterior left hemisphere, as in the four patients presented here, there is no deficit in object recognition.

Lateral Tachistoscopic Study of Face Processing

The finding of an almost exclusive involvement of the right hemisphere in face identification, except for the activation of the left temporal pole, contradicts the results of a similar tachistoscopic experiment I conducted on normal subjects (Sergent, 1984), in which a significant right visual field advantage had prevailed. I have since collected additional data to clarify this issue. In this experiment, all the subjects who participated in the PET study were also tested in a tachistoscopic experiment, using exactly the same procedure and equipment. The only difference was that in the tachistoscopic study, the stimuli were presented laterally, and were half the size used in the PET study. To compensate for this factor, subjects saw the stimuli at half the distance they saw them during the PET study, so that, in terms of retinal size, the stimuli subtended the same visual angle. In addition, the stimuli were also presented for 1 second, as in the PET study, and eye fixation was monitored in such a way that stimulus presentation occurred only when the subjects were fixating properly. (Any deviation of more than 0.5 degree of visual angle from fixation during the 1-second exposure would interrupt presentation, and the trial would be discarded.) In spite of the similarity of the procedures in the two studies, the results of the divided visual field experiment failed to confirm the dominant involvement of the right hemisphere in the face identification task (see Table 5.2), whereas the other tasks (i.e., the grating discrimination and the face gender categorization) produced patterns of visual field asymmetry consistent with the results of the PET study. The object categorization task did yield a pattern of visual field asymmetry consistent with the results of the PET study, a predominant involvement of the left hemisphere, but the visual field difference was not significant.

This is rather puzzling and embarrassing, because the PET study had clearly shown that, in these subjects, the face identification task engaged essentially right-hemisphere structures, and the involvement of the left hemisphere was limited to the left fusiform gyrus, which was also involved in the processing of objects and the most anterior part of the temporal cortex, most likely reflecting the evocation of the name associated with each face, which was not necessary in performing the task. That is, the inference of a left-hemisphere superiority in the identification of faces that could justifiably be made on the basis of the results of the tachistoscopic study does not correspond to what was actually going on in the brain of these subjects. This makes one wonder how reliable the findings of tachistoscopic studies are with respect to the contribution of the cerebral hemispheres to cognitive functions.

I must still explain why a right visual field advantage obtained in the face identification task. One factor could be the fact that subjects responded with their right hand. This was made necessary because, during the PET study, the intravenous injection of the radioactive solution was made in the left arm, so the right hand was used in both the PET and the tachistoscopic studies. This factor is unlikely to be the explanation, because in the face gender categorization a left visual field advantage prevailed even though the subjects also responded with their right hand. Another possible explanation would be that the last stage of processing was taking place in the left anterior temporal cortex, as suggested by the PET results, thereby accounting for the superiority of the left hemisphere in the task. This cannot explain the results either, however. If this were the case, it would imply that information initially projected to the left hemisphere would first have to

TABLE 5.2. Mean Reaction Time (RT, in msec), Percentage of Errors, and Standard Deviation (SD) in the Divided Visual-Field Study as a Function of Task and Visual Field. (LVF=left visual field, RVF=right visual field)

	Gratings		Gender		Face Identity		Objects	
	LVF	RVF	LVF	RVF	LVF	RVF	LVF	RVF
RT	740	740	722	757	941	922	774	764
% Errors	2.4	1.8	0.6	0.9	7.5	4.2	3.3	3.1
SD	124	118	109	127	131	129	101	105

TABLE 5.3. Mean Reaction Time (in msec) in the Face Identity and the Object Categorization Tasks, as a Function of Visual Field and Order of Presentation of the Stimuli.

	Face Identity			Objects	
Presentation	LVF	RVF		LVF	RVF
First	1037	1068		851	836
Second	845	776		697	692

be transferred to the right hemisphere (to the right parahippocampal gyrus) and then transferred back to the left anterior temporal cortex, whereas information projected to the right hemisphere would have direct access to the right parahippocampal gyrus and would, thus, not need the initial transfer.

A third explanation comes from a difference between the PET and the tachistoscopic studies. The 40 faces were presented twice, once in each visual field in the tachistoscopic study, but only once centrally in the PET study. I re-examined the data using only the first presentation of each face in each visual field, and the results, shown in Table 5.3, indicated a strong interaction of Order of presentation × Visual Field. That is, a right-hemisphere advantage obtained in the first presentation, consistent with the results of the PET study, but, after the subjects had seen the face once, a left-hemisphere advantage prevailed. This, at least, suggests that the left hemisphere is not incapable of processing faces, although it remains unclear how it does so.

Sergent and Signoret (1992b) conducted an experiment on prosopagnosic patients that may be revealing in this respect . We had them learn the associations between 12 faces and their respective names, and after a great many trials, each patient eventually succeeded in correctly naming each face. The day following criterion, we tested them on this task, and they performed almost perfectly, with responses of 11 or 12 correct. This suggests that they had been able to establish the proper connection between a face and its name. We then replaced the 12 pictures with a different version of each face, equally recognizable for a normal subject. None of the patients was able to name correctly these new faces, and their performance did not differ from chance. Given the right-hemisphere lesions of these patients, one may assume that the learning of the name-face association was accomplished by the left hemisphere, which could achieve some level of efficiency with a fair amount of training. However, the left hemisphere proved unable to extract from the new faces the configurations that uniquely described each one, suggesting that the left hemisphere does not have the capacity to process faces in a configurational manner and is not able, on its own, to identify faces. Obviously, this is in contrast with the conclusions that could be derived from findings of tachistoscopic experiments showing a right visual field advantage in face identification. In particular, it indicates that experiments that use only a few faces, presented repeatedly in the same format, may have little in common with the conditions under which one normally has to recognize faces. Finding a left-hemisphere superiority in such experiments may not prove that the left hemisphere can identify faces. Indeed, when prosopagnosic patients are tested in such conditions, they are able to learn to identify faces, but only if the faces are repeatedly presented in exactly the same format. Such learning does not extend to other views of the same faces and cannot, therefore, be considered   true identification.

IMPLICATIONS AND CONCLUSIONS

In the three preceding sections, data bearing on hemisphere specialization in face identification were reported from two populations with three different techniques. If one were to consider each pattern of results separately, different conclusions would be drawn from each. From the prosopagnosic patients, one would conclude that the right hemisphere alone is both necessary and sufficient to perform the identification of faces, because the lesion was restricted to the right hemisphere in three patients and involved only the pole of the left temporal lobe, in addition to the anterior right temporal lobe, in the fourth patient. It must be noted that the finding of a unilateral right-hemisphere lesion is not necessarily the rule in prosopagnosia (cf. Meadows, 1974; A. Damasio, 1985), but the fact that it occurs suggests that damage to the left hemisphere is not necessary to produce a prosopagnosic disturbance. From the PET study of normal subjects, one would also conclude that the right hemisphere is necessary to the identification of faces, because the involvement of the right parahippocampal gyrus was clearly detected only in the face categorization task. Yet, activation was found in the left fusiform gyrus and in the left anterior temporal cortex, suggesting that these areas also participate in the processing of faces. Nonetheless, because the left fusiform gyrus was also activated in the object categorization task, and because prosopagnosia and visual object agnosia are dissociable impairments, it could be argued that the involvement of the left fusiform gyrus was not indispensable to the identification of faces and reflected visual analysis of the facial stimuli considered as visual patterns only, and not as facial configurations as such. Note, however, that such a suggestion relies on findings from brain-damaged patients and could not be made on the basis of the PET results alone. Finally, from the divided visual field study of the normal subjects, taking the global pattern of results, one would conclude that the left hemisphere is more adept at identifying faces, because a right visual field superiority obtained. Only because this finding was in disagreement with the results of the PET study were the data split into two parts to uncover one possible source of discrepancy, but, in usual practice, such an examination would not have been performed.

All this seems to leave a rather ambivalent impression regarding our capacity to understand the cerebral lateralization of functions. The findings from prosopagnosic patients and from the PET study on normal subjects lead to conclusions that depart from what one would infer from the results of at least some tachistoscopic experiments. Although one would tend to rely more on the former two sources of information, they are not immune from difficulties of methodology and interpretation. For instance, inquiring about the location of the lesions responsible for prosopagnosia and asking what cortical structures normally underlie the processing of faces are two distinct questions, which may not necessarily have the same answer. In a dynamic system such as the brain, local damage may affect the functional integrity of adjacent and remote structures spared by the lesion. Moreover, if the right hemisphere performs operations that are essential for the initial operations on faces, damage to the posterior right hemisphere may prevent other structures, including those in the left hemisphere, from performing their normal functions. In this sense, findings from brain-damaged patients may indicate that a lesion in specific areas of the right hemisphere disables the face-recognition system, but they cannot tell us which areas normally participate in the identification of faces (Sergent, 1984). In addition, one sometimes sees patients with lesions invading the same territory as the lesions found in prosopagnosic patients, yet these patients have little difficulty recognizing faces.

The PET technique itself is replete with methodological problems that bear on data acquisition, analysis, localization of foci of activation, and interpretation (Evans, Beil, Marrett, Thompson, & Hakim, 1988; Fox, Perlmutter, & Raichle, 1985; Raichle, 1990). On a purely cognitive level, the subtraction method in which one compares the activation associated with two tasks differing by a component operation produces results that must be interpreted with considerable caution (Sergent, Zuck, Lévesque, & MacDonald, 1992). First, the finding of well-localized foci of activation may suggest that only these "highlighted" areas are involved in the realization of a given operation, and this could promote a modern type of phrenology that would emphasize the "modularity" of the brain. However, several aspects of the procedure must be taken into account before jumping to such conclusions. By subtracting a control condition from an experimental condition, one eliminates areas of activation that were elicited by the experimental task, which may then give a partial or biased view of the actual involvement of cerebral structures in the task in question. Consider, for instance, the object categorization task. The results of the PET study indicated involvement of the left occipito-temporal area in its realization, which is consistent with findings from brain-damaged patients (e.g., McCarthy & Warrington, 1990), but the results of the divided visual field study showed no hemisphere difference in this task, even if there was a trend toward a left-hemisphere advantage. However, the results of the PET study were obtained by subtracting the grating condition from the object condition, and, in doing so, concealed right-hemisphere activation that was present in the grating task. It would, thus, be misleading to conclude, from the results of the PET study on object categorization, that the right hemisphere was not involved, and, in fact, there was activation of the posterior right hemisphere for the initial perceptual operations preceding the semantic categorization. The absence of a visual field difference in the divided visual field study is therefore not in contradiction with the PET results, because the initial operations may have been performed faster in the right hemisphere than in the left, whereas the semantic categorization proper may have called for specialized areas of the posterior left hemisphere. What this apparent contradiction suggests, therefore, is that the pattern of PET activation derived by subtraction reflects the performance of one component operation of a given task, whereas the pattern of results obtained in lateral tachistoscopic studies (or other behavioral experiments) reflect the whole performance of the task, encompassing each component operation, some of which may not be specific to the main processing demand of the task (such as semantic categorization in the present task).

Second, the PET technique is a very "noisy" procedure, and the actual count of relevant emitted positrons is less than one tenth the total number of emitted positrons. It is only through group averaging that one can obtain sufficient data, and stringent statistical criteria must be used to ensure the validity of the findings. However, changes in CBF are observed in many more areas than those reaching a statistically reliable difference, and all the areas where CBF changes are judged insignificant are considered as not participating in the realization of the task. Whether these changes are truly insignificant cannot be known, but one can think of several reasons why true participation of such areas would fail to be reliably detected. For instance, perhaps not all areas of the brain have the same level of metabolism when they are activated; or some structures (such as the hippocampus) may be organized in such a way that their activation is spread over a larger extent than other structures that are more focally organized; or a given structure may be involved in some subjects but not in others depending on the strategy they develop in performing the task; or some areas initially involved in the performance of a task may be bypassed with repetition of the same operation.

Third, the subtraction method assumes a purely serial and unidirectional processing of information, which has been disputed on both theoretical and empirical grounds. In addition, it assumes that, when subjects are requested to perform a given task, they execute only the operations that are strictly relevant and use only the information pertinent to the task. This assumption is likely to be invalid: The Stroop test provides a clear illustration that subjects are unable to refrain from processing additional aspects of a stimulus even when they are instructed not to. As a result, a "control" task may comprise more operations than the experimenter assumes because subjects may engage in automatic processing of various aspects of a stimulus depending on their training and expertise (see Sergent, Zuck, Levesque, & MacDonald, 1992, for illustration and discussion). As a result, the control task may activate, to a certain extent, some cerebral areas that are not directly relevant to its performance, which, in turn, may raise the threshold for activation difference of these areas between the control and the experimental tasks and prevent actual involvement of these areas in the experimental task from showing a statistically reliable CBF change.

Fourth, PET data are essentially static and cumulative and do not allow direct inference about the dynamic and interactive properties of cerebral processing (cf. Felleman & Van Essen, 1991). For instance, with respect to the involvement of the left fusiform gyrus in the face identification task discussed earlier, it cannot be determined whether its activation reflects prior processing by the right hemisphere (which findings from the prosopagnosic patients would suggest) or direct access (which findings from the divided visual field study would suggest). In addition, what is considered in computational models as a single operation may require the involvement of several cerebral structures and, perhaps, the conjoint inhibition or deactivation of other structures. At present, there is no rationale or method capable of clarifying this problem, and one may be tempted to attribute to each focus of activation a specific function without actually being able to specify how the different foci relate to one another. One generally assumes that each component operation of a given task has a single corresponding cerebral structure that performs it, and therefore attributes to the activated area the function implied by this operation. Such a strategy, however, is open to misinterpretation.

Suppose, for instance, that one examines the phonological processing of words in a rhyming task. The subjects may very well engage in vocalization of the words to determine what they sound like, which results in activation of Broca's area. This does not mean, however, that Broca's area is the "site" of the phonological decision, and its involvement would be marginal compared to the actual processing demands of the task (see Sergent et al., 1992).

All of these considerations seem to cast a rather gloomy outlook on the possibility of ever achieving a comprehensive understanding of the functional organization of the brain and of the communication and cooperation of the two hemispheres in the realization of mental functions. The addition of new techniques does not eliminate the methodological difficulties associated with inferring the neurobiological substrates of cognitive functions; instead, it raises further questions and problems. By understanding better the various parameters inherent in these techniques and identifying their strengths and weaknesses, we will be able to get deeper, and with less risk of error, into the highly complex and interactive cerebral structures that sustain human mental processes.

ACKNOWLEDGMENTS

The work reported in this chapter is supported by the E.J.L.B. Foundation, the National Institute of Mental Health, the Medical Research Council of Canada, and the Natural Sciences and Engineering Research Council of Canada.

REFERENCES

Benton, A.L., Hamsher, K., Varney, N.R., & Spreen, O. (1983). *Contributions to neuropsychological assessments.* New York: Oxford University Press.

Broca, P. (1861). Perte de la parole, ramollissement chronique et destruction partielle du lobe antérieur gauche du cerveau [Loss of speech, chronic softening and partial destruction of the anterior lobe of the brain]. *Bulletin de la Société d'Anthropologie, 2,* 235-237.

Bruce, V., & Young, A.W. (1986). Understanding face recognition. *British Journal of Psychology, 77,* 305-327.

Damasio, A. (1985). Prosopagnosia. *Trends in Neuroscience, 8,* 132-135.

Damasio, A., Damasio, H., Tranel, D., & Brandt, J.P. (1991). The neural regionalization of neural access: Preliminary evidence. *Cold Harbor Spring Symposium of Quantitative Biology, 55,* 1039-1047.

De Renzi, E. & Spinnler, H. (1966). Facial recognition in brain damaged patients: An experimental approach. *Neurology, 16,* 145-152.

Ellis, A.W., Young, A.W., & Critchley, E.M.R. (1989). Loss of memory for people following temporal damage. *Brain, 112,* 1469-1484.

Evans, A.C., Beil, C., Marrett, S., Thompson, C.J., & Hakim A. (1988). Anatomical-functional correlation using an adjustable MRI-based region of interest atlas with positron emission tomography. *Journal of Cerebral Blood Flow and Metabolism, 8,* 513-530.

Evans, A.C., Marrett, S., Collins, L., & Peters, T.M. (1989). Anatomical-functional correlative analysis of the human brain using three-dimensional imaging systems. *Proceedings of the Society of Photographic and Optical Instrumentation and Engineering, 1092,* 264-274.

Felleman D.J., & Van Essen, D.C. (1991). Distributed hierarchical processing in the primate cerebral cortex. *Cerebral Cortex, 1,* 1-47.

Fox, P.T., Mintun, M.A., Reiman, E.M., & Raichle, M.E. (1988). Enhanced detection of focal brain responses using intersubject averaging and change-distribution analysis of subtracted PET images. *Journal of Cerebral Blood Flow and Metabolism, 8,* 642-653.

Fox, P.T., Perlmutter, J.S., & Raichle, M.E. (1985). A stereotactic method of anatomical localization for positron emission tomography. *Journal of Computer Assisted Tomography, 9,* 141-153.

Hamsher, K., Levin, H., & Benton, A. (1979). Facial recognition in patients with focal brain lesions. *Archives of Neurology, 36,* 837-839.

Hécaen, H. (1972). *Introduction à la neuropsychologie* [Introduction to neuropsychology]. Paris: Masson.

Kertesz, A. (1979). Visual agnosia: The dual deficit of perception and recognition. *Cortex, 15,* 403-419.

Levy, J., Trevarthen, C., & Sperry, R.W. (1972). Perception of bilateral chimeric figures following hemisphere deconnexion. *Brain, 95.* 61-78.

Marr D. (1982). *Vision.* San Francisco: W.H. Freeman.

Marzi, C., & Berlucchi, G. (1977). Right visual field superiority for accuracy of recognition of famous faces in normals. *Neuropsychologia, 15,* 751-756.

McCarthy, R.A. & Warrington, E.K. (1990). *Cognitive neuropsychology. A clinical introduction.* London: Academic Press.

Meadows, J.C. (1974). The anatomical basis of prosopagnosia. *Journal of Neurology, Neurosurgery, and Neuropsychiatry, 37,* 489-501.

Mintun, M., Fox, P.T., & Raichle, M.E. (1989). A highly accurate method of localizing neuronal activity in the human brain with positron emission tomography. *Journal Cerebral Blood Flow and Metabolism, 9,* 96-103.

Patterson, K.E., & Bradshaw, J.L. (1975). Differential hemispheric mediation of non-verbal visual stimuli. *Journal of Experimental Psychology: Human Perception and Performance, 1,* 246-252.

Petersen, S.E., Fox, P.T., Posner, M.I., Mintun, M., & Raichle, M.E. (1989). Positron emission tomographic studies of the processing of single words. *Journal of Cognitive Neuroscience, 1,* 153-170.

Posner, M.I., Petersen, S.E., Fox P.T., & Raichle M.E. (1988). Localization of cognitive operations in the human brain. *Science, 240,* 1627-1631.

Quagliano, A., & Borelli, G.B. (1867). Emiplegia sinistra con amaurosi, guaragione, perdita totale della percezione dei colori e della memoria delle configurazione degli oggletti. [Left hemiplegia with blindness, aphasia, complete loss of color perception and of memories of facial configurations]. *Giornale d'Oftalmologia Italiano, 10,* 106-117.

Raichle, M.E. (1990). Images of the functioning human brain. In H. Barlow, C. Blakemore, & M. Weston-Smith (Eds.) *Images and Understanding* (pp. 284-296). Cambridge, England: Cambridge University Press.

Raichle, M.E., Martin, W.R.W., Herscovitch , P., Mintun, M.A., & Markham, J. (1983). Brain blood flow measured with intravenous H_2O. II. Implementation and validation. *Journal of Nuclear Medicine, 24,* 790-798.

Rizzolatti, G., Umiltà, C., Berlucchi, G. (1970). Demostrazione di differenze funzionali fra gli emisferi cerebrali dell'uomo normale per mezzo della tecnica dei tempi di reazione [Demonstration of functional differences of normal human cerebral hemispheres with the method of reaction times]. *Archiva Fisiologica, 68,* 96-97.

Searle, J. (1984). *Minds, brains and science: The 1984 Reith Lectures.* London: British Broadcasting Corporation.

Sergent, J. (1984a). Inferences from unilateral brain damage about normal hemispheric functions in visual pattern recognition. *Psychological Bulletin, 96,* 99-115.

Sergent, J. (1984b). Configural processing of faces in the left and the right cerebral hemispheres. *Journal of Experimental Psychology: Human Perception and Performance, 10,* 554-572.

Sergent, J. (1989). Structural processing of faces. In A.W. Young and H.D. Ellis (Eds.), *Handbook of research on face processing* (pp. 57-91). Amsterdam: North-Holland, .

Sergent, J. (1990b). The neuropsychology of visual image generation: Data, method and theory. *Brain and Cognition, 13,* 98-129.

Sergent, J. (1990a). Furtive incursions into bicameral minds. *Brain, 113,* 537-579.

Sergent, J., & Signoret, J.L. (1992a). Functional and anatomical decomposition of face processing: Evidence from prosopagnosia and PET study of normal subjects. *Philosophical Transactions of the Royal Society, London,* Series B, *335,* 55-62.

Sergent, J., & Signoret, J.L. (1992b). Varieties of functional deficits in prosopagnosia. *Cerebral Cortex, 2,* 375-388.

Sergent, J., Ohta, S., & MacDonald, B. (1992). Functional neuroanatomy of face and object processing: A positron emission tomography study. *Brain, 115,* 15-29.

Sergent, J., Zuck, E., Lévesque, M., & MacDonald, B. (1992). A positron emission tomography study of letter and object processing: Empirical findings and methodological considerations. *Cerebral Cortex, 2,* 68-80.

Warrington, E.K. (in press). Associative visual agnosias. In D. Ottoson, P.E. Roland, & B. Gulyás, (Eds.), *The functional organization of the human visual cortex,* London: Macmillan Press.

Warrington, E.K., & James, M. (1967). An experimental investigation of facial recognition in patients with unilateral cerebral lesions. *Cortex, 3,* 317-326.

6   Parameters of the Bilateral Effect

David B. Boles
Rensselaer Polytechnic Institute

The term *bilateral effect* is used in two senses in the literature on hemispheric differences. One sense is the overall processing advantage sometimes observed when the same stimulus is presented simultaneously to both visual fields, as opposed to only one field (Hellige, 1991). However, another sense of the term refers to the increase in a field difference, or asymmetry, that is found when different stimuli are presented to the two fields, as compared to a single stimulus to one field or the other (Boles, 1979, 1983, 1987, 1990; Healey, Waldstein, & Goodglass, 1985; McKeever, 1971). It is the latter type of bilateral effect that is the focus of this chapter.

There are two major reasons why the bilateral effect is of importance in the study of hemispheric differences. First, the cause of the bilateral effect is itself of theoretical interest, because it is now known to reflect an interaction between the hemispheres in the processing of information. Second, on a purely empirical level, any method that increases the size of obtained asymmetries deserves attention as a means of increasing the power of experimental manipulations.

In this chapter, I first discuss the generality of the bilateral effect. Then I summarize research on 13 possible hypotheses of the effect, leading to one as the most likely explanation. An anatomical mechanism and locus is then suggested. Finally, the chapter closes with a treatment of several parameters of the bilateral effect. These include how displays have to be constructed to obtain the effect; the size of the effect, both in absolute terms and in comparison to other influences on visual field (VF) asymmetry; and the relative reliabilities of VF differences found with bilateral and unilateral displays.

GENERALITY OF THE BILATERAL EFFECT

Any discussion of the bilateral effect must begin with the visual modality, which has received considerably more attention than the auditory and tactile modalities. In one common type of visual bilateral display, two stimuli are shown, one to each side of a fixation point, with a central arrowhead pointing to the stimulus the subject is to recognize. Alternatively, the two items may be accompanied by a central stimulus such as a digit, and the subject is to recognize all three stimuli. In contrast, a unilateral display typically involves only a single stimulus presented at random to one field or the other.

Formal observations that bilateral visual displays produce larger field differences date back to the early 1970s, when Walter McKeever showed that the right visual field (RVF) advantage found in recognizing words was magnified if bilateral displays were used in place of the more traditional unilateral displays

(McKeever, 1971). This effect has since been found on numerous occasions (Boles, 1979, 1983, 1987, 1990; Healey et al., 1985).

At about the same time, there were qualitative reports, often no more than a sentence or two in published papers, asserting the existence of a similar phenomenon in other sensory modalities. Even as early as 1964, Kimura had suggested that bilateral displays increase asymmetry in the auditory modality. These, of course, are known as *dichotic* presentations, and they typically involve the presentation of a small number of pairs of disparate stimuli to the two ears, followed by free report.

In the tactile modality, Witelson (1974) suggested that bilateral stimulation of the two hands is necessary if lateral differences are to be reliable; these are known as *dichhaptic* presentations. A typical stimulation procedure is to present a single pair of stimuli simultaneously to the two hands, for a limited period of time, both of which the subject is to report.

Accordingly, although the empirical aspects of the bilateral effect are best understood in the visual modality, there is reason to think that the effect exists in other modalities. If so, it can fairly lay claim to being one of the fundamental phenomena of laterality research.

Other reasons for considering it a fundamental phenomenon is that the effect generalizes across stimulus types and dependent measures. Boles (1987) reported experiments illustrating the generality of the effect across stimulus types: in this case, words and bargraphs. Examples of individual stimuli are shown in Fig. 6.1. In word displays, two words were presented, each representing the word name of a number, and the subject responded to the one pointed to by a central arrowhead in a reaction time (RT) task. In bargraph displays, two bargraphs were presented, with each representing a number, accompanied by a central arrowhead, again in a RT task. The subject was told that the bottom reference line represented 0, the middle line 4, and the top line 8.

FIG. 6.1. Examples of bargraph and word stimuli used in Boles (1987).

TABLE 6.1 RTs (in msec) From Boles (1987).

| | Bargraphs | | Words | |
	Bilateral	Unilateral	Bilateral	Unilateral
LVF	832	692	736	567
RVF	876	696	717	567
Difference	-44	-4	+19	0

TABLE 6.2 Word Recognition Results (in Percentage Correct) From Boles (1983, Experiment 1).

	Bilateral	Unilateral
RVF	53.9	64.3
LVF	43.9	61.2
difference	+10.0	+3.1

TABLE 6.3 Hypotheses Regarding the Bilateral Effect

A. Noninteraction Hypotheses

    1. Directional reading
    2. Order of report
    3. Improved fixation control
    4. Increased task complexity (demand)
    5. Increased motivation
    6. Disruption of orienting
    7. Locus certainty

B. Hemispheric Interaction Hypotheses

    1. Disparity in arrival time
    2. Storage of ipsilateral stimulus
    3. Selective processing
    4. Mutual inhibition
    5. Neglect of ipsilateral side
    6. Homolog activation

These stimulus types were used in different experiments, both in the described bilateral format, and with corresponding unilateral displays mixed in. Unilateral displays consisted of only a single stimulus, presented at random to one field or the other, with no arrowhead. Regardless of the display type, subjects recognized the required number and responded on RT keys; for example, with the keys labeled as *odd* or *even*. The results were clear-cut and quite typical of this type of research (see Table 6.1). Bargraphs produced a strong left visual field (LVF) advantage, consistent with right-hemisphere spatial processing. However, they did so only when the displays were bilateral. Conversely, words showed a RVF advantage, consistent with left-hemisphere verbal processing, but again, they did so only when the displays were bilateral.

Both of these outcomes illustrate the bilateral effect, and indicate that it generalizes across stimulus types. It also generalizes across dependent measures. These examples were of RT asymmetries, but the early work on the phenomenon used accuracy (percent correct) measures. For example, Table 6.2 shows the results of an experiment I reported in 1983 (Boles, 1983, Experiment 1). In the study, horizontally oriented words, such as *bear* and *lane*, were presented either bilaterally, with a digit at the fixation point, or unilaterally, as a single word to one field. The subject was to recognize all stimuli shown, which, for bilateral trials, were two words and the central digit. Again, the bilateral effect was evident, with a significant RVF advantage found only for the bilateral displays.

Clearly, if a phenomenon generalizes across modalities, stimulus types, and dependent measures, it has a fair claim to being a fundamental one in its field. The next question to be addressed, then, is "What causes it?".

CAUSE OF THE BILATERAL EFFECT

In the early literature on the phenomenon, no fewer than 13 hypotheses were proposed or implied. To be sure, not all of these were mutually exclusive, but they were distinct in their emphases, and they constituted a large body of potential explanations requiring experimental investigation. As indicated in Table 6.3, there are two broad classes of hypotheses. The first, *noninteraction hypotheses*, essentially propose that the effect is an artifact of the way bilateral displays are processed by subjects. The second set are the *hemispheric interaction hypotheses*. These propose that the effect is due to some type of interaction between the hemispheres, either inhibitory or facilitatory in nature, depending on the hypothesis. From a theoretical standpoint, these are the more interesting ones, and they represent the tie to the theme of this volume, on interhemispheric transfer, integration, and cooperation.

Certain of the noninteraction hypotheses can be discarded quickly on the basis of information already described. First, the bilateral effect is not due to a directional reading artifact. This suggestion was made by Hines (1972), and stated that following fixation on a central point, a reading scan might proceed to the right given a bilateral display, producing better recognition of the RVF stimulus. Presumably, the scan would not take place for a unilateral stimulus, resulting in a null field effect. The hypothesis was plausible at the time, given that relevant experiments to that point had exclusively used word stimuli; however, the directional reading hypothesis clearly cannot be correct in light of what we know today, that bilateral displays of bargraphs magnify a LVF advantage.

Another possibility that can be discarded quickly is that the effect is an order of report artifact (Mackavey, Curcio, & Rosen, 1975). Such an explanation can only apply if both stimuli in a bilateral display are recalled. In that case, it could be that a consistent tendency to report from one field first could produce something that looks very much like the bilateral effect. However, as we have seen, the bilateral effect is also obtained in partial report, where only one stimulus must be recognized, the one pointed to by a central arrowhead.

A third possibility, also discredited, is that control over eye fixation is better when bilateral displays are used, and that better fixation control simply allows asymmetries to be found (McKeever, Suberi, & VanDeventer, 1972). The idea here is that if the subject's eyes are wandering all over the display, which the hypothesis implies is the case for unilateral displays, then any measure of asymmetry will be invalid, and field effects will tend to be reduced or nonexistent. Bilateral displays presumably produce better eye fixation, and consequently larger field effects. However, the bilateral effect is typically found when unilateral and bilateral trials are mixed randomly within a block of trials, as in the example of the word and bargraph experiments already noted. In such cases the subject has no way of knowing what type of trial is coming up, and control over eye fixation should be identical for the two types of trials. Nevertheless, the bilateral effect is found, eliminating this hypothesis from consideration.

Another possibility is that the effect is somehow an artifact of the sheer number of stimuli presented in a display. Perhaps, if you increase the load, you increase the field asymmetry. Three of the hypotheses of the bilateral effect propose some variation on this theme. One states directly that it is due to increased demand on lateralized processors (Witelson, 1974). Another states that it is due to the increased motivation of subjects confronted by multiple-stimulus displays (Olson, 1973). And, the third suggests that the presentation of multiple stimuli disrupts attentional orienting to any one of them, producing the effect in some unknown way (Boles, 1979).

All of these hypotheses, however, were ruled out by experiments that equated the number of stimuli shown in the bilateral and unilateral displays. Experiment 3 from Boles (1983) serves as an illustration. Only a single word was shown, but the position of the accompanying digit was varied: it was either at the fixation point (central presentation), or in the same field as the word (peripheral presentation). When presented centrally, the display was a type of bilateral display, because portions of the digit overlapped the visual midline. In other words, both fields were stimulated, to at least a minimal degree. When the digit was placed in the same field as the word, however, the display was strictly unilateral. When this experiment was performed, a RVF advantage was found only for the center digit condition (Table 6.4). Of particular note is that overall

TABLE 6.4 Word Recognition Results (in Percentage Correct) from Boles
(1983, Experiment 3)

	Center Digit	Side Digit
RVF	37.5	31.1
LVF	28.9	29.5
difference	+8.6	+1.6

accuracy was almost identical in the center- and side-digit conditions, tending, if anything, to be slightly greater with central digits. The result indicates that the bilateral effect cannot somehow be attributed to an increased level of difficulty with bilateral displays.

Experiments like these (see also Boles, 1979) indicate that the bilateral effect is found even when the number of stimuli (and level of difficulty) is equated across the bilateral and unilateral conditions. As such, the results go against hypotheses that link the effect to the number of stimuli or to difficulty levels, as in the increased demand, increased motivation, and disrupted orienting accounts of the effect.

The last type of experiment is critically important to understanding the cause of the bilateral effect, because it demonstrates two other things. The somewhat less important conclusion is that the bilateral effect cannot be attributed to locational certainty as to where stimuli will be presented. That is, the words can be in either field or both fields, but as long as the display is made a bilateral one (with at least a digit overlapping the midline), the effect is still obtained. This argues against yet another hypothesis, suggested by Heron (1957), that locational certainty influences the direction and strength of VF asymmetry. The second point is the more important one, however. This is that it appears to be specifically the bilateral nature of the display that produces the result that is termed the *bilateral effect*. Again, the positioning of the digit in this type of experiment was critical, with asymmetry found when the digit overlapped the midline and stimulated both hemispheres. In some way, large field differences appear to emerge when the two hemispheres are simultaneously stimulated.

The outcome therefore serves as support for a class of hypotheses that can be called *hemispheric interaction hypotheses* (see Table 6.3). Hemispheric interaction hypotheses are exactly what they sound like: they propose that there is some type of interaction, either inhibitory or facilitatory, of one hemisphere on the other when both are stimulated. The specific mechanisms that are proposed vary. Two were effectively eliminated by studies that appeared in the literature long ago. One states that it is a disparity in arrival time of the two stimuli at a lateralized processor that is responsible for the effect. For example, given a bilateral display of words, the RVF word would presumably arrive at left-hemisphere verbal processors before a LVF word, due to the time taken by interhemispheric transfer. The hypothesis proposes that prior entry goes hand in hand with higher accuracy, producing the pronounced RVF advantage in word recognition. However, the hypothesis was tested by McKeever (1971) , who reported that a 20-msec head start for the LVF stimulus was not sufficient to eliminate the large RVF advantage in word recognition found with bilateral displays. It was further reported that in pilot data, a 40-msec head start was not enough (McKeever & Huling, 1971). Certainly, the latter figure is greater than most estimates of interhemispheric transfer time (Bashore, 1981), and so should have been enough to allow prior entry of the LVF stimulus.

A second hemispheric interaction hypothesis is that large VF differences emerge with bilateral displays because the stimulus projected to the hemisphere less capable of processing it is held in temporary storage pending processing of the other stimulus (Springer, 1971). This memory fades and produces the effect. However, this explanation clearly cannot account for bilateral effects found with partial report techniques, requiring the recognition of only one of the two stimuli, and thus is not tenable.

The remaining four hemispheric interaction hypotheses were all tested in experiments reported in Boles (1990). The selective processing hypothesis proposes that information is degraded as it is transferred between hemispheres, and lateralized processors selectively respond to the least degraded stimulus (McKeever & Huling, 1971). It was tested by experimentally degrading word stimuli. If the hypothesis was correct, then an intact LVF word paired with a sufficiently degraded RVF word, should result in the lateralized word processor responding to the intact LVF word. The result should be an elimination of the large RVF advantage found for word recognition. In the reported experiment, words were degraded by randomly deleting an average of 27% of the VDT pixels that comprised their outlines (Boles, 1990, Experiment 1).

The results are reproduced in Fig. 6.2. The comparison of interest is that between the two bottom points, to the right. These correspond to displays in which the word to be responded to was intact, but was paired with a degraded word. Under the hypothesis, the VF difference should be eliminated: that is, an

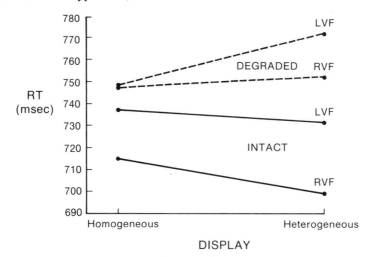

FIG. 6.2. RT results from Boles (1990, Experiment 1). The bilateral stimuli were intact or degraded words, in homogeneous (two intact or two degraded) or heterogeneous (one intact and one degraded) displays.

intact LVF word should be processed in preference to a degraded RVF word, much the same as an intact RVF word should be processed in preference to a degraded LVF word. Yet, if anything, this comparison produced the largest VF difference in the experiment. Notice, also, that there is a large main effect of degradation, so the manipulation seems to have been effective in testing the hypothesis.

Two other hemispheric interaction hypotheses are similar in their proposed mechanisms and can be discussed together. According to the mutual inhibition hypothesis (Boles, 1979, with partial derivation from Mackavey et al., 1975), a stimulus presented directly to a hemisphere activates that hemisphere proportional to the hemisphere's ability to process the stimulus. The activation is also proposed to inhibit the opposite hemisphere. For example, suppose two bargraphs are presented. Activation will be greater in the "spatial" right hemisphere, according to the hypothesis. Mutual inhibition, therefore, will produce a greater effect in the left hemisphere. The result is a relative activation of the right hemisphere, and a relative inhibition of the left hemisphere.

The similar hypothesis states that there is neglect of the ipsilateral side following bilateral stimulation (Heilman & Watson, 1977; Mackavey et al., 1975). According to this explanation, bilateral stimuli cause competition for a common orienting system, which is resolved in favor of the hemisphere that is more capable of processing its stimulus. Two bargraphs would presumably result in orientation toward the right hemisphere stimulus: that is, the LVF bargraph. Input to the left hemisphere would be neglected.

These two hypotheses make a common prediction. If a bilateral display of bargraphs is presented, there should be better processing of LVF stimuli due either to relative activation of the right hemisphere and relative inhibition of the left hemisphere or to orienting toward the LVF and neglecting the RVF. A probe stimulus that is then presented to one VF or the other should show the effects of this activation-inhibition, or orientation-neglect, mechanism.

The hypotheses were tested by presenting a light patch probe to one field or the other at a short delay following a bargraph display (Boles, 1990, Experiment 4). On two thirds of the trials, only bargraphs were presented, half bilateral and half unilateral displays. On one third of the trials, similar bargraph displays were used, but they were also accompanied by a lateralized light patch probe. Subjects were to respond to a bargraph unless a probe appeared, in which case they withheld the bargraph response and hit a single RT key to the probe. Stimulus onset asynchronies (SOA) of 0, 183, and 350 msec were used for the delay between the bargraph display and the probe. The prediction is that at some brief delay after the presentation of the bargraphs, responses to LVF probes should be speeded, while responses to RVF probes should be slowed.

The results were straightforward: In no condition was there a VF difference in RT to the probes. The bilateral effect for the bargraphs was found, however, with bilateral displays producing a significant LVF asymmetry of 35 msec, and unilateral displays producing a nonsignificant LVF asymmetry of only 5 msec. These results are very difficult to reconcile with any proposed mechanism of the bilateral effect that proposes an influence over a whole hemisphere or VF, such as those suggested by the mutual inhibition and neglect hypotheses.

Finally, we arrive at the last hemispheric interaction hypothesis, and the only one that, to date, appears to have any support. This is the homolog activation hypothesis (Witelson, 1974). It states that different stimuli presented simultaneously to the two hemispheres may activate homologous areas and disrupt the transfer of information between hemispheres. Presumably, the greater the similarity of the processes required by the stimuli, the greater the chance of homolog activation and the greater the chance of a large VF difference. The hypothesis was tested in a lexical decision experiment, using word and nonword stimuli (Boles, 1990, Experiment 3). In previous research, the word stimuli in lexical decision studies have produced RVF advantages in RT or errors, whereas the nonword stimuli have produced no field effect (Chiarello, Senehi, & Soulier, 1986; Hardyck, Chiarello, Dronkers, & Simpson, 1985; Leiber, 1976; St. Denis, 1987). The interaction between stimulus type and VF suggests that the two types do require somewhat different processes. If so, there is a fairly straightforward prediction about the field effects to be found for different pairings of the stimulus types in bilateral displays. Bilateral words should produce homolog activation and result in a significant RVF advantage, but all other conditions should result in a reduced or nonexistent field difference. That is, a word paired with a nonword should result in activation of nonhomologous areas, producing a reduced RVF advantage if the subject responds to the word. Nonwords, however, don't seem to depend on lateralized processing, and thus, no field effect should be seen regardless of whether they are paired with a word or a nonword.

In the experiment, bilateral displays of words and nonwords were used, and subjects classified the item pointed to by a central arrowhead as a word or nonword. The error results were quite straightforward, as shown in Table 6.5. The only significant RVF advantage was found for words paired with words. No other field effect was significant, and the difference between conditions was supported by a significant three-way interaction of field, stimulus type, and distractor type. The interaction was also significant in the RT data in a way that was generally consistent with the error results, although not nearly as pronounced. The results are viewed as supportive of the homolog activation hypothesis.

One must wonder, of course, why a central digit and a lateralized word produce the bilateral effect when a paired word and nonword do not. When the lexical decision results were published, I suggested that the reason might be that words and digits are processed by the same or overlapping anatomical areas.

TABLE 6.5. Percentage Error Results From Boles (1990, Experiment 3).

	Word Stimulus		Nonword Stimulus	
	Word Distractor	Nonword Distractor	Word Distractor	Nonword Distractor
LVF	25.1	14.9	22.0	17.4
RVF	17.8	15.9	18.9	13.7
difference	+7.3	-1.0	+3.1	+3.7

Therefore, when paired in a bilateral display, homologous areas of the two hemispheres might be activated. This hypothesis has since been supported by recent factor analytic work in which lateral difference scores for a visual digit recognition task and two visual word recognition tasks loaded together on a common factor (Boles, 1992). The outcome indicates that similar lateralized processes underlie visual digit and word recognition. It should also be re-emphasized that the nonword stimuli in the lexical decision task failed to produce the RVF advantage shown by words. In contrast, in the factor analytic studies, both digits and words produced RVF advantages.

With regard to the findings on homolog activation, it is interesting that similar results were reported in the auditory modality years earlier by K. McFarland, M. L. McFarland, Bain, and Ashton (1978). They used dichotic stimuli consisting of word targets to one ear paired with various types of distractor stimuli to the other ear. What they found was that when the distractors were words, a much larger REA was found than when the distractors consisted of white noise or crowd noise.

Together, these results support the homolog activation hypothesis of the bilateral effect, and suggest that the effect is due to a disruption of information transfer between hemispheres when stimulation is bilateral and involves similar stimulus types. It should be emphasized that the stimulus types must be similar. When this type of experiment is conducted with pairs displayed in homologous versus nonhomologous locations of the VFs, the interaction with type of pairing is not found. This was tested in an experiment that presented bargraphs in homologous or various types of nonhomologous relationships, but bilaterally in all cases. The LVF superiority that was obtained in responding to the bargraphs did not vary with homology of location (Boles, 1990, Experiment 2).

The latter finding may be an important one for localizing the anatomical substrate of the bilateral effect. Specifically, the results suggest that the anatomical locus is to be found at cortical levels beyond those at which a retinotopic organization is to be found. Otherwise, to the extent that homologous activation produces the bilateral effect, one might expect homology of location to be effective in producing it.

In this regard, Marzi (1986) has reviewed evidence, most of it from experiments using monkeys, that a strong retinotopic organization is present in areas corresponding to the human occipital lobe. Specifically, the receptive fields for neurons at levels V1 - V3 are all relatively small, and cross the vertical meridian at most 4-5 degrees to the ipsilateral side (this crossover occurring in area V3). Crossover of the visual meridian is made possible by the transfer of information across the corpus callosum. Now, if the mechanism of the bilateral effect occurred at these early levels, we might expect that homologous activation by location would produce the effect, yet, as noted, it does not.

A second prediction that is made by occipital-level transfer is that the size of the bilateral effect should be different for stimulus eccentricities of less than 5 degrees than it is for eccentricities of more than 5 degrees. According to Marzi's review, at less than 5 degrees, transfer is possible at occipital levels, so there should be an opportunity for homolog activation to have an effect on the resultant asymmetry. At greater than 5 degrees, transfer is not possible at these levels, and homolog activation should have no effect, in which case the VF difference should be reduced.

In the bargraph homology experiment just described, eccentricities of 3.5 and 6.6 degrees were used. Although no analysis was reported on the effect of eccentricity in the original research report (Boles, 1990), Table 6.6 shows the outcome when trials using homologous displays are represented: There was no significant interaction between VF and eccentricity (for RT, $F[1,15]= .29$; for percentage correct, $F[1,15]= .09$). The LVF advantage was robust at both eccentricities, yielding a significant main effect of VF (in RT, $F[1,15]= 5.62$, $p <$ .05; in percentage correct, $F[1,15]= 12.30$, $p < .005$).

Further tests of the eccentricity prediction are provided by the comparative experiments described further on. The size of the bilateral effect did not vary, whether the eccentricity was ~1.4 versus 6.4 degrees. The conclusion from these studies is that because the effect can be obtained with eccentricities greater than 5 degrees, the early occipital levels of processing cannot be those underlying the bilateral effect.

Where are the critical levels, then? A partial answer may be provided by considering the cortical levels at which retinotopic organization has been lost. By the time information reaches the posterior parietal, middle temporal, and inferotemporal cortices, the receptive fields overlap into the ipsilateral VF to a very great extent. For example, Marzi (1986) reported that a lateralized stimulus will activate at least 70% of the neurons in the ipsilateral inferotemporal cortex. In other words, at these higher levels, retinotopic organization has largely been lost. This suggests that the homolog activation involved in the bilateral effect, and the accompanying cross-commissural interaction between hemispheres, is at cortical levels beyond the occipital cortex: in parietal and temporal areas, or perhaps beyond. Interestingly, using different logic, Marzi likewise suggested that much of the transfer of visual information takes place beyond levels V1 - V3 in the monkey.

In summary, it appears likely that the major loci of hemispheric interaction, as evidenced in the bilateral effect, can be regarded as anterior to occipital sites.

PARAMETERS OF THE BILATERAL EFFECT

Having discussed the causes of the bilateral effect, I now pass on to what I have termed the *parameters* of the effect. The first has already been mentioned, namely, that the critical display factor appears to be the use of a bilateral display, in which stimuli requiring similar processing produce activation of homologous areas of the hemispheres. Beyond this, I first cover data on the size of the effect, both in terms of the magnitudes of asymmetries emerging from bilateral versus unilateral displays, and in comparison to other variables that have been proposed to affect VF differences. Finally, I compare the reliability of VF differences found using bilateral vs. unilateral displays.

To examine the size of the effect, I make reference to six experiments in two papers (Boles, 1983, 1987). These are not the only ones that could be examined, but I believe them to be reasonably representative. The first three studies used percentage correct as the dependent measure. The values appearing in Table 6.7 under the Bilateral and Unilateral headings are the field differences, a + indicating a RVF advantage in recognizing the stimuli, and a - indicating a LVF advantage. As indicated, the bilateral displays produced much larger RVF advantages, amounting to about 4:1 or 5:1 in ratio terms, and 6.4% in absolute terms.

In the RT studies (Table 6.8), the picture is much the same. Here, the ratio is about 5:1 or 6:1 overall, and the absolute difference is 24 msec. In fact, it practically makes no sense to talk about ratios with these data, because the unilateral field differences were rarely significantly different from zero.

These results make a case that when a study is conducted with the intent of finding field differences, consideration should be given to the use of a bilateral methodology. It is certainly not impossible to get a significant field difference with unilateral methods (the literature amply shows that), but, on an a priori basis, a bilateral display provides a much better shot at one.

There is a second way to approach the issue of the size of the bilateral effect, namely in a comparative manner. That is, how does the effect of display type stack up against other variables that have been proposed to affect VF differences? One of the most obvious yardsticks for comparison would be the effect of stimulus type. In general, stimuli requiring verbal processing should produce a right field advantage, and stimuli requiring spatial processing should produce a left field advantage. This well-replicated effect of the type of stimulus or processing provides one comparison that can be made. Other variables that have been proposed as having strong influences on field asymmetries are the so-called input variables (Christman, 1989; Sergent & Hellige, 1986). These are factors relating to the quality of the stimuli rather than how they are organized in the display. Specifically, the eccentricity of stimuli, their duration, their luminance or contrast, and their size are all variables that have been proposed to affect asymmetries.

Recently, I undertook three experiments that compared the effect sizes of all of these input variables to the effect sizes of the stimulus and display-type variables (Boles, 1994). All three experiments were RT studies that also looked at the percentage of errors, and all used both unilateral and bilateral displays. The stimulus types were two that have been much-used in my laboratory (Boles, 1986, 1987, 1989, 1990, 1991), involving the odd-even classification of word names of numbers, or of bargraphs (Fig. 6.1). The manipulation of stimulus type was within Experiment 1 (words vs. bargraphs), and also between Experiments 2 (words) and 3 (bargraphs). All experiments manipulated the input variables of eccentricity and duration, and the variables of luminance/contrast and size were also manipulated in Experiments 2 and 3. Most of the manipulations were made in fully mixed blocks of trials, with the exception of stimulus type in Experiment 1, and luminance, which were blocked variables.

TABLE 6.6. Eccentricity Results From Boles (1990, Experiment 2). RT in msec With Percentage of Errors in Parentheses.

	Eccentricity	
	3.5°	6.6°
LVF	803 (12.5)	818 (9.1)
RVF	844 (16.7)	872 (14.8)
difference	-41 (-4.2)	-54 (-5.7)

TABLE 6.7 The Size of the Bilateral Effect in Percentage Correct (Boles, 1983): A + Designates a RVF Advantage; - Designates a LVF Advantage. The Ratio in Parentheses is Based on the Mean Asymmetries.

Experiment	Stimuli	Bilateral	Unilateral	Ratio	Absolute Difference
1	words	+10.0	+3.1	3.2	6.9
2	words	+6.0	+0.7	8.6	5.3
3	words	+8.6	+1.6	5.4	7.0
M		+8.2	+1.8	(4.6)	6.4

TABLE 6.8 The Size of the Bilateral Effect in RT (Boles, 1987): A + Designates a RVF Advantage; - Designates a LVF Advantage. The Ratio in Parentheses is Based on the Mean Asymmetries.

Experiment	Stimuli	Bilateral	Unilateral	Ratio	Absolute Difference
1	bargraphs	-44	-4	11.0	40
2	letters	+24	+11	2.2	13
3	words	+19	0	-	19
M of absolute values		29	5	(5.8)	24

Briefly, the input variables were manipulated as follows. The greater of two eccentricities was 6.4 degrees for all stimuli. Because of display limitations that required the plotting of words and bargraphs on different coordinate systems, the lesser eccentricity was not perfectly matched between the stimulus types, but was fairly similar: 1.1 degrees for words, and 1.6 degrees for bargraphs. The durations used were 50 msec and 150 msec. Low and high luminance values were 0.28 nits and 1.24 nits, an approximately 1:4 ratio. (Contrast was not independently manipulated but of course covaried with the luminance; stimuli were presented against a dark background on the cathode ray tube, in a semi-dark environment.) Stimulus sizes, manipulated in separate experiments for words and bargraphs, were 3.8 and 7.7 degrees for words, and 6.3 and 13.4 degrees for bargraphs.

The results appear in Tables 6.9 through 6.14. In all tables a + means an effect in the direction predicted by the modal result in the literature (Christman, 1989): for example, with decreasing eccentricity, an increase in a RVF advantage or a decrease in a LVF advantage. A - means that the effect went in the direction opposite the literature: for example, with a decrease in size, a decrease in a RVF advantage (in RT or errors) or an increase in a LVF advantage. These values, in other words, are arithmetic values of the interaction of each independent value with VF, with a plus sign indicating that it went in the expected direction, and a minus meaning it went in the unexpected direction.

As the variable of central interest to this chapter, display type effects are shown first, in Table 6.9. As indicated, the VF × Display Type interaction was significant in Experiments 1 (percentage of errors) and 2 (RT), and strong, consistent trends were seen for RT in all experiments. Taking RT as the more sensitive measure, the effect size was +16 msec, reasonably close to the +24 msec figure found for the experiments in Boles (1987) discussed earlier.

Table 6.10 shows the results of the stimulus type manipulation. Experiment 1 produced a strong VF × Stimulus Type interaction for both RT and percentage of errors, and the between-experiment comparison also produced a significant effect for RT. For RT, the effect size was +25 msec. This effect would be expected to be large because it is bidirectional in nature: that is, the VF differences for words and bargraphs are in opposite directions of one another, and so are additive with respect to effect size.

TABLE 6.9 Display Type Effect Size: A + Indicates Greater Bilateral than Unilateral Asymmetry (Averaged Over Stimulus Types in Experiment 1). RT Effect in msec; %E Effect in Percent Errors.

Experiment	Manipulation	RT Effect	%E Effect
1	Unilateral vs.bilateral	+14	+3.3*
2	Unilateral vs.bilateral	+22*	+1.1
3	Unilateral vs.bilateral	+12	+2.0
M		+16	+2.1

*p<.05

TABLE 6.10. Effect of Stimulus Type: A + Indicates that Words Showed a Greater LVF-RVF Difference Than Bargraphs. RT Effect in msec; %E Effect in Percent Errors.

Experiment	Manipulation	RT Effect	%E Effect
1	Bars vs. Wor	+26*	+2.3*
2	Words	+24*	+1.4
3	Bars		
M		+25	+1.9

*p<.05

The effects of eccentricity are shown in Table 6.11. A significant effect was found for only one comparison: RT in Experiment 3. The result is somewhat odd in that it was found for bargraphs, yet no such effect was found in Experiment 1 (+3 msec taking the bargraphs alone). It should also be noted that the eccentricity variable was not found to influence VF asymmetry in the homology-by-location experiment discussed previously. Nevertheless, averaged over these three experiments, the effect size was +11 msec.

Table 6.12 shows the VF × Duration interaction. It was not significant for any comparison, and the overall effect size for RT was -1 msec.

Luminance/contrast effects are represented in Table 6.13. The only significant comparison was in a direction opposite to that claimed in the literature, in Experiment 3 errors. The overall effect size for RT was -3 msec.

Finally, the results from the size manipulations are shown in Table 6.14. Again, only one comparison was significant, and it was in the direction opposite the modal result in the literature (Experiment 1 RT). The average effect size for RT was -24 msec.

A summary of all the effect sizes is provided in Table 6.15, ranked in order of size as indicated on the RT measure. From this comparative analysis, it appears that display type (unilateral vs. bilateral) had the second largest influence on VF asymmetry among those manipulated. Only stimulus type produces a larger effect, and, as indicated, it has the advantage of being a bidirectional effect.

The input variables, in contrast, fared very poorly as modifiers of VF asymmetry. Within this group, eccentricity produced results that were the most consistent with those claimed in the literature (Christman, 1989; Sergent & Hellige, 1986), yet it did so in only one comparison, in an experiment using bargraphs as stimuli (Experiment 3), and it failed to do so in two other experiments that used bargraphs as stimuli (Experiment 1 and the homology experiment). The other input variables, size and luminance/contrast, produced results opposite those expected from the literature, though in only one comparison each. Thus, it would appear that the input variables do not count for much as influences on VF asymmetry. It is possible, of course, that if the manipulations of these variables were taken to extremes, more consistent effects might appear, but the ranges of the manipulations used in Experiments 1-3 are rather typical in laterality research.

A final parameter of the bilateral effect, and one that has not been reported previously, is the relative reliability of asymmetries emerging from bilateral and

TABLE 6.11 Eccentricity Effect: A + Indicates that the Smaller Eccentricity Showed a Greater LVF-RVF Difference than the Larger Eccentricity. RT Effect in msec; %E Effect in Percent Errors.

Experiment	Manipulation	RT Effect	%E Effect
1	6.4 versus ~1.4deg	+2	+1.3
2	6.4 versus 1.1deg	+3	+0.4
3	6.4 versus 1.6deg	+27*	+0.7
M		+11	+0.8

*p<.05

TABLE 6.12 Duration Effect: A + Indicates That the Longer Stimuli Showed a Greater LVF-RVF Difference than the Briefer Stimuli RT Effect in msec; %E Effect in Percent Errors.

Experiment	Manipulation	RT Effect	%E Effect
1	50 versus 150msec	-12	+1.3%
2	50 versus 150msec	+6	+0.8%
3	50 versus 150msec	+3	+1.0%
M		-1	+1.0

Table 6.13 Luminance/Contrast Effect: + Indicates That High Luminance/Contrast Stimuli Showed a Greater LVF-RVF Difference Than Low Luminance/Contrast Stimuli. RT Effect in msec; %E Effect in Percent Errors.

Experiment	Manipulation	RT Effect	%E Effect
2	0.28 nits versus 1.24 nits	+6	-0.1%
3	0.28 nits versus 1.24 nits	-11	-2.5%*
M		-3	-1.3

*p<.05

TABLE 6.14 Size Effect Size. A + Indicates That the Smaller Stimuli Showed a Greater LVF-RVF Difference Than the Larger Stimuli. RT Effect in msec; %E Effect in Percent Errors.

Experiment	Manipulation	RT Effect	%E Effect
2	7.7 deg versus 3.8 deg.	-30*	-0.4%
3	13.4 deg versus 6.3 deg.	-18	+0.8%
M		-24	+0.2

*p<.05

unilateral displays. I reported the reliabilities of VF differences using bilateral displays alone in an earlier paper (Boles, 1984). There, results from five word recognition experiments were shown, in which the trials could be split evenly into first and second halves. The experiments were part of a larger set of 14 that were analyzed for sex differences. For the five, reliabilities were calculated by splitting the data files into first and second halves, separately calculating asymmetries for each subject in each half, and correlating the asymmetry scores across subjects. The mean reliability, uncorrected for halving the trials was +.71, with a range of +.41 to +.91.

Subsequently, I have re-examined those five studies. Two of them also used unilateral displays. Those two, labeled Experiments 2 and 7 in Boles (1984), showed uncorrected reliabilities of +.46 and +.56, respectively, for bilateral displays, and +.26 and -.32 for unilateral displays (see Table 6.16, top half). Hence, there is some indication from earlier results that there is at least moderate reliability when displays are bilateral, but virtually no reliability using unilateral displays.

The comparative experiments just described provide a further opportunity to contrast the reliabilities of the two display types. The RT data were taken as being the more sensitive of the measures, but otherwise much the same kind of analysis was conducted as has been described for the two studies that measured accuracy. The outcomes are shown in Table 6.16 (bottom half).

Again, the bilateral reliabilities were respectable, whereas the unilateral ones left something to be desired. The median reliability for bilateral displays over all four comparisons is +.65. If the Spearman-Brown formula is applied to correct for halving the trials, this increases to a respectable +.79. The median reliability for the unilateral displays, in contrast, is -.03.

At the very least, these results indicate that in studying individual differences in lateralization, one is much better off using bilateral displays, because they clearly provide more reproducible VF differences at the level of the individual subject.

CONCLUSIONS

The *bilateral effect* may be defined as the larger field asymmetries found using bilateral displays compared to unilateral displays. It has been argued that it generalizes across modalities, stimulus types, and dependent measures, thus representing one of the fundamental phenomena of lateralization research. A critical feature of the effect is that the display must have an aspect of bilaterality, even if only at the midline. The most likely cause of the effect is the activation of homologous areas of the two hemispheres by stimuli requiring similar processing, which disrupts communication between the hemispheres by a process of hemispheric interaction. The locus of the interaction appears to be anterior to the occipital areas, perhaps in parietal and temporal regions. Turning to some of the parameters of the effect, the bilateral effect averages about 6% in percentage-

TABLE 6.16. Reliability of VF Differences. %C studies (Boles, 1983)

Experiment	Stimuli	N	Uncorrected test-retest reliability	
			Bilateral	Unilateral
2	words	19	+.46	+.26
7	words	15	+.56	-.32

RT studies (present results)

Experiment	Stimuli	N	Uncorrected test-retest reliability	
			Bilateral	Unilateral
1	words	16	+.56	-.16
	bars	16	+.68	+.11
2	words	23	+.61	-.45
3	bars	14	+.74	+.15

correct terms, and about 24 msec in RT (or an approximately 5:1 ratio compared to unilateral asymmetries). In comparative terms, it may be the second largest influence on field asymmetry, after that of stimulus type. Finally, bilateral displays produce VF differences with much higher reliability than those found with unilateral displays. In cited studies, bilateral reliabilities were shown to approach +.80, while unilateral reliabilities were found to be essentially zero.

REFERENCES

Bashore, T.R. (1981). Vocal and manual reaction time estimates of interhemispheric transmission time. *Psychological Bulletin, 89*, 352-368.

Boles, D.B. (1979). *The bilateral effect: Mechanisms for the advantage of bilateral over unilateral stimulus presentation in the production of visual field asymmetry.* Unpublished doctoral disseration, University of Oregon, Eugene.

Boles, D.B. (1983). Hemispheric interaction in visual field asymmetry. *Cortex, 19*, 99-114.

Boles, D.B. (1984). Sex in lateralized tachistoscopic word recognition. *Brain and Language, 23*, 307-317.

Boles, D.B. (1986). Hemispheric differences in the judgment of number. *Neuropsychologia, 24*, 511-519.

Boles, D.B. (1987). Reaction time asymmetry through bilateral vs. unilateral stimulus presentation. *Brain and Cognition, 6*, 321-333.

Boles, D. B. (1989). Do visual field asymmetries intercorrelate? *Neuropsychologia, 27*, 697-704.

Boles, D.B. (1990). What bilateral displays do. *Brain and Cognition, 12*, 205-228.

Boles, D.B. (1994). An experimental comparison of stimulus type, display type, and input variable contributions to visual field asymmetry. *Brain and Cognition, 24*, 184-197.

Boles, D.B. (1992). Factor analysis and the cerebral hemispheres: Temporal, occipital, and frontal functions. *Neuropsychologia, 11*, 963-988.

Boles, D.B. (1991). Factor analysis and the cerebral hemispheres: Pilot study and parietal functions. *Neuropsychologia, 29*, 59-91.

Chiarello, C., Senehi, J., & Soulier, M. (1986). Viewing conditions and hemisphere asymmetry for the lexical decision. *Neuropsychologia, 24*, 521-529.

Christman, S. (1989). Perceptual characteristics in visual laterality research. *Brain and Cognition, 11*, 238-257.

Hardyck, C., Chiarello, C., Dronkers, N.F., & Simpson, G.V. (1985). Orienting attention within visual fields: How efficient is interhemispheric transfer? *Journal of Experimental Psychology: Human Perception and Performance, 11*, 650-666.

Healey, J.M., Waldstein, S., & Goodglass, H. (1985). Sex differences in the lateralization of language discrimination vs language production. *Neuropsychologia, 23*, 777-789.

Heilman, K.M., & Watson, R.T. (1977). The neglect syndrome: A unilateral defect of the orienting response. In S. Harnad, R.W. Doty, L. Goldstein, J. Jaynes, & G. Krauthamer (Eds.), *Lateralization in the nervous system* (pp. 285-302). New York: Academic Press.

Hellige, J.B. (1991). Cerebral laterality and metacontrol. In F.L. Kitterle (Ed.), *Cerebral laterality: Theory and research* (pp. 117-132). Hillsdale, NJ: Lawrence Erlbaum Associates.

Heron, W. (1957). Perception as a function of retinal locus and attention. *American Journal of Psychology, 70*, 38-48.

Hines, D. (1972). Bilateral tachistoscopic recognition of verbal and nonverbal stimuli. *Cortex, 8*, 315-322.

Kimura, D. (1964). Left-right differences in the perception of melodies. *Quarterly Journal of Experimental Psychology, 16*, 355-358.

Leiber, L. (1976). Lexical decisions in the right and left cerebral hemispheres. *Brain and Language, 3*, 443-450.

Mackavey, W., Curcio, F., & Rosen, J. (1975). Tachistoscopic word recognition performance under conditions of simultaneous presentation. *Neuropsychologia, 13*, 27-33.

Marzi, C.A. (1986). Transfer of visual information after unilateral input to the brain. *Brain and Cognition, 5*, 163-173.

McFarland, K., McFarland, M.L., Bain, J.D., & Ashton, R. (1978). Ear differences of abstract and concrete word recognition. *Neuropsychologia, 16*, 555-561.

McKeever, W.F. (1971). Lateral word recognition effects of unilateral and bilateral presentation, asynchrony of bilateral presentation and forced order of report. *Quarterly Journal of Experimental Psychology, 23*, 410-416.

McKeever, W.F., & Huling, M.D. (1971). Bilateral tachistoscopic word recognition as a function of hemisphere stimulated and interhemispheric transfer time. *Neuropsychologia, 9*, 281-288.

McKeever, W.F., Suberi, M., & VanDeventer, A.D. (1972). Fixation control in tachistoscopic studies of laterality effects: Comments and data relevant to Hines' experiment. *Cortex, 8,* 473-479.

Olson, M.E. (1973). Laterality differences in tachistoscopic word recognition in normal and delayed readers in elementary school. *Neuropsychologia, 11,* 343-350.

Sergent, J., & Hellige, J.B. (1986). Role of input factors in visual-field asymmetries. *Brain and Cognition, 5,* 200-222.

Springer, S.P. (1971). Ear asymmetry in a dichotic detection task. *Perception and Psychophysics, 10,* 239-241.

St. Denis, G. (1987). *Primed lateralization of the memory codes involved in reading with covarying familiarity and SOA.* Unpublished master's thesis, Rensselaer Polytechnic Institute, Troy, NY.

Witelson, S.F. (1974). Hemispheric specialization for linguistic and nonlinguistic tactual perception using a dichotomous stimulation technique. *Cortex, 10,* 3-17.

7 Independence Versus Integration of Right and Left Hemisphere Processing: Effects of Handedness

Stephen D. Christman
University of Toledo

A substantial amount of research demonstrating asymmetries between the left and right cerebral hemispheres in perceptual, cognitive, and emotional processing has accumulated since the 1960s. Typical approaches in this research have included examining the information processing ability of a single hemisphere at a time by employing lateralized presentation of input in normal populations. The performance of clinical populations such as commissurotomy patients and stroke patients with unilateral brain damage has also been examined. Although the resulting theories provide adequate accounts of the functioning of the isolated hemispheres, relatively little work has been devoted to the issue of how the hemispheres interact in the course of normal performance where *both* hemispheres have access to the relevant input. This situation has led to an unfortunate lack of contact between theories of cerebral lateralization and mainstream theories of cognitive psychology (e.g., see Hellige, 1990).

One problem with extrapolating from neuropsychological findings to general theories of normal cognition lies precisely in the fact that most theories of hemispheric specialization strictly apply only to the functioning of the hemispheres in isolation. Because cognitive experimentation usually involves central presentation of input and/or exposure durations that allow for eye movements that provide both hemispheres with equivalent access to input, it is not obvious how knowledge of the performance characteristics of individual cerebral hemispheres can inform models of psychological processes in which the two hemispheres work together. This is an important issue, because the question of the extent to which cognitive functions operate in an independent, modular fashion is a central debate in cognitive science (e.g., Fodor, 1983). Although these modules may in many cases be defined functionally, as opposed to spatially (e.g., Haugeland, 1978), the left and right cerebral hemispheres are salient candidates for spatially defined neural modules. Consequently, knowledge of how the hemispheres interact may be important in the debate over the modular organization of mind.

An equally important issue in attempts to integrate neuropsychological and cognitive theories concerns the question of individual differences in performance. Neuropsychological theories have long recognized the importance of individual differences in patterns of hemispheric specialization of function, although, as discussed further on, the typical approach to this issue has been to restrict the subject population so that individual differences will be minimized. The situation in cognitive psychology is, if anything, worse. An informal survey of a half dozen cognitive psychology textbooks sitting on my bookshelf revealed that only one text had a subject index heading for individual differences. Fortunately, this situation appears to be improving, as witnessed by the recent introduction of a journal devoted to this topic, *Learning and Individual Differences*. In fact, a recent review article in this journal focussing on the relationship between patterns of cerebral hemispheric asymmetry and individual differences in cognition concluded that there is a connection (O'Boyle & Hellige, 1989), but further research is plainly required. It is clear that any complete theory of general psychological function needs to take into account both the manner in which left-hemisphere (LH) and right-hemisphere (RH) processes interact and the nature of individual differences in information processing.

METHODS IN STUDYING INTERHEMISPHERIC INTERACTION

One method employed in addressing the issue of interhemispheric interaction has involved presenting lateralized input to both hemispheres and examining how the hemispheres interact during the course of processing. In some cases, identical input is presented simultaneously to both hemispheres; the nature of performance on bihemispheric trials is then compared to the nature of performance on unihemispheric trials to determine whether the mode of processing of one hemisphere or the other dominates on bilateral trials (e.g., Hellige, Jonsson, & Michimata, 1988; Hellige, Taylor, & Eng, 1989; Jones, 1982; Levy & Trevarthen, 1976). This concept has been referred to as *metacontrol*. Of particular interest is the finding that the hemisphere with the superior processing ability is not necessarily the one that assumes metacontrol; for example, Hellige et al. (1989) employed a consonant-vowel-consonant (CVC) identification task and showed that under conditions of bilateral presentation, the less efficient strategy associated with the right hemisphere dominated and was applied to both LH and RH stimuli. Hellige and associates have extended this paradigm to examine the qualitative nature of performance for foveally presented stimuli and have found that the pattern of errors for central presentations also resembled that for RH, but not LH, presentations (Hellige, Cowin, & Eng, 1991). This counterintuitive finding may represent a case of interhemispheric cooperation: because the more efficient LH strategy, based on phonetic processing, is not available to the right hemisphere, both hemispheres may adopt the less efficient RH strategy because it is available to both.

A similar approach employing simultaneous bilateral input involves presenting different input to the two hemispheres to examine how dividing processing between the hemispheres affects task performance (Banich & Belger, 1990; Davis & Schmit, 1973; Dimond & Beaumont, 1971, 1972b; Liederman, Merola, & Martinez, 1985; Merola & Liederman, 1988; L. Miller, 1983; Sereno & Kosslyn, 1991). A general trend found in these studies is that increasing task difficulty leads to greater relative advantage for between- versus within-hemisphere division of input. This is consistent with the notion that, as the processing resources required by a given task exceed the resources available within a single hemisphere, the between-hemisphere division of processing becomes beneficial by doubling the pool of available resources (e.g., Friedman & Polson, 1981).

Finally, research has also employed the presentation of successive bilateral stimuli, in which the two stimuli are to be compared or integrated (Banich & Belger, 1991; Beaumont & Dimond, 1975; Christman, 1991a; Kleinman & Little, 1973; Lordahl et al., 1965). This technique often, although not invariably, yields better performance when the two stimuli are presented to the same hemisphere. This result is consistent with the notion that when the stimuli can be processed one at a time (as opposed to simultaneously), the processing load at any one moment is reduced, and the advantage for between-hemisphere division of processing found with simultaneous bilateral presentation is reduced or reversed. In addition, within-hemisphere processing may generally be superior in situations requiring memorial processing.

Although these approaches offer valuable techniques for addressing the issue of interhemispheric interaction, they still suffer from two drawbacks. First, they rely on the lateralized presentation of input, creating non-ecological viewing conditions. This is an especially important issue when considering the nature of interhemispheric interaction because the interhemispheric transfer of information may be greater when input is presented closer to the fovea (Berardi & Fiorentini, 1987). This leads to the possibility that the nature of interhemispheric interaction may differ under parafoveal and foveal viewing conditions. Study of interhemispheric interaction under more ecological conditions of input (e.g., foveal, binaural) could have important implications regarding the relevance of neuropsychological findings for models of normal human cognition.

Second, with relatively few exceptions, only right-handed subjects (with no left-handed relatives in their immediate family) have been employed in studies examining interhemispheric interaction. Handedness is a readily available behavioral correlate of individual differences in degree of lateralization. Research examining individual differences in lateralization has primarily focused on performance asymmetries between the left and right visual fields, ears, and hands, with the general conclusion that personal and/or familial sinistrality is associated with lesser lateralization of function (e.g., smaller performance asymmetries between the left and right visual fields; see Beaton, 1985). Research has also indicated that the corpus callosum (the bundle of nerve fibers connecting the two hemispheres) is larger in left-handers (Witelson, 1985; 1989), suggesting important potential differences in the nature of interhemispheric connectivity as a function of handedness.

INDIVIDUAL DIFFERENCES IN INTERHEMISPHERIC INTERACTION

The fact that sinistrality is associated with both lesser lateralization of function and a thicker corpus callosum suggests that processing in subjects with personal or familial sinistrality may involve greater interhemispheric interaction. This pattern does not entail any *a priori* difference in absolute levels of ability. Research suggests that there are few, if any, differences in general intellectual function (e.g., as measured by tests of verbal and performance IQ) as a function of handedness (e.g., Hardyck & Petrinovich, 1977). Rather, the behavioral and anatomical characteristics associated with sinistrality may indicate a situation involving greater coordination between specific LH and RH processes. Such a state could lead to relative advantages in situations where multiple subcomponents of a complex task, some of which are localized to the left hemisphere and others that are localized to the right, need to interact and be coordinated for optimal performance. Similarly, such a state could lead to relative disadvantages in situations (e.g., dual-task conditions) where separate LH and RH processes need to be carried out in parallel, without interaction or interference.

To date, few studies have looked explicitly at the role of handedness in mediating characteristics of interhemispheric interaction. Dimond and Beaumont (1972a) presented pairs of identically colored stimuli to the left, the right, or both hemispheres and found that performance was impaired when the input was divided between hemispheres. This effect was stronger in right-handed than in left-handed subjects, suggesting relatively greater interhemispheric integration in left-handers. Beaumont and Dimond (1973) presented meaningless paired-associate duograms (vowel-consonant), with one member directed to one hemisphere, and the second member being presented either to the same hemisphere or to the other one. No differences were found between these conditions or between right- and left-handed subjects. Beaumont and Dimond (1975) required subjects to match pairs of abstract shapes that were presented to the same or different hemispheres and also found no differences between conditions as a function of handedness, although left-handed subjects exhibited superior performance overall. These failures to find any effects related to interhemispheric integration may be related to the finding by Kleinman and Little (1973) that meaningless information is less readily transmitted between hemispheres than meaningful information.

Honda (1982) examined effects of handedness on the inhibition of reaction time in double stimulation situations (where two stimuli are presented, but only the second is responded to). The data obtained were consistent with the view that in right-handers, movements of the right hand are controlled by the left hemisphere, whereas movements of the left hand are controlled by both hemispheres; in left-handers, however, there is bilateral control of both hands. Verillo (1983) examined the subjective magnitude of vibrotactile stimulation when conditioning and test stimuli were presented to the same versus different hands in right-, mixed-, and left-handers. Presentation of the conditioning stimulus to one hand affected the perception of the test stimulus presented to the other hand in right- and left-handers, but not in mixed-handers. Potter and Graves (1988) had subjects compare stimuli presented simultaneously to both sides of the body. Better interhemispheric transfer performance was shown by left-handers for motor and tactile tasks.

L. Miller (1983) found evidence for *lesser* interhemispheric integration in left-handers in a unilateral versus bilateral word recognition task. The author pointed out, however, that the presence of both floor effects (the overall performance of left-handers was poor) and differences among subgroups (e.g., the strongest evidence for hemispheric independence was found for left-handers with an inverted writing posture and with no left-handed relatives) limit the generalizability of the findings. Moreover, the lower overall performance level of the left-handers suggests they may have been at a disadvantage under conditions requiring bihemispheric processing (i.e., the simultaneous recognition of bilateral words).

Finally, a study performed by Berry, Hughes, and Jackson (1980) involved left- and right-handers performing two different tasks either independently or simultaneously. The two tasks were chosen so as to represent LH versus RH processes, with the LH task involving speech and mathematical processing and the RH task involving a variation of the WAIS Block Design subtest. There were no differences between handedness groups when each task was performed alone; however, when subjects performed them both simultaneously, left-handers exhibited a greater decline in performance. The authors interpreted their results as reflecting greater interhemispheric interference in left-handers, arising from their lesser degree of lateralization.

Taken together, these results indicate that handedness can influence characteristics of interhemispheric interaction. Although the results suggest that many factors can affect the nature of this interaction (e.g., whether or not non-right-handed subject groups are broken down into left- versus mixed-handers; whether the task is primarily sensory, perceptual, or cognitive), there is at least suggestive evidence that left- and/or mixed-handedness is typically associated with greater degrees of interhemispheric integration.

The current framework represents an extension of ideas originally proposed by Kinsbourne (e.g., Kinsbourne & Hicks, 1978). Kinsbourne proposed the notion of *functional cerebral distance* to account for the intertask interactions observed during dual-task performance. Specifically, Kinsbourne argued that the lateralization of different functions in the two cerebral hemispheres allowed for the reduction of interference between such tasks when performed concurrently; that is, if subjects have to perform two processes at once, to the extent to which the neural substrates underlying the processing demands of the separate tasks are relatively isolated from each other, there will be less intertask interference. Due to the greater interhemispheric connectivity displayed by left-handers, LH and RH processes are expected to be less functionally isolated from each other in them, and greater interference between tasks is predicted.

PILOT STUDIES

The experiments described in this chapter attempt to extend this hypothesis to task situations in which both hemispheres jointly participate in the processing required by the task at hand. The working hypothesis of these studies is that subjects exhibiting lesser degrees of cerebral lateralization (i.e., non-right-handers) should be relatively superior at complex tasks requiring *integration* of LH and RH processes; conversely, subjects exhibiting greater degrees of lateralization (i.e., right-handers) should be relatively better in dual-task situations that require *independent* execution of LH and RH processes.

Two pilot studies provide support for this hypothesis. The first investigated handedness among musicians. A number of previous studies have investigated handedness in musicians versus nonmusicians (Byrne, 1974; Gotestam, 1990; Oldfield, 1969), with the general finding that musicians are more likely to be left- and/or mixed-handed compared to nonmusicians. Christman (1993a) re-examined handedness in musicians as a function of the instrument they play. The goal of the study was to determine if the relative roles of the left and right hands in playing musical instruments that require bimanual activity were related to direction and/or degree of handedness. There is evidence suggesting that fine motor movements of the hands, such as those involved in playing musical instruments, are primarily under the control of the contralateral hemisphere in right-handers and under relatively greater bilateral control in left-handers (Honda, 1982; Kimura & Vanderwolf, 1970; Parlow & Kinsbourne, 1981). In some instruments (e.g., keyboard instruments), the activities of the two hands are independent; that is, the activity of one hand has no *a priori* constraint on the activity of the other hand. In other instruments (e.g., strings, woodwinds), however, the activities of the two hands need to be coordinated (e.g., on a string instrument, the string being fretted by the left hand determines which string is to be bowed by the right hand). Thus, performance on the former versus latter types of instruments might best be accomplished with relatively independent versus coordinated hemispheric control of movement of the two hands, respectively.

Christman (1993b) tested the hypothesis that musicians with mixed handedness (and therefore with presumably greater interhemispheric integration) should be more prevalent among those musicians who play instruments requiring greater bimanual coordination. The results supported the hypothesis (see Table 7.1). Although the two groups did not differ in overall *direction* of handedness ($F<1$) (i.e., performers of bimanual coordinated instruments were no more likely to be left-handed than performers of bimanual independent instruments), the musicians who played instruments requiring greater bimanual coordination showed an overall weaker *degree* of handedness ($p<.03$) (i.e., had a weaker absolute strength of handedness, regardless of direction). This suggests that relatively greater interhemispheric coordination of fine motor activity is beneficial for competent performance of selected instruments, which could account for the greater overall proportion of left-handedness among musicians found by previous researchers.

These results also point out an important qualification in using the term "left-handed"; namely, that what may be most important is degree, not direction, of

Table 7.1 Handness Scores as a Function of Instrumental Category

Instrumental Category	Average	Average of Absolute Values
Bimanual: Integrated	61.3	77.6
Bimanual: Independent	69.4	84.6
Unimanual	67.0	84.9

handedness. In general, however, left-handers are less likely than right-handers to exhibit strongly consistent hand preference (i.e., to report exclusive use of the preferred hand for *all* activities surveyed by typical handedness inventories). This fact is reflected by the growing trend in the literature to replace use of the term "left-handed" with "non-right-handed".

A second study, providing evidence for greater interhemispheric integration in subjects with personal or familial sinistrality, focused on tasks requiring same-different judgements (Christman, 1992). In two of the tasks from Experiment 1, subjects decided whether a verbal component of a foveally presented stimulus was the same as or different than the spatial component. For example, subjects saw a line drawing of a face that was either smiling or frowning; written across the center of the face was either the word *happy* or *sad*. Subjects judged whether or not the facial expression of a schematic face matched the word it contained in it. A second task involved Stroop-type stimuli for which subjects had to indicate whether the color name matched the actual color of the stimulus. In a third task, subjects judged whether the local dimension of a stimulus matched the global dimension, using the hierarchical letter stimuli developed by Navon (1977). The fourth task required subjects to judge whether or not the left and right halves of complex geometric objects were the same, defined as being mirror images of each other (i.e., making the figure left-right symmetrical). Examples of the stimuli are shown in Fig. 7.1. Because verbal, local, and right hemispace judgements are typically better performed by the left hemisphere, and spatial, global, and left-hemispace judgements are better performed by the right hemisphere, these tasks presumably require interhemispheric integration. Therefore, subjects with personal or familial sinistrality were hypothesized to be better at them.

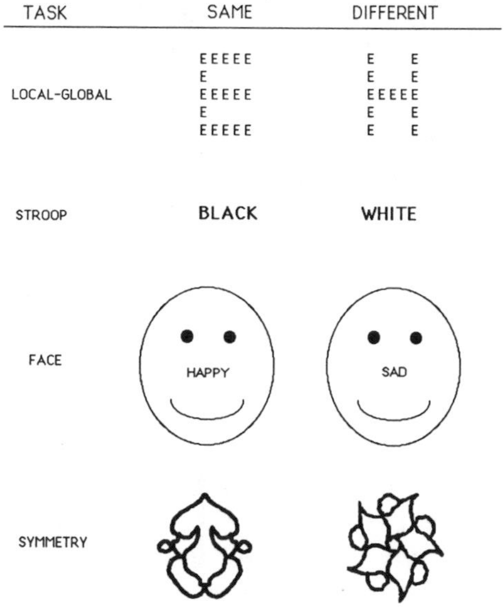

FIG. 7.1. Examples of stimuli employed in same-differnt tasks (Christman, 1992).

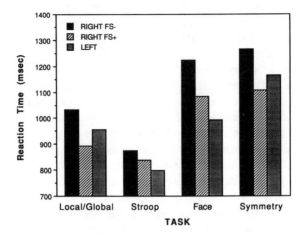

FIG. 7.2. Reaction time data for *same* judgments as a function of task. Experiment 1 (error bars indicate mean standard error).

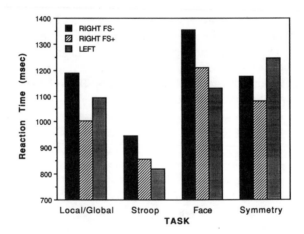

FIG. 7.3. Reaction time data for *different* judgments as a function of task. Experiment 1 (error bars indicate mean standard error).

Results for the verbal/spatial and local/global tasks supported the hypothesis: reaction times (RTs) for left-handers and right-handers with familial sinistrality (FS$^+$) were significantly faster than for right-handers without familial sinistrality (FS$^-$) for the local/global ($p<.05$), Stroop ($p<.03$), and face ($p<.01$) tasks (see Fig. 7.2 and 7.3 for from same and different trials, respectively). I suggest that the symmetry task yielded no differences between subject groups ($F<1$). The failure of the sinistral groups to exhibit an advantage on this task may have arisen from two factors. First, the symmetry task required interhemispheric integration of perceptual information, whereas the other three tasks required the transfer of higher level cognitive information. This is consistent with the observation that the regions of the corpus callosum that are larger in left-handers are those regions involved in the transfer of more abstract information; those callosal regions (e.g., the splenium) involved in the transfer of sensory information do not differ between handedness groups (Habib, Gayraud, Regis, & Oliva, 1990; Witelson, 1989). Second, the relative disadvantage shown by left-handed subjects may be related to findings of greater left-right confusion among left-handers (e.g., Hannay, Ciaccia, Kerr, & Barrett, 1990). The fact that sinistrality was *not* associated with a performance advantage in the symmetry task is useful in ruling out the possibility that sinistrality was simply associated with a general RT advantage, regardless of the specific nature of the task.

In Experiment 2, I sought to replicate these findings. The local/global and facial tasks from the first experiment were repeated, along with two other same-different tasks involving judgments of physical versus name identity in pairs of letters. The letter matching tasks were adapted from the work of Posner, Boies, Eichelman, & Taylor (1969), with physical matching "same" responses only to structurally identical letter pairs (e.g., AA), and the name identity task requiring "same" responses to letter pairs shairing a common name (e.g., AA and Aa). The latter two tasks were chosen because, although they still involve same-different judgments, they do not require the same degree of explicit interhemispheric integration, and can presumably be adequately performed intrahemispherically. The results for the local/global and facial tasks replicated those of the first experiment (see Figs. 7.4 and 7.5): Comparison of the performance of the FS⁻ right-handers with that of left-handers revealed marginally superior performance on the local/global task ($p<.065$) and significantly better performance on the facial task ($p<.05$) in left-handers. Data from the FS⁺ right-handers fell between those of the other two groups. On the two letter-matching tasks, on the other hand, there were no differences at all among the handedness groups (all $Fs<1$). These results are useful in ruling out the possibility that the superiority of the subjects with personal or familial sinistrality arose simply from an overall advantage in performing tasks requiring same-different judgments, regardless of the degree of interhemispheric integration instead. Rather, the results suggest that the advantage shown by subjects with personal and familial sinistrality arises from an explicit advantage in the integration of LH and RH processes.

Experiment 3 concentrated on local versus global processing, a task with a rich tradition in cognitive psychology. Left- and right-handed subjects participated in each of three tasks: the foveal same-different task employed in the aforementioned studies, a focused attention task in which subjects had to explicitly identify the letter appearing at a given level (with separate blocks run requiring responses to the local versus global levels), and a parafoveal divided attention task in which subjects had to describe whether a given target letter was present at either level.

The focused attention task was chosen to serve as a complement to the same-different task: Whereas the same-different task requires explicit integration

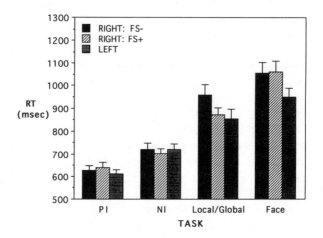

FIG. 7.4. Reaction time data for *same* judgments as a function of task. Experiment 2 (error bars indicate mean standard error).

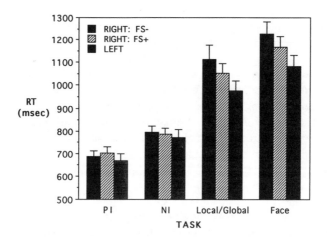

FIG. 7.5. Reaction time data for *different* judgments as a function of task. Experiment 2 (error bars indicate mean standard error).

of information occurring at the local and global levels, under conditions of focused attention, subjects must ignore one of the levels. A typical finding with this paradigm is that subjects *cannot* ignore the irrelevant level, leading to interference effects when the information at the two levels is incongruent. This leads to a situation where greater independence of local versus global processing (and of LH versus RH processing) should lead to decreased interference between the two levels. Thus, although left-handers were again hypothesized to exhibit superior performance on the same-different task, right-handers were expected to outperform left-handers on the focused attention task, where greater independence between LH and RH processes is advantageous. Indeed, Robertson, Lamb, and Zaidel (1993) reported that split-brain patients, who exhibit maximal degrees of interhemispheric independence, show greatly reduced interference effects in focused attention paradigms. Finally, the divided attention task utilized left and right visual field presentations and served to provide an estimate of the degree of lateralization for local versus global processing. This allowed for an examination of how the degree of lateralization is related to the degree of interhemispheric interaction.

The results for the same-different task (see Fig. 7.6) yielded a nonsignificant advantage for left-handers ($p<.10$). Although a significant advantage for left-handers on the local/global same-different task was obtained in the Experiment 1 only, there were marginal trends of an advantage for left-handers in both other experiments. An analysis of the combined data for left- and right-handers from all three experiments yielded a highly significant overall advantage for left-handers ($p<.007$), suggesting that valid differences as a function of handedness do exist for this task.

In the focused attention task (see Fig. 7.7), left-handers exhibited significantly greater interference from the irrelevant level for both locally and globally focused conditions ($p<.001$). This result is consistent with the framework in which patterns of lesser interhemispheric interaction (as in right-handed and split-brain subjects) result in lower interference from irrelevant levels in local/global processing.

The results for the divided attention task showed no effects at all of handedness: Both left- and right-handers exhibited equivalent LH versus RH specialization for the processing of local versus global information, respectively (see Fig. 7.8). This result suggests that the degree of lateralization is unrelated to the degree of interhemispheric interaction. Finally, no significant correlations between the same-different RTs and the focused attention RTs were obtained. This strongly suggests that the phenomenon of interhemispheric integration versus independence should not be considered to be opposite sides of the same coin. That is, although left-handers as a whole exhibited both greater interhemispheric integration and lesser interhemispheric independence, the left-handers who showed the *most* integration were not necessarily the same ones who exhibited the *least* independence. This implies that facilitative and/or integrative interaction between the hemispheres may involve separate mechanisms from those involved in

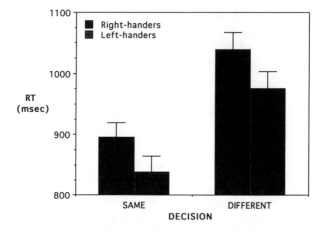

FIG. 7.6. Reaction time data for same-different tasks as a function of subject handedness. Experiment 3 (error bars indicate mean standard errors).

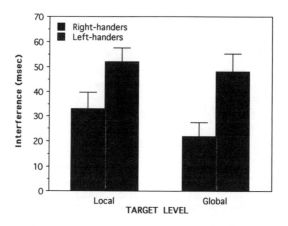

FIG. 7.7. Interference data (incongruent RT minus congruent RT) for focused attention task as a function of target level and subject handedness. Experiment 3 (error bars indicate mean standard error).

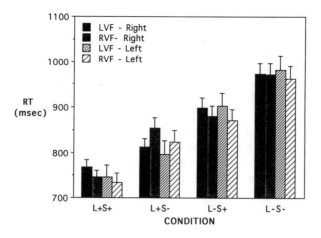

FIG. 7.8. Reaction time data for divided attention task as a function of stimulus type, visual field, and subject handedness. Experiment 3 (error bars indicate mean standard error).

inhibitory and/or independent interhemispheric interaction.

RELATED FINDINGS

Certain reports of individual differences in the mainstream cognitive psychology literature may be explained in terms of the framework developed in this chapter. MacLeod, Hunt, and Mathews (1978) reported individual differences in performance on a task developed by Clark and Chase (1972) in which a subject first observes a sentence, such as Plus Is Above Star, and then a picture showing a plus sign above or below a star. The subject's task is to indicate, as rapidly as possible, whether or not the sentence is a true description of the picture. MacLeod et al. examined individual differences in the verification of such sentence-picture relationships, and isolated a small group of subjects who exhibited a qualitatively different pattern of performance than the others. The majority of subjects adopted a strategy of converting the picture into a propositional format for comparison with the initial sentence; a small subset of subjects, on the other hand, appeared to adopt the opposite strategy of converting the sentence into a pictorial format for comparison with the subsequent picture. The subset of subjects employing the pictorial strategy were found to exhibit faster verification RTs, as well as significantly higher spatial ability. Future research could attempt to determine whether subjects employing the pictorial strategy are more likely to exhibit personal or familial sinistrality: perhaps pictorial codes are better integrated interhemispherically than are linguistic codes, leading non-right-handers to more readily adopt the pictorial strategy.

Although some researchers (e.g., Levy, 1969; E. Miller, 1971; Nebes, 1971) have reported that left-handers have poorer spatial ability than right-handers (and, hence, would *not* be expected to comprise the pictorial strategy subset), there are several reasons to question the generalizability of this finding. First, several studies have failed to find evidence for spatial deficits among non-right-handers (e.g., Fennel, Satz, Van den Abell, Bowers, & Thomas, 1978; Hardyck, 1977; Hardyck, Petrinovich, & Goldman, 1976). Second, some studies have indicated that handedness and gender variables interact in their relationship to measures of spatial ability (e.g., Kocel, 1976; McKeever, Seitz, Hoff, Marino, & Diehl, 1983). Because MacLeod et al. (1978) did not break their spatial strategy group down by gender composition, handedness and gender may have been confounded. For example, their spatial strategy group may have consisted primarily of left-handed males. Finally, Geschwind & Galaburda (1985) suggested that the relation between handedness and spatial ability may display bimodal effects; that is, non-right-handed subjects may be overrepresented at *both* ends of the spectrum of spatial ability .

Similarly, Yee and Hunt (1991) have recently reported individual differences in Stroop interference effects. Some subjects exhibited strong interference from the presence of color words while naming color patches, while other subjects showed little or no interference. The current hypothetical framework predicts that right-handers should show less interference than non-right-handers, assuming that the hemispheric mechanisms for naming the color versus naming the word are more independent in right-handers.

Finally, Ward (1985) reported individual differences in the tendency to process the dimensions of multidimensional stimuli in a separable versus an integral manner. The dimensions of his stimuli can be roughly construed as being analogous to the local/global dimensions of hierarchical stimuli. He reported that although some subjects could process the information from the two dimensions in an independent and separable manner, other subjects displayed a tendency to process the two dimensions in an integrated manner. This finding echoes the current findings of handedness differences in local/global processing, with right-handers being more likely to exhibit independent processing of the two levels, and left-handers being more likely to show integrated processing. The possibility that left-handers may, indeed, have been overrepresented in the integrated processing group in Ward's study is strengthened by Ward's finding that those subjects exhibited greater field dependence than the subjects who processed the stimulus dimensions in a more separable manner. Numerous studies have reported left-handers to be more field dependent that right-handers (e.g., O'Connor & Shaw, 1978; Silverman, Adevai, & McGough, 1966).

Recent work on aspects of interhemispheric processing of spatial frequency information may also be informed by investigation into the influence of individual differences. For example, Berardi and her associates (Berardi, Bodis-Wollner, Fiorentini, Giuffre, & Morelli, 1989; Berardi & Fiorentini, 1987) have presented psychophysiological and behavioral evidence that lower spatial frequencies are more readily transferred interhemispherically than are higher frequencies. This leads to the possibility that the extent of this preferential transfer of low-frequency information could be relatively greater in non-right-handers, leading to a situation in which the processing resources of both hemispheres could be more readily brought to bear on input. Although Christman (1991) found no differences among handedness groups in a task requiring same-different judgments on pairs of low-spatial-frequency stimuli presented successively, tasks involving simultaneous presentation or a deeper processing of the input may yield such differences. If so, this could help account for previous reports of advantages for left-handed subjects in both foveal and lateralized processing of lower spatial frequency information (Christman, 1989; 1991a). Given the evidence for important hemispheric differences in the processing of spatial frequency information (e.g., Kitterle, Christman, & Hellige, 1990; Sergent, 1982), examination of individual differences in this area could generate interesting insights.

The current theoretical framework may also shed light on a recent report of increased accident-related injury risk among left-handers. Coren (1989) found that left-handers (especially males) were significantly more likely than right-handers to have suffered an injury requiring medical attention while driving a vehicle. Coren interprets this result in terms of "implicit and explicit biases of the environment toward maximal convenience of the right-handed majority" (p. 1040-1041). There are two potential problems with this explanation. First, of the five categories of accidental injury, the difference in risk between left- and right-handers was significant only for accidents involving vehicles. It is not clear why environmental biases should act more strongly in conjunction with motor vehicles than with other tools and household objects. Second, given the evidence for greater ambilateral hand skill among at least certain subgroups of left-handers, along with extensive bimanual training and practice at operating a vehicle, it seems unlikely that an uncoordinated right hand is solely responsible for left-handers increased risk for traffic accidents. An alternative explanation derives from viewing driving as often constituting a dual-task situation: one task involving operating the vehicle, and the other "task" taking the form of some sort of verbal activity (e.g., talking to a passenger, listening to the radio, talking on a car phone, etc.). In this situation, the right-hander may have an advantage in keeping the demands of the spatial (RH) driving task independent from those of the verbal (LH) task, preventing crosstalk and mutual interference. In left- or mixed-handers, on the other hand, the two hemispheres may not be as able to carry out their separate tasks independently, and may integrate their processing by focussing on one of the two tasks; clearly, if the verbal activity dominates, the risk for spatial inattention (and consequent accident) would greatly increase.

It is important to note that the predictions of greater dual-task interference in left-handers when the two tasks tap processing resources from within a single hemisphere may be limited to situations in which there is neither response uncertainty nor competition (i.e., in the scenario described, although individuals are carrying out two tasks concurrently, explicit responses to the two tasks are not necessarily carried out concurrently). Pashler and O'Brien (1993) have recently demonstrated that when subjects must respond concurrently to two tasks, the obtained interference does not depend on whether the two tasks are lateralized to the same or opposite hemispheres; rather, the locus of interference appears to arise at some central bottleneck in response selection. Their study, however, employed only right-handed subjects, so the question of whether left-handers may exhibit interhemispheric dual-task interference under conditions of response uncertainty remains unaddressed. Similarly, left- and right-handers may differ in the characteristics of the central bottleneck in response selection. Future work will need to address the nature of interference as a function of response variables, as well as stimulus and task variables.

The current framework could be extended to issues of linguistic processing. There is evidence for independent and parallel processing of intonational information by the right hemisphere and phonetic information by the left hemisphere (Blumstein & Cooper, 1974; Hartje, Willmes, & Weniger, 1985). Similarly, along with a wealth of data supporting LH specialization for syntactic processing, evidence points to RH specialization for the processing of thematic, metaphoric, and pragmatic information (e.g., Brownell, Michel, Powelson, & Gardner, 1983; Hough, 1990; Kaplan, Brownell, Jacobs, & Gardner, 1990). In normal discourse, the interplay between the structural and conceptual levels of information clearly plays a crucial role in understanding. Although these two levels are often in concordance, certain forms of discourse feature a dissociation between the two levels: for example, in sarcasm, the speaker's utterance is literally false, and the listener must utilize contextual information to arrive at the correct non-literal interpretation. The hypothesis developed in this chapter suggests that left- and right-handers should differ in the nature of interaction among these different levels of processing. Specifically, left-handers may exhibit greater sensitivity to mismatches between the syntactic and pragmatic content of utterances which arises from the greater integration of LH and RH processing. Similarly, when the structural and conceptual levels are concordant, left-handers may achieve quicker and/or greater comprehension by taking advantage of the complementary redundancy between the two levels.

A recent report by Iverson and Bever (1989) provides intriguing data in this area. They tested right-handed subjects, with or without left-handed relatives, on their comprehension of auditory essays. For some essays, presentation was monaural, for others, the function words were presented to one ear and the content words were presented to the other ear. Presumably, the former condition required less interhemispheric integration and the latter required more. In the monaural condition, subjects without left-handed relatives exhibited superior comprehension, whereas in the switching condition, subjects with left-handed relatives exhibited superior performance. Although this study did not compare left- and right-handers, right-handers with familial sinistrality have been shown to exhibit less lateralization than those without (for a review, see McKeever, 1990), suggesting, in accordance with the pilot data presented earlier, that left-handers and FS[+] right-handers may exhibit similar patterns of hemispheric interaction.

SUMMARY AND IMPLICATIONS

The proposed theoretical framework addresses the nature and importance of individual differences in processing ability in terms of the pattern and degree of cerebral lateralization. Its goal is to provide contact between neuropsychological theories of handedness and models of mainstream cognition by exploring the implications of cerebral lateralization for performance under ecological conditions of nonlateralized input. It goes beyond previous research by stressing a systems approach, placing a greater analytic emphasis on *how* different functions are lateralized, as opposed to simply *what* functions are lateralized. Although performance differences between right-handed and non-right-handed subjects for input presented directly to the left and right hemispheres are well-documented, such findings have provided relatively little insight into the nature of possible differences between such subject groups under more ecologically valid conditions in which both hemispheres have equivalent access to input. Thus, the emphasis of the current approach is not on LH *versus* RH skills, but rather on the interaction between LH and RH skills.

Such research could play a vital role in reconciling and synthesizing theories of cerebral laterality with more general theories of information processing and individual differences in performance and ability. Currently, individual differences in performance in both neuropsychological and cognitive research are typically treated as random error variance to be ignored and collapsed over (although there have been intriguing developments recently in this regard; e.g., see Kim, Levine, & Kertesz, 1990). However, if variations in the degree and nature of interhemispheric interaction affect the manner in which various subcomponents of task processing are coordinated, then individual differences in cerebral lateralization and interaction could be an important variable of interest in the design and interpretation of research in a great many areas of psychological inquiry, above and beyond issues of strictly neuropsychological interest. For example, if individual differences in handedness are found to affect patterns of performance in conditions of non-lateralized presentation of input, then researchers interested in questions of general information processing may want to pay closer attention to patterns of handedness among their subjects, an issue that has typically been of concern only to laterality researchers. Because handedness can be easily assessed by questionnaire, it provides a readily available measure of individual differences that could be employed as a simple adjunct to mainstream psychological experimentation.

Similarly, the current hypothesis could have important practical implications for vocational issues related to job-specific skills. Non-right-handers have been found to be overrepresented in some occupations, and the proposed research could shed light on what abilities such persons possess that make them better suited for certain professions. For example, left-handers have been found to be over-represented among architects (Peterson & Lansky, 1977). A successful architect may need to balance the spatial/aesthetic demands of designing an attractive-looking structure with the more analytic demands required by considerations of functionality (e.g., number and purpose of rooms, wiring and ventilation requirements, etc.). If the spatial and analytic requirements require RH and LH processes, respectively, then left-handers may possess an advantage in integrating these constraints to achieve an optimal balance. A similar line of reasoning may help account for a similar overrepresentation of left-handers among college students majoring in art (Mebert & Michel, 1980).

Finally, the research on this topic could shed light on the debate concerning the concept of *hemisphericity*. Bogen, DeZure, Tenhouten, and Marsh (1972) devised the term hemisphericity to refer to the hypothesized tendency for people to rely more on the mode of processing of one hemisphere more than on the other. The idea of hemisphericity has come under conceptual attack (Beaumont, Young, & McManus, 1984; Hardyck & Haapanen, 1979). One of the main critiques that Beaumont et al. levelled against the theoretical basis of hemisphericity is that "it seems to ignore the fact that the cerebral hemispheres work together in normal people, forming a single integrated system" (p. 205). The hypothesis developed in the current proposal suggests that what is important may not be tendencies to prefer the use of one hemisphere over another (a simplistic notion to begin with, because most complex tasks presumably require the resources of both hemispheres); rather, an important factor in determining individual differences in cognitive style may be the extent to which the processing abilities of the left and right cerebral hemispheres operate in a relatively integrated versus an independent manner.

REFERENCES

Banich, M., & Belger, A. (1990). Interhemispheric interaction: How do the hemispheres divide and conquer a task? *Cortex, 26*, 77-94.

Banich, M., & Belger, A. (1991). Inter- versus intrahemispheric concordance of judgements in a nonexplicit memory task. *Brain and Cognition, 15*, 131-137.

Beaton, A. (1985). *Left side, right side: A review of laterality research*. New Haven: Yale University Press.

Beaumont, G., & Dimond, S. (1973). Transfer between the cerebral hemispheres in human learning. *Acta Psychologica, 37*, 87-91.

Beaumont, G., & Dimond, S. (1975). Interhemispheric transfer of figural information in right- and non-right-handed subjects. *Acta Psychologica, 39*, 97-104.

Beaumont, J.G., Young, A., & McManus, I. (1984). Hemisphericity: A critical review. *Cognitive Neuropsychology, 1*, 191-212.

Berardi, N., Bodis-Wollner, I., Fiorentini, A., Giuffre, G., & Morelli, M. (1989). Electrophysiological evidence for interhemispheric transmission of visual information in man. *Journal of Physiology, 411*, 207-225.

Berardi, N., & Fiorentini, N. (1987). Interhemispheric transfer of visual information in humans: Spatial characteristics. *Journal of Physiology, 384*, 633-647.

Berry, G., Hughes, R., & Jackson, L. (1980). Sex and handedness in simple and integrated task performance. *Perceptual and Motor Skills, 51*, 807-812.

Blumstein, S., & Cooper, W. (1974). Hemispheric processing of intonation contours. *Cortex, 10*, 146-158.

Bogen, J., DeZure, R., Tenhouten, W., & Marsh, J. (1972). The other side of the brain IV: The A/P ratio. *Bulletin of the Los Angeles Neurological Societies, 37,* 49-61.

Brownell, H., Michel, D., Powelson, J., & Gardner, H. (1983). Surprise but not coherence: Sensitivity to verbal humor in right-hemisphere patients. *Brain and Language, 18,* 20-27.

Byrne, B. (1974). Handedness and musical ability. *British Journal of Psychology, 65,* 279-281.

Christman, S. (1989). Temporal integration of form as a function of subject handedness and retinal locus of presentation. *Neuropsychologia, 27,* 1373-1382.

Christman, S. (1991). *Negative evidence for differences among gender and handedness groups in inter-hemispheric transfer of visual information.* Paper presented at the 19th annual meeting of the International Neuropsychological Society, San Antonio, TX.

Christman, S. (1993a). Handedness in musicians: Bimanual constraints on performance. *Brain and Cognition, 22,* 266-272.

Christman, S. (1993b). *Integration versus independence of bihemispheric processing of foveally presented input.* Manuscript submitted for publication.

Clark, H., & Chase, W. (1972). On the process of comparing sentences to pictures. *Cognitive Psychology, 3,* 472-517.

Coren, S. (1989). Left-handedness and accident-related injury risk. *American Journal of Public Health, 79,* 1040-1041.

Davis, R., & Schmit, V. (1973). Visual and verbal coding in the interhemispheric transfer of information. *Acta Psychologica, 37,* 229-240.

Dimond, S., & Beaumont, G. (1971). Use of two cerebral hemispheres to increase brain capacity. *Science, 232,* 270-271.

Dimond, S., & Beaumont, G. (1972a). Processing in perceptual integration between and within the cerebral hemispheres. *British Journal of Psychology, 63,* 509-514.

Dimond, S., & Beaumont, G. (1972b). Hemisphere function and color naming. *Journal of Experimental Psychology, 96,* 87-91.

Fennel, E., Satz, P., Van den Abell, T., Bowers, D., & Thomas, R. (1978). Visuospatial competency, handedness and cerebral dominance. *Brain and Language, 5,* 206-214.

Fodor, J. (1983). *The modularity of mind.* Cambridge, Mass.: MIT Press.

Friedman, A., & Polson, M. (1981). The hemispheres as independent resource systems: Limited-capacity processing and cerebral specialization. *Journal of Experimental Psychology: Human Perception and Performance, 7,* 1031-1058.

Geschwind, N., & Galaburda, A. (1985). *Cerebral lateralization.* Cambridge: MIT Press.

Gotestam, K.O. (1990). Lefthandedness among students of architecture and music. *Perceptual and Motor Skills, 70,* 1323-1327.

Habib, M., Gayraud, D., Regis, J. & Oliva, A. (1990, May). *The corpus callosum is larger in right-handed females and non-right-handed males.* Paper presented at the meeting TENNET, Montreal.

Hannay, H.J., Ciaccia P., Kerr, J., & Barrett, D. (1990). Self-report of right-left confusion in college men and women. *Perceptual and Motor Skills, 70,* 451-457.

Hardyck, C. (1977). Handedness and part-whole relationships: A replication. *Cortex, 13,* 177-183.

Hardyck, C., & Haapanen, R. (1979). Educating both halves of the brain: Educational breakthrough or neuromythology? *Journal of School Psychology, 17,* 219-230.

Hardyck, C., & Petrinovich, L. (1977). Left-handedness. *Psychological Bulletin, 84,* 385-404.

Hardyck, C., Petrinovich, L., & Goldman, R. (1976). Left-handedness and cognitive deficit. *Cortex, 12,* 266-279.

Hartje, W., Willmes, K., & Weniger, D. (1985). Is there parallel and independent hemispheric processing of intonational and phonetic components of dichotic speech stimuli? *Brain and Language, 24,* 83-99.

Haugeland, J. (1978). The nature and plausibility of cognitivism. *Behavioral and Brain Sciences, 2,* 215-260.

Hellige, J. (1990). Hemispheric asymmetry. *Annual Review of Psychology, 41,* 55-80.

Hellige, J., Cowin, E., & Eng, T. (1991, February). *Processing of CVC syllables from LVF, RVF, and foveal locations.* Paper presented at the 19th Annual Meeting of the International Neuropsychological Society, San Antonio, TX.

Hellige, J., Jonsson, J., & Michimata, C. (1988). Processing from LVF, RVF and BILATERAL presentations: Examinations of metacontrol and interhemispheric interaction. *Brain and Cognition, 7,* 39-53.

Hellige, J., Taylor, A., & Eng, T. (1989). Interhemispheric interaction when both hemispheres have access to the same stimulus information. *Journal of Experimental Psychology: Human Perception and Performance, 15,* 711-722.

Honda, T. (1982). Effects of handedness on the inhibition of reaction time in double stimulation situations. *Japanese Psychological Research, 24,* 43-47.

Hough, M. (1990). Narrative comprehension in adults with right- and left hemisphere brain-damage: Theme organization. *Brain and Language, 38,* 253-277.

Iverson, P., & Bever, T. (1989). *Auditory lexical segregation, comprehension and familial handedness.* (Cognitive Science Technical Report No. 45). Rochester, NY: University of Rochester, Department of Psychology.

Jones, B. (1982). The integrative action of the cerebral hemispheres. *Perception & Psychophysics, 32,* 423-433.

Kaplan, J., Brownell, H., Jacobs, J., & Gardner, H. (1990). The effects of right hemisphere damage on the pragmatic interpretation of conversational remarks. *Brain and Language, 38*, 315-333.

Kim, H., Levine, S., & Kertesz, S. (1990). Are variations among subjects in lateral asymmetry real individual differences or random error in measurement? Putting variability in its place. *Brain and Cognition, 14*, 220-242.

Kimura, D., & Vanderwolf, C. (1970). The relation between hand preference and the performance of individual finger movements by the left and right hands. *Brain, 93*, 769-774.

Kinsbourne, M., & Hicks, R. (1978). Functional cerebral space: A model for overflow, transfer, and interference effects in human performance. In J. Requin (Ed.), *Attention and performance VII* (pp. 345-362). Hillsdale, NJ: Lawrence Erlbaum Associates.

Kitterle, F., Christman, S., & Hellige, J. (1990). Hemispheric differences are found in the identification, but not the detection, of low versus high spatial frequencies. *Perception & Psychophysics, 48*, 297-306.

Kleinman, K., & Little, R. (1973). Inter-hemispheric transfer of meaningful visual information in normal human subjects. *Nature, 241*, 55-57.

Kocel, K. (1976). Cognitive abilities: Handedness, familial sinistrality, and sex. *Annals of the New York Academy of Sciences, 280*, 233-243.

Levy, J. (1969). Possible basis for the evolution of lateral specialization of the human brain. *Nature, 224*, 614-615.

Levy, J., & Trevarthen, C. (1976). Metacontrol of hemispheric functions in human split-brain patients. *Journal of Experimental Psychology: Human Perception and Performance, 2*, 299-312.

Liederman, J., Merola, J., & Martinez, S. (1985). Interhemispheric collaboration in response to simultaneous bilateral input. *Neuropsychologia, 23*, 673-683.

Lordahl, D., Kleinman, K., Levy, B., Massoth, N., Pessin, M., Storandt, M., Tucker, R., & Vanderplas, J. (1965). *Psychonomic Science, 3*, 245-246.

MacLeod, E., Hunt, E., & Matthews, N. (1978). Individual differences in the verification of sentence-picture relationships. *Journal of Verbal Learning and Verbal Behavior, 17*, 493-507.

McKeever, W. (1990). Familial sinistrality and cerebral organization. In S. Coren (Ed.), *Left-handedness: Behavioral implications and anomalies* (pp. 373-412). Amsterdam: Elsevier.

McKeever, W., Seitz, K., Hoff, A., Marino, M., & Diehl, J. (1983). Interacting sex and familial sinistrality characteristics influence both language lateralization and spatial ability in right handers. *Neuropsychologia, 21*, 661-668.

Mebert, C., & Michel, G. (1980). Handedness in artists. In J. Herron (ed.), *Neuropsychology of left-handedness*. New York: Academic Press.

Merola, J., & Liederman, J. (1988, January). *The extent to which between-hemisphere division of inputs improves performance depends on task difficulty*. Paper presented at the 16th annual meeting of the International Neuropsychological Society, New Orleans, LA.

Miller, E. (1971). Handedness and the pattern of human ability. *British Journal of Psychology, 62*, 111-112.

Miller, L. (1983). Hemifield independence in the left handed. *Brain and Language, 20*, 33-43.

Navon, D. (1977). Forest before trees: The precedence of global features in visual perception. *Cognitive Psychology, 9*, 353-383.

Nebes, R. (1971). Handedness and perception of part-whole relations. *Cortex, 8*, 350-356.

O'Boyle, M., & Hellige, J. (1989). Cerebral hemisphere asymmetry and individual differences in cognition. *Learning and Individual Differences, 1*, 7-35.

O'Connor, K., & Shaw, J. (1978). Field dependence, laterality and the EEG. *Biological Psychology, 6*, 93-109.

Oldfield, R. (1969). Handedness in musicians. *British Journal of Psychology, 60*, 91-99.

Parlow, S., & Kinsbourne, M. (1981). Handwriting posture and manual motor asymmetry in sinistrals. *Neuropsychologia, 19*, 687-696.

Pashler, H., & O'Brien, S. (1993). Dual-task interference and the cerebral hemispheres. *Journal of Experimental Psychology: Human Perception and Performance, 19*, 315-330.

Peterson, J., & Lansky, L. (1977). Left handedness among architects: Partial replication and some new data. *Perceptual and Motor Skills, 45*, 1216-1218.

Posner, M., Boies, S., Eichelman, W., & Taylor, R. (1969). Retention of visual and name codes of single letters. *Journal of Experimental Psychology Monograph, 79*, 1-16.

Potter, S., & Graves, R. (1988). Is interhemispheric transfer related to handedness and gender? *Neuropsychologia, 26*, 319-325.

Robertson, L., Lamb, M. & Zaidel, E. (1993). Interhemispheric relations in processing hierarchical patterns: Evidence from normal and commissurotomized subjects. *Neuropsychology, 7*, 525-542.

Sereno, A., & Kosslyn, S. (1991). Discrimination within and between hemifields: A new constraint on theories of attention. *Neuropsychologia, 29*, 659-676.

Sergent, J. (1982). The cerebral balance of power: Confrontation or cooperation? *Journal of Experimental Psychology: Human Perception and Performance, 8*, 253-272.

Silverman, A., Adevai, G., & McGough, W. (1966). Some relationships between handedness and perception. *Journal of Psychosomatic Research, 10*, 151-158.

Verillo, R. (1983). Vibrotactile subjective magnitude as a function of hand preference. *Neuropsychologia, 21*, 383-395.

Ward, T. (1985). Individual differences in processing stimulus dimensions: Relation to selective processing abilities. *Perception & Psychophysics, 37*, 471-482.

Witelson, S. (1985). The brain connection: The corpus callosum is larger in left-handers. *Science, 229,* 665-668.

Witelson, S. (1989). Hand and sex differences in the isthmus and genu of the human corpus callosum. *Brain, 112,* 799-835.

Yee, P., & Hunt, E. (1991). Individual differences in Stroop dilution: Tests of the attention-capture hypothesis. *Journal of Experimental Psychology: Human Perception and Performance, 17,* 715-725.

8 Individual Differences in Characteristic Arousal Asymmetry: Implications for Cognitive Functioning

Susan C. Levine
University of Chicago

This chapter addresses the question of whether individual differences in asymmetry scores on laterality tests are related to individual differences in cognitive functioning. Such a relation might be expected based on various clinical findings, notably reports that patients with unilateral brain damage show particular cognitive deficits that are associated with the laterality of their lesion (e.g., Hécaen, 1962; Milner, 1968; Milner, Branch, & Rasmussen, 1964; Warrington, James, & Kinsbourne, 1966) Despite such expectations, prior research has generally failed to uncover a consistent relation between measures of hemispheric specialization and measures of cognitive functioning in normal subjects (see review by Beaumont, Young, & McManus, 1984). In the studies reported in this chapter, laterality scores are viewed as reflecting both characteristic hemispheric arousal asymmetry and patterns of hemispheric specialization (Levy, Heller, Banich, & Burton, 1983b). This approach, combined with the use of cognitive tasks that differentially involve the left and right cerebral hemispheres, appears to yield more positive findings.

INDIVIDUAL DIFFERENCES IN CHARACTERISTIC AROUSAL ASYMMETRY: BACKGROUND

Numerous explanations have been proposed to account for the extreme variability in perceptual asymmetries among normal dextrals on standardly used laterality tasks (e.g., dichotic listening and lateralized tachistoscopic presentation). These include unreliability of asymmetry scores indexed by laterality tasks (Chiarello, Dronkers, & Hardyck, 1984; Colbourn, 1978; Satz, 1977; Schwartz & Kirsner, 1984, Teng, 1981), individual differences in hemispheric specialization (Boles, 1989; Shankweiler & Studdert-Kennedy, 1975), asymmetric pathway dominance (Hellige, Bloch, & Taylor, 1988) and individual differences in characteristic hemispheric arousal asymmetry (Levy et al., 1983b). The relative merits and shortcomings of these various hypotheses are reviewed elsewhere (Kim & Levine, 1991b; Kim, Levine, & Kertesz, 1990), and will not be discussed in detail here.

Briefly, the hypothesis that variations in asymmetry scores are attributable to unreliability is problematic because similar variations are observed when highly reliable tasks are used (e.g., Levine & Levy, 1986; Wexler, Halwes, & Heninger,

1981). Further, the hypothesis that individual differences in asymmetry scores are attributable to variations in underlying hemispheric specialization is problematic because the proportion of normal dextrals with a reversed direction of asymmetry far exceeds that predicted by clinical data obtained from brain damaged patients (e.g., Rasmussen & Milner, 1977; Wada & Rasmussen, 1960).

Levy et al.'s (1983b) hypothesis that variations in dextrals' asymmetry scores on laterality tasks are largely attributable to variations in characteristic arousal asymmetry appears to have the strongest empirical support (e.g., Kim & Levine, 1991a, 1991b; Kim et. al., 1990; Levine, Banich, & Kim, 1987; Levine, Banich, & Koch-Weser, 1988; Luh, Ruekert, & Levy, 1991). According to this hypothesis, a subject's perceptual asymmetry on a standard laterality task is a joint function of his or her pattern of hemispheric specialization and his or her characteristic arousal asymmetry. It is further hypothesized that hemispheric specialization is relatively stable both across dextrals as a group and within individual subjects. In contrast, characteristic arousal asymmetry is hypothesized to be highly variable across subjects, but highly stable within individual subjects. Some of the research findings from our laboratory supporting these findings are reviewed here. Following this review, I report the results of a set of studies that address the question of whether individual differences in characteristic arousal asymmetry are related to individual differences in cognitive functioning.

REVIEW OF RESEARCH SUPPORTING CHARACTERISTIC AROUSAL ASYMMETRY

Levy et al. (1983b) hypothesized that a subject's perceptual asymmetry on a standard laterality task was a joint function of his or her pattern of hemispheric specialization and his or her characteristic arousal asymmetry. That asymmetry scores are influenced by underlying patterns of hemispheric specialization is reflected by findings that mean asymmetry scores across subjects shift in expected directions for left-hemisphere (LH), nonlateralized, and right-hemisphere (RH) tasks. The finding that individual subjects maintain the same position relative to other subjects in the distributions of asymmetry scores on an array of laterality tasks would support the hypothesis that asymmetry scores are also influenced by individual differences in characteristic arousal asymmetry. Figure 8.1 displays hypothetical results one might obtain for subjects whose asymmetry scores reflect both hemispheric specialization and characteristic arousal asymmetry (Kim et al., 1990).

Our studies, using dichotic listening and bilateral tachistoscopic presentation of a range of stimuli, have borne out this pattern. In one study (Kim et. al., 1990), 4- and 5-letter words that were the names of common objects, line drawings of common objects, photographs of chairs, and photographs of faces were presented for bilateral tachistoscopic viewing. In addition, the free vision chimeric face task of Levy, Heller, Banich, and Burton (1983a) was given to each subject. On this task each chimera consisted of one-half of an individual's face with a smiling pose and the other half with a neutral pose. The subject's task on each of 36 trials was to decide which of two mirror-imaged chimeras looked

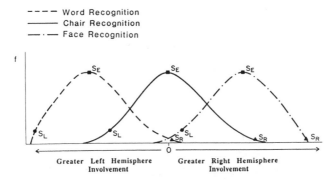

FIG. 8.1. Asymmetry scores predicted by a strong version of the arousal hypothesis of a right hemisphere aroused subject (SR), a symmetrically aroused subject (SE), and a left hemisphere aroused subject (SL), on a left hemisphere specialized word recognition task, a nonlateralized chair recognition task, and a right hemisphere specialized face recognition task.

happier, the one with the smile on the left or the one with the smile on the right. Results showed a significant right visual field (RVF) advantage for the recognition of words, significant left visual field (LVF) advantages for the recognition of line drawings and faces, a significant leftward bias on the free vision face task, and no significant asymmetry for the recognition of chairs. Further, on dividing subjects on the basis of their asymmetry scores on the nonlateralized chair task, we found significant group differences in asymmetry scores on the other three tachistoscopic tasks, as well as on the free vision face task. Thus, the group that showed a LVF advantage on the chair task (Group LChair) showed larger LVF scores and smaller RVF scores on all the tachistoscopic tasks than the group that showed a RVF advantage on the chair task (Group RChair). In addition, Group LChair showed a larger leftward bias on the facebook task than Group RChair (Fig. 8.2).

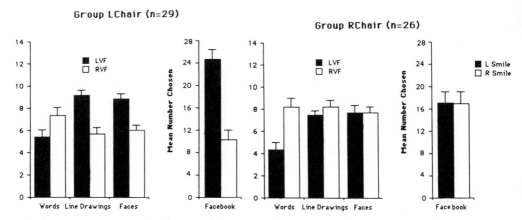

FIG. 8.2. Mean number of LVF and RVF correct responses for the tachistoscopic tasks and mean number of leftward and rightward responses for the free-vision facebook task for Group LChair and Group RChair.

To investigate further the hypothesis that laterality scores reflect characteristic arousal asymmetry, we performed a principal components analysis on subjects' asymmetry score on all five laterality tasks. This analysis revealed two principal components with eigenvalues greater than unity. The first component (PC1) was characterized by high and homogeneous loadings of all five tasks in the same direction. This component accounted for 45.2% of the total variance in subjects' asymmetry scores. A median split of subjects based on this component indicated that the asymmetry scores of subjects with high PC1 scores were displaced toward the right on all five laterality tasks relative to those of subjects with low PCl scores (see Fig. 8.3). The emergence of this component supports the hypothesis that subjects' asymmetry scores reflect individual differences in characteristic arousal asymmetry.

The second principal component (PC2), which accounted for 23.9% of the total variance, was characterized by opposite loadings on the face tasks

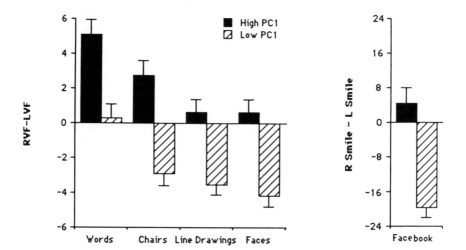

FIG. 8.3. Mean asymmetry scores for the tachistoscopic tasks (RVF-LVF) and facebook task (R Smile - LSmile) of high and low PC1 Groups as defined by a median-split on the first principal component scores.

(tachistoscopic face recognition task and the free vision face task) and the object recognition tasks (tachistoscopic chair and line drawing tasks). This may reflect individual differences in hemispheric involvement in processing faces versus non-faces (Luh, Rueckert, & Levy, 1991). This component is not discussed in detail here, because it is not directly relevant to the issue of characteristic arousal asymmetry. (For further discussion, see Kim et al., 1990.)

In addition to this study, a meta-analytic review by Kim and Levine (1991b) lends strong support to Levy et al.'s (1983b) hypothesis that individual differences in asymmetry scores largely reflect characteristic arousal asymmetry. Meta-analyses were carried out on studies that have reported correlations between subjects' asymmetry scores on LH- and RH- specialized tasks. These analyses showed positive correlations among asymmetry scores on visually presented laterality tasks and among asymmetry scores on auditory laterality tasks (asymmetry scores computed as R - L for both left and right hemisphere specialized tasks), and these correlations were more positive when stimuli were presented bilaterally than when they were presented unilaterally. Thus, at least for bilaterally presented visual and auditory laterality tasks, a significant amount of the between-subjects variability in asymmetry scores appears to reflect non-stimulus specific individual differences in perceptual asymmetry, or what Levy et al. (1983b) referred to as *characteristic arousal asymmetry.*

We next addressed the question of whether these individual differences are related to individual differences in cognitive functioning. A priori, one might hypothesize that subjects whose characteristic arousal asymmetry favors the right hemisphere might perform better on RH-specialized tasks such as certain types of face recognition and attentional tasks, and that subjects whose characteristic arousal asymmetry favors the left hemisphere might perform better on LH-specialized tasks, such as word recognition. Although less likely, for certain tasks performance may be better when characteristic arousal asymmetry is discordant with the specialized hemisphere. Such a situation may result in attention to stimuli being more evenly distributed across perceptual space.

As noted previously, prior studies aimed at uncovering the relation between hemispheric specialization and cognitive task performance generally have not yielded positive findings (Beaumont et al., 1984). This review pointed out that, for the most part, the cognitive indices that have been used in these studies have been taken from IQ tests. In such studies, it is commonly assumed that those tasks that are verbal in nature differentially involve the left hemisphere, and those tasks that are more spatial in nature differentially involve the right hemisphere. However, even with clinical populations such global measures have not been good indices of lesion laterality (Beaumont et al., 1984). Thus, it is not surprising that in our own laboratory we found no relation between normal subjects' characteristic arousal asymmetry and their performance on cognitive tasks such as digit span, verbal fluency, mental rotation, and recognition memory for a series of faces (Kim et al., 1990).

In view of these negative findings, we decided to use more discreet cognitive tasks that have been shown to differentially involve one hemisphere or the other in normal adults to investigate whether there is a relation between individual differences in arousal asymmetry and cognitive task performance. This has proven to be a better approach in studying the relationship between lesion laterality and cognitive task performance in brain-damaged patients (e.g., Beaumont et al., 1984). Moreover, one of our prior studies suggested that this approach might yield positive results with normal subjects. In particular, we found that subjects with characteristic arousal asymmetry in favor of the right hemisphere needed a shorter mean exposure duration to correctly recognize faces than subjects with characteristic arousal asymmetry in favor of the left hemisphere. Whereas this was true for recognition of face photographs presented in the upright orientation, a task that shows a significant LVF-RH advantage, it was not true of the same face photographs presented in the inverted orientation, a task on which performance in the two visual fields does not differ (Levine et al., 1988).

Perceptual Asymmetry and Performance on Left- and Right-Hemisphere Specialized Tasks

We carried out a set of studies addressing the question of whether characteristic arousal asymmetry is related to performance on LH- and RH-specialized tasks. In view of Kim and Levine's (1991a) findings, in all of the studies we used bilaterally presented laterality tasks to assess individual differences in characteristic arousal asymmetry. As a starting point, we hypothesized that performance level on a particular task would be better when characteristic arousal asymmetry was concordant with the hemisphere specialized for the cognitive processes underlying that task.

Our first study tested the hypothesis that subjects with characteristic arousal asymmetry in favor of the right hemisphere have a performance advantage on an attentional task that differentially involves the right hemisphere. Our second study tested the hypothesis that subjects with characteristic arousal asymmetry in favor of the left hemisphere have a performance advantage on a word recognition task that differentially involves the left hemisphere. Our third study examines the relations among arousal asymmetry, strategy choice, and performance level on a task involving numerical comparison.

Experiment 1: Attentional Orienting. In this study, carried out by Levine, Yen and Kim (1992), we addressed the question of whether subjects who differ in characteristic arousal asymmetry also differ in their capacity to orient to peripheral visual stimuli following valid and invalid peripheral locational cues. In particular, we tested the hypothesis that subjects with characteristic arousal asymmetry in favor of the right hemisphere would have faster reaction times (RTs), in general, than subjects with characteristic arousal asymmetry in favor of the left hemisphere.

This hypothesis is based on findings of faster simple RTs among subjects with larger leftward biases on Levy et al.'s (1983a) free vision face task (Burton & Levy, 1991; Wirsen, Klinteberg, Levander, & Schalling, 1990), by findings that simple reaction is increased more by RH than LH damage (Benson & Barton, 1970; De Renzi & Faglioni, 1965; Howes & Boller, 1975), and by findings that the right hemisphere is more effective in orienting attention across space than the left hemisphere (Heilman & Van den Abell, 1980). These data suggest that the right hemisphere plays a more important role in regulating certain aspects of attention and vigilance than does the left hemisphere (for a review, see Heilman & Watson, 1977; Mesulam, 1981).

The subjects in this experiment were 36 right-handed subjects from the University of Chicago community. On each trial of the attention task, subjects began by viewing a small central fixation box and two large boxes, one to the left of center and one to the right. A trial consisted of the outline(s) of the left, the right, or both large peripheral boxes becoming bold for 250 msec. Then, after an interstimulus interval (ISI) of 50, 200 or 500 msec, a small black target appeared in the center of the left or right peripheral box. The subject's task was to press a key on the computer keyboard with the right index finger as quickly as possible following presentation of the target stimulus. Three different types of experimental trials were given: valid trials, invalid trials, and neutral trials. Valid trials were those on which the target stimulus appeared at the center of the cued square, invalid trials were those on which the target stimulus appeared at the center of the square in the field opposite the cued square, and neutral trials were those on which both sides were cued and the stimulus appeared at the center of each peripheral box 50% of the time (see Fig. 8.4).

In addition to this attention task, subjects' characteristic arousal asymmetry was assessed through three lateralized tachistoscopic tasks and one free vision

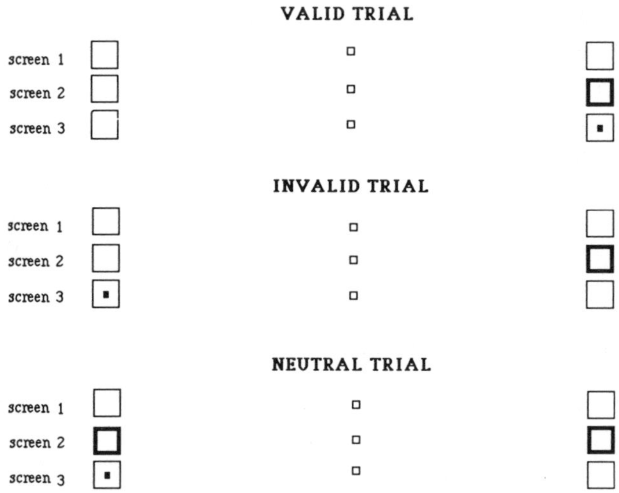

FIG. 8.4. Lateralized Attention Paradigm: Valid Trials: Those on which the target stimulus appeared at the center of the cued square (50% of experimental trials); Invalid Trials: Those on which the target stimulus appeared at the center of the square in the field opposite to the cued square (25% of experimental trials); Neutral Trials: Those on which both peripheral boxes were cued and the stimulus appeared at the center of each box 50% of the time (25% of experimental trials).

laterality task. The tachistoscopic tasks involved recognizing bilaterally presented photographs of chairs, photographs of faces, and vertically aligned words typed in black capital letters. Each stimulus card had a central fixation symbol, as well as two stimuli of the same kind placed equidistant from the midline, one in the LVF and the other one in the RVF.   Trials were blocked by stimulus type so that the chair task was given first, followed, in counterbalanced order, by the face task and the word task. On the chair task as well as on the face task, subjects selected the stimuli seen from a 12-item choice array. On the word task, subjects verbally reported whatever words or letters they had seen. Exposure duration was varied from trial to trial to maintain performance level at approximately 50% correct for each stimulus type. However, the exposure duration was never less than 10 msec or greater than 200 msec.

Following the tachistoscopic tasks, subjects were given Levy et al.'s (1983a) free vision chimeric face task. The subject's task on each trial was to decide which of two mirror-imaged chimeras looked happier. Rightward responses were those in which the chimera with the smile to the subject's right was chosen as looking happier, and leftward responses were those for which the chimera on the left was designated as happier. *Can't decide* responses were allowed in the event that the subject could not make a decision.

Consistent with Posner and Cohen's (1980) findings, our results showed that, compared to other trial types, subjects responded faster to valid and neutral trials at the 50 msec ISI, faster to neutral trials at the 200 msec ISI, and faster to invalid trials at the 500 msec ISI. This switch from faster responding on valid trials to faster responding on invalid trials is characterized by Posner and Cohen as reflecting inhibition of attentional return to the cued position at longer ISIs.

The results also showed that in certain conditions, LVF warning cues were more effective than RVF warning cues on the attention task. In particular, in the 200 msec ISI condition, trials with LVF warning signals were responded to significantly faster than trials with RVF warning signals. In the 500 msec condition trials with LVF warning signals were responded to faster only on invalid trials. Thus, in the 500 msec ISI condition, subjects responded faster to RVF target stimuli preceded by LVF warnings than to LVF target stimuli preceded by RVF warnings. These results are consistent with Heilman and van den Abell's (1980) findings that the attentional orienting capacity of the right hemisphere is superior to that of the left.

We next tested the hypothesis that subjects with characteristic arousal asymmetry in favor of the right hemisphere have faster RTs, in general, than subjects with characteristic arousal asymmetry in favor of the left hemisphere. Individual subjects' arousal asymmetries were indexed by performing a principal components analysis on asymmetry scores on the three tachistoscopic tasks and Levy et al.'s (1983b) free vision face task. As in previous studies, all four tasks loaded in the same direction on the first component, consistent with the hypothesis that characteristic arousal asymmetry affects subjects' asymmetry scores. Subjects were divided into three groups on the basis of their principal component scores, a LH arousal group (high PC1), an intermediate group (middle PC1 group) and a

RH arousal group (low PC1). Consistent with our first hypothesis, an analysis of variance showed that subjects in the RH arousal group responded faster than subjects in the LH arousal group (309 msec vs. 362 msec, $p<.05$). The mean reaction time of the intermediate arousal group (323 msec) was closer to that of the RH arousal group, but did not differ significantly from either of the other groups.

Thus, for an attentional orienting task on which LVF-RH cues are more effective than RVF-LH cues, at least in some conditions, we have evidence that subjects with RH arousal asymmetry have a performance advantage. This finding is consistent with results reported by Wirsen et al. (1990) with normal subjects on simple reaction time. In addition, they are consistent with the finding that simple reaction time to auditory stimuli is faster in patients with unilateral LH than unilateral RH lesions (Howes & Boller, 1975).

Experiment 2: Processing of Bilateral Redundant and Nonredundant Words. This study, carried out by Levine, Bogner, Taylor, and Kim, addressed the question of whether subjects with characteristic arousal asymmetry in favor of the left hemisphere show a performance advantage in processing bilaterally presented word stimuli, a task that has previously been shown to differentially involve the left hemisphere in right-handed subjects.

Forty-nine right-handed subjects, drawn from the University of Chicago community, were shown 20 pairs of bilateral redundant words (the same word presented simultaneously in each visual field; [BVF]) and 20 pairs of bilateral nonredundant words (different words presented simultaneously in each visual field; see Fig. 8.5 for example of stimuli). The stimuli were randomly intermixed so that on any given trial subjects did not know whether a redundant or nonredundant word pair would be presented. We also examined the types of errors made by subjects in the two arousal groups.

An analysis of variance with visual field of presentation as a within subjects factor, revealed a highly significant effect of visual field ($p<.0001$), such that BVF

BILATERAL REDUNDANT TRIAL   BILATERAL NON-REDUNDANT TRIAL

```
F               F       G                       O
R               R       L                       R
U       *       U       O          +            G
I               I       B                       A
T               T       E                       N
```

FIG. 8.5. Example of bilateral redundant word trial and bilateral non-redundant word trial.

performance was superior to both RVF and LVF performance, and RVF performance was superior to LVF performance. The finding of superior performance on RVF than LVF nonredundant trials supports differential LH involvement in that task. The finding that performance on BVF trials is superior to LVF nonredundant and RVF nonredundant trials reflects an advantage of redundant over conflicting information in the two visual fields.

In order to address the question of whether subjects with characteristic arousal asymmetry in favor of the right or left hemisphere differ in performance on a word recognition task, a LH-specialized task, subjects were divided by median split on the basis of their asymmetry score on the bilateral nonredundant word recognition task. Unlike Experiment 1, subjects in this study were not given multiple laterality tasks, so we were forced to rely on the asymmetry scores from one task. A comparison of the performance of these groups in the bilateral redundant condition revealed higher word recognition scores for the group with characteristic arousal asymmetry in favor of the left hemisphere than in the group with characteristic arousal asymmetry in favor of the right hemisphere ($p = .05$). This difference in bilateral redundant performance is more marked for subjects with extreme arousal asymmetries, that is, those with arousal asymmetry scores that were ± 1 SD from the mean ($p < .005$).

We next examined the types of errors made on words presented in the LVF and RVF both by the group of subjects as a whole and by the two median split groups. In particular, we calculated the relative numbers of errors that were first-letter errors (e.g., *rake* for *fake*) and last-letter errors (e.g., *lean* for *leaf*). Although subjects typically make more last-letter than first-letter errors, the discrepancy between these two error types has been found to vary for the two visual fields. Levy et al. (1983b) hypothesized that a wider gap between the relative numbers of last-letter errors and first-letter errors, as is typically found for words presented in the LVF-RH, reflects more sequential letter-by-letter encoding. In contrast, a narrower gap between last-letter and first-letter errors, typically found for words presented in the RVF-LH is thought to reflect more holistic encoding. In agreement with previous findings (Hellige, Jonsson, & Michimata, 1988; Levy et al., 1983b), the whole group of subjects showed a wider difference between the relative number of first- and last-letter errors for words presented in the LVF-RH than for words presented in the RVF-LH. However, we found no significant difference in the qualitative error patterns between the two arousal groups, defined either by median split or ± 1 SD. The absence of such a difference suggests that the left and right hemispheres of the two arousal asymmetry groups are similarly specialized for word recognition. Thus, the performance advantage in favor of the group with arousal asymmetry in favor of the left hemisphere appears to be attributable to the greater arousal level allocated to the more specialized left hemisphere and not to a qualitative difference between the arousal groups in the nature of the specialized processes of the two hemispheres for visual word recognition.

Experiment 3: Numerosity Judgements using Digital versus Spatial Representations of Number. The results of Experiments 1 and 2, considered together, show that for an attentional task that differentially involves the right hemisphere, the RH-arousal group has a performance advantage. In contrast, for a word recognition task that differentially involves the left hemisphere, the LH-arousal group has a performance advantage.

The final study carried out by Levine, Fernandez, Tang, and Stigler (in preparation), provides some preliminary information about the interaction of arousal asymmetry, strategy choice, and performance level on a task. This study clearly shows that there is a complex and most likely dynamic relation between hemispheric involvement in a particular task and performance level on that task. In particular, this relation appears to be influenced by strategy choice, characteristic arousal asymmetry, and, no doubt, a multiplicity of other factors.

In this study, two groups of subjects were tested, one on a numerosity judgment task involving digit stimuli and the other on a numerosity judgment task involving block stimuli. Figure 8.6 depicts a trial from each task. Trials consisted of pairings of different numerosities between 1 and 10. On both the digit and the block tasks subjects pressed a key on the computer keyboard if the peripheral numerosity was larger than the center numerosity and did not respond if the reverse was true. The same numerosity comparisons were presented in each condition. Following the numerosity judgment task, subjects were given the free vision facebook task (Levy et al., 1983b).

We were particularly interested in the strategies that subjects adopted on

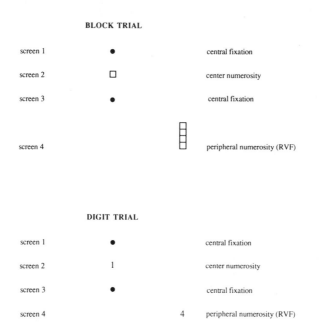

FIG. 8.6. Example of block numerosity judgment trial and digit numerosity judgment trial.

the block task. Strategies were identified by correlating each subject's RTs on block task problems to the mean RTs obtained on corresponding problems by the group of subjects who did the digit task. Based on the level of these correlations, subjects were then divided by median split into two groups, referred to as the like-digit group and the unlike-digit group. The like-digit group included the half of subjects with higher correlations between reaction times on corresponding block task and digit task problems (mean $r = .52$, $SD = .17$). This group of subjects appeared to make numerosity judgments on the block task in a manner similar to that used by the subjects who made numerosity judgments on the digit task. The unlike-digit group included the half of subjects with lower correlations between reaction times on corresponding block and digit problems (mean $r = -.09$, $SD = .25$). This group appeared to make numerosity in a different manner than subjects who made numerosity judgments on the digit task, perhaps on the basis of a visual comparison of the columns of blocks.

Independent of the strategy group that subjects were placed in, each subject was placed in an arousal asymmetry group based on a median split of subjects' asymmetry scores on the free vision facebook task: Mean asymmetry was calculated as (# faces with smile on right judged happier - # of faces with smile on left judged happier)/36. Thus, the 50% of subjects that showed the greatest tendency to choose the face with the smile on the left as happier were placed in the group with characteristic arousal asymmetry in favor of the left side of space (and the right hemisphere), and the other 50% of subjects were placed in the group with characteristic arousal asymmetry in favor of the right side of space (and left hemisphere). Mean asymmetry scores were -.62 ($SD = .18$) for the RH-aroused group and .21 ($SD = .35$) for the LH-aroused group.

Data analyses showed an overall RVF advantage on the block numerosity task ($p < .002$). Thus, based on the results of our prior studies, one might hypothesize that LH-aroused subjects would be at an advantage compared to RH-aroused subjects. However, our results showed a more complex relationship, in that performance level on the task was influenced by the strategies subjects adopted as well as their characteristic arousal asymmetries.

Overall, subjects in the unlike-digit group had faster overall reaction times than subjects in the like-digit group ($p < .0001$). We hypothesized that subjects in the unlike-digit group would have faster RTs on across-column comparisons (e.g., a trial such as 3 vs. 7, where one numerosity, 3, involves a single column of blocks and the other numerosity, 7, involves two columns of blocks) than on within column comparisons (e.g., a trial such as 6 vs. 10, where both numerosities involve two columns of blocks), because of the obvious spatial difference in the across column comparison. In contrast, we hypothesized that subjects in the like-digit group would not show this RT difference. In fact, this was the case: Subjects in the unlike digit group had significantly faster RTs on the across- than on the within-column comparisons ($p < .04$) whereas subjects in the like-digit group did not show this pattern. Unpredicted, however, was the finding that subjects in the like-digit group had significantly faster RTs on the within- than across-column comparisons ($p<.02$). The reason for this is not clear, but the difference in the RT patterns of the two groups provides further support for the contention that these groups are adopting different strategies on the block numerosity judgment task.

Results also show that the strategy adopted is not related to characteristic arousal asymmetry group. In particular, approximately 50% of subjects in each arousal asymmetry group were classified as taking a like-digit strategy and 50% as taking an unlike-digit strategy. However, the effectiveness of the strategy adopted appears to be highly related to arousal asymmetry: RTs of RH-aroused and LH-aroused subjects who adopted the more efficient unlike-digit strategy did not differ. However, when the less optimal like-digit strategy was adopted, there was a significant difference between the RTs of LH-aroused and RH-aroused subjects. This difference is characterized by slower RTs of RH-aroused than LH-aroused subjects in the like-digit group, particularly on RVF-LH trials.

To summarize, the results of Experiment 3 indicate that the hypothesis that LH-aroused subjects should on average, perform better on LH-specialized tasks and RH-aroused subjects should, on average, perform better on RH-specialized tasks is too simplistic. It is also important to take into account the strategy adopted by the subject in performing a task in analyzing the relation between arousal asymmetry and performance on cognitive tasks. Although strategy choice was not found to be related to characteristic arousal asymmetry, the adaptiveness of a particular strategy choice was found to be related to characteristic arousal asymmetry.

CONCLUSIONS

The results of this set of studies indicate that there is a relation between the characteristic hemispheric arousal asymmetry of normal subjects and performance level on certain RH- and LH-specialized tasks. The pattern of these findings is consistent with the well-known literature on brain-damaged patients in which particular patterns of deficit have been associated with lesion laterality. The results of Experiment 3 suggest that the relation between hemispheric involvement and performance level in normals may have been elusive in past studies because it is modifiable by the strategy a subject adopts in performing a task. In particular, certain strategy-arousal group combinations appear to be detrimental to task performance. In our study, for example, RH-aroused subjects who adopted a like-digit strategy performed particularly poorly. Moreover, our findings clearly show that subjects with different arousal asymmetry patterns do not necessarily adopt what appear to be optimal strategies. Future studies need to focus more on the influences of strategy choice on the performance level of subjects with different patterns of hemispheric arousal. Furthermore, an interesting open question remains regarding the extent to which performance on a task can be improved by training subjects with different characteristic arousal asymmetry patterns to adopt more optimal strategies.

REFERENCES

Beaumont, J.G., Young, A.W., & McManus, I.C. (1984). Hemisphericity: A Critical Review. *Cognitive Neuropsychology, 1,* 191-212.

Benson, D.F., & Barton, M.I. (1970). Disturbances in constructional ability. *Cortex, 6,* 19-46.

Boles, D.B. (1989). Do visual field asymmetries intercorrelate? *Neuropsychologia, 27,* 697-704.

Burton, L.A., & Levy, J. (1991). Effects of processing speed on cerebral asymmetry for left and right oriented faces. *Brain and Cognition, 15,* 95-105.

Chiarello, C., Dronkers, N.F., & Hardcyk, C. (1984). Choosing sides: On the variability of language lateralization in normal subjects. *Neuropsychologia, 22,* 363-373.

Colburn, C.J. (1978). Can laterality be measured? *Neuropsychologia, 16,* 283-289.

DeRenzi, E. & Faglioni, P. (1965). The comparative efficiency of intelligence and vigilance tests in detecting hemispheric cerebral damage. *Cortex, 1,* 410-433.

Hécaen, H. (1962). Clinical symptomatology in right and left hemisphere lesions. In V.B. Mountcastle (Ed.), *Interhemispheric relations and cerebral dominance* (pp. 215-243). Baltimore, MD: Johns Hopkins University Press.

Heilman, K.M., & Van Den Abell, T. (1980). Right hemisphere dominance for attention: The mechanism underlying hemispheric asymmetries of inattention (neglect). *Neurology, 30,* 327-330.

Heilman, K.M., & Watson, R.T. (1977). Mechanisms underlying the unilateral neglect syndrome. *Advances in Neurology, 18,* 93-106.

Hellige, J.B., Bloch, M.I., & Taylor, A.K. (1988). Multitask investigation of individual differences in hemispheric asymmetry. *Journal of Experimental Psychology: Human Perception and Performance, 14,* 176-187.

Hellige, J.B., Jonsson, J.E., & Michimata, C. (1988). Processing from LVF, RVF and bilateral presentations: Examinations of metacontrol and interhemispheric interaction. *Brain and Cognition, 7,* 39-53.

Howes, D., & Boller, F. (1975). Simple reaction time: Evidence for focal impairment from lesions of the right hemisphere. *Brain, 98,* 317-332.

Kim, H., & Levine, S.C. (1991). Sources of between subject variability in perceptual asymmetries: A meta analytic review. *Neuropsychologia, 29,* 877-888.

Kim, H., & Levine, S.C. (1991). Inferring patterns of hemispheric specialization for individual subjects from laterality data: A two-task criterion, *Neuropsychologia, 29,* 93-105.

Kim, H., & Levine, S.C. (1991). Sources of between-subjects variability in asymmetry scores: A meta-analytic review. *Neuropsychologia, 29,* 877-888.

Kim, H., Levine, S.C., & Kertesz, S. (1990). Are variations among subjects in lateral asymmetry real individual differences or random error in measurements? Putting variability in its place. *Brain and Cognition, 14,* 230-242.

Levine, S.C., Banich, M.T., & Kim, H. (1987). Variations in arousal asymmetry: Implications for face processing. In D. Ottoson (Ed.) *Duality and unity of the brain* (pp. 207-222). Wenner-Oren Center International Symposium Series.

Levine, S.C., Banich, M.T., & Koch-Weser, M.P. (1988). Face recognition: A general or specific right hemisphere capacity? *Brain and Cognition, 8,* 303-325.

Levine, S.C., & Levy, J. (1986). Perceptual asymmetry for chimeric faces across the lifespan. *Brain and Cognition, 5,* 291-306.

Levine, S.C., Yen, S., & Kim, H. (1992, February). *Lateralized attentional orienting: Effects of individual differences in characteristic perceptual asymmetry.* Presented at the Twentieth Annual International Neuropsychology Conference, San Diego, CA.

Levy, J., Heller, W., Banich, M., & Burton, L. A. (1983b). Are variation among right-handed individuals in perceptual asymmetries caused by characteristic arousal differences between hemispheres? *Journal of Experimental Psychology: Human Perception and Performance, 9,* 329-359.

Levy, J. Heller, W., Banich, M., & Burton, L.A. (1983a). Asymmetry of perception in free-viewing of chimeric faces. *Brain and Cognition, 2,* 404-414.

Luh, K.E., Rueckert, L.M., & Levy, J.L. (1991). Perceptual asymmetries for free viewing of several types of chimeric stimuli. *Brain and Cognition, 16,* 83-103.

Mesulam, M.M. (1981). A cortical network for directed attention and unilateral neglect. *Annals of Neurology, 10,* 309-325.

Milner, B. (1968). Visual recognition and recall after right temporal-lobe excision in man. *Neuropsychologia, 6,* 191-209

Milner, B., Branch, C., & Rasmussen, T. (1964). Observations on cerebral dominance. In A.V.S. de Rueck & M. O'Conner (Eds.), *Disorders of language* (pp. 200-222), London: Churchill.

Posner, M.I.,& Cohen, Y. (1980). Attention and the control of movements. In G.E. Stelmach & J. Requin (Eds.), *Tutorials in motor behavior* (pp. 243-258), Amsterdam: North Holland.

Rasmussen, T., & Milner, B. (1977). The role of early left-brain injury in determining lateralization of cerebral speech functions (pp. 355-369). *Annals of the New York Academy of Sciences, 299.*

Satz, P. (1977). Laterality tests: An inferential problem. *Cortex, 13,* 208-212.

Schwartz, S., & Kirsner, K. (1984). Can group differences in hemispheric asymmetry be inferred from behavioral laterality indices? *Brain and Cognition, 3,* 57-70.

Shankweiler, D., & Studdert-Kennedy, M. (1975). A continuum of lateralization for speech perception. *Brain and Language, 2,* 212-225.

Teng, E.L. (1981). Dichotic ear differences is a poor index for the functional asymmetry between the cerebral hemispheres. *Neuropsychologia, 19,* 235-240.

Wada, J., & Rasmussen, T. (1960). Intra-carotid injection of sodium amytal for the lateralization of cerebral speech dominance. *Journal of Neurosurgery, 17,* 266-282.

Warrington, E.K., James, M., & Kinsbourne, M. (1966). Drawing disability in relation to the laterality of cerebral lesion. *Brain, 89,* 53-82.

Wexler, B.E., Halwes, T., & Heninger, G.R. (1981). Use of a statistical significance criterion in drawing inferences about hemispheric dominance for language function from dichotic listening data. *Brain and Language, 13,* 13-18.

Wirsen, A., Klinteberg, S., Levander, S., & Schalling, D. (1990). Differences in asymmetric perception of facial expression in free-vision chimeric stimuli and reaction time. *Brain and Cognition, 12,* 229-239.

9 Interhemispheric Interaction: Mechanisms of Unified Processing

Marie T. Banich
University of Illinois at Urbana-Champaign

The major quest in the field of cognitive neuroscience is to understand how the neural wiring of the brain constrains and shapes the information processing capacity of the human mind. One of the primary features of the neurological organization of the human brain is lateral asymmetry. Not only are the cerebral hemispheres distinct in anatomical structure (e.g., Geschwind & Levitsky, 1968) and biochemical affinity (e.g., Oke, Keller, Mefford, & Adams, 1978), but they differ in their functional specialization, as well. The left hemisphere excels at processing material in a verbal, analytic, and sequential manner, and the right excels at processing material in a nonverbal, holistic, and spatial manner (e.g., Sperry, 1974). Thus, it is important for the agenda of cognitive neuroscience to consider how this aspect of brain organization affects human information processing.

One of the ways in which the functional specialization of the hemispheres has been demonstrated most dramatically is by research with split-brain patients. These are individuals with intractable epilepsy, in whom the hemispheres have been surgically disconnected by severing the corpus callosum, the nerve fiber tract connecting the two halves of the brain. Such surgery allows the cognitive abilities and emotional proclivities of each hemisphere to be explored in isolation. Research on these patients has not only left an extensive legacy of empirical data, but has had considerable impact on the the way in which lateralization of function is conceptualized. Because findings from these studies provided information about the functioning of a hemisphere in isolation, researchers absorbed an inherent bias to conceive of the hemispheres of normal individuals as processing information in an independent manner. Such a bias is exemplified by such statements as, "The right hemisphere is specialized for processing faces," when, in actuality, a typical finding is that the right hemisphere is only 10% more accurate than the left at recognizing faces.

This bias is further compounded by the standard research methods for demonstrating asymmetry of function because, typically, performance of one hemisphere is pitted against that of the other. Generally, perceptual information is directed simultaneously to both hemispheres and the accuracy or speed of processing of material directed to one hemisphere is compared to that directed to the other. Thus, the research paradigms employed have emphasized differences in hemispheric function and have provided little evidence of how such processing might be coordinated.

This gap in our knowledge becomes more glaring in light of the inconsistencies in patterns of perceptual asymmetries observed across studies. For example, although a left visual field (LVF) advantage is usually obtained for face processing tasks, a right visual field (RVF) advantage can be acquired under other conditions. The variability of results across studies has frustrated some researchers in the field who despair that laterality findings are neither robust nor stable. Rather than illustrating that undertaking research in this area is tenuous, these results may be taken as an indication that hemispheric processing in normal individuals is governed by a dynamic, as opposed to a static, system. With the exception of a handful of tasks (e.g., speech production), most tasks can be performed by either hemisphere. However, the hemispheres differ in the manner in which they perform. To use face recognition as an example, it appears that when an overall gestalt of the face must be considered, a right-hemisphere (RH) advantage is found (e.g., Young & Ellis, 1976). In contrast, when one must discriminate between faces that differ on only one feature, a left-hemisphere (LH) advantage emerges (Sergent, 1982). Thus, in normal individuals the 250 million nerve fibers of the corpus callosum allow the hemispheres to work together, so that each can bring its own special expertise to bear on the problem or material at hand.

What remains a mystery, however, is how the hemispheres work as a unified entity. This gap in our knowledge is especially striking given that there is a consensus among researchers in the area that an understanding of the mechanisms and means by which the hemispheres coordinate processing remains a major unanswered question (Hellige, 1990; Wyke, 1982). The research in our laboratory directly addresses these questions by focusing on explicating the nature of the dynamic interactions of the hemispheres in normal individuals and by attempting to understand the implications of such interactions for human information processing.

The findings of the research I review in the following pages can be most aptly summarized as saying that, "The sum of the parts does not equal the whole." The functioning of the hemispheres in isolation, whether derived from research on split-brain patients or inferred in normal individuals from directing information initially to only one hemisphere, does not provide an adequate characterization of how the hemispheres act as an integrated unit. The validity of this statement is demonstrated in two major ways. First, I will show that the processing power of the hemispheres working together can surpass that of the separate capabilities of each hemisphere added together. Second, I will demonstrate that there are many conditions in which the dynamic interaction of the hemispheres cannot be surmised by observing the processing of each hemisphere alone.

ASPECTS OF INTERHEMISPHERIC PROCESSING

One could view interhemispheric processing as merely a simple shuttling mechanism allowing for passive transport of information between the hemispheres. The evidence provided in this chapter presents a much different viewpoint. It suggests that interhemispheric processing has much broader implications for human information processing, both in the ways it enhances processing and the ways in which it constrains processing. When attempting to uncover the mechanisms of interhemispheric processing, it is important to consider that it is a means for coordinating activity between two specialized processing systems, the cerebral hemispheres. Certain advantages and disadvantages are always conferred by a system composed of specialized processors or modules. The main advantage of having specialized processors is that performance can be enhanced by allowing tasks to be performed in more than one way and by allowing for parallel processing of different aspects of information. The main disadvantage is that, at some point, the outcomes of these separate processes must be translated into a common code or coordinated to yield a unified response (see Nelson & Bower, 1990, for a discussion of these issues as they relate to parallel computers).

Considering these points had led me to hypothesize that interhemispheric interaction plays a much larger role in human information processing than simply being a means of keeping the hemispheres in synchrony with one another. In particular, the advantages of interhemispheric processing can be observed most clearly when all the information required to perform a task is available simultaneously. It is under these conditions that the parallel processing capabilities permitted by interhemispheric communication become most apparent and allow for levels of performance that might not otherwise be possible. Furthermore, these increases in processing capability are, by and large, independent of asymmetries in hemispheric processing. These issues are addressed in the first part of the chapter. To complement this picture, one also needs to examine the codes and means by which information is shared between the hemispheres. These issues are addressed in the second half of the chapter.

The Influence of Interhemispheric Processing on Information Processing Capabilities

The Hypothesis: Interhemispheric Processing Aids Performance When Tasks are Computationally Complex. In this section of the chapter it will be argued that interhemispheric interaction is a means whereby the overall processing capacity of the brain is enhanced. Furthermore, such enhancement is viewed as being most apparent when tasks are taxing. One means of determining the influence and effects of interhemispheric interaction on human information processing is to compare task performance when interhemispheric processing is required to situations when it is not. This can be accomplished by contrasting performance in a condition in which information is divided between the hemispheres to performance in a situation in which all the information required for a task is initially directed to only one hemisphere.

The findings of studies employing this experimental approach have been equivocal. Sometimes, performance is superior when information is directed initially to only one hemisphere, *a within-hemisphere advantage* (Beaumont & Dimond, 1973, 1975; Bradshaw, Nettleton, & Patterson, 1973; Dimond, 1969; Dimond & Beaumont, 1974; Dimond, Gibson, & Gazzaniga, 1972; Kleinman & Little, 1973; Leiber, 1982; Liederman, 1986; Liederman, Merola, & Martinez,

1985; Lordahl et al., 1965), and sometimes it is superior when processing is divided between the hemispheres, an *across-hemisphere advantage* (Davis & Schmit, 1971, 1973; Dimond, 1971; Dimond & Beaumont, 1971, 1972a, 1972b; Liederman, Merola, & Hoffman, 1986; Merola & Liederman, 1985; Miller, 1981, 1983). Because there had been no explanation for these conflicting results, I attempted to devise a theory that might account for them.

Generalizing across studies, it appeared that an across-hemisphere advantage emerged when all information was presented simultaneously. When there was an interstimulus interval (ISI) between presentation of different pieces of information, a within-hemisphere advantage was observed. Such patterns appeared to occur regardless of the stimuli employed (e.g., words or faces). I hypothesized that such findings reflect the aid of interhemispheric processing to task performance under conditions in which the processing load is high. The ISI condition can be considered a low-load condition because the presentation of information is dispersed temporally. In contrast, the no-ISI condition represents a higher processing load or a more demanding condition because all the information is presented concurrently.

The suggestion that interhemispheric processing aids task performance under high load conditions is also consistent with findings in split-brain patients. These patients, who cannot transfer information via the cortical commissures, exhibit greater and greater decrements in performance as the difficulty of a task increases (Kreuter, Kinsbourne, & Trevarthen, 1972). The most revealing aspect of these results for the hypothesis at hand is that such decrements, which were much more severe than those observed in normal subjects, occurred even when both tasks were lateralized to the same hemisphere (e.g., reciting the alphabet and tapping with the right hand, both of which rely on the left hemisphere). This is important because, in general, the capacity of a single hemisphere of a split-brain patient to perform a task for which it is specialized is not compromised much compared to that of normal subjects. The fact that performance of split-brain patients under dual-task conditions is so much poorer than that of normal individuals implies that normal individuals decrease heavy processing loads by distributing them across the hemispheres. When the cortical commissures are severed, however, no such distribution is possible and performance plummets.

Methodological Considerations in Testing the Hypothesis. The hypothesis that interhemispheric processing aids performance when tasks are computationally complex was made by generalizing across studies employing diverse methodologies. However, before an empirical test of the hypothesis could be undertaken, a number of methodological issues needed to be addressed. In many previous studies, there were other factors besides interhemispheric processing that could have influenced the pattern of results. It was worth considering the role that two factors, in particular, played in contributing to the across-hemisphere advantage observed under no-ISI conditions.

First, scanning habits related to reading might have influenced the pattern of results in some studies. In these studies, the two items presented on within-hemisphere trials were presented in the same visual field, equally displaced from midline, but with one positioned above the other. In contrast, on across-hemisphere trials, one item was presented in each visual field on the same y coordinate and equally laterally displaced from midline. Thus, on across-hemisphere trials, a postperceptual left-to-right scanning strategy, similar to that typically utilized in reading, could be employed. In contrast, on within-hemisphere trials a top-to-bottom scanning strategy, which is much less typical, had to be employed. Thus, poorer performance on within- than across-hemisphere trials might have occurred, not because interhemispheric processing aids task performance, but because of scanning habits related to reading. A second consideration is that in most experiments the perceptual processing load was not equated on within- and across-hemisphere trials. On across-hemisphere trials, only one item was presented in each visual field, and thus the perceptual processing load on each hemisphere was a single item. In contrast, on within-hemisphere trials, two items were presented in a visual field, so that in these conditions the perceptual processing load on the hemisphere was double that on across-hemisphere trials. Thus, the advantage on across-hemisphere trials might not be due to coordination of processing between the hemispheres, but might derive, rather, from the fact that the number of inputs per hemisphere on across-hemisphere trials was half that on within-hemisphere trials.

To avoid these issues, I constructed arrays consisting of three items. They were located at what would be the vertices of an inverted triangle. Two items, which were never identical, were presented, one in each visual field, equally above and equally lateral from central fixation (2.8°). The third item was displaced an equal distance below midline as the top two, but less laterally displaced (1.4°). In addition, an additional item, whose report was used to ensure central fixation, was placed in the middle of the array (see Fig. 9.1). The subject's task was to decide, as quickly but also as accurately as possible, whether the bottom item matched either of the top two. Half of the trials contained a match and half did not. On half of the match trials, the matching items were positioned in the same visual field (within-hemisphere trials) and on half they were positioned in opposite visual fields (across-hemisphere trials). Furthermore, for half of the trials the bottom item was positioned in the LVF (b-LVF) and for half it was in the RVF (b-RVF).

The advantages of these arrays are that all matching items are aligned along a diagonal, which reduces the possibility that scanning habits related to reading will influence the results. Furthermore, the perceptual processing load is equated on within- and across-hemisphere trials. In both cases, one item is initially directed to one hemisphere, and two items are initially directed to the other (compare within LVF and across b-LVF trials). Thus, any advantage observed for across-hemisphere trials cannot be attributed to a division of inputs between the hemispheres. Finally, a comparison between information initially directed to different hemispheres is ensured because subjects must determine whether the two items match. If subjects just have to report the identity of items, and not reach a decision about them, it is not at all clear that the hemispheres ever need to communicate on across-hemisphere trials. In contrast, requiring a match decision guarantees that communication occurs on across-hemisphere trials.[1]

Empirical Investigations of the Hypothesis. As an initial step in determining whether interhemispheric processing aids performance when tasks are computationally complex, we examined performance on two tasks (Banich, 1985; Banich & Belger, 1990). In one, subjects had to make a perceptual identity decision, determining whether two letters were the same (e.g., *A* and *A*). In the other, subjects had to make a name identity decision, determining if an upper- and a lower-case letter had the same name (e.g., *A* and *a*). The latter task is more complex computationally than the former because it must entail at least one additional step in processing. Not only must perceptual processing be performed on the letters, but these perceptual patterns must then be transformed into some other code (e.g., phonemic) for a match decision to be reached. Also suggesting that the name identity task is the more difficult of the two tasks, mean reaction time (RT) for it is usually significantly longer than RT for the physical identity task (e.g., Posner & Mitchell, 1967), a finding that we also obtained.

Consistent with the hypothesis that interhemispheric processing is useful when tasks are difficult, an across-hemisphere advantage was obtained for the name identity task, whereas a within-hemisphere advantage was obtained for the physical identity task. Furthermore, it was demonstrated that the within-hemisphere advantage obtained for the physical identity task was not limited to the specific type of stimuli employed, namely, letters. A within-hemisphere advantage was also found for a physical identity task in which digits were used as stimuli.

Further evidence that across-hemisphere processing enhances performance when tasks are difficult came from two additional tasks in which digits were employed as stimuli and in which more than a simple physical identity match was required. In one, the summation task, subjects decided if the bottom item plus one of the top items equaled 10 or more. In the other task, the ordinal task, subjects decided if the bottom item was less in value than one of the top items (Banich & Belger, 1990). Both experiments yielded an across-hemisphere advantage. The

---

[1]A possible problem with such arrays, however, is that although items on within- and across-hemisphere trials are displaced an equal distance from midline, the actual distance between matching items is greater on across- than within-hemisphere trials. To determine whether this was a possible confound, I investigated whether performance on within-hemisphere trials relative to across-hemisphere trials varied as a function of the eccentricity of the bottom item: The more laterally displaced the bottom item, the greater the distance between matching items on within-hemisphere trials as compared to across-hemisphere trials. Thus, if the distance between matching items is important, then the more lateral the bottom item, the poorer performance on within-hemisphere trials should be relative to across-hemisphere trials. Suggesting that the distance between matching items was not a problematic factor, performance on within-hemisphere trials relative to across-hemisphere trials was the same whether the eccentricity of the bottom item was 1.05, 1.4 or 1.75 degrees from midline (Banich, 1985).

FIG. 9.1. Examples of match and mismatch arrays for the physical-identity letter task.

results of all of these studies can be found in Table 9.1. They clearly illustrate that when a task requires a decision more difficult than one of simple physical identity, an across-hemisphere advantage is obtained. This suggests that interhemispheric processing aids performance when tasks are difficult, at least when difficulty is manipulated by the complexity of the decision process.

If an hypothesis is to be useful, it should be able to explain a broad variety of phenomena. In all the studies described so far, however, computational complexity has only been manipulated in one manner, namely, by the number of steps required in the decision process. With this in mind, we (Belger & Banich, 1992) recently investigated whether other manipulations of task complexity have similar effects on the influence of interhemispheric processing on task performance. If computational complexity affects interhemispheric processing,

TABLE 9.1. Mean Reaction Time and Percentage of Errors (in Parentheses) for the Various Tasks.

	TRIALTYPE			
	Within LVF	Within RVF	Across b-LVF	Across b-RVF
Physical-identity task - letters	600 (12.2)	652 (18.1)	676 (16.9)	640 (13.1)
Name-identity task - letters	790 (17.3)	854 (24.4)	778 (15.7)	711 (11.9)
Physical-identity task - digits	576 (13.6)	624 (13.9)	631 (15.5)	600 (11.9)
Ordinal task - digits	718 (9.2)	777 (12.8)	702 (8.8)	683 (5.1)
Summation task - digits	697 (6.2)	752 (10.6)	668 (8.2)	639 (4.5)

then it should have analogous effects on performance, regardless of the stage of information processing (e.g., encoding and comparison vs. decision-making) that is manipulated.

In the study designed to address this question, we varied complexity in two manners: (a) by varying the number of inputs to be encoded and compared to the target and (b) by manipulating the complexity of the decision process. Each subject performed three tasks. The first, a physical identity letter task, was identical to the one we have used previously. Subjects were presented with three letters in an inverted triangle configuration and had to decide if the bottom letter of the array was identical to either of the top two. The second task was a 5-letter physical identity task, in which subjects had to decide if the bottom letter matched any of four letters, rather than just two. This manipulation increases the computational complexity of the task at a level other than that of decision making. Complexity is increased, not only because subjects must encode more items, but because they must also make more comparisons between the bottom item and the top ones before a decision can be reached. Our goal in using this task was to determine whether increasing the number of items to be processed would yield an across-hemisphere advantage, as has been found with tasks for which computational complexity is increased at the decision level.

The third task employed was a five-letter name identity task, which differed from the five-letter physical identity task in only one way. Stimulus arrays in the five-letter physical identity task consisted of five uppercase letters, enabling subjects to make a decision simply on the basis of physical features. However, in the five-letter name identity task, the bottom letter was in lowercase, whereas all four others were in uppercase. Under such conditions, subjects are unable to make a simple physical identity comparison, but have to transform the uppercase and lowercase letters to a common code to reach a decision. Thus, an additional stage of processing, or computation, is required to make the name identity decision, as compared to the physical identity decision.

The results of the experiment indicated that increasing task difficulty by adding computations in the encoding and comparison stages causes interhemispheric processing to be beneficial to task performance, just as had been observed for adding computations in the decision process. For the three-letter physical identity task, we obtained a within-hemisphere advantage of marginal significance, which, importantly, did not differ significantly from the within-hemisphere advantage we had obtained previously with this task. Unlike this pattern, the five-letter physical identity task yielded a significant across-hemisphere advantage, indicating that with increased task difficulty at the encoding and comparison stages, interhemispheric processing became beneficial to task performance. Thus, using a different manipulation of complexity than had been used previously, these results confirmed the hypothesis that as the computational complexity of a task increases, interhemispheric processing aids task performance.

Not surprisingly, we also found that the five-letter name identity task yielded a significant across-hemisphere advantage. This result was to be expected because we had previously obtained a significant across-hemisphere advantage for a three-item name identity task. Interestingly, the size of the across-hemisphere advantage for the five-letter name identity task was greater than that observed for the five-letter physical identity task, suggesting that the effects of different types of computational complexity (in the encoding and comparison stage vs. the decision-making stage) had separable effects on interhemispheric processing. This study, then, provides evidence that computational complexity is, indeed, a variable that influences how interhemispheric interaction affects task performance.

Insights Into the Mechanisms by Which Interhemispheric Processing Aids Task Performance. Given these findings, we would like to be able to determine the mechanism by which interhemispheric processing aids task performance when tasks are complex. One possibility is that interhemispheric interaction allows the processing load to be distributed so that the hemispheres can work in parallel, each performing a particular set of operations. Such an idea is consonant with the viewpoint that, at least to some degree, the hemispheres have their own separate resources (e.g., Friedman & Polson, 1981; Hellige & Wong, 1983).

Evidence for such parallel processing comes from examining the pattern of performance on across-hemisphere trials. Unlike previous methodologies, in which there was only one type of across-hemisphere trial, the methodology we employ has two. Differences in performance on these two types of trials provide insights into the manner in which interhemispheric processing can aid task performance. In particular, the pattern of results on across-hemisphere trials suggests that processing is divided so that one hemisphere is responsible primarily for one aspect of processing (e.g., perceptual processing), and the other is responsible primarily for another aspect of processing (e.g., decision-making).

To investigate these issues, we need to determine which hemisphere makes the match decision on different trial types (within LVF, within RVF, across b-LVF, across b-RVF). On within-hemisphere trials, this determination is relatively straightforward, because the hemisphere contralateral to the visual field of presentation of the two matching digits is more likely to do so. However, on across-hemisphere trials, it is possible for either hemisphere to make the match decision. The hemisphere making the decision could either be the one contralateral to the visual field in which the two items are presented, or contralateral to the visual field in which only one is. If the hemisphere contralateral to the visual field of presentation of two items makes the match decision, this would suggest that the majority of processing on across-hemisphere trials is performed by one hemisphere. I refer to as this possibility as the *concentration* model, because most of the processing is concentrated within one hemisphere. In contrast, if the hemisphere contralateral to the visual field of presentation of only one item makes the match decision, this would suggest that processing is distributed across the hemispheres, because one hemisphere performs the majority of the perceptual processing (two items as opposed to one) and the other hemisphere makes the match decision. I call this the *distribution* model. If interhemispheric processing is a means of dispersing the processing load, as posited earlier, then the latter model should be a better description of performance.

A hint as to which model is correct can be obtained by characterizing the results on across-hemisphere trials under the assumptions of each model and determining how parsimonious the pattern is with that observed on the within-hemisphere trials. That is, one can assume that the concentration model is correct and determine whether the pattern of results on across-hemisphere trials under these assumptions "makes sense" with regard to the pattern observed on within-hemisphere trials, and, likewise for the distribution model.

Under the assumptions of the concentration model, the hemisphere making the match decision on across-hemisphere trials is the one contralateral to the visual field of presentation of two items rather than one. Thus, the match decision would be made by the left hemisphere on across b-RVF trials and by the right hemisphere on across b-LVF trials. If we assume that the distribution model, in which the hemisphere making the match decision on across-hemisphere trials is the one contralateral to the visual field of presentation of only one item, the left hemisphere makes the match decision on across b-LVF trials, and the right hemisphere makes the match decision on across b-RVF trials (see Fig. 9.2). Thus, each model makes different assumptions as to which hemisphere makes the match decision on each of the across-hemisphere trials. We can now examine the empirical data from the point of view of each model.

As an example of what each model implies with regard to the empirical data, refer back to the data in Table 9.1 for the letter physical-identity task. Assume, first, that the concentration model is correct. In this case, on across b-RVF trials, the match decision is made by the left hemisphere. This would yield, for trials on which the left hemisphere makes the match decision, an across-hemisphere advantage of approximately 12 msec (compare within RVF and across b-RVF trials). In contrast, for trials on which the right-hemisphere makes the match decision, there would be a within-hemisphere advantage of about 76 msec (compare within LVF and across b-LVF). Thus, under the assumptions of the concentration model, a large asymmetry in interhemispheric processing is observed. Information processing by the left hemisphere would be faster when it must receive information from the right than when it receives all the information directly. In contrast, performance would be much slower for the right hemisphere when it must receive information from the left hemisphere than when all the information is received directly. Given that there is no evidence of 60 msec differences in interhemispheric transfer depending on direction, from the right hemisphere to the left or vice versa, the concentration model seems unlikely to be a good description of how processing occurs on these trials.

In the distribution model, the pattern of results on across-hemisphere trials is much more consistent with that observed on the within-hemisphere trials. Once again, we use the data from the physical identity tasks for letters to evaluate how parsimonious the model is. In the distribution model, the effect of interhemispheric processing is similar regardless of which hemisphere makes the

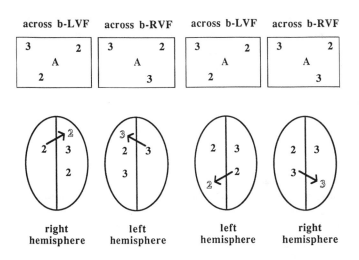

FIG. 9.2. Processing of across-hemisphere trials under the concentration and distribution models.

match decision. Because the left hemisphere is assumed to make the match decision for across b-LVF trials, there is a within-hemisphere advantage for trials on which the left hemisphere makes the match decision (compare within RVF and across b-LVF trials). Likewise, there is a within-hemisphere advantage for trials on which the right hemisphere makes the match decision (compare within LVF and across b-RVF trials). Thus, on the basis of parsimony, it appears that the distribution model is a more apt description of processing on across-hemisphere trials than the concentration model. In fact, the pattern of results on across-field trials for all the experiments listed in Table 9.1 are more parsimonious with that observed on within-field trials under the assumptions of the distribution model than under the assumptions of the concentration model.

The fact that the distribution model is a better description of performance than the concentration model is important, because it suggests that, indeed, interhemispheric interaction allows processing to be dispersed over as much neural space as possible. In this model, the hemisphere that must do the majority of the perceptual encoding (i.e., the hemisphere contralateral to the visual field of presentation of two items) does not have to perform another aspect of the task, namely, the match decision. Thus, this analysis suggests that interhemispheric processing may provide a performance advantage by dividing different aspects or stages of processing across the hemispheres. Such a suggestion is consistent with the proposal made by Liederman (Liederman, 1986; Liederman et al., 1986) that dividing inputs (as compared to directing them to just one hemisphere) will lead to a performance advantage when inputs to each hemisphere require just one kind of processing.

Further evidence of how well the distribution model characterizes performance on across-hemisphere trials comes from two additional experiments. In one (Banich, Stolar, Heller, & Goldman, 1992), two groups of subjects were given the digit matching task. One group performed the task after being induced into a sad mood state, and the other did so after being induced into a neutral mood state. It had been found previously that induction of a sad mood state selectively interferes with the processing of RH trials (Ladavas, Nicoletti, Umilta & Rizzolatti, 1984). Consistent with these findings, we found that the RTs to within LVF trials was significantly longer for the sad-mood induced group than for the neutral-mood-induced group. However, the RTs of the two groups did not differ for within RVF trials.

The concentration and distribution models provide very different predictions of the pattern that should be observed on across-hemisphere trials. The concentration model assumes that the match decision is made by the right hemisphere on across b-LVF trials, and by the left hemisphere on across b-RVF trials. Thus, if this model is correct, RH dysfunction in the sad-mood induced group should be indicated by significantly longer RTs to across b-LVF trials than those observed for the neutral-mood-induced group. Furthermore, RTs to across b-RVF trials should not differ between the two groups. In contrast, the distribution model predicts the opposite: RT for the sad-mood-induced group should be significantly longer than for the neutral-mood induced group for across b-RVF trials but not across b-LVF trials. It is this latter pattern that we observed.

Additional evidence for the validity of the distribution model comes from a study (Banich, Goering, Stolar, & Belger, 1990) in which interhemispheric processing in left- and right-handers was compared (this study is discussed in more detail later on in another context). Although the right-handers did not exhibit a significant difference in RT to within-LVF and within-RVF trials, responses of the left-handers were significantly faster to within-RVF trials than to within-LVF trials. Under the assumptions of the distribution model, the left hemisphere makes the match decision on across b-LVF trials and the right does so on across b-RVF trials. Thus, this model would predict that, for left-handers, RT to across b-LVF trials should be substantially faster than to across b-RVF trials. This is exactly what we observed. Both of these studies, then, provide independent evidence that the distribution model is a good characterization of performance on across-hemisphere trials.

A question raised by these data is how the distribution model would be implemented in the brain. It is important to realize that just because the distribution model provides a good representation of the data, this does not imply that there resides, somewhere in the brain, a piece of neural tissue that "decides" which hemisphere makes the match decision. Rather, the model could be considered completely compatible with the notion that each hemisphere relays the information it receives to its partner, after which a horse race ensues to determine which hemisphere will make the match decision. In this scenario, the distribution model provides a good characterization of performance, because the hemisphere initially receiving only one item can make the match decision more quickly than the hemisphere that receives two items. The beauty of describing the results in this way is that no a priori rule need be invoked as to how to across-field trials will be processed. Thus, there is no need to assume that one hemisphere "knows" it is to make a decision and the other "knows" that it should not. This description of interhemispheric processing contrasts with others suggesting that when identical information is provided to the hemispheres, one dominates performance (e.g., Hellige, Taylor, & Eng, 1990). Thus, our results suggest that the hemispheres need not work in a manner in which one is the "master" and the other is the "slave".

The Degree to Which Hemispheric Specialization Influences Interhemispheric Processing. If one posits that interhemispheric processing is useful because it allows for a dispersion of the load during high-load tasks, it would be of interest to determine how hemispheric specialization constrains or influences this dispersion. Data from the studies I have described here suggest that it has a surprisingly small influence. The pieces of evidence are numerous. First, interhemispheric processing differs for tasks that, nonetheless, yield equivalent perceptual asymmetries (as determined by performance on within-field trials). For example, the physical identity letter tasks yields a significant within-hemisphere advantage and the name identity letter task yields a significant across-hemisphere advantage, yet for both tasks, a RH advantage of approximately 60 msec is found.[2] Likewise, similar patterns of interhemispheric processing can be associated with very different perceptual asymmetries. The name identity task with letters and a spelling task (discussed further on) yield an across-field advantage of equivalent magnitude, even though right-handers exhibit a significant visual field asymmetry on within-field trials for the former task but not the latter. Thus, the degree to which a task is lateralized appears to vary orthogonally with the effect of interhemispheric processing on task performance (Banich, 1986).

Other support for the independence of interhemispheric processing and lateralized performance comes from findings that, across subjects, the degree of asymmetry exhibited on a task is uncorrelated with the size of the within- or across-hemisphere advantage. Still another way we have examined this issue is to compare interhemispheric processing in two groups of subjects who usually exhibit different patterns of lateralized performance, left-handers and right-handers (Banich et al., 1990, Experiment 1). In one experiment, performance on the physical identity digit matching task was compared for 54 left-handed and 32 right-handed subjects. Suggesting that interhemispheric processing did not differ between the groups, they exhibited a within-hemisphere advantage of equal magnitude. However, the size of the perceptual asymmetries exhibited by the two groups on within-field trials was also equal. This raised the possibility that interhemispheric processing did not differ between the groups because lateralization of function did not. We do not think this interpretation very likely because other research indicates that differences in perceptual asymmetry between handedness groups are not a requirement for observing differences in interhemispheric processing (e.g. Levy & Wagner, 1984; Moscovitch & Smith, 1979). To investigate this issue further, Banich et al. (1990, Experiment. 2) performed another study in which subjects heard a three-letter word and, 1 second later, saw a triangular display of letters (see Fig. 9.3). Their task was to decide if the bottom letter and one of the top two were the second and third letter of the target word, respectively. On this task, the right-handers exhibited no visual field asymmetry, but the left-handers exhibited a significant RVF advantage for within-field trials. Despite this difference in lateralized processing between the groups, both groups exhibited across-hemisphere advantage, which were identical in magnitude. These findings are consistent with a set of studies, relatively ignored, in which no differences in interhemispheric processing are reported when comparing left- and right-handers (Beaumont & Dimond, 1973, 1975; Dimond & Beaumont, 1972a, 1974; Liederman, 1989; Piccirilli, Finali & Sciarma, 1989).

---

[2] A right-hemisphere advantage for the name-identity task might seem counter-intuitive since it is often assumed that this task must be performed by converting the letters into a phonemic code, which is then used to make the match decision. In such a case, one would expect a left-hemisphere advantage, since the left hemisphere is superior to the right at processing phonemic information (e.g., Levy and Trevarthen, 1977). However, the task may also be performed using a case-transformation strategy, and in such a case a right-hemisphere advantage is observed (Boles and Eveland, 1983).

Thus, at least when all the information required for a task is presented simultaneously, the effect of interhemispheric interaction on task performance appears to be independent of asymmetric processing. Such findings are consistent with the idea that interhemispheric communication aids task performance by dividing processing over as much neural space as possible. This conception makes the lack of a difference between interhemispheric processing in left- and right-handers more understandable. Regardless of the degree of lateralization in brain organization, dividing processing over a wider expanse of neural regions is useful. This suggestion does not preclude the possibility that there are certain conditions under which hemispheric specialization would constrain interhemispheric processing. For example, if only one hemisphere is capable of performing a specific aspect of a task (e.g., programming a verbal output), the manner in which processing can be divided between the hemispheres may be limited. Under these conditions, interhemispheric processing of left- and right-handers might indeed differ if certain aspects of a task were bilateralized for left-handers, but constrained to a single hemisphere in right-handers. However, most tasks can be accomplished in multiple ways (e.g., face recognition via a feature strategy or a gestalt strategy). In such cases, interhemispheric interaction may provide a flexible means of providing for the most efficient division of a difficult processing load.[3]

Stimulus Attributes that Influence Interhemispheric Processing

The experiments discussed so far have investigated interhemispheric interaction as a monolithic entity. The question addressed was, "How does interhemispheric processing affect task performance?" To gain a more complete picture of interhemispheric processing, it is also desirable to determine which aspects of task performance or which attributes of the stimuli being processed are most affected by interhemispheric processing. Supporting the possibility that interhemispheric processing might be affected by stimulus attributes, information transferred between the hemispheres can be of different forms. For example, certain callosal signals appear to be sensory in nature (Milner & Lines, 1982; Rugg, Lines, &

---

[3] These findings might cause one to re-examine the utility of some of the methodologies employed in laterality research, such as the dual-task paradigm for determining the independence or non-independence of resources. Our results provide the possibility that when the overall processing load is high, as in the dual-task condition, it may be better to divide portions of a single task across the hemispheres. However, under the single-task condition, which is a lighter load, that same task may be performed better by just one hemisphere. Thus, the same task may not be performed the same way in regards to the hemispheres under single- and dual-task conditions. The precaution generally taken to avoid such a possibility is to employ a task that only one hemisphere is capable of performing (e.g., phonetic analysis, which can only be performed by the left hemisphere). However, even though the rhyme decision can only be made by the left hemisphere, other aspects of the task that are required to make the rhyme decision (e.g., grapheme analysis) can be performed by both hemispheres and hence could be processed differently under single- and dual-task conditions. As will become clearer in the next section of the paper, interhemispheric effects may vary with task manipulations even when the final decision can only be performed by one hemisphere.

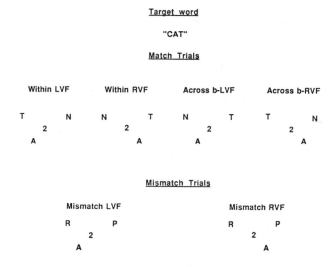

Fig. 9.3. Example of match and mismatch arrays for the spelling task.

Milner, 1984), whereas others are nonsensory and have been hypothesized to be motoric. These findings raise the possibility that interhemispheric coordination could occur anytime from early sensory processes through to the decision stage, whose end is signaled by the selection of a motor response.

We have investigated such issues by utilizing a method in which performance is compared between trials on which information is directed to only one hemisphere (unilateral trials) and trials on which redundant information is directed simultaneously to both hemispheres (bilateral trials; e.g., Hellige, Jonsson, & Michimata, 1988; Hellige & Michimata, 1989a, 1989b; Hellige et al., 1989). Previously, this methodology has been used to investigate how bihemispheric processing affects task performance, and whether performance on bilateral trials is more similar to that observed on unilateral LVF or unilateral RVF trials. The goal of this latter enterprise is to determine which hemisphere ultimately controls the output of processing when the information received allows either to do so. We have used this method not in service of this goal, but, rather, to determine how processing in the hemispheres is integrated to yield a final response and how different stages or aspects of processing contribute to the influence of bihemispheric processing on task performance.

As a first step in this endeavor, we examined how different aspects of redundancy affect bihemispheric processing (Banich & Karol, 1992). In our task, subjects decided whether either of two words in a display rhymed with a previously presented target word. The effect that different types of information have on bihemispheric processing was investigated by having two classes of trials: those in which the words were redundant in some manner and those in which they were not. Furthermore, redundant trials were of two types, those on which the words seen were identical (Same-Word/Same-Decision; e.g., target word *key*, stimuli *bee* + *bee*), and those on which each word had a distinct identity but both of which led to the same decision in regards to the target (different-word/same-decision, e.g., target word *key*; stimuli *bee + sea*). For nonredundant trials, the information projected to each visual field not only had a distinct identity but also led to different decisions (different-word/different-decision, e.g., target word *key*, stimuli *bee + cat*). (see Fig. 9.4). Both unilateral and bilateral trials were constructed in this manner. On bilateral trials, one word was projected to each visual field, whereas on unilateral trials both words were presented in the same visual field. Half of the unilateral and half of the bilateral trials contained a match and half did not.

This experiment allows us to determine the relative influence that different aspects of information have on bihemispheric performance. If bihemispheric processing is strongly influenced by whether the hemispheres receive identical information, then performance on same-word/same-decision trials should differ from performance on different-word/same-decision trials, because the information presented to the hemispheres is identical in the former case but not the latter. In contrast, if decision processes have a large influence on bihemispheric processing, then performance on same-word/same-decision and different-word/same-decision trials should be similar, because the decision in both types of trials is the same. In this case, one would also expect that performance on different-word/different-decision trials should vary from that for the other two types of bilateral trials,

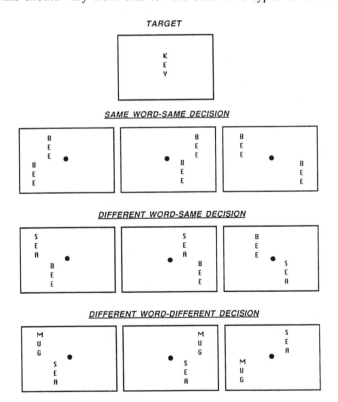

FIG. 9.4. Example of bilateral match trials in the Banich and Karol experiments.

because in these trials the information projected to the two hemispheres does not lead to the same decision, whereas on same-word/same-decision and different-word/same-decision trials it does.

This particular pattern can then be compared to performance on unilateral trials. If the pattern observed on bihemispheric trials is specific to interhemispheric processing, then it should differ from that observed on unilateral trials. On the other hand, if the effects result from patterns of facilitation or interference that occur any time two types of words are presented on the screen, then the pattern for unilateral and bilateral trials should not differ.

The results obtained provide information on two different aspects of bihemispheric processing. First, they let us examine whether the functioning of each hemisphere in isolation is a good predictor of the functioning of the hemispheres as a coordinated unit. The evidence obtained from these studies concurs with that of studies discussed in the previous section in indicating that the sum of the parts does not predict the whole. The second issue addressed is whether certain attributes of an item influence bihemispheric processing more than others. The results indicate that stimulus attributes do not take precedence over one another as much as they appear to interact to influence bihemispheric processing.

First, I discuss whether bihemispheric processing can be predicted on the basis of the performance of each hemisphere in isolation. The results of this study are presented in Table 9.2. Of most relevance to this question are the data for the rhyme trials. For LVF trials, it matters little whether identical or nonidentical words are presented. In contrast, for RVF trials, performance is much superior when identical rather than nonidentical words are presented. Of most importance, the pattern on the bilateral trials differed from that observed on both RVF and LVF trials. Whether words were identical or not did influence performance on bilateral trials, unlike the findings for LVF trials. Furthermore, the advantage for same-word/same-decision trials over different-word/same-decision trials observed on bilateral trials was reduced in size significantly, compared to that observed on RVF trials.

To further explore whether bihemispheric processing could be predicted on the basis of performance when all material was directed to one hemisphere, we next went about determining more specifically the locus of the advantage for same-word/same-decision trials over different-word/same-decision trials. Two major possibilities presented themselves. First, it might be that faster responses are observed for same-word/same-decision than different-word/same-decision trials because information on either side of the midline is equivalent perceptually. Another reason for the superior performance on same-word/same-decision trials could be that the words are semantically equivalent (rather than perceptually equivalent). Thus, it may be that bihemispheric processing is easier when the information presented to the two hemispheres has the same meaning, compared to when it does not. Because the words in the two visual fields on same-word/same-decision trials were identical, they were both perceptually equivalent and semantically equivalent, as well as redundant regarding the decision to which they led. Likewise, on different-word/same-decision trials, information was both perceptually distinct and semantically distinct, but redundant with regard to the decision engendered. Thus, faster RTs to same-word/same-decision than different-word/same-decision trials could have occurred either because of perceptual redundancy or because of semantic redundancy.

We attempted to differentiate between these two possibilities by performing the experiment again, except that this time the two words were no longer equivalent perceptually. This was accomplished by presenting one word in one font and in lowercase, and the other word in a different font and in uppercase. If lack of perceptual redundancy caused RT to different-word/same-decision trials to be slower than to same-word/same-decision trials, then no difference in RT between these trial types should be found because the words were perceptually distinct in both cases. On the other hand, if the lack of semantic redundancy impeded processing on different-word/same-decision trials, then responses to same-word/same-decision trials should be faster than to different-word/same-decision trials, because the semantic information is redundant in the former case, and distinct in the latter.

The results clearly illustrated, once again, that the stimulus attributes that affect bihemispheric processing are distinct from those affecting unilateral processing. For unilateral trials, the pattern of performance was not affected by the case/font manipulation. For RVF trials, performance on same-word/same-decision trials was superior to that on different-word/same-decision trials, just as in the previous experiment. Likewise, the pattern on LVF trials was the same as that observed previously. Responses to same-word/same-decision and different-word/same-decision trials were equivalent. The pattern for bilateral trials, however, was quite different. In this experiment, the responses to same-word/same-decision trials were no faster than to different-word/same-decision trials (see Table 9.3). Thus, a critical point to emerge from these studies is that the factors affecting the interaction of the hemispheres are different than those affecting the processing of each hemisphere in isolation. Although the pattern on unilateral trials was the same in the two experiments, there were very important differences between the two experiments in the pattern of performance observed on bilateral trials.[4] They very strongly suggest that it is almost impossible to predict what factors govern bihemispheric processing by examining situations in which information is directed, at least initially, to only one hemisphere. These results are consistent with those discussed in the previous section (e.g., Banich & Belger, 1990; Belger & Banich, 1992) in illustrating that the performance of each hemisphere separately cannot be used to predict the pattern of the system as a whole. What, however, do the results tell us about the attributes that influence bihemispheric processing? They suggest that neither perceptual characteristics

---

[4] It should be noted that differences between the two experiments cannot be attributed to differences in the manner in which the fonts were processed by each hemisphere. An analysis of unilateral trials on the basis of font of presentation (Chicago upper-case vs. Los Angeles lower-case: Macintosh computer) yielded no main effect of font nor interaction of font with visual field of presentation.

Table 9.2. Mean RTs (msec) and Error Rates (in Parentheses) for Bilateral and Unilateral Trial Types.

Trial Type	Rhyme	No-Rhyme
LVF same-word/same-decision	1018 (19.1)	1007 (18.8)
LVF same-word/different-decision	1033 (17.4)	1077 (23.9)
RVF same-word/same-decision	841 (8.3)	987 (18.8)
RVF same-word/different-decision	1020 (23.3)	1044 (18.8)
Bilateral same-word/same-decision	898 (19.1)	1096 (18.8)
Bilateral same-word/different-decision	961 (20.8)	1069 (16.1)

alone nor semantic characteristics alone are critical in influencing bihemispheric processing. Rather, these two factors appear to interact. If the longer RTs to the bilateral different-word/same-decision trials than to the same-word/same-decsion trials in the first experiment had been due to the fact that the words were semantically distinct, then the same pattern should have emerged when the words were printed in different fonts and cases. This is clearly not what we observed. Likewise, if the longer RTs to different-word/same-decision than same-word/same-decision trials occurred solely because the items on the different-word/same-decision trials were perceptually distinct, then one would make two predictions. First, when words were perceptually distinct, no difference should be observed between same-word/same-decision and different-word/same-decision trials. This, indeed, was observed. However, one would expect also that whenever words were perceptually distinct, processing should be longer than when they were perceptually similar. Because the two studies were performed with different groups of subjects, a meaningful comparison could not be made.

To investigate this issue, two additional experiments were performed. In these, performance on bilateral same-word/same-decision and different-word/same-decision trials were compared to a baseline or reference point of performance on single-item unilateral trials. In the first additional experiment, items were presented in the same font and case. We replicated our findings that on bilateral trials responses to same-word/same-decision trials were faster than responses to different-word/same-decision trials. In addition, we found that, although responses on same-word/same-decision trials took no longer than responses to unilateral trials, responses of different-word/same-decision trials did. These findings lead to the strong prediction that if it is the lack of perceptual redundancy alone that leads to elongated RTs on different-word/same-decision trials, then when words are printed in different fonts and cases, RTs should be longer than to unilateral trials regardless of whether the same word or different

Table 9.3 Mean RT's (msec) and Error Rates (in Parentheses) for Bilateral and Unilateral Trial Types.

Trial Type	Rhyme	No-Rhyme
LVF same-word/same-decision	1097 (36.2)	1071 (11.1)
LVF same-word/different-decision	1109 (24.6)	1168 (15.5)
RVF same-word/same-decision	1010 (15.9)	1068 (17.2)
RVF same-word/different-decision	1145 (29.9)	1172 (19.5)
Bilateral same-word/same-decision	1054 (18.1)	1111 (24.7)
Bilateral same-word/different-decision	1069 (20.8)	1115 (14.1)

words are presented to the hemispheres. In an experiment designed to test this prediction, we found that it was not borne out. Responses to both same-word/same-decision and different-word/same-decision trials were as fast as to unilateral trials (see Table 9.4).

To what conclusions do these findings lead? Apparently, when the hemispheres are presented with information that differs in semantic content, processing is easier when the overall perceptual characteristics of the words, embodied in our experiment by font and case, are also distinct. It appears, therefore, that the similarity of overall perceptual characteristics in the first of our additional experiments caused an interference effect when the words presented to the two hemispheres had different meanings. However, when the words were not perceptually distinct, as in our second additional experiment, there was no interference if the words presented to the two hemispheres had different meanings. Hence, bihemispheric processing is not influenced solely by information's perceptual characteristics nor by its semantic characteristics, but rather by some interaction of the two.

One interesting implication of this result is that it suggests that the bihemispheric processing of information may not be well characterized by a simple stage model, in which perceptual analysis precedes semantic processing. If perceptual analysis were totally distinct from semantic processing, then one should not have observed the interaction found in these two experiments. If these two stages were independent, then the lack of semantic redundancy should have impeded performance both when the words were printed in the same font and also when they were printed in different fonts. We observed, however, that semantic redundancy influenced performance in the former case, but not in the latter. Our findings raise the possibility, therefore, that interhemispheric exchange of information operates in a cascade fashion (see McClelland, 1979), such that processing initiated at one stage continuously influences successive stages until the final response is made.

Taken as a whole, the results of these experiments suggest that the dynamic nature of interhemispheric interaction influences performance to a greater degree than one might infer from the processing of information directed to an individual hemisphere. Furthermore, it indicates that even when only one hemisphere is capable of making a final decision about an item (as was the case in our study,

TABLE 9.4. Mean RTs (in msec) and Error Rates (in Parantheses) for Bilateral and Single-Item Unilateral Trials.

Trial Types	Same case/same font		Different case/different font	
	Match	Mismatch	Match	Mismatch
Unilateral LVF	1298 (17.1)	1272 (5. 8)	1057 (19.4)	1026 (7.3)
Unilateral RVF	1364 (12.0)	1303 (3.5)	1040 (16.1)	1010 (4.0)
Bilateral Same-Word/Same-Decision	1334 (12.2)	1440 (11.7)	1044 (11.4)	1128 (14.5)
Bilateral Different-Word/Same-Decision	1417 (16.6)	1532 (8.9)	1052 (11.0)	1127 (11.6)

because only the left hemisphere could make a rhyme decision; cf. Rayman & Zaidel, 1991), other attributes of a stimulus may still influence bihemispheric processing. We are now doing a study in which the nature of the task requirements are changed so that both hemispheres are capable of making the final decision (a decision about whether a digit is larger or smaller in value than a target). This will allow us to investigate whether the influence of factors affecting coordination of processing between the hemispheres (e.g., physical redundancy, semantic redundancy) remains constant or interacts with the nature of the decision process

The Relationship Between Interhemispheric Processing and Memorial Processing

As mentioned in the beginning of this chapter, the effect of interhemispheric interaction on performance seems to vary depending on whether there is an ISI interposed between presentations of the items to be compared. These findings raised the possibility that interhemispheric effects might differ between tasks with a memory component and those without. As a first step in investigating interhemispheric processing under conditions in which there is a memory component, Banich and Shenker (in press) investigated interhemispheric effects for memory of a particular item. Previous research (e.g., Dimond et al., 1972; Kleinman & Little, 1973; Leiber, 1982; Lordahl et al., 1965) had shown that when subjects were explicitly asked to decide if an item had been viewed previously, performance was either better when the item had been projected initially to the same hemisphere than when it had been projected to the opposite hemisphere, or it was no worse. We also investigated interhemispheric effects for judgments of item frequency, because we wished to determine if interhemispheric effects could be found for subjective judgements and because item recognition and item frequency appear to rely on different neural substrates, which allows for the possibility that interhemispheric transfer of information might differ for these tasks. In particular, it has been found that memory for recognition of nonsense figures relies differentially on temporal regions of the right hemisphere. Thus, patients with right, but not left, temporal lobe lesions are impaired at deciding whether a nonsense shape had been viewed previously. However, if these patients correctly remember that an item has been seen, they are unimpaired at estimating item frequency. In contrast, damage to frontal regions of the brain does not interfere with the ability to remember that an item has been viewed previously, but does interfere with the ability to estimate frequency of occurrence (Smith & Milner, 1988). This ability does not rely on an asymmetrical neural substrate, however, because these deficits are observed after either right or left frontal lesions. Thus, there is a double dissociation between the ability to recognize objects and the ability to judge their frequency of occurrence.

To investigate interhemispheric processing for item identity and item frequency, subjects viewed a "presentation" series of nonsense shapes in either the RVF or the LVF. A particular nonsense shape could appear one, five, or nine times within the series, and was always presented in the same visual field. The order of presentation of specific items was random, such that if a particular nonsense shape appeared more than once, it did not appear successively within the series (i.e., if an item appeared nine times, it was not presented nine times, one after another, in the presentation series). Subjects were then given a test series consisting of the items previously viewed and an equal number that had never been seen. For each item, they were to determine whether it had been viewed previously (old/new decision). Of those items viewed previously, half were presented in the same visual field as in the presentation list and half were presented in the opposite visual field. Thus, the within-hemisphere advantage was determined by contrasting performance when the probe item was presented in the same visual field as originally viewed to performance when the probe was presented in the opposite visual field. Then, the size of the within-hemisphere advantage was determined for each of the presentation frequencies (one, five, and nine). After deciding whether an item had been viewed previously, subjects were also asked to provide an estimate of the frequency of presentation of the item. Thus, we could compare estimates of item frequency when initial presentation and probe were directed to the same hemisphere and to opposite hemispheres.

We found that the effect of frequency of presentation on interhemispheric processing differed for accuracy of item identity and judgments of item frequency. In particular, the size of the within-hemisphere advantage for item recognition did not change with increasing frequency of presentation. This was not the case for estimates of item frequency, however. We found that for lower frequencies of presentations (i.e., five times), the estimated item frequency was higher when both the initial and the subsequent presentation were directed to the same visual field as compared to when they were presented to opposite visual fields. This within-hemisphere advantage, however, disappeared for higher frequencies of presentations (i.e., nine times).

It is important to note that the judgments of item frequency were independent of the ability to discriminate between familiar and novel stimuli. For example, even though there were no significant differences in estimates of item frequency for presentation frequencies of nine items for within- and across-hemisphere trials, a significantly greater ability to discriminate between novel and previously presented items (as measured by d') was found for within-hemisphere trials as compared to across-hemisphere trials. This led us to suggest that the differences in frequency estimates on within- and across-hemisphere processing is driven by how "familiar" the item seems: the more familiar, the higher the estimate. Thus, information obtained via callosal relay would seem less familiar, leading to an underestimation of frequency. Such a suggestion is consonant with the work of Jacoby (1988), who suggested that exposure to an item can influence judgments about particular dimensions of that item. For example, words that subjects have previously viewed are rated as being of longer duration than words not viewed previously (Witherspoon & Allan, 1985). Such a result is analogous to our finding that designs presented to and probed in the same hemisphere are considered to have occurred more frequently than words presented to and probed in opposite hemispheres.

Because we obtained interhemispheric effects for judgments, we wanted to determine if the effects would also occur when the emphasis was not put on explicit remembering. Recent evidence suggests that the recall of longer term information might differ depending on whether or not subjects must explicitly remember that they have previously encountered an item. For example, although amnesic subjects cannot explicitly remember whether they have viewed information previously, they nonetheless do so implicitly. So, although they can perform at chance levels in stating whether they have seen a particular item previously, the exposure to that word will still prime their performance on tasks (e.g., stem completion) that do not require that they remember they saw the item previously (e.g., Graf, Squire, & Mandler, 1984). It is not hard to imagine that interhemispheric effects might be influenced by whether one has to explicitly remember an experience with an item. It might be that that because one has to explicitly remember the previous encounter with an item, which hemisphere initially encodes the information would be of large consequence, whereas for implicit memory tasks, whether processing was performed by the same hemisphere that did the initial encoding is insignificant, because memory for the initial encoding itself is less important. On the other hand, requiring the transfer of information from one hemisphere to the other, might have just as large an influence on nonexplicit memory tasks..

To investigate whether interhemispheric effects could also be found for nonexplicit memory tasks, Banich and Belger (1991) presented lines of different lengths and asked subjects to rate how long the lines were on a scale of 1 to 10. Half of the lines were presented in the LVF and half in the RVF. No differences were found in mean ratings, variance of ratings, or accuracy of ratings (how close the judgments of line length were to the actual length) for items presented in the LVF as compared to those in the RVF. Thus, both hemispheres appear to use the same rating scale in judging the lines and to be equally adept at making such classifications.

Next, subjects were asked to rate the lines again. This time, half were presented in the same visual field as initially viewed and half were presented in the opposite visual field. Because subjects are asked only to rate the lines again, and not to remember if or when the item was viewed previously, the task can be considered a test of implicit memory. Typically, effects of implicit memory are shown by demonstrating that responses to a set of stimuli previously encountered are different than to stimuli to which the subject has not been exposed. In the present study, a variation of this logic was used. Rather than varying whether an item was encountered previously, we varied whether the hemisphere making the judgment had previously made a judgment for that item. We compared concordance of line length ratings for items whose initial and subsequent exposure were directed to the same hemisphere to the concordance when the exposures were to different hemispheres. In the first case, any influence of the first exposure on the subsequent rating occurs directly, whereas in the latter case it must occur

TABLE 9.5. Differences in Average Line Length Rating as a Function of Initial and Subsequent Field of Presentation.

	Initial field	
Subsequent field	LVF	RVF
LVF	.1645	.3081
RVF	.3026	.0987

via callosal relay. Thus, a greater concordance for ratings when items are viewed twice by the same hemisphere than by opposite hemispheres would suggest that callosal transfer also influences information needed for non-explicit memory tasks.

We found that the concordance of ratings was higher for items presented in the same visual field than for those in opposite visual fields (see Table 9.5). Specifically, the mean difference in ratings of line length between initial and subsequent presentation was less for items presented to the same hemisphere than for items presented to opposite hemispheres.[5]

The results of these studies illustrate a number of points. First, the dissociation between interhemispheric effects for an item's identity as compared to its frequency of presentation underscores the fact that interhemispheric transfer of information is not a unitary phenomenon. Second, interhemispheric effects can be found not only for explicit decisions about items and their attributes, but for subjective judgments of items, as well. This assertion is supported by the finding of interhemispheric effects not only for judgments of item frequency, but also for concordance of judgments of relative length. Finally, the higher concordance of length ratings found when lines are projected initially and subsequently to the same visual field, as compared to the concordance when stimuli are projected to opposite visual fields, indicates that interhemispheric effects may be rather ubiquitous, and can even be found for implicit memory tasks.

GENERAL CONCLUSIONS

The research described here explores how asymmetric processing of the hemispheres and hemispheric interaction influence the cognitive competence of the human mind. My co-workers and I have attempted to add to our knowledge of interhemispheric processing in two main ways: by examining its effect on task performance and by determining the role that particular aspects of information,

---

[5] The results of our study cannot be attributed to spatial cueing effects. One could argue that ratings of items would be more similar or accuracy of recognition greater if the initial and subsequent presentation of an item occurs in the same spatial location than if it does not. Thus, processing on within-field trials might benefit relative to across-hemisphere trials because spatial location could act as a cue for reminding about the initial presentation in the former trial type but not the latter. In all the memory studies we perform such an explanation for the results is precluded by having the initial presentation (or series of presentations) placed in a different location within the visual field than the subsequent presentation or probe (e.g., displaced above midline vs. displaced below midline). This is done both for items presented initially and subsequently in the same visual field and those presented initially and subsequently in opposite visual fields. Furthermore, because the means and variances of the initial ratings of items did not differ as a function of visual field, the higher concordance on same vs. opposite hemisphere trials cannot be said to result from baseline differences in hemispheric processes.

such as their perceptual and semantic characteristics or the type of decision (explicit recognition vs. subjective judgment) play in bihemispheric processing.

The results of this research program have provided some insights into the nature of interhemispheric processing. First, they suggest that interaction between the hemispheres allows for flexibility of processing, which enhances the ability to analyze information. In particular, interhemispheric processing appears to be a means whereby heavy processing loads are dispersed across large expanses of neural tissue. Such dispersion seems to have the effect of making computationally complex tasks easier to tackle. Second, our results reveal that distinct aspects of information, such as their semantic and perceptual attributes, have different influences on bihemispheric processing. These results also illustrate that the relaying of such attributes may not occur in discrete stages. Third, our results indicate that interhemispheric processing may also be affected by how people process information, that is, whether they must recall seeing an item or whether they must rate its frequency of occurrence.

The results of these investigations are likely to have broader implications for our understanding of neurocognitive functioning. For example, a major question in neurobiology revolves around the "binding" problem of how information from diverse brain regions is combined. There is much evidence that different aspects of information are processed in somewhat separate modules in the brain. For example, parietal regions of the brain appear to be particularly sensitive to the spatial location of items without much regard to identity. In contrast, temporal regions are very sensitive to item identity but not to spatial location. Nonetheless, our brains have the ability to locate a particular item in a particular location. Thus, information about item location must somehow be bound to information about item identity. How this occurs is not well understood.

Comprehending the information exchange between the hemispheres has the possibility of providing clues to solving this problem. Although information exchange between the hemispheres is likely to have particular characteristics due to the specific ways in which cognitive and emotional functions are lateralized, it may provide some general principles for conceptualizing the manner in which information is integrated in the brain. For example, the research described here strongly suggests that how information is processed within a particular brain region (e.g., a hemisphere) may provide only a sketchy picture of the way in which that information affects overall performance. Such realizations may, on the surface, appear to be disheartening because they suggest that our task is much more challenging than it had originally appeared. However, appreciating the complexity of information processing in the human brain is a prerequisite to understanding it.

ACKNOWLEDGMENTS

I thank, first, the students who have pursued with me the ideas discussed in this chapter: Aysenil Belger, Darcie Karol, Joel Shenker, and Neal Stolar. They made the endeavor more challenging and more fun. I would also like to acknowledge the support that made possible the research discussed in this chapter: an Arnold O.

Beckman Research Award from the Research Board at the University of Illinois, Biomedical Research Support Grants 1-5-61030 and 1-5-60850 administered through the School of Life Sciences at the University of Illinois, and a Beckman Fellowship for the Fall of 1989 at the University of Illinois Center for Advanced Study. Finally, I thank Wendy Heller for comments on this manuscript, for steadfast encouragement while I was pursuing this research, and for more than a decade of discussing ideas.

REFERENCES

Banich, M.T. (1985). *The nature and time course of interhemispheric communication.* Unpublished doctoral dissertation, University of Chicago.

Banich, M.T. (1986). Independence of interhemispheric interaction and asymmetric processing in humans [Abstract] *Society for Neuroscience, 12.*

Banich, M.T., & Belger, A. (1990). Interhemispheric interaction: How do the hemispheres divide and conquer a task? *Cortex, 26,* 77-94.

Banich, M.T, & Belger, A. (1991). Inter- versus intrahemispheric concordance of judgements in a non-explicit memory task. *Brain and Cognition, 15,* 131-137.

Banich, M.T., & Karol, D.L. (1992). The sum of the parts does not equal the whole: Evidence from bihemispheric processing. *Journal of Experimental Psychology: Human Perception and Performance, 18,* 763-784.

Banich, M.T., & Shenker, J.I. (in press). Dissociations in memory for item identity and item frequency: Evidence form hemispheric interactions. *Neuropsychologia.*

Banich, M.T., Goering, S., Stolar, N., & Belger, A. (1990). Interhemispheric processing in left- and right-handers. *International Journal of Neuroscience, 54,* 197-208.

Banich, M.T., Stolar, N., Heller, W., & Goldman, R. (1992). A deficit in right-hemisphere performance after induction of a depressed mood. *Neuropsychiatry, Neuropsychology, and Behavioral Neurology, 5,* 20-27.

Beaumont, J.G., & Dimond, S.J. (1973). Transfer between the cerebral hemispheres in human learning. *Acta Psychologica, 37,* 87-91.

Beaumont, J.G., & Dimond, S.J. (1975). Interhemispheric transfer of figural information in right and non-right-handed subjects. *Acta Psychologica, 39,* 97-104.

Belger, A., & Banich, M.T. (1992). Interhemispheric interaction affected by computational complexity. *Neuirpsychologia, 30,* 923-931.

Boles, D.B., & Eveland, D.C. (1983). Visual and phonetic codes and the process of generation in letter matching. *Journal of Experimental Psychology: Human Perception and Performance, 9,* 657-675.

Bradshaw, J.L., Nettleton, N.C., & Patterson, K. (1973). Identification of mirror-reversed and non-reversed facial profiles in same and opposite visual fields. *Journal of Experimental Psychology, 99,* 42-48.

Davis, R., & Schmit, V. (1971). Timing the transfer of information between the hemispheres in man. *Acta Psychologica, 35*, 335-346.

Davis, R., & Schmit, V. (1973). Visual and verbal coding in the interhemispheric transfer of information. *Brain, 95*, 347-356.

Dimond, S.J. (1969). Hemisphere function and immediate memory. *Psychonomic Science, 16*, 111-112.

Dimond, S.J. (1971). Hemisphere function and word registration. *Journal of Experimental Psychology, 87*, 183-186.

Dimond, S.J., & Beaumont, G. (1971). Use of two cerebral hemispheres to increase brain capacity. *Nature, 232*, 270-271.

Dimond, S.J., & Beaumont, G. (1972a). Hemisphere function and color naming. *Journal of Experimental Psychology, 96*, 87-91.

Dimond, S.J., & Beaumont, G. (1972b). Processing in perceptual integration between and within the cerebral hemispheres. *British Journal of Psychology, 63*, 509-514.

Dimond, S.J., & Beaumont, G. (1974). Hemisphere function and paired-associate learning. *British Journal of Psychology, 65*, 275-278.

Dimond, S.J., Gibson, A.R., & Gazzaniga, M.S. (1972). Cross-field and within-field integration of visual information. *Neuropsychologia, 10*, 379-381.

Friedman, A., & Polson, M.C. (1981). The hemispheres as independent resource systems: Limited-capacity processing and cerebral specialization. *Journal of Experimental Psychology: Human Perception and Performance, 7*, 1031-1058.

Geschwind, N., & Levitsky, W. (1968). Left-right asymmetry in temporal speech regions. *Science, 161*, 186-187.

Graf, P., Squire, L.R., & Mandler, G. (1984). The information that amnesic patients do not forget. *Journal of Experimental Psychology: Learning, Memory, and Cognition, 10*, 164-178.

Hellige, J.B. (1990). Hemispheric asymmetry. *Annual Review of Psychology, 41*, 55-80.

Hellige, J.B., Jonsson, J.E., & Michimata, C. (1988). Processing from LVF, RVF, and bilateral presentations: Examination of metacontrol and interhemispheric interaction. *Brain and Cognition, 7*, 39-53.

Hellige, J.B., & Michimata, C. (1989a). Categorization versus distance: Hemispheric differences for processing spatial information. *Memory and Cognition, 17*, 770-776.

Hellige, J.B., & Michimata, C. (1989b). Visual laterality for letter comparison: Effects of stimulus factors, responses factors, and metacontrol. *Bulletin of the Psychonomic Society, 27*, 441-444.

Hellige, J.B., Taylor, A.K., & Eng, T.L. (1989). Interhemispheric interaction when both hemispheres have access to the same stimulus information. *Journal of Experimental Psychology: Human Perception and Performance, 15*, 711-722.

Hellige, J.B., & Wong, T.M. (1983). Hemispheric-specific interference in dichotic listening: Task variables and individual differences. *Journal of Experimental Psychology:General, 2*, 218-239.

Jacoby, L. (1988). Memory observed and memory unobserved. In U. Neisser & E. Winograd (Eds.), *Remembering reconsidered: Ecological and traditional approaches to the study of memory* (pp. 145-177). Cambridge, England: Cambridge University Press.

Kleinman, K.M., & Little, R.W. (1973). Inter-hemispheric transfer of meaningful information in normal human subjects. *Nature, 241*, 55-57.

Kreuter, C., Kinsbourne, M., & Trevarthen, C. (1972). Are deconnected cerebral hemispheres independent channels? *Neuropsychologia, 10*, 453-461.

Ladavas, E., Nicoletti, R., Umilta, C., & Rizzolatti, G. (1984). Right hemisphere interference during negative affect: A reaction time study. *Neuropsychologia, 22*, 479-485.

Leiber, L. (1982). Interhemispheric effects in short-term recognition memory for single words. *Cortex, 18*, 113-124.

Liederman, J. (1986). Interhemispheric interference during word naming. *International Journal of Neuroscience, 30*, 43-56.

Liederman, J. (1989). The advantage of between-hemisphere division of inputs: Generalizability across handedness, populations and procedural variations. *Journal of Clinical and Experimental Neuropsychology, 11*, 37.

Liederman, J., Merola, J., & Hoffman, C. (1986). Longitudinal data indicate that hemispheric independence increases during early adolescence. *Developmental Neuropsychology, 2*, 183-201.

Liederman, J., Merola, J., & Martinez, S. (1985). Interhemispheric collaboration in response to simultaneous bilateral input. *Neuropsychologia, 23*, 673-683.

Lordahl, D.S., Kleinman, K.M., Levy, B., Massoth, N.A., Pessin, M.S., Storandt, M., Tucker, R., & Vanderplas, J.M. (1965). Deficits in recognition of random shapes with changed visual fields. *Psychonomic Science, 3*, 245-256.

Levy, J., & Trevarthen, C. (1977). Perceptual, semantic, and phonetic aspects of elementary language processes in split-brain patients. *Brain, 100*, 105-118.

Levy, J., & Wagner, N. (1984). Handwriting posture, visuomotor integration and lateralized reaction time parameters. *Human Neurobiology, 3*, 157-161.

Lordahl, D.S., Kleinman, K.M., Levy, B., Massoth, N.A., Pessin, M.A., Storandt, M., Tucker, R., & Vanderplas, J.M. (1965). Deficits in recognition of random shapes with changed visual fields. *Psychonomic Science, 3*, 245-256.

McClelland, J. (1979). On the time relations of mental processes: An examination of systems of processes in cascade. *Psychological Review, 86*, 287-330.

Merola, J., & Liederman, J. (1985). Developmental changes in hemispheric independence. *Child Development, 56*, 1184-1194.

Miller,L.K. (1981). Perceptual independence of the hemifields in children and adults. *Journal of Experimental Child Psychology, 32*, 298-312.

Miller, L.K. (1983). Hemifield independence in the left-handed. *Brain and Language, 20*, 33-43.

Milner, A.D., & Lines, C.R. (1982). Interhemispheric pathways in simple reaction time to lateralized light flash. *Neuropsychologia, 20*, 171-179.

Moscovitch, M., & Smith, L.C. (1979). Differences in neural organization between individuals with inverted and noninverted handwriting postures. *Science, 205*, 710-712.

Nelson, M.E., & Bower, J.M. (1990). Brain maps and parallel computers. *Trends in Neuroscience, 13*, 403-408.

Oke, A., Keller, R., Mefford, I., & Adam, R.N. (1978). Lateralization of norepinephrine in the human thalamus. *Science, 200*, 1411-1413.

Piccirilli, M., Finali, G., & Sciarma, T. (1989). Negative evidence of differences between right- and left-handers in interhemispheric transfer of information. *Neuropsychologia, 27*, 1023-1026.

Posner, M.I., & Mitchell, R.F. (1967). Chronometric analysis of classification. *Psychological Review, 74*, 392-409.

Rayman, J., & Zaidel, E. (1991). Rhyming and the right hemisphere. *Brain and Language, 40*, 89-105.

Rugg, M.D., Lines, C.R., & Milner, A.D. (1984). Visual evoked potentials to lateralized visual stimuli and the measurement of interhemispheric transmission time. *Neuropsychologia, 22*, 215-225.

Sergent, J. (1982). About face: left-hemisphere involvement in processing physiognomies. *Journal of Experimental Psychology: Human Perception and Performance, 8*, 1-14.

Smith, M.L. & Milner, B. (1988). Estimation of frequency of occurrence of abstract designs after frontal or temporal lobectomy. *Neuropsychologia, 26*, 297-306.

Sperry, R.W. (1974). Lateral specialization in the surgically separated hemispheres. In F. Schmitt & F. Worden (Eds.), *The neurosciences: Third study program*, Cambridge,MA.: MIT Press.

Witherspoon, D., & Allan, L.G. (1985). The effects of a prior presentation on temporal judgements in a perceptual identification task. *Memory and Cognition, 13*, 101-111.

Wyke, M. (1982). Interhemispheric integration in man. *Psychological Medicine, 12*, 225-230.

Young, A.W., & Ellis, H.D. (1976). An experimental investigation of developmental differences in the ability to recognize faces presented to the left and right cerebral hemispheres. *Neuropsychologia, 14*, 495-498.

10 Hemispheric Specialization and Cooperation in Processing Complex Visual Patterns

Lynn C. Robertson
University of California, Davis

Neuropsychological investigations of functional hemisphere differences in patients have long shown that there is an asymmetry in performance on visual spatial tasks (De Renzi, 1982). Early work with commissurotomy patients demonstrated that stimuli presented to the left hemsiphere of such subjects would be matched using details, and stimuli presented to the right hemisphere would be matched with reference to the whole (Nebes, 1978). Other studies in patients with left- (LH) or right-hemisphere (RH) lesions, together with clinical observation, demonstrated that LH damage disrupted performance on the details of a visual pattern, and RH damage disrupted performance on the configuration (Kaplan, 1983). It was not surprising, then, that patients with LH damage were more likely to miss the local *H* in a form such as that shown in Fig. 10.1, and patients with RH damage were more likely to miss the global *S* (Delis, Robertson, & Efron, 1986). Consistently, studies with normals have shown that presentation of such figures in the right visual field (RVF) produced faster reaction times (RTs) for local information than when presented in the left visual field (LVF), whereas the reverse was true for global information (Martin, 1979; Robertson, Lamb, & Zaidel, 1993; Sergent, 1982; Van Kleek, 1989).

These findings are discussed in detail in the following sections and are relevant to a broad range of issues that cross the disciplinary boundaries of neuropsychology, cognitive psychology, cognitive science, and cognitive neuroscience. Perhaps, the relevance of the results to the different areas can be represented best by a series of questions: Do the hemispheres differentially compute gestalts and parts or wholes and details, and what anatomical regions in the right and left hemispheres produce a global/local hemisphere asymmetry (a long-standing question in neuropsychology)? Is there evidence for parallel processing within processing components biased toward global or local levels as parallel distributed processing (PDP) models in cognitive science would predict? If so, what computations occur within each module and what cognitive and neural systems support them (a question most pertinent to cognitive neuroscience)? As a general rule, is global information available before local information in higher order cognition (a question motivated by Navon's, 1977 global precedence theory in cognitive psychology)? The discussion that follows is organized into sections that are structured around each of these questions.

FUNCTIONAL HEMISPHERIC DIFFERENCES AND GLOBAL/LOCAL PROPERTIES

Following decades of research in both patient populations and normals, it is clear that the two hemispheres in the human brain process information differently. Although dichotomous theories abounded early on, more recently the questions have been refined to examine the functions of several different components that contribute to asymmetric effects. For instance, early theories of visual spatial asymmetries suggested that the right hemisphere was specialized for gestalt, holistic analysis and the left hemisphere was specialized for detailed, analytic analysis. Many theorists attempted to force all cognitive deficits associated with one hemisphere or the other into this framework. They soon discovered that this was an impossible task. For instance, how could one explain why patients with pure alexia due to LH damage were able to read only in a letter-by-letter fashion, if LH-damaged patients were more likely to miss the elements of complex patterns? A general theory of hemispheric laterality had difficulty with such facts.

Nevertheless, there are lateralized deficits in visual spatial processing that are both reliable and at least broadly consistent with the whole versus element distinction (although this nomenclature is called into question at the end of this section). Patients with LH damage are likely to draw the outline of the pattern in Fig. 10.2 leaving out the inner details, whereas patients with RH damage are likely to draw the elements, but miss the overall configuration (Robertson & Lamb, 1991). Likewise, damage to one or the other hemisphere often produces distinctive types of deficits on other neuropsychological tests requiring perceptual organization skills, such as the Block Design test, in which red and white blocks must be arranged to form a standard pattern. Patients with LH damage are likely to place the blocks in the proper configuration but miss the elements, whereas patients with RH damage arrange the elements properly but in the wrong configuration (Ben-Yishay, Diller, Mandelberg, Gordon, & Gerstman, 1971; Kaplan, 1976, 1983). This pattern of performance is consistent with the drawings of hierarchically structured patterns shown in Fig. 10.3 done by patients with RH or LH strokes in acute stages (Delis et al. 1986). A later study by Kramer, Kaplan, Blusewicz & Preston (1991) showed that performance differences on Block Design and on global/local patterns were positively correlated.

The first indication that hierarchical patterns could be used to evaluate functional hemispheric differences was reported by Martin (1979), who found that reaction time (RT) for discriminating local forms was better in the RVF than the LVF. Later, Sergent (1982) observed the same effect using a more elaborate design with the same type of patterns, and she also demonstrated that global patterns were processed faster in the LVF than in the RVF. There was a crossover interaction between level and field. Although this interaction has not always reached significant levels in studies of normals (Alivisates & Wilding, 1982; Boles, 1984), the reported means have always been in the expected direction. A meta-analysis by Van Kleek (1989) supported this observation quantitatively. The Level

HHHH
H
HHHH
H
HHHH

FIG. 10. 1. Example of a hierarchically organized pattern with a global *S* created from local *H*s.

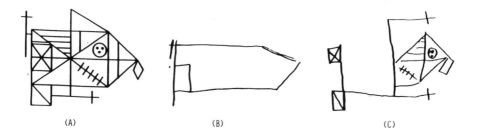

(A)   (B)   (C)

FIG. 10. 2. Drawings of the pattern in (A) by a left-hemisphere-damaged patient (B) and a right-hemisphere-damaged patient (C).

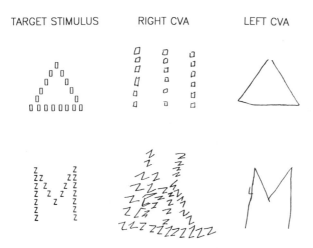

FIG. 10. 3. Drawings of the target stimuli by right- and left-hemisphere-damaged patients.

× Field interaction in normals was also observed by my colleagues and me in a study in which bilateral presentation was interspersed with unilateral presentation (Robertson et al. 1993; Boles, this volume, Chapter 6) has shown that this procedure produces more consistent field asymmetries in normals.

The most reliable evidence for the performance asymmetry has been found in brain-damaged patient groups. Patient groups with LH damage in temporal-parietal (T-P) regions consistently respond to local patterns more slowly than to global patterns, and patient groups with RH damage in the analogous vicinity respond to global patterns more slowly than to local patterns (Lamb, Robertson, & Knight, 1990; Robertson & Lamb, 1991; Robertson, Lamb, & Knight, 1988). Converging evidence from patients who have undergone full commissurotomy to control intractable epilepsy shows a global advantage when patterns are presented in the LVF and a local advantage when they are presented in the RVF (Robertson et al., 1993). These data are discussed in more detail in the discussion of processing components.

In sum, the evidence from normals and patient populations clearly demonstrates a functional difference between the right and left hemispheres in responding to global and local levels of hierarchically constructed stimuli. It must be emphasized that the type of pattern showing such consistent effects is one in which wholes are parts of other wholes. In the pattern in Fig. 10.1, there are details or features (i.e., lines and angles) on a small scale within a local whole, and there are details or features (i.e., lines and angles) on a larger scale within a global whole. The patterns in Figs. 10.1, 10.2, and 10.3 contain perceptual objects embedded within other perceptual objects. The global and local levels of such patterns are probably processed differently from local lines and angles that connect to make a recognizable form. The line of a desk that differentiates it from its background is logically different than the drawer within the desk. This distinction should be kept in mind when evaluating theories of hemispheric laterality for visual patterns. A global H and a local H are both gestalts, wholes, or configurations with their own sets of details. They are self-contained forms at different levels of stimulus structure and relative spatial scale.

ANATOMICAL CORRELATES

With the advent of in vivo methods for determining the location and extent of anatomical damage in the human brain, the question of which neural regions support the observed performance asymmetry in responding to hierarchically structured patterns could be addressed with more precision than before. By using RT measures with groups of stable patients (at least 6 months after injury, so that complications due to diascesis were diminished), we found that the asymmetric performance of groups with unilateral LH or RH damage depended on the specific cortical regions involved (namely posterior left or right association areas including temporal area 22 and portions of adjacent caudal parietal areas 39 and 40, which we designated as T-P); could be observed in the first few hundred milliseconds of processing; and persisted well beyond the acute stage. The asymmetry was observed in high-functioning stable patients when sensitive measures were used (Lamb, Robertson, & Knight, 1989; 1990; Robertson et al., 1988). Asymmetric performance was not found in groups with lateral inferior parietal damage (IPL), including rostral portions of areas 39 and 40 and portions of area 7, nor in groups with lesions centered in dorsolateral prefrontal cortex (areas 9 and 46) (Robertson et al., 1988; Robertson, Lamb, & Knight, 1991). Left T-P groups had longer response times to local than to global forms relative to controls (whether the control groups were normals or groups with lesions in different locations), and right T-P groups had longer response times to global than to local forms.

   In one of the early studies of this asymmetry, we asked subjects to focus attention on one level or the other, independent of stimulus location, and to judge the identity of local forms by pressing one of two keys in one block of trials and to judge global forms in another block (Lamb et al., 1989). The targets were always *H* or *S*, whether they occurred at the global or the local level. The data are plotted in Fig. 10.4. To more easily compare data across studies, difference scores are presented (calculated by subtracting local RT from global RT). The horizontal line at zero represents an absence of global or local advantage. Bars above the line represent a global advantage, and bars below the line represent a local advantage. As can be seen in Fig. 10.4, subjects with T-P involvement showed the Global/local × Hemisphere dissociation. They were significantly different from controls in opposite directions depending on the side of the lesion. A nonsignificant global advantage in normal controls was enhanced in left T-P groups and absent in right T-P groups. Relative to normals, the two T-P groups split in opposite directions.

   Another study used a divided attention procedure in which one of two targets appeared at one level or the other; subjects did not know in advance which level would contain the target from one trial to the next (Robertson et al., 1988). In this study normals showed a slight, nonsignificant local advantage, as shown in Fig. 10.5, whereas groups with T-P involvement diverged from normals, as in the previous study. In contrast, groups with damage limited to the left or right inferior parietal lobe or dorsolateral frontal regions performed at comparable levels to one another, and were not significantly different from normal controls. The left parietal and T-P groups had equal lesion volume in this study, a situation that could not be achieved for subjects with lesions on the right. Although there was some anatomical overlap between the left and right posterior groups, no parietal patient had a cortical lesion extension into the superior temporal gyrus. Involvement of this area appears to be required to produce the Global/local × Hemisphere dissociation.

PROCESSING COMPONENTS

The evidence discussed in the two previous sections with normal subjects using RVF and LVF presentation and with patient groups with LH and RH lesions is

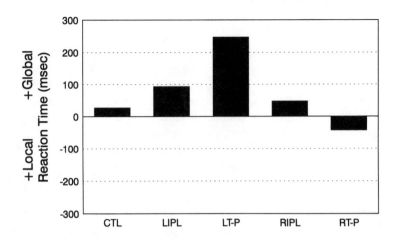

FIG. 10. 4. Mean global reaction time advantage (above 0) or local reaction time advantage (below 0) for controls (CTL) and patient groups (L = left hemisphere, R = right hemisphere, IPL = inferior parietal lobe, T-P = temporal-parietal).

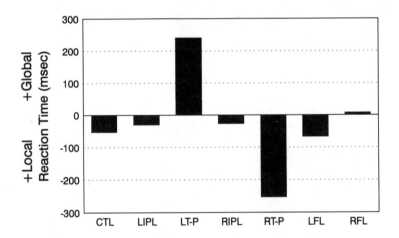

FIG. 10. 5. Mean global reaction time advantage (above 0) or local reaction time advantage (below 0) for controls (CTL), and patient groups (L = left hemisphere, R = right hemisphere, IPL = inferior parietal lobe, T-P = temporal-parietal, FL = frontal lobe).

consistent with a a multi-component processing system. One processing component on the left is biased toward local information, and one on the right is biased toward global information. The findings do not mean that the components are dedicated to either global or local levels exclusively, although this cannot be ruled out entirely. Rather, relative to some baseline, the right hemisphere discriminates global information faster than local, and the left hemisphere discriminates local information faster than global. This conclusion has been supported recently in patients with full commissurotomy, for whom hemispheric transfer was limited to subcortical pathways (Robertson et al., 1993). As with the focal lesion groups, commissurotomized subjects were slower at one level or the other depending on the field of presentation.

We also discovered a third component, which supports the interaction between global and local levels and similarity. In normals, there is an effect of the global form on the local response that depends on how similar the global and local forms are to each other (Lamb & Robertson, 1989; Navon, 1977). For example, a global H and a local H are the most similar to one another. Response to a local H is faster when the global stimulus is the same or similar (e.g., block letters H or A) than when they are different. Within reasonable limits of visual acuity, when subjects are directed to local patterns, they are faster when the global and local levels are similar or consistent than when they are different or inconsistent (see Fig. 10.6). Conversely, when responding to the global patterns, there is no effect of consistency. This has been called Stroop-like interference (Pomerantz, 1983) but I question this connection further on.

In addition to the asymmetries discussed in the previous sections, T-P damage, but not IPL damage, disrupts the normal interference effect observed with hierarchical patterns and does so equally whether damage is on the right or the left (i.e., whether there is a global or a local advantage). In fact, T-P damage eliminates the interaction shown in Fig. 10.6 completely (Lamb et al., 1989). Conversely, Avishi Henik, Marvin Lamb and I used the Stroop test and found that color-name interference was normal (1993). The elimination of interference between global and local levels occurs whether the pattern is presented centrally, in the field ipsilateral to the lesion, or in the contralateral field.

It is of interest to note that the P300 of both auditory and visual scalp evoked potentials is also eliminated or substantially reduced in the same patients. This occurs over both the T-P region of damage and the homologous region on the opposite side (Knight, Scabini, Woods, & Clayworth, 1989). Partly on the basis of this finding Yamaguchi and Knight (in press) suggested that the P300 represents cortical-cortical synchronization across hemispheres. Although the cognitive correlates of the P300 are debatable, the fact that it is reduced or eliminated over both T-P regions in patients with unilateral T-P damage correlates with the elimination of normal interactions between global and local levels when stimuli are presented in either the ipsilateral or contralateral field. This correspondence between the electrophysiological and behavioral indices lends weight to the notion that the global interference effect is supported by cortical-cortical communication.

The hypothesis that the interaction represents a disconnection between asymmetrically represented functions was recently tested in three patients with full commissurotomy (L.B., N.G., & A.A.). Both surgical reports and more recent magnetic resonance images confirmed that the corpus callosum and the anterior and posterior commissures were fully sectioned in these patients (see Bogen, Schultz, & Vogel, 1988). As predicted, local performance on hierarchical patterns was better when they were presented in the RVF (which connects directly to the left hemisphere) than when they were presented in the LVF, and global performance was better when they patterns were presented in the LVF (which connects directly to the right hemisphere) than when they were presented in the RVF. Normals also showed the typical interaction between global and local levels and consistency. Patients, however, showed no hint of this interaction (F value for this effect was less than 1 in each of the three cases analyzed individually). The collapsed data are shown in Fig. 10.7 for controls and split-brain patients.

Given that both full commissurotomy and unilateral T-P lesions eliminated the global interference effect, we can safely conclude that intact cortical-cortical pathways between posterior regions of the two hemispheres support the normal interference effect. This conclusion is also consistent with data collected in a patient with deep bilateral posterior inferior lesions that would also disrupt posterior callosal transfer (Humphreys, Riddoch, & Quinlan, 1985). The normal interference effect was absent in this patient who was tested using a similar design to the one we used with unilateral T-P groups and commissurotomized patients.

Other evidence has demonstrated that unilateral parietal damage that does not extend into T-P regions does not alter the normal pattern of performance, nor does unilateral dorsolateral frontal damage (Lamb et al., 1989). These data further support the conclusion that the critical connections are through posterior regions of the corpus callosum that connect the temporal and parietal areas in each hemisphere to each other.

I have suggested that the function of this right-left pathway is to integrate global and local levels (Robertson & Lamb, 1991), but this cannot be said conclusively. This cortico-cortical pathway could be involved in interference, which would be consistent with theories suggesting that the corpus callosum functions as an inhibitory system. However, we have shown that RT in normals is faster when the global and local levels are similar to each other than when they are not (Lamb et al., 1990). This finding questions an interference interpretation. Similar items do not increase RT to identify the local item. Rather, similar items seem to facilitate local identification. Consistent with the idea that hemisphere transfer represents processes separate from those that produce a global or local advantage, other studies have shown that the level advantage can be affected independently of the interference effect. Navon and Norman (1983) reported that global advantage in normals could remain constant while the interference effect varied, and our studies with normals, under different conditions than those of Navon and Norman, showed that the level advantage could vary without affecting the magnitude of the interference effect (Lamb & Robertson, 1989). Patient data

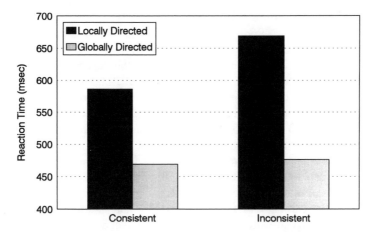

FIG. 10. 6. Typical effects of consistency in locally directed and globally directed conditions.

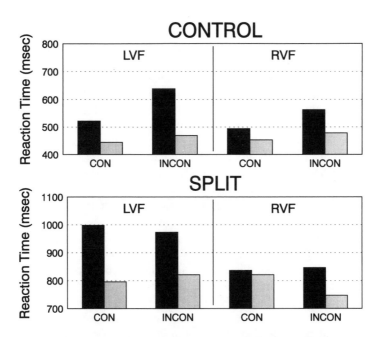

FIG. 10. 7. Mean reaction time for globally directed (light bars) and locally directed (dark bars) conditions as a function of consistency for RVF and LVF presentation for normal controls and patients with full commissurotomy (split). Con= consistent, Incon=inconsistent.

support this independence, as well (Lamb et al., 1989): There can be a global advantage in left T-P groups with no interference effect and a local advantage in right T-P groups with no interference effect. The independence of the interference effect and the level advantage was further supported in normals in a study in which a correlational analysis was performed between the magnitude of the global advantage and magnitude of the global interference (Robertson et al., 1993) and there was no correlation between the two measures. These results can be seen in Fig. 10.8 where the scatterplot of global interference (local RT for inconsistent letters minus local RT for consistent letters) against level advantage (global RT minus local RT) is shown for a group of 31 normal subjects. Given that the size of the corpus callosum varies enormously, especially through the isthmus where T-P regions would be connected (see Witelson, this volume, Chapter 2), it is possible that the lack of correlation is due to signals between pathways being biased toward either global or local analysis. For the advantage and interference effects to be uncorrelated the signal would be randomly timed and vary according to the strength and number of connections. This hypothesis is speculative and deserves further investigation, but it is consistent with both the behavioral and the neuroanatomical data.

PARALLEL PROCESSING IN ASYMMETRIC MODULES

Do the asymmetric processes biased toward global or local levels operate in parallel? I cannot conclusively say they do, but there is evidence that is consistent with this suggestion. My colleagues and I tested young normals in a preliminary experiment in the same design used with commissurotomized patients, but with fewer trials and more subjects. We presented hierarchical patterns in the LVF, the RVF, or both visual fields simultaneously. A small central fixation point preceded each display, and one of the three types of displays was presented randomly for 100 msec. In one block of trials, subjects were globally directed and in another they were locally directed. It was emphasized that on bilateral trials, patterns in the LVF and the RVF would by the same. Mean RT is presented in Fig. 10.9. Note that there was a global advantage in all conditions. This was expected because the stimuli were purposely constructed to make the global letter more salient than the local. Also note that the global advantage was larger in the LVF than the RVF, consistent with hemispheric differences in level bias. More important for the present concern, global RT in the bilateral condition was equal to unilateral presentation in the LVF, and local RT in the bilateral condition was equal to the unilateral presentation in the RVF. Conversely, bilateral global RT was significantly faster than unilateral RVF global RT, whereas bilateral local RT was significantly faster than LVF local RT. These effects are consistent with parallel processes that ignore redundant information in the opposite field. They are also consistent with a model in which the less efficient hemisphere is inhibited, or the more efficient activated, according to task demands. If the task is to identify global information, the left hemisphere may be less activated than the right in anticipation

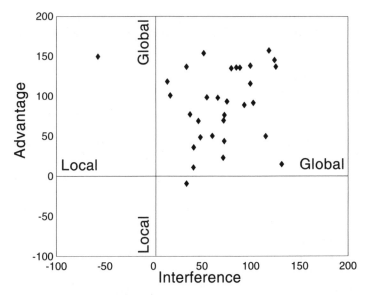

FIG. 10. 8. Scatter plot representing the amount of level advantage (globally directed reaction time minus locally directed reaction time) as a function of the amount of global interference (consistent minus inconsistent reaction time for the locally directed condition) for 31 normal subjects.

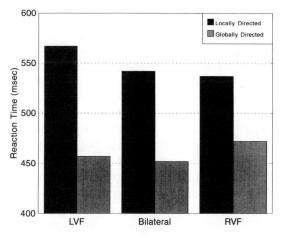

FIG. 10. 9. Mean reaction times for globally directed and locally directed conditions for right visual field (RVF), left visual field (LVF) and bilateral presentation.

of the pattern, and if the task is to identify local information, the right hemisphere may be less activated than the left. Again, these are hypotheses that need more study.

COMPUTATIONS

What parameters of the stimulus are important in producing the Global/local × Field asymmetry in hierarchical patterns, and what computations are employed by each asymmetrically represented component? In 1982, Sergent suggested that the hemispheres differed in their responses to different spatial frequencies at the global and local levels. She hypothesized that the hemispheres did not differ in primary visual function, but that a higher order process was lateralized so that the right hemisphere was more efficient at processing lower spatial frequencies and the left hemisphere was more efficient at processing higher frequencies. This hypothesis was based on the results of her studies using hierarchical patterns and visual field presentation in normals in which a RVF advantage was found for local letters and a LVF advantage was found for global letters. The fundamental frequency in a global form is lower than that in a local form. We later found that performance asymmetries due to left or right T-P lesions for such patterns occurred over a wide range of visual angles (between 6° and 12°; Lamb et al., 1990). These data demonstrated that the asymmetrical components were responding to some relative difference between global and local levels and, by extension, that relative spatial frequency may be the critical parameter.

Recent experiments using sinusoidal gratings containing a single spatial frequency and RVF or LVF presentation in normals have shown that low frequencies are responded to faster in the LVF than in the RVF, and high frequencies are responded to faster in the RVF than in the LVF, but only when subjects must discriminate frequency gratings that are presented above threshold (Kitterle, Christman, & Hellige, 1990; Kitterle & Kaye, 1985; Kitterle & Selig, 1991). Asymmetric performance does not occur when simple detection is required. A subsequent study by Christman, Kitterle, and Hellige (1991) showed that the asymmetry occurred for both absolute and relative spatial frequencies. The relatively high frequency of a compound stimulus with three gratings produced a RVF advantage. When the same absolute frequency was the relatively low frequency, a LVF advantage occurred.

These directional asymmetries appear to be multimodal. Responses to relative auditory frequencies show a similar asymmetry when dichotically presented. Ivry and Lebby (1993) and Lebby, Ivry, Robertson, and Shimamura (1991) found that the highest frequency of a set of high-frequency tones presented among lower frequency tones produced better performance when presented to the right ear than to the left, whereas the lowest of the set of higher frequencies produced better performance when presented to the left ear than to the right. As in vision, this effect was observed under conditions where discrimination between tones was required. Ivry and Lebby (1993) have suggested that there are separate attentional filters that are superimposed on the sensory signal, one represented in the right hemisphere and one in the left. The filter can be thought of as a skewed Gaussian distribution placed over the frequency channels represented by the sensory cortex. According to this model, the asymmetry is due to the skew of the curves being in opposite directions for the two hemispheres. It is assumed that the skew does not change, although its peak position over the sensory representation can. The RH mechanism filters out high-frequency information, and thus enhances lower frequency information, whereas the LH mechanism filters out low-frequency information and enhances high. Ivry and Robertson (1993) conclude that the two filters accept as input a modulated form of the sensory representation, producing the effects of relative frequency. Because attentional selection is required, the effects will only be observed when a task other than detection is required. In detection, one can utilize the sensory representation directly and need not employ a relative measure.

The evidence that the asymmetry was superimposed on the sensory signal and was only one step removed from primary sensory representation in the visual cortex is discussed at length by Robertson (1992) and Robertson and Lamb (1991). In the Lamb et al. (1989) study discussed early in the section on anatomical correlates, normals and patient groups were tested with hierarchical patterns presented in the LVF, in the RVF, or centrally. Identification of the global form was required in one block of trials and identification of the local form in another. The data for central presentation were shown in Fig. 10.4. There was only a slight (nonsignificant) global advantage for controls with the right T-P group showing a local advantage and the left T-P group a global advantage. Fig. 10.10 shows the data for peripheral presentation for the same experiment. A global advantage was evident for normal controls in these conditions. This would be expected, because local forms would be more difficult to see due to the lower resolution of peripheral vision. Right and left T-P groups still diverged from normals, but right T-P showed no level advantage under these conditions. However, the difference between controls and right T-P was similar for central (Fig. 10.3) and peripheral (Fig. 10.10) presentation, and the asymmetry was superimposed on the sensory signal. This was confirmed in a subsequent study that showed that between 6° and 12° of visual angle (the stimulus as a whole was made larger or smaller) left T-P and right T-P groups diverged from controls as before (Lamb et al., 1990).

GLOBAL PRECEDENCE

In 1977, Navon claimed that the visual system analyzed global features before local features, all else being equal. In his initial studies, he equated RT for large and small letters, but found that when he placed them in a hierarchical structure, global forms were more rapidly identified than local. Furthermore, inconsistent global forms (e.g., a global S created from local Hs) increased local response more than a consistent global form, but consistency had no effect on global RT (see Fig. 10.6). On the basis of the two effects (global advantage and global interference), Navon

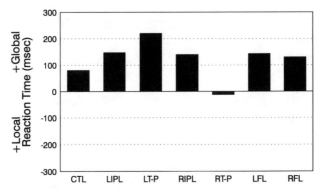

FIG. 10. 10. Mean global reaction time advantage (above 0) or local reaction time advantage (below 0) for controls (CTL) and patient groups (L = left hemisphere, R = right hemisphere, IPL = inferior parietal lobe, T-P = temporal-parietal, FL = frontal lobe)

concluded that global advantage and global interference emerged from the same underlying process. Global information was available first and therefore interfered with local identification. Global RT was unaffected across consistency because local identification was not available at the time global identification was made.

The data I have discussed, from both normals and brain-damaged groups, demonstrate a far more complex set of operations than Navon then suspected. Navon's logic was reasonable at the time, but subsequent experimental findings called into question any simple answers concerning the issue of global or local precedence in the human visual system, even evidence from normals (Hoffman, 1980; Kinchla & Wolfe, 1979; Miller, 1981; Pomerantz, 1983). To address the issues of level precedence, the first question should concern at what stage of analysis global or local advantage is hypothesized to occur. We know that primary visual cortex responds to low frequencies before high, and global forms have a lower fundamental frequency than do local. If global advantage were due entirely to this stage of analysis, then global precedence would be a reasonable theory. The use of simple detection, rather than discrimination, has the potential to reveal global precedence at this stage of analysis. However, to progress from the sensory representation to identification requires several steps. I have discussed neuropsychological data showing that differences in global and local availability can be found beyond the sensory stage, but are asymmetrically represented. A mechanism biased toward global information is disrupted by right T-P damage, and one biased toward local information is disrupted by left T-P damage. The evidence supports the idea that these biases are due to higher order analyses superimposed on the sensory signal and occur when discrimination tasks are required (Ivry & Robertson, 1993; Lebby et al., 1991; Robertson, in press; Robertson & Lamb, 1991; Sergent, 1982).

A different mechanism is responsible for the interaction between levels, and normal performance relies on intact connections between T-P regions through the corpus callosum. Global advantage and global interference can be stochastically independent (see Fig. 10.8). The consistency effects that lengthened local response in Navon's (1977) paradigm reflect a different cognitive process than those that determined the time to identify forms at the global or local levels.

This conclusion is not meant to fault Navon. He did not have access to the enriched set of data that have been collected since his original paper. In fact, his paradigm has proven extremely useful in uncovering not only cognitive mechanisms that respond to hierarchically organized patterns, but also the neural mechanisms that support them. The latter application was not evident in 1977. Also, Navon was correct in stating that there is global precedence in the visual system. However, there is also local precedence, and the amount of interference (or facilitation) is not directly related to the temporal advantage in identifying one level or the other when discrimination is required. In fact, it is debatable whether or not the interference effect reflects interference at all. Our data suggest that facilitation is a more likely candidate, and I hypothesize that the interaction between global and local levels is due to integrative processes between component hemispheric operations.

CONCLUSION

The findings I have discussed have relevance for several questions that cross disciplines. They support the claim, in neuropsychology, that hemispheric laterality for visual spatial information can be observed in relatively early visual processes, but ones that are a step removed from cortical sensory input (Sergent, 1982, 1987). Converging evidence from several laboratories suggests that this asymmetry is multimodal and is linked to the relative fundamental frequencies in duplex patterns. The fact that field asymmetries in normals cross modalities and have been associated with T-P regions is consistent with the animal literature demonstrating that the T-P junction is a multimodal region receiving direct inputs from visual, auditory, and somatosensory cortices (see Seltzer & Pandya, 1978).

The evidence also suggests that a far more complex set of cognitive operations is activiated in responses to hierarchical forms than previous cognitive theories suggested. Furthermore, the data demonstrate that either/or questions in cognitive psychology (e.g., is there a global or a local advantage in the visual system, is the advantage due to top-down or bottom-up processes, etc.) may not be very useful. The visual system includes both global and local precedence, and the RT advantage depends on the stage of analysis, on the stimulus parameters, and on the task demands. Also, measuring interference effects to determine what can be ignored and what cannot may not always be the best way to address such issues; grouping interference effects under umbrellas, such as Stroop-interference, may blur important distinctions. Interference or facilitation can be associated with different pathways than identification processes, and the activated pathways may depend, at least in part, on the stimulus features.

I have discussed a rather limited set of data focused on patterns of performance in response to stimuli having at least two levels of structure. Although the focus seems narrow, in fact, the findings as a whole are applicable to a broad range of research interests. Since the early 1980s, we have come much closer to understanding the role of input mechanisms in hemisphere laterality, resulting in models that make distinct predictions. We have been able to capitalize on the development of in vivo methods and have begun to isolate regions in the human brain that are responsible for visual-spatial lateralization and callosal transfer effects. We have addressed concerns about the applicability of patient research to normal cognitive functioning by using converging evidence from several populations, including normals. As a result, we have been able to question existing cognitive theories and to develop new theories of normal perceptual analysis. We have obviously only scratched the surface. Current theories are bound to evolve as discoveries are made, but progress has been made in understanding both the cognitive and neural mechanisms associated with a common type of perceptual organization.

ACKNOWLEDGMENTS

This manuscript was supported by the Medical Research Service of the Department of Veterans Affairs and by grant award AA06637 to the author.

REFERENCES

Alivisates, B., & Wilding, J. (1982). Hemispheric differences in matching Stroop-type letter stimuli. *Cortex, 18*, 5-22.

Ben-Yishay, Y., Diller, L., Mandelberg, I., Gordon, W., & Gerstman,L.J. (1971). Similarities and differences in block design performance between older normal and brain injured persons: A task analysis. *Journal of Abnormal Psychology, 78*, 17-25.

Bogen, J.E., Schultz, D.H., & Vogel, P.J. (1988). Completeness of callostomy shown by magnetic resonance imaging in the long term. *Archives of Neurology, 45*, 1203-1205.

Boles, D.B. (1984). Global versus local processing: Is there a hemispheric dichotomy? *Neuropsychologia, 22*, 445-455.

Christman, S., Kitterle, F.L. & Hellige, J. (1991). Hemispheric asymmetry in the processing of absolute versus relative spatial frequency. *Brain and Cognition, 16*, 62-73.

Delis, D.C., Robertson, L.C., & Efron, R. (1986). Hemispheric specialization of memory for visual hierarchical stimuli. *Neuropsychologia, 24*, 205-204.

DeRenzi, E. (1982). *Disorders of space exploration and cognition.* New York: Wiley.

Hoffman, J.R. (1980). Interaction between global and local levels of a form. *Journal of Experimental Psychology: Human Perception and Performance, 6*, 222-234.

Humphreys, G.W., Riddoch, M.J. & Quinlan, P.T. (1985). Interactive processes in perceptual organization: Evidence from visual agnosia. In M.I. Posner & O.S.M. Marin (Eds.). *Attention and Performance XI* (pp. 301-318). Hillsdale, NJ: Lawrence Erlbaum Associates.

Ivry, R.B., & Lebby, P.C. (1993). Hemispheric differences in auditory perception are similar to those found in visual perception. *Psychological Science, 4,* 41-45.

Ivry, R.B., & Robertson, L.C. (In preparation). *Hemispheric asymmetries in vision and audition.* Cambridge, MA: MIT Press.

Kaplan, E. (1983). Process and achievement revisited. In S. Wapner & B. Kaplan (Eds.), *Toward a holistic developmental psychology* (pp. 143-156). Hillsdale, NJ: Lawrence Erlbaum Associates.

Kinchla, R.A., & Wolfe, J.M. (1979). The order of visual processing: "Top-down," "bottom-up," or "middle-out." *Perception & Psychophysics, 25,* 225-231.

Kitterle, F.L., & Kaye, R.S. (1985). Hemispheric symmetry in contrast and orientation sensitivity. *Perception and Psychophysics, 37,* 391-396.

Kitterle, F.L., Christman, S., & Hellige, J. (1990). Hemispheric differences are found in the identification, but not detection, of low versus high spatial frequencies. *Perception & Psychophysics, 48,* 297-306.

Kitterle, F.L., & Selig, L.M. (1991). Visual field effects in the discrimination of sine-wave gratings. *Perception & Psychophysics, 50,* 15-18.

Knight, R. T., Scabini, D., Woods, D. L., & Clayworth, C. C. (1989). Contribution of temporal-parietal junction to the human auditory P3. *Brain Research, 502,* 109-116.

Kramer, J.H., Kaplan, E., Blusewicz, M.J., & Preston, K.A. (1991). Visual hierarchical analysis of block design configural errors. *Journal of Clinical and Experimental Neuropsychology, 13,* 455-465.

Lamb, M.R., & Robertson, L.C. (1989). Do response time advantage and interference reflect the order of processing of global and local level information? *Perception & Psychophysics, 46,* 254-258.

Lamb, M.R., Robertson, L.C., & Knight, R.T. (1989). Effects of right and left temporal parietal lesions on the processing of global and local patterns in a selective attention task. *Neuropsychologia, 27,* 471-483.

Lamb, M.R., Robertson, L.C. & Knight, R.T. (1990). Component mechanisms underlying the processing of hierarchically organized patterns: Inferences from patients with unilateral cortical lesions. *Journal of Experimental Psychology: Learning, Memory & Cognition, 16,* 471-483.

Lebby, P., Ivry, R., Robertson, L.C., & Shimamura (1991, November). *Laterality effects in the processing of high- and low-frequency auditory stimuli.* Paper presented at the annual meeting of the Society for Neuroscience, New Orleans, LA.

Martin, M. (1979). Hemisphere specialization for local and global processing. *Neuropsychologia, 17,* 33-40.

Miller, J. (1981). Global precedence in attention and decision. *Journal of Experimental Psychology: Human Perception and Performance, 7,* 1161-1185.

Navon, D. (1977). Forest before trees: The precedence of global features in visual perception. *Cognitive Psychology, 9,* 353-383.

Navon, D., & Norman, J. (1983). Does global precedence really depend on visual angle? *Journal of Experimental Psychology: Human Perception and Performance, 9*, 955-965.

Nebes, R.D. (1978). Direct examination of cognitive function in the right and left hemispheres. In M. Kinsbourne (Ed.), *Asymmetrical function of the brain*. Cambridge, England: Cambridge University Press.

Pomerantz, J.R. (1983). Global and local precedence: Selective attention in form and motion perception. *Journal of Experimental Psychology: General, 112*, 516-540.

Robertson, L.C. (1992). The role of perceptual organization and search in attentional disorders. In D.I. Margolin (Ed.). *Cognitive neuropsychology in clinical practice*. New York: Oxford University Press.

Robertson, L.C., & Lamb, M.R. (1991). Neuropsychological contributions to theories of part/whole organization. *Cognitive Psychology, 23*, 299-330.

Robertson, L.C., Lamb, M.R., & Knight, R.T. (1988). Effects of lesions of temporal-parietal junction on perceptual and attentional processing in humans. *Journal of Neurosciences, 8*, 3757-3769.

Robertson, L.C., Lamb, M.R., & Knight, R.T. (1991). Normal global-local analysis in patients with dorsolateral frontal lobe lesions. *Neuropsychologia, 29*, 959-967.

Robertson, L.C., Lamb, M.R., & Zaidel, E. (1993). Interhemispheric relations in processing hierarchical patterns: Evidence from normal and commissurotomized subjects. *Neuropsychology, 7*, 325-342.

Seltzer, B., & Pandya, D.N. (1978). Afferent cortical connections and architectonics of the superior temporal sulcus and surrounding cortex in the rhesus monkey. *Brain Research, 149*, 1-24.

Sergent, J. (1982). The cerebral balance of power: Confrontation or cooperation? *Journal of Experimental Psychology: Human Perception and Performance, 8*, 253-272.

Sergent, J. (1987). Failures to confirm the spatial-frequency hypothesis: Fatal blow or healthy complication? *Canadian Journal of Psychology, 41*, 412-428.

Van Kleek, M. (1989). Hemisphere differences in global versus local processing of hierarchical visual stimuli by normal subjects: New data and a meta-analysis of previous studies. *Neuropsychologia, 27*, 1165-1178.

Yamaguchi, S., & Knight, R. T. (in press). Anterior and posterior association cortex contributions to the somatosensory P300. *Journal of Neuroscience*.

11 Spatial-Frequency Selectivity in Hemispheric Transfer

Frederick L. Kitterle
Stephen F. Austin State University

Stephen Christman
Jorge S. Conesa
University of Toledo

Research in our laboratory has been concerned with characterizing the differences between the left and the right cerebral hemispheres in the processing of spatial-frequency information (Christman, Kitterle, & Hellige, 1992, Kitterle, Christman, & Conesa, 1993; Kitterle, Christman, & Hellige, 1991; Kitterle, Hellige, & Christman, 1992; Kitterle & Selig, 1991). These experiments were motivated by the work of Sergent (1982, 1983, 1985), who advanced the *spatial-frequency hypothesis* . According to this hypothesis, the cerebral hemispheres differ in the efficiency with which they process spatial-frequency information. Specifically, the right hemisphere (RH) is more efficient in processing low spatial frequencies, whereas the left hemisphere (LH) is more efficient in processing high spatial frequencies.

The spatial-frequency hypothesis derives from two sources. One is research on the influence of input factors on hemispheric differences in visual information processing. A typical finding is that degrading the perceptual quality of the visual information affects the processing of stimuli presented in the right visual field (RVF) more adversely than the processing of stimuli presented in the left visual field (LVF). This implies that the quality of visual input can influence the magnitude and direction of hemispheric asymmetries. Moreover, the quality of visual input is of critical importance, because it determines the way in which stimulus input may be analyzed by and represented in the visual system. Consequently, differences in procedure that influence the quality of visual input may account for the contradictory findings among studies.

The other source is based on both psychophysical and electrophysiological research that indicates that the visual system may analyze a visual stimulus in terms of its spatial-frequency Fourier components (see Weisstein, 1980 for a review). This research suggests that the visual system contains multiple channels, each of which responds to a different range of spatial-frequency contained within the visual stimulus. The spatial-frequency hypotheses suggests that the two cerebral hemispheres differ in the efficiency with which they process spatial-frequency information. The left hemisphere is more efficient at processing high spatial-frequency ranges and the right is more efficient at processing low spatial frequencies. However, a given task may depend on information from either the low or the high spatial-frequency range. Thus, according to the spatial-frequency hypothesis, the direction of hemispheric asymmetries will be jointly determined by the spatial-frequency information contained in the visual stimulus, that is, information available for higher level processing, and the information required for a specific task.

The results of several experiments that have tested the spatial-frequency hypothesis have been mixed (see Christman, 1989). In a review, Kitterle and Christman (1991) have noted that the failure to replicate may be attributed to several factors: failure to control for changes in mean luminance, failure to control the bandwidth of spatial frequencies in the stimulus, the nature of task, and others. Moreover, beyond these difficulties, Sergent (1987) has pointed out an additional, twofold difficulty: it is not possible to specify, a priori, the procedural variables that would result in a given visual field superiority, nor is it possible to determine which spatial frequencies convey the relevant information to optimize performance on a given task.

Our experiments have attempted to circumvent some of these difficulties. We have used a psychophysical task in which subjects were required either to detect the presence of a sine-wave grating or to identify whether it was of high or low spatial frequency (Kitterle et al., 1991). Because the gratings were sinusoidal rather than square-wave, and modulated about the mean luminance of the display screens, we were able to control the spatial frequency content of the visual input and also ensure that no mean luminance changes accompanied the presentation of the gratings. Thus, we were able to specify the spatial frequency content available in the visual input. By varying the nature of the psychophysical task, we were able to determine not only the spatial frequency required for a task, but also whether additional computations were necessary beyond simply registering the presence of a spatial-frequency. That is, in the detection task all that is required is that one be aware that a grating was presented, not that one identify which grating was presented. However, the requirements of the identification task are different. In this case, not only must the presence of a grating be detected, but the subject must also determine whether it is of low or high spatial-frequency. Kitterle et al. (1991) showed that hemispheric asymmetries occur for identification, but not for detection. Low spatial-frequency gratings were identified faster when presented in the LVF than RVF, whereas, the opposite was found for high spatial-frequency gratings; these were identified faster when presented in the RVF than in the LVF. The direction of the interaction between spatial frequency and visual field supports the spatial-frequency hypothesis and indicates that hemispheric asymmetries arise at a computational stage in processing in which the outputs of spatial-frequency channels are compared.

Subsequent research explored the processing of complex gratings that contain a range of spatial frequencies (Christman et al., 1991; Kitterle et al., 1992). Two important conclusions can be drawn from these studies. The first is that processing a target spatial frequency is influenced by other components in the pattern.   For example, Christman et al. (1991) showed that hemispheric asymmetries depend on both relative and absolute spatial frequency.   A target spatial frequency that is the lowest component in a compound stimulus will lead to a LVF advantage. However, if it is the highest spatial frequency of a component, a RVF advantage is obtained.   Other work indicates that the processing of a target spatial frequency in a compound grating can be inhibited by other components in the pattern (see Kitterle et al., 1993), and the magnitude of inhibition depends on the spatial frequency of the target and the visual field of presentation.   Subjects in this study were required to determine the orientation of one of the components (the target grating) of a compound grating that consisted of both low and high spatial-frequency sinusoidal gratings.   The pattern was presented in either the LVF or the RVF.   The results of this study showed that low spatial-frequency gratings interfered with the processing of the high spatial-frequency target.   Although the effect was found for both visual field presentations, interference was greatest when the compound pattern was presented in the LVF.   When the target grating was of low spatial frequency, a considerably smaller interference effect from the high spatial-frequency component was found for the RVF presentations.

A second conclusion is that in a compound grating containing more than one spatial frequency, task requirements can focus attention on different spatial-frequency ranges.   For example, Kitterle et al. (1992) showed that a task requiring processing in the low spatial-frequency range yields a LVF advantage.   However, when the task depends on processing in the high spatial-frequency range, a RVF advantage emerges.   In this experiment, subjects were shown one of four patterns on a given trial (a 1 c/deg square-wave grating, a 1 c/deg sine-wave grating, a 3 c/deg square-wave grating, and a 3 c/deg sine-wave grating).   In one task the subjects judged whether a target had wide or narrow bars, independent of whether it was a square-wave or sine-wave grating.   In the other task the subjects determined whether a pattern had sharp (square-wave) or fuzzy (sine-wave) edges independent of the width of the bars.   The former task resulted in a LVF advantage because the spatial frequencies were relatively low.   However, the latter task yielded a RVF advantage, because subjects had to process the high spatial frequencies to determine if a sharp edge was present.

The finding that hemispheric differences exist in the processing of spatial-frequency information suggests the involvement of hemispheric communication.   Such a mechanism is necessary in order to ensure that spatial-frequency information is shared between the hemispheres.   Obviously, however, input factors, task demands, and the costs versus the benefits of hemispheric interaction determine whether one hemisphere will carry out processing of visual information independent of the other or whether they will interact.   For example, in central viewing both hemispheres have access to the available spatial-frequency information.   It might be reasonable to expect that the hemispheres will distribute the processing of visual information in a way that maximizes the efficiencies of each hemisphere.   In this case, the RH will be involved in processing the low spatial-frequency information and the LH will process the high spatial frequencies. At some point in the processing sequence, information from the two hemispheres will need to be shared in arrive at an integrated percept.   Clearly, information transfer may serve the function of providing a unified perception across the vertical midline.   An understanding of the conditions under which transfer can and cannot occur may help to provide further insight into the role of input factors on the magnitude and direction of cerebral laterality effects.   For example, we argued earlier that input factors affect the quality of the visual input available for further processing.   It may also be the case that input factors determine the likelihood of information transfer between the two hemispheres.   Thus, it is important to our understanding of the role of the two cerebral hemispheres in the processing of visual information and the effects of input factors on laterality effects to characterize the nature of the hemispheric transfer of spatial-frequency information and the interaction between the hemispheres in the processing of spatial frequency.

HEMISPHERIC TRANSFER

Three different kinds of experiments have addressed the issue of hemispheric transfer of spatial-frequency information.   In an electrophysiological study, Berardi and Fiorentini (1987a) determined the temporal and spatial characteristics of visual information transmitted across the corpus callosum in cats by recording directly from the corpus callosum and in split-chiasm cats by means of visual evoked potentials (VEPs) and single unit recordings at the border of areas 17 and 18 of the cerebral cortex.   Because the neural fibers crossing to the opposite side of the cortex were severed, the only way for visual input from one eye to reach the contralateral hemisphere was through the corpus callosum.   Thus, a direct comparison could be made between the transfer of information through the geniculocortical system and that transmitted via the corpus callosum.   Using threshold to suprathreshold levels of contrast, Berardi and Fiorentini (1987a) found that the amplitudes of the signals were lower in the callosal pathways than in the geniculate pathways.   Moreover, the high spatial and high temporal frequencies were more strongly attenuated for the callosal than for the geniculocortical pathway.   These results imply that the crosstalk between hemispheres is abolished at low contrasts and high spatial frequencies.   Based on these findings, Berardi and Fiorentini (1987a) suggested that a transfer of learning and discrimination between the hemispheres is obtained only for high contrast patterns.

  Fiorentini and Berardi (1987b) explored phase discrimination as a function of retinal position for gratings presented in the LVF and RVF.   Earlier research had shown that phase discrimination was better for LVF than RVF presentations (Fiorentini and Berardi, 1984).   If spatial-frequency information is transferred, then one should find no differences between the LVF and RVF when the patterns are presented close to the vertical midline.   Moreover, if there is selective transfer of spatial-frequency information, then hemispheric differences in phase discrimination for higher spatial-frequency patterns should remain unaffected by retinal position unless the contrast of the patterns is raised significantly. Psychophysical studies with humans confirm this prediction (Berardi and Fiorentini, 1987b).   For compound gratings presented 5° from fixation, a right-hemisphere (RH) advantage was found. However for patterns with a fundamental spatial frequency of 2 c/deg or lower presented close to the vertical meridian, the RH advantage disappeared. A second experiment investigated the transfer of learning of spatial phase. In earlier work, Fiorentini and Berardi (1981) had shown that performance on phase discrimination progressively improved with practice. In fact, performance remained constant, even after weeks. However, if the gratings were shifted to a new orientation or if the spatial frequencies of the training patterns was changed, then performance dropped to chance level. Transfer of learning was specific to spatial frequency and phase. Berardi and Fiorentini (1987b) found that transfer of learning was obtained for gratings of 2 c/deg or lower when presented close to the vertical meridian and symmetrically located on either side of it. No transfer was found for non-overlapping regions on the same side of the vertical meridian. They also found interocular transfer of learning for gratings 2 c/deg or less if they were presented close to the vertical meridian and symmetrically placed on either side.

In a related paper, Berardi, Bodis-Wollner, Fiorentini, Giuffre, and Morelli (1989) presented electrophysiological evidence for the interhemispheric transfer of spatial-frequency information. They showed that the VEPs for a low spatial-frequency grating presented on one side of the vertical meridian was reduced by the presence of a higher contrast grating of the same spatial frequency symmetrically placed on the opposite side of the vertical meridian, provided that both gratings were close to the vertical midline. The effect of the higher contrast grating on the VEP was progressively reduced with increasing distance from the vertical midline. The interference effect vanished for spatial frequencies greater than 4 c/deg and for temporal frequencies greater than 10 Hz. It was not found for low spatial frequencies if both gratings were presented on the same side of the vertical meridian to spatially adjacent retinal regions. Moreover, the interference effect was also found for dichoptic presentations. Thus, interference appears to reflect interhemispheric cross-talk between symmetric regions of the visual field across the vertical meridian.

THE PRESENT STUDIES

Berardi et al. (1989) noted that besides reducing the amplitude of the VEP to the reference grating, the interference grating increased the psychophysical contrast threshold to the reference grating. This result is of particular interest given the numerous reviews that indicate virtually no effect of an adapting grating on the threshold of a test grating when the two are presented to spatially adjacent, noncontiguous retinal regions. However, it appears that when two gratings of similar low spatial frequency stimulate symmetrical regions on the two sides of the vertical meridian, they can interact. As the spatial frequency of the two adjacent gratings increased, the observed interactions decreased. Thus, the implication of the psychophysical work of Berardi et al. (1989) and the electrophysiological studies mentioned earlier is that low spatial-frequency information is more readily transferred across the corpus callosum than is high spatial-frequency information, particularly at low contrast levels. This conclusion is supported by other research that indicates that a LVF advantage for discriminating the phase relationship between two low spatial-frequency gratings in a compound pattern disappears when the grating pattern is moved closer to the vertical midline; this is not the case for high spatial-frequency gratings. Presumably, at closer eccentricities the transfer of spatial-frequency information is more likely.

In the experiments reported in this chapter, we have explored the transfer of spatial-frequency information using two different kinds of experiments. The first experiment was concerned with spatial-frequency adaptation and determined the effect of the spatial and temporal frequency of an adapting grating on the reaction time (RT) to a low contrast test grating. The second experiment employed a redundant signals procedure to explore spatial-frequency interactions across the vertical meridian. In one study, subjects were required to respond as quickly as possible to the presentation of a grating in the LVF, RVF, both visual fields (VFs), or neither. In a second study, the simple RT task was modified, and subjects were required to identify whether a target grating was presented. A grating was presented in the LVF, RVF, both VFs, or neither. Before describing the rationale for these experiments, we discuss our general methodology.

General Methods and Procedure

In these experiments, a Picasso Image Generator under computer control was used to present the horizontally oriented sinusoidal gratings on the face of two Tektronix 608 monitors (P-31 phosphor). A black matte screen was placed in front of the two spatially adjacent monitors, and the screens of both monitors were visible through the square openings in the surround. A fixation point was placed midway between the openings. At a viewing distance of 57 cm, the dimension of each openings was 4.5 deg × 4.5 deg, and the inner edge of each opening was .5 deg from the fixation point. With the exception of the mean luminance of the monitors, the experimental room was dark. The mean luminance of the monitors was 10 cd/m^2. The contrasts used in each experiment are noted below. Throughout the course of this study, luminance calibrations were made daily to ensure that the monitors were matched in mean luminance and that there was no drift in contrast levels. Additional calibrations were made to ensure that similar spatial frequencies simultaneously presented on the monitors were in phase. A chin rest was used to stabilize vision and the importance of responding quickly and accurately was stressed. Only right-handed males with normal or corrected to normal vision and no familial history of sinistrality participated in the experiments.

EXPERIMENT 1: ADAPTATION TO LATERAL GRATINGS

As already noted, hemispheric interaction between two gratings of the same spatial frequency can be obtained when both are of low spatial frequency, close to the vertical midline, and flickered at a low temporal frequency. Thus, in the present experiment we measured the time it took subjects to detect a sine-wave grating presented in one visual field when a high contrast grating of the same spatial frequency was (adapted condition) or was not (unadapted condition) presented in the contralateral visual field.

Based on earlier research, we expected interhemispheric interaction would be obtained for low but not high spatial-frequency gratings. To test this, we briefly flashed either a low (1 c/deg) or high (9 c/deg) spatial-frequency grating for 100 msec in either the LVF or the RVF. The grating was near threshold (85% detectability) and horizontally oriented. Subjects were required to depress a response key as quickly as possible to indicate that they detected the grating. The gratings were masked down to circular apertures which at a viewing distance of 57 cm, subtended a visual angle of 5.5 deg with the inner edge .5 deg from fixation. The trials were blocked as follows: in one session the time to detect the target grating was determined in the absence of an adapting grating (no-adapt condition). In the adapt-left and adapt-right conditions, the target grating was presented in the visual field contralateral to the adapting grating. Typically, each condition was replicated 40 times.

For the adapt-left and adapt-right conditions, at the beginning of each trial, the adapting grating was presented for 2 sec while the subject fixated a small red LED. At the end of two sec, a tone was sounded. Then, after a random foreperiod, the target was presented. Subjects were instructed to react as quickly and accurately as possible. In order to reduce false positives, subjects were instructed that 15% of the trials would be blank. Six right-handed male subjects with normal vision participated in this study. They were naive about the purpose of the study and received payment for their participation.

In Fig. 11.1A, RT is plotted as a function of target spatial-frequency for the 1 c/deg adapting grating, which was at a contrast of 40% and flickered at 5 Hz. Figure 11.1B summarizes the results for the 9 c/deg adapting grating. Note that for both the adapt and no-adapt conditions shown in Figs 11.1 A and B, there is virtually no difference in RT for LVF and RVF presentations, consistent with the findings of earlier research (see Kitterle and Christman, 1990 for a review). With regard to Fig 11.1A, note that the 1 c/deg adapting grating has a marked influence on RT to the 1 c/deg target and no effect on RT to the 9 c/deg grating. On the other hand, in Fig. 11.1B, there is virtually no difference between the adapted and unadapted conditions for either the 1 c/deg or the 9 c/deg targets. Thus, it appears that our results support earlier work; namely, when a target and adapting grating are presented to different visual fields, it is the low and not the high spatial-frequency adapting grating that influences target detection. As already noted, the interhemispheric transfer of spatial-frequency information is not only dependent upon the spatial frequency of the grating but also on its temporal frequency. Figures 11.2A and B summarize the results of an experiment designed to explore the effect of this variable on the action of the 1 c/deg adapting grating. In Fig. 11.2A, RT is plotted as a function of target spatial frequency when the adapting

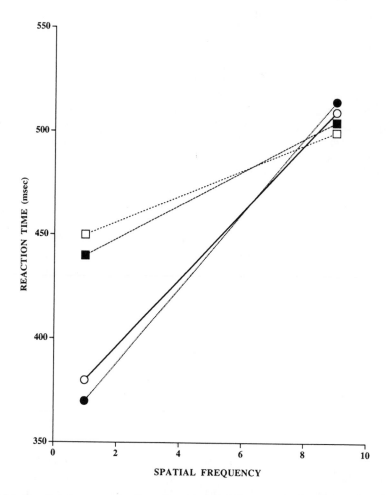

Fig. 11.1A. Reaction time as a function of target spatial frequency in the absence (no adapt, circles) or presence (adapt, squares) of a 1 c/deg adapting grating of 40% contrast presented in the contralateral visual field. Open symbols indicate adapting grating in LVF and test grating in the RVF whereas, filled symbols indicate adapting grating in RVF, test grating in LVF.

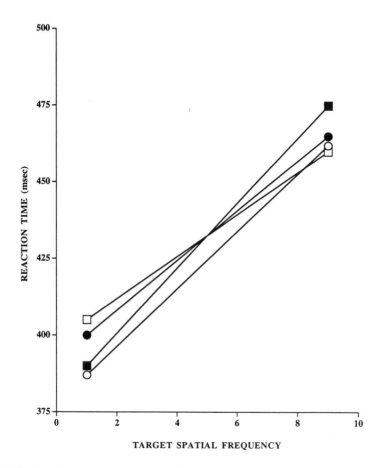

Fig. 11.1B. Reaction time as a function of target spatial frequency in the absence (no adapt, circles) or presence (adapt, squares) of a 9 c/deg adapting grating of 40% contrast presented in the contralateral visual field.

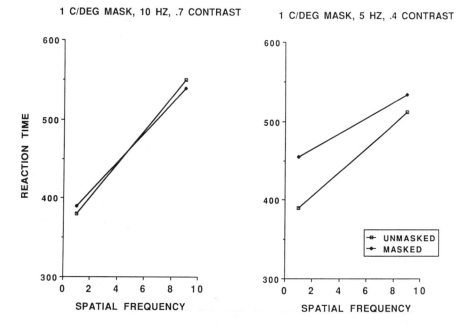

Fig. 11.2 A and B. (A). (left) RT as a function of target spatial frequency for 1 c/deg and 9 c/deg targets in the absence (no-adapt) or the presence (adapt) of a 1 c/deg mask at 10 Hz and .7 contrast. (B). (right) RT as a function of target spatial frequency for 1 c/deg and 9 c/deg targets in the absence (no-adapt) or the presence (adapt) of a 1 c/deg mask at 5 Hz and .4 contrast.

grating is flickered at 5 Hz. Figure 11.2B plots the effect of the same grating at 10 Hz. As in Fig. 1A, the 1 c/deg adapting grating influences RT to the 1 c/deg target but not to the 9 c/deg grating. However, it is readily apparent that the influence of the adapting grating on target detection is found only when the grating is flickered at 5 Hz. There is virtually no difference between the adapt and no-adapt conditions when the adapting field flicker rate is 10 Hz.

Discussion

In preliminary work, we found consistent evidence for threshold elevation for low but not high spatial-frequency adaptation for F.L.K. (the first author of this chapter), who is a highly practiced psychophysical observer. However, for one of the other authors, J.S.C., the results were highly variable. Therefore, we chose RT as an indicator of spatial-frequency interaction instead of measuring contrast thresholds for lateralized gratings under the adapt and no-adapt conditions, because it was an easier task for subjects who were not highly practiced. Our decision to use RT was also guided by the fact that RT has been successfully used in prior studies to reveal properties of spatial-frequency channels under adapted and unadapted conditions (Harwerth and Levi, 1978; Brietmeyer and Ganz,1975; Parker, 1980; Parker and Salzen, 1982; Tolhurst, 1975).

Before we can conclude that the results of this study provide further behavioral evidence that the transfer of spatial-frequency information is selective we need to consider an alternative explanation. The reason is that studies of visual adaptation to sinusoidal gratings have shown adaptation effects are obtained when test and adapting field are superimposed but not when they are spatially adjacent (rather than overlapping). Thus, it might be argued that our results do not reflect hemispheric transfer, but are due instead, to the superposition of the adapting and test fields that result from unsteady fixation and eye movements. The results of our study allow us to reject this hypothesis. Adaptation effects have been found at spatial frequencies greater than 9 c/deg as well as at the very low spatial frequencies. Thus, if eye movements produced superposition of the test and adapting gratings, then the increase in RT found for 1 c/deg stimuli should have been found for the 9 c/deg stimuli, also, but it was not. It might be argued that the eye movement effects are more salient at low rather than high spatial frequencies. However, we did not find any influence of the 1 c/deg grating when it was flickered at a high rate. In contrast, adaptation effects at a similar low spatial frequency and high temporal frequency have been obtained for superimposed stimuli. Thus, the spatial- and temporal-frequency selectivity of our adaptation effects argue against any eye movement or superposition effect. It is, however, possible that the effects we have observed are consistent with the hypothesis of bilateral representation of the vertical midline.

Berardi et al. (1989) have shown that an interaction between gratings on the two sides of the vertical midline can occur when one of the components is 2.5 deg from the other. If our results were due to the bilateral representation of the vertical meridian, then we would have to posit that the nasal-temporal overlap extends more than 2 deg along the horizontal meridian. In addition, we would also need to assume that bilateral representation is highly asymmetrical, because interactions are not found when the two stimuli are within the area of bilateral representation with one above the other. There is no evidence to support this assumption (Bunt et al., 1977; Hess, Negishi and Creutzfeldt, 1975). Moreover, the fact that the two gratings must be accurately aligned in order to observe interactions is consistent with the properties of callosal receptive fields (Berlucchi and Rizzolatti, 1968). Berardi et al. (1989) also noted that the receptive field of callosal recipient neurons is made up of two areas juxtaposed at the vertical meridian, one provided by direct input from the lateral geniculate nucleus and the other coming from callosal input. As they pointed out, the response to a stimulus of moderate contrast mediated by the direct input can be suppressed by the callosal input in the presence of a stimulus of much higher contrast. Berardi et al. (1989) further suggested that the interactions between the two stimuli arise at the border between V1 and V2.

Our results are consistent with those of Berardi et al. (1989): a low spatial-frequency adapting grating in one visual field elevated the threshold contrast necessary to elicit an evoked potential to a grating of similar spatial frequency presented in the contralateral visual field, provided that both were presented close to the vertical midline and aligned with respect to phase. A similar finding was not obtained with high spatial-frequency gratings. The fact that more contrast was needed to elicit an evoked potential implies that the adapting grating reduced the contrast of the test grating. The results we have obtained are consistent with the interpretation that the adapting grating lowered the effective contrast of the test grating because lower contrast stimuli are responded to less quickly than those of higher contrast (Harwerth and Levi, 1978). Our results also indicate that the transfer of low spatial-frequency information is dependent on temporal frequency: at 10 Hz, the adapting grating had virtually no effect on RT to the test grating. Thus, low spatial and low temporal frequencies are more readily transferred than are high ones.

The results of this study may provide further insight into the effects of input variables on hemispheric asymmetry. For example, it might explain why the LVF advantage found for more eccentric presentations disappears for tasks requiring low spatial-frequency information when the target is relatively close to fixation. On the other hand, it may explain why the RVF advantage is independent of target locationin tasks which require the processing of high spatial-frequency information. Hemispheric transfer of spatial-frequency information would occur in the former situation, but not in the latter. It may also explain why hemispheric asymmetries found with stimuli presented close to fixation under relatively long durations disappear when exposure duration is lengthened. Very brief exposures are represented by high temporal frequencies, which are not transferred as readily as low temporal frequencies.

EXPERIMENT 2: REDUNDANT STIMULUS TRIALS

The selective nature of the adaptation effects in Experiment 1 provided insight into the transfer of spatial and temporal frequency information. An alternative way to explore the transfer of spatial-frequency information between the two hemispheres is to utilize the redundant signals paradigm (Bjork & Murray, 1974; Fournier & Eriksen, 1990; Miller, 1982; Raab, 1962). In this paradigm, subjects are typically required to monitor two distinct channels for information that may be in the same modality (e.g., vision: color and form) or different modalities (e.g., vision and audition: a tone and a flash), and to react as quickly as possible when a signal is presented on either channel. Thus, on each trial a tone, or a light, or both are presented. The last condition is called a redundant stimulus trial, because information relevant to the task could be based on either visual or auditory information, and one modality (e.g., vision) does not add any information relevant to the subject's task in the other modality (audition). The typical finding has been referred to as a *redundant signals effect*: RTs to redundant trials are typically faster than RTs to either target presented alone.

There have been two alternative interpretations of this finding: *separate activation* and *coactivation*. Separate activation theories assume that information on each channel accumulates with time on parallel, independent channels until a criterion is reached; then, a response is generated. RT on redundant trials reflects the results of a race in which the "winner" is the faster of the two channels (e.g.,

Raab, 1962). Consequently, the redundant trials effect results from statistical facilitation or probability summation, because there are two chances to detect the target on redundant trials, whereas there is only one chance on the nonredundant trials.

In contrast to the separate activation or *race* model, coactivation models describe the redundant stimulus effect as the result of the components of each channel combining (summating) to influence responding on a single trial. That is, activation from different channels combines to satisfy a single criterion. Coactivation models differ in how and where in the processing stream these separate responses combine (Miller, 1991, 1982; Mordkoff and Yantis, 1993; Mordkoff and Miller, 1993; Mordkoff and Yantis, 1991). As a result, activation builds much faster, on average, when it is provided by two sources rather than one and, thus, leads to faster RTs on redundant trials. Although both the separate activation and coactivation explanations can account for the speeded RT in the redundant target condition, coactivation models predict greater reduction in RT in the redundant target condition beyond that expected to arise from simple probability summation. Miller (1982) has developed a mathematical framework for determining the presence of coactivation under such conditions.

Evidence exists to support both the separate activation and the coactivation models. Miller (1982) elaborated on the experimental conditions that result in these different modes of processing redundant signals. Support for separate activation models has been found in studies using a parity criterion, in which different responses are required for information arriving on different channels. On the other hand, support for coactivation is found when the same response is made to signals on different channels. Miller (1982) argued that the former situation requires that the activation on each channel be kept separate whereas the latter does not and, consequently, encourages coactivation.

We adapted this framework to address the issue of interhemispheric interaction by considering each hemisphere to be providing information that can influence RT to a target. Thus, in the context of a simple detection task, we were able to contrast conditions in which a sinusoidal stimulus was presented to a single visual field with conditions in which sinusoidal stimuli were presented to both visual fields. The latter condition provides bilateral stimulation and can be thought of as a redundant target trial because a single target is sufficient for the detection response.

Based on the foregoing discussion, we would expect redundant trials to result in faster responding than single trials. The question this experiment addressed was whether bilateral trials produce coactivation. To the extent that they do, this would support the contention that information from the two targets initially presented to separate hemispheres was, at some locus in processing, being combined. Such a demonstration would therefore provide evidence for some form of interhemispheric interaction. Conversely, an absence of coactivation for bilateral presentations would indicate that the information presented to the two hemispheres remains independent and that RTs simply reflect the faster of the two independent processes.

The specific design of this experiment was guided by the findings of Berardi and Fiorentini (1987), who reported that low- but not high-spatial-frequency information presented to symmetric points about the vertical meridian of the visual field is readily transferred interhemispherically. Our stimulus set consisted of all possible combinations of high- and low-frequency stimuli, and unilateral and bilateral presentation. Thus, there were two same conditions, in which the spatial frequencies presented to the two visual fields were the same (i.e., either both high or both low) and two mixed conditions, in which the gratings presented to the visual fields differed.

The question of interest was whether the bilateral presentations would provide evidence for coactivation relative to the unilateral baselines. In particular, we predicted that coactivation would be obtained for the same bilateral presentation of low-frequency information to both hemispheres, which, as just noted, is readily transferred interhemispherically. Conversely, coactivation was not expected for the same bilateral presentation of high-frequency information, which, in accordance with the aforementioned findings of Berardi and Fiorentini (1987a), is not readily transferred between the hemispheres.   The mixed conditions in which the gratings in the visual fields differed in spatial frequency, provided an opportunity to assess whether coactivation could be obtained across spatial-frequency channels and whether the transfer of low-spatial-frequency information is asymmetrical.   That is, given that low spatial frequencies are transferred, are they more readily transferred from the left hemisphere to the right hemsiphere or vice versa.   Although we did not find any evidence for transfer asymmetries in Experiment 1, it might be the case that asymmetries exist for coactivation, when hemispheric communication is facilitory, but not for adaptation, when it is inhibitory.

We assessed the possible presence of coactivation by employing the procedure developed by Miller (1982), which consists of comparing the RT distribution for the bilateral target condition with the fastest half of the combined RT distribution for the single target conditions. This procedure allows us to parcel out the decrease in RT in the redundant target condition that would be expected by probability summation alone; any residual decrease in RT is then assumed to reflect some form of coactivation between the two redundant targets. It should be noted here that although aspects of Miller's coactivation model have been called into question (e.g., Fournier & Eriksen, 1990), the focus of these questions is whether Miller's procedure possesses sufficient power to detect subtle forms of coactivation; consequently, Miller's test is a conservative one, so any demonstration of coactivation derived from it is valid.

Data Analysis

Miller (1982) has shown that separate activation models must obey the following rule which is known as the *race model inequality*.   The inequality concerns the entire distribution of RTs to single and redundant stimulus trials as follows:

$$P(RT < t/T_1 \text{ and } T_2) \leq P(RT < t/T_1) + P(RT < t/T_2) \quad (1)$$

where t is the time since stimulus onset and T_1 and T_2 refer, respectively, to the target presented in location 1 and location 2.   In the context of the present experiment T1 and T2 refer to gratings presented in the LVF and RVF, respectively.   The left side of this inequality corresponds to the cumulative probability distribution (CDF) of RT on the redundant stimulus trials, and the two terms on the right side correspond to the CDFs for the two single stimulus trials. Thus, the race model places an upper bound on the speed of redundant target responses throughout the entire distribution.   If the observed facilitation exceeds the inequality, then all separate activation models can be rejected.   That is, with coactivation the fastest response to redundant stimuli could be faster than the fastest response to either stimulus alone.

In the present experiment, we determined whether our data violated the inequality in Eq. 1. It should be noted that the inequality can only be violated when t is relatively small. For large values of t the left side of the equation goes to 1, and the right side reaches asymptote at 2.   Coactivation models predict violations of the inequality for small values of t.   Thus, they predict more redundant signal responses in the fastest range than can be explained by considering the number of responses to either signal. The observed violations of the inequality, then, should appear at the low end of the redundant signal CDF.

Method

In this experiment there were eight stimulus conditions: four of these used bilateral presentations (both stimuli were low, both were high, the LVF stimulus was low and RVF stimulus high, and the LVF stimulus high and the RVF stimulus low).   In the other four conditions, either a high- or low spatial-frequency grating was presented in the LVF or RVF. Each condition included 40 trials. At the beginning of a trial, a fixation cross appeared. At a variable foreperiod following the onset of the cross, one of the eight conditions or a blank trial was presented, and subjects were instructed to react as quickly and accurately as possible when they detected a stimulus.   There was a 1.5 sec intertrial interval.   The stimuli consisted of horizontally oriented gratings of 1 c/deg and 9 c/deg.   They were flashed for 150 msec and at a contrast of 10%. Eight subjects participated in this experiment.

Results

The data for each subject were analyzed according to the procedure outlined by Miller (1982).   CDFs were computed for each condition; the results are shown in Figs. 11.3A-D. Figure 11.3A illustrates the data for the 1 c/deg grating.   It is readily apparent that RTs to bilateral trials are significantly faster than the fastest of the single stimulus presentations. This finding violates the inequality presented by Miller (1982) and, thus, provides evidence for coactivation. In contrast to this finding, note that in Fig. 11.3B where the data are shown for the 9 c/deg grating, the bilateral trials and the sum of the two single trial curves are virtually identical over a considerable range of the CDFs.   There is no evidence in these data for coactivation.   Figure 11.3C presents the results for the condition in which the 1 c/deg grating was presented to the LVF and the 9 c/deg grating was presented to the RVF; Fig. 11.3D illustrates the opposite condition.   It is clear in these data, as in Fig 11.3B, that there is no evidence for coactivation.   Thus, the only condition in which the information from the two hemispheres coactivates a response is when both stimuli are of low spatial-frequency and both are close to the vertical midline.

EXPERIMENT 3: IDENTIFICATION

In contrast to the detection experiment just described, the next experiment determined the effect of redundancy on identification.   In this experiment, as in the previous one, eight stimulus conditions were employed.   In one condition of this experiment, however, subjects were required to depress one response key to indicate that a low spatial-frequency grating was presented and another to indicate that it was not presented.   In another condition, which was run on a different day, they were required to depress one key to indicate that a high spatial-frequency grating was presented and another key if it was not.   For both conditions, the keys were counterbalanced across subjects.

Results

The data were analyzed as in Experiment 2 and are presented in Fig. 11.4A-D.   In Fig. 11.4A, the condition in which the 1 c/deg stimulus was used, there is a clear evidence of coactivation.   However, in Fig. 11.4B, there is no evidence for coactivation with the high-spatial-frequency (9 c/deg) targets.   In addition, as seen in Fig. 11.4C, it is clear that responses to a low-spatial-frequency target are not coactivated by a high-spatial-frequency component.   Moreover, the response to a high-spatial-frequency target is not coactivated by a low-spatial-frequency component, as evidenced in Fig. 11.4D. Coactivation only occurs for the low-spatial-frequency target in the same condition.

Discussion

The results of this experiment indicate that coactivation occurs for low spatial frequencies only.   As we have noted, the fact that coactivation occurs indicates that information from the two hemispheres must be combined to jointly influence RT.   The fact that we have found coactivation for low, but not high, spatial frequencies provides additional behavioral evidence for the selective transfer of spatial-frequency information.   Moreover, it is clear that coactivation occurs for both detection and identification.   It is not task specific in these experiments.   However, there is specificity in the transfer of low-spatial-frequency information because coactivation was not found for the mixed conditions.   That is, low-

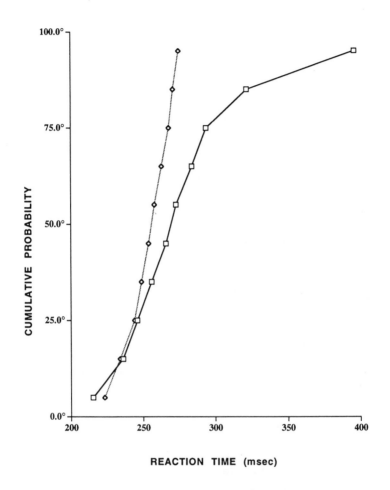

Fig. 11.3A. Cumulative probability density functions for detection RTs for redundant signals of a 1 c/deg grating in the LVF and a 1 c/deg grating in the RVF (squares) and sum of single presentations of a 1 c/deg grating in the LVF and a 1 c/deg grating in the RVF (diamonds).

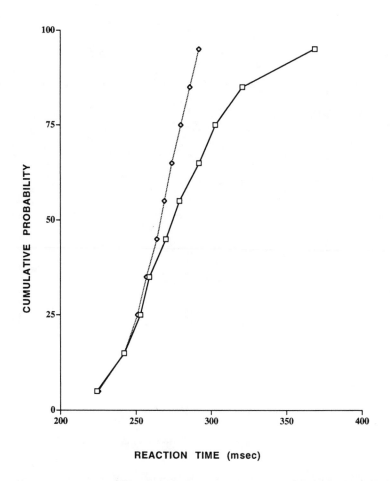

REACTION TIME (msec)

Fig. 11.3B. Cumulative probability density functions for detection RTs for redundant signals of a 9 c/deg grating in the LVF and a 9 c/deg grating in the RVF (squares) and sum of single presentations of a 9 c/deg grating in the LVF and a 9 c/deg grating in the RVF (diamonds).

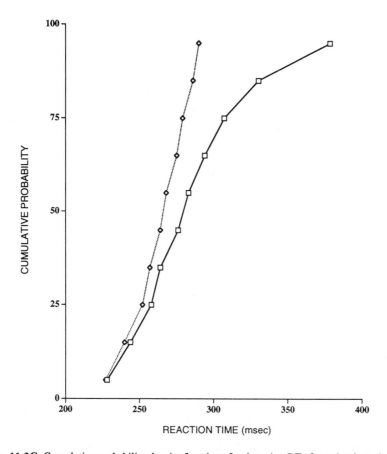

Fig. 11.3C. Cumulative probability density functions for detection RTs for redundant signals of a 1 c/deg grating in the LVF and a 9 c/deg grating in the RVF (squares) and sum of single presentations of a 1 c/deg grating in the LVF and 9 c/deg grating in the RVF (diamonds).

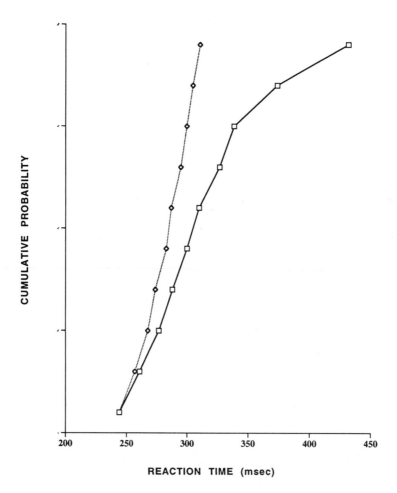

Fig. 11.3D. Cumulative probability density functions for detection RTs for redundant signals of a 1 c/deg grating in the RVF and a 9 c/deg grating in the LVF (squares) and sum of single presentations of a 1 c/deg grating in the RVF and 9 c/deg grating in the LVF (diamonds).

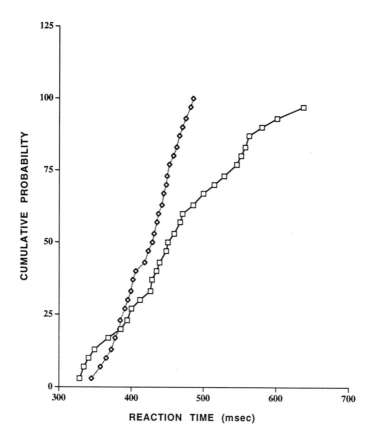

Fig. 11.4A. Cumulative probability density functions for identification RTs for redundant signals of a 1 c/deg grating in the LVF and a 1 c/deg grating in the RVF (squares) and sum of single presentations of a 1 c/deg grating in the LVF and a 1 c/deg grating in the RVF (diamonds).

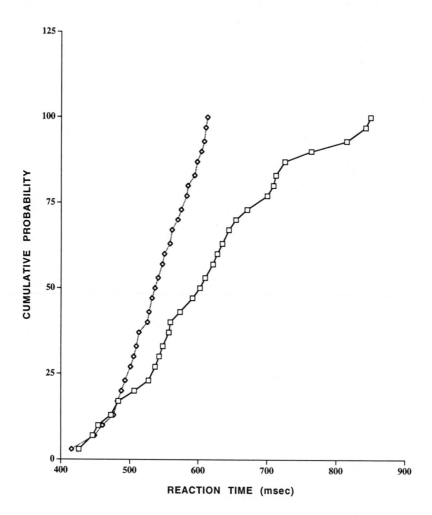

Fig. 11.4B. Cumulative probability density functions for identification RTs for redundant signals of a 9 c/deg grating in the LVF and a 9 c/deg grating in the RVF (squares) and sum of single presentations of a 9 c/deg grating in the LVF and a 9 c/deg grating in the RVF (diamonds).

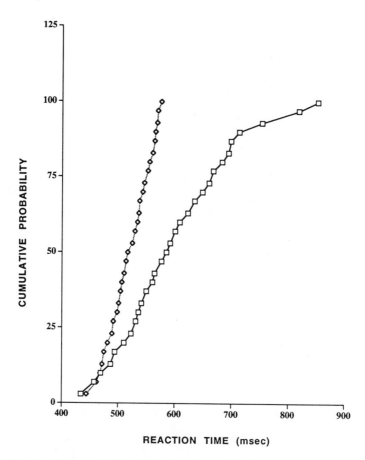

Fig. 11.4C. Cumulative probability density functions for identification RTs for redundant signals of a 1 c/deg grating in the LVF and a 9 c/deg grating in the RVF (squares) and sum of single presentations of a 1 c/deg grating in the LVF and 9 c/deg grating in the RVF (diamonds).

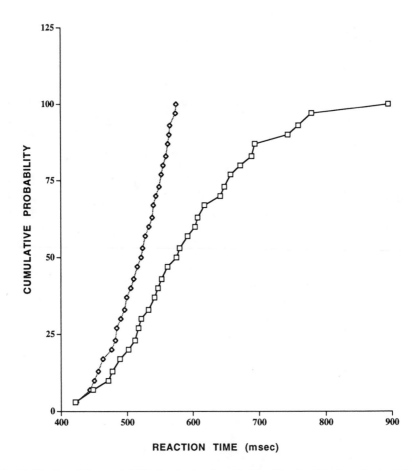

Fig. 11.4D. Cumulative probability density functions for identification RTs for redundant signals of a 1 c/deg grating in the RVF and a 9 c/deg grating in the LVF (squares) and sum of single presentations of a 1 c/deg grating in the RVF and 9 c/deg grating in the LVF (diamonds).

spatial-frequency information in one hemisphere does not combine with information from high-spatial-frequency channels in the contralateral hemisphere to conjointly influence RT.

When low spatial-frequency information is transferred, it may either inhibit the response to the stimulus in the contralateral visual field, as the adaptation experiments have shown, or, it may facilitate the response, as the redundant stimulus experiments have shown, when low-spatial-frequency stimuli in both visual fields can coactivate a response. The findings of inhibition and facilitation in the hemispheric transfer of low-spatial-frequency information in early visual processing may have important implications for studies that use bilateral stimulus presentations. Clearly, our earlier results reinforce the importance of considering the nature of visual input in assessing the generality of findings from such studies (e.g., Kitterle et al., 1992). The ease with which spatial-frequency information can be transferred must influence the magnitude of laterality effects.

REFERENCES

Berardi, N., Bisti, S., & Maffei, L. (1987b). The transfer of visual information across the corpus callosum: spatial and temporal properties in the cat. *Journal of Physiology, 384,* 619-632.

Berardi, N., Bodis-Wollner, I., Fiorentini, A., Guiffre, G., & Morelli, M. (1989). Electrophysiological evidence for interhemispheric transmission of visual information in man. *Journal of Physiology, 411,* 207-225.

Berardi, N., & Fiorentini, A., (1987a). Interhemispheric transfer of visual information in humans: Spatial characteristics. *Journal of Physiology, 384,* 633-647.

Berardi, N., & Fiorentini, A., (1988). Functional dissociation of the hemispheres in the discrimination of complex gratings near the vertical meridan. *Vision Research, 28,* 491-496.

Bjork, E.L., & Murray, J.T. (1974). On the nature of input channels and visual processing. *Psychological Review, 84,* 472-484.

Bradshaw, J. L., & Nettleton, N.C. (1983). *Human cerebral asymmetry.* Englewood Cliffs, NJ: Prentice-Hall.

Brietmeyer, B.G., & Ganz, L. (1975) Simple reaction times as a measure of the temoral response properties of transient and sustained channels. *Vision Research, 15,* 1411-1412.

Breitmeyer, B. & Ganz, L. (1977). Temporal studies with flashed gratings: Inferences about human transient and sustained channels. *Vision Research, 16,* 861-865.

Bunt, A.H., Minckler, D.S., & Johanson, G.W. (1977) Demonstration of bilateral projection of the central retina of the monkey with horseradish peroxidase neuronography. *Journal of Comparative Neurology, 171,* 619-630.

Campbell, F.W. & Robson, J. (1968). Application of Fourier analysis to the visibility of gratings. *Journal of Physiology, 197,* 551-566.

Christman, S. (1987). Effects of perceptual quality on hemispheric asymmetries in visible persistence. *Perception & Psychophysics, 41,* 367-374.

Christman, S. (1989). Perceptual characteristics in visual laterality research. *Brain and Cognition, 11,* 239-257.

Christman, S., Kitterle, F. L., & Hellige, J. B. (1991). The effects of absolute and relative spatial-frequency on hemispheric asymmetry. *Brain and Cognition, 16,* 62-73.

Duncan, J. (1984). Selecive attention and the organization of visual information. *Journal of Experimental Psychology: General, 113,* 501-517.

Efron, R. (1990). *The decline and fall of hemispheric specialization.* Hillsdale, NJ: Lawrence Erlbaum Associates.

Fiorentini, A., & Berardi, N. (1981). Learning in grating waveform discrimination: specificity for orientation and spatial-frequency. *Vision Research, 21,* 1149-1158.

Fiorentini, A. & Berardi, N. (1984). Right-hemisphere superiority in the discrimination of spatial phase. *Perception, 13,* 695-708.

Fournier, L.R., & Eriksen, C.W. (1990). Coactivation in the perception of redundant targets. *Journal of Experimental Psychology Human Perception and Performance, 16,* 538-550.

Graham, N. (1980). Spatial-frequency channels in human vision: detecting edges without edge detectors in Harris, C. S. (Ed.), *Visual coding and adaptatability* (pp. 215-262). Hillsdale: NJ: Lawrence Erlbaum Associates.

Harris, C. S. (Ed.) (1980). *Visual Coding and Adaptatability.* Hillsdale: NJ: Lawrence Erlbaum Associates.

Harwerth, R.S., & Levi, D.M. (1978) Reaction time as a measure of suprathreshold grating detection. *Vision Research 18,* 1579-1586.

Hellige, J. B.(1993). *Hemispheric Asymmetry.* Cambridge, MA: Harvard University Press.

Hess, R., Negishi, K., & Creutzfeldt, O. (1975) The horizontal spread of intracortical inhibition in the visual cortex. *Experimental Brain Research, 22,* 415-419.

Kennedy, H., Dehay, C., & Bullier, J. (1986). Organization of the callosal connections of visual areas V1 and V2 in the macaque monkey. *Journal of Comparative Neurology, 247,* 398-415.

Kitterle, F. L. (1986). Psychophysics of lateral tachistoscopic presentation. *Brain & Cognition, 5,* 131-162.

Kitterle, F. L., & Christman, S. (1991). Hemispheric symmetries and asymmetries in the processing of sine-wave gratings. In F. L. Kitterle (Ed.). *Cerebral laterality: Theory and research* (pp. 201-224). Hillsdale, NJ: Lawrence Erlbaum Associates.

Kitterle, F. L., Christman, S., & Conesa, J. (1993). Hemispheric differences in the interference among components of compound gratings. *Perception & Psychophysics, 54,* 785-793.

Kitterle, F. L., Christman, S., & Hellige, J.B. (1991). Hemispheric differences are found in the identification, but not the detection, of low vs. high spatial frequencies. *Perception & Psychophysics, 48*, 297-306.

Kitterle, F. L., Hellige, J. B., & Christman, S. (1992). Visual hemispheric asymmetries depend upon which spatial frequencies are task relevant. *Brain and Cognition, 80*, 308-314.

Kitterle, F. L., & Jones, R. (1986). A programmable, multifunction dual-channel waveform generator for visual psychophysics. *Behavior Research Methods, Instruments, & Computers, 18*, 571-581.

Kitterle, F. L., & Selig, L. (1991). Visual field effects in the discrimination of sine-wave gratings. *Perception & Psychophysics, 50*, 15-18.

Miller, J. (1982). Divided attention: Evidence for coactivation with redundant signals. *Cognitive Psychology, 14*, 247-279.

Miller, J. (1991). Channel interaction and the redundant targets effect. *Journal of Experimental Psychology, 17,* 160-169.

Mordkoff, J.T., & Miller, J. (1993). Redundancy gains and coactivation with two different targets: The problem of target preferences and the effects of display frequency. *Perception & Psychophysics, 53*, 527-535.

Mordkoff, J. T., & Yantis, S. (1991). An interactive race model of divided attention. *Journal of Experimental Psychology, 17*, 520-538.

Mordkoff, J.T., & Yantis, S. (1993). Dividing attention between color and shape: evidence of coactivation. *Perception & Psychophysics, 53*, 357-366.

Parker, D.M. (1980). Simple reaction times to the onset, offset and contrast reversal of sinusoidal gratings. *Perception & Psychophysics, 28*, 365-368.

Parker, D.M., & Salzen, E.A. (1982). Evoked potential and reaction times to the offset and contrast reversal of sinusoidal gratings. *Vision Research, 22*, 205-207.

Raab, D.(1962). Statistical facilitation of simple reaction times. *Transactions of the New York Academy of Sciences, 24*, 574-590.

Sergent, J. (1982a). The cerebral balance of power: Confrontation or cooperation? *Journal of Experimental Psychology: Human Perception and Performance, 8*, 253-272.

Sergent, J. (1982b). Influence of luminance on hemispheric processing. *Bulletin of the Psychonomic Society, 20*, 221-223.

Sergent, J. (1982c). Theoretical and methodological consequences of variations in exposure duration in visual laterality studies, *Perception & Psychophysics, 31,* 451-461.

Sergent, J. (1983). Role of input in visual hemispheric asymmetries. *Psychological Bulletin, 93*, 481-512.

Sergent, J. (1984). Role of contrast, lettercase, and viewing conditions in a lateralized word-naming task. *Perception & Psychophysics, 35*, 489-498.

Sergent, J. (1985). Influence of task and input factors on hemispheric involvement in face processing. *Journal of Experimental Psychology: Human Perception and Performance, 11*, 846-861.

Sergent, J. (1987). Failures to confirm the spatial-frequency hypothesis: Fatal blow or healthy complication? *Canadian Journal of Psychology, 41*, 412-428.

Sergent, J. & Hellige, J. (1986). Role of input factors in visual-field asymmetries. *Brain and Cognition, 5*, 174-199.

Thomas, E.A.C., & Ross, B.H. (1980). On approporiate procedures for combining probability distributions. *Journal of Mathematical Psychology, 21*, 136-152.

Tolhurst, D.J. (1975). Reaction times in the detection of gratings by human observers: A probabilistic mechanism. *Vision Research, 15*, 1143-1149.

Van Essen, D.C., Newsome, W.T., & Bixby, J.L. (1982) The pattern of interhemispheric connections and its relationship to extra striate visual areas in the macaque monkey. *Journal of Neuroscience, 2*, 265-283.

Weisstein, N. (1980). The joy of Fourier Analysis. In C. S. Harris. (Ed.), *Visual coding and adaptability*. Hillsdale, NJ: Lawrence Erlbaum Associates.

12 Coordinating the Different Processing Biases of the Left and Right Cerebral Hemispheres

Joseph B. Hellige
University of Southern California

Many tasks can be performed reasonably well by both cerebral hemispheres, although the hemispheres are biased to handle the tasks in qualitatively different ways. For example, both hemispheres are able to identify a visually presented consonant-vowel-consonant (CVC) nonsense trigram. However, the two hemispheres appear to go about the task in different ways. Lacking phonetic processing ability, the right hemisphere processes the trigram as three individual letters, beginning with the first letter and proceeding sequentially to the third letter. The left hemisphere, on the other hand, supplements or replaces this sequential, letter-by-letter mode of processing with a mode of processing that causes attention to be distributed more evenly across all three letters. A likely possibility is that the more even distribution of attention characteristic of the left hemisphere is related to the use of phonetic processes that treat the CVC trigram as a single linguistic unit. The fact that the two hemispheres are biased toward different modes of processing raises important questions about what mode of processing emerges when both hemispheres have equivalent access to incoming stimulus information. The present chapter deals with some of these questions.

Hellige (1991) argued for the concept of metacontrol as one way for the intact brain to deal with the situation just outlined. The term *metacontrol* was introduced by Levy and Trevarthen (1976) to refer to the neural mechanisms that determine which hemisphere will attempt to control cognitive operations. In studies with split-brain patients, they found that one hemisphere or the other often tended to assert control over processing when both hemispheres were given an equal chance and that the hemisphere asserting control was not always the one with greater ability. A particularly relevant illustration of this comes from a study reported by Levy, Trevarthen, and Sperry (1972). In one of the tasks, they presented split-brain patients with a pattern consisting of three vertically oriented *X*'s and squares, with each hemisphere being shown a different ordering of stimuli. For example, the left hemisphere might have seen (from top to bottom) *X*, *X*, □ at the same time that the right hemisphere saw □, □, *X*. On each trial, the patient was forced to choose one specific ordering from a set of eight possibilities. When patients were free to point to the response with either hand (note that voluntary movements of each hand are controlled primarily by the contralateral cerebral hemisphere), patients had a strong preference to respond with the right hemisphere. However, when the left hemisphere was forced to assume control of responding by requiring a verbal description of the stimulus order, the level of performance attained by the left hemisphere was superior to that achieved by the right hemisphere in the free-response condition. That is, there was a clear dissociation between hemispheric ability and hemispheric assertion of control.

Recent research reported by my colleagues and me indicates that a similar dissociation can occur in neurologically intact individuals, at least with respect to the dominance of the mode of cognitive processing favored by one hemisphere or the other (e.g., Hellige, 1987, 1991; Hellige, Cowin, and Eng, 1991; Hellige, Jonsson, and Michimata, 1988; Hellige and Michimata, 1989a, 1989b; Hellige, Taylor, and Eng, 1989). The most striking example of a dissociation between hemispheric ability and the dominance of one hemisphere's preferred mode of processing has come from studies of CVC recognition. Accordingly, it is these studies and their recent extensions that are considered in this chapter. I begin by reviewing the nature and reliability of the very counterintuitive dissociation we have observed. This is followed by (a) a description of studies using rotated CVC stimuli which provide an interesting lead about the counterintuitive dissociation and (b) recent data suggesting that there are reliable individual differences in which hemisphere's mode of processing is utilized when both hemispheres are given an equal chance to process the stimuli. With this as a backdrop, the chapter concludes with a discussion of the conditions under which metacontrol mechanisms might serve to coordinate the different processing biases of the two hemispheres in the intact brain.

PROCESSING CVC SYLLABLES FROM VARIOUS LOCATIONS

Hellige et al. (1989) had right-handed university students identify visually presented CVC stimuli, with the CVC on each trial being presented briefly to the left visual field (LVF, and thereby, the right hemisphere), to the right visual field (RVF, and thereby, the left hemisphere), or to both visual fields and hemispheres simultaneously (redundant bilateral trials). Illustrations of these three viewing conditions are given in Fig. 12.1. One purpose of their experiments was to replicate a qualitative difference reported by Levy, Heller, Banich, and Burton (1983) in the mode of CVC processing favored on LVF versus RVF trials. In order to do this, stimulus duration was titrated from trial to trial in order to maintain an error rate of approximately 50%, averaged across all three visual field conditions. The resulting errors were classified into three types: (a) first-letter errors (FEs), which occurred when the first letter of the CVC was missed but the third letter was correct (correctness of the middle letter was ignored); (b) last-letter errors (LEs), which occurred when the last letter of the CVC was missed but the first letter was correct (again correctness of the middle letter was ignored); and (c) other errors (OEs), which consisted of all other types of errors. Following Levy et al., for each visual field condition, the number of errors of each type was divided by the total number of errors for that condition, producing normalized

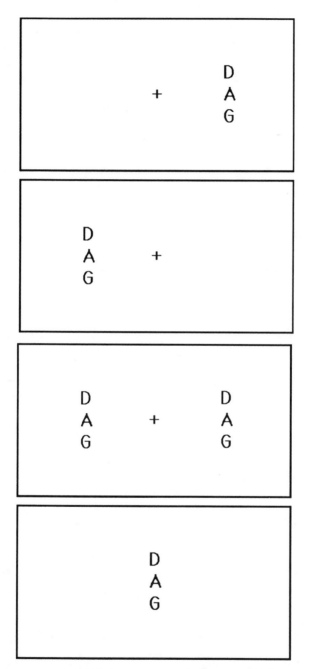

FIG. 12.1. Illustrations of the same CVC stimulus presented in different viewing conditions. From top to bottom: RVF, LVF, Redundant bilateral, and center.

values that show the qualitative error pattern corrected for any visual field differences in overall error rate.

In an analysis restricted to LVF and RVF trials, Hellige et al. (1989) found that the overall error rate was significantly lower on RVF trials than on LVF trials, consistent the with hypothesized left-hemisphere (LH) superiority for processing linguistic stimuli. Of more importance, in each of two experiments, Hellige et al. replicated Levy et al. (1983) by finding evidence of a qualitative difference in the modes of processing favored on LVF and RVF trials. This is illustrated in the upper panel of Fig.12.2, which shows the normalized percentages of FEs, OEs, and LEs from one of our experiments. Note that on LVF trials, subjects failed to identify the last letter far more often than the first letter so that there were many more normalized LEs than normalized FEs. On RVF trials, this difference was significantly reduced. Levy et al. (1983; see also Levy and Kueck, 1986) argued that the LVF pattern occurs because the right hemisphere processes the letters individually and in sequence, whereas the difference between normalized FEs and LEs is reduced on RVF trials because the left hemisphere supplements or replaces a letter-by-letter mode of processing with a phonetic mechanism that distributes attention more evenly across all letter positions. Note that whatever the mode of processing favored on RVF trials, it leads to better performance than the mode of processing favored on LVF trials.

A second purpose of the experiments reported by Hellige et al. (1989) was to compare performance on redundant bilateral trials with performance on LVF and RVF trials. Note that each hemisphere simultaneously receives exactly the same stimulus information on bilateral trials, so that the bilateral viewing condition does not create any obvious bias in favor of one hemisphere or the other. It is intuitively appealing to suppose that when the two hemispheres are biased in favor of qualitatively different ways of performing a task, the brain will spontaneously engage in the mode of processing associated with superior performance, as long as the viewing conditions do not create a bias toward one hemisphere or the other. With respect to the processing of CVC syllables, this intuitively appealing hypothesis leads to the expectation that the qualitative pattern of errors on redundant bilateral trials will be similar to the pattern obtained on RVF trials. In fact, the results obtained by Hellige et al. (1989) are quite different from this. Although the overall error rate on bilateral trials was as low as or slightly lower than the overall error rate on RVF trials (which might be expected with presentation of two identical copies of the same CVC), the qualitative error pattern on bilateral trials was very different from the pattern obtained on RVF trials. In fact, in each of two experiments, Hellige et al. found that the qualitative error pattern on bilateral trials was virtually identical to the pattern obtained on LVF trials (see the upper panel of Fig.12.2).

Hellige, Cowin, and Eng (1994) considered the possibility that this counterintuitive pattern of results was related to the use of redundant bilateral stimulation as the method of creating a viewing condition that was not biased toward one hemisphere or the other. It is true that exactly the same stimulus

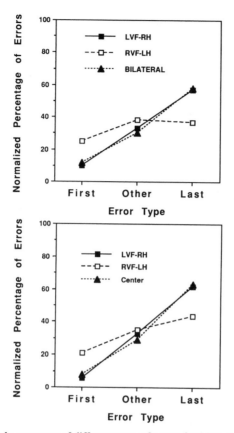

FIG. 12.2. Normalized percentage of different types of errors for LVF, RVF and bilateral trials in the upper panel and for LVF, RVF and center trials in the lower panel. The results shown in the upper panel are from Hellige et al. (1989), Experiment 2 and the results shown in the lower panel are from Hellige, Cowin, & Eng (1994), Experiment 1. (First = first-letter errors; Last = last-letter errors; Other = other errors).

information is presented to both hemispheres on bilateral trials. However, it is possible that with two presentations of the same stimulus, subjects are biased to begin processing the LVF stimulus first and that it is this scanning bias that predisposes the brain toward the mode of processing characteristic of LVF trials. A post-exposure scanning bias of this sort could be particularly likely in processing verbal material because of the left-to-right scanning that ordinarily occurs when reading English. With this in mind, we reasoned that the pattern of results should be very different if redundant bilateral trials were replaced by the presentation of a single CVC to the center of the visual field as an alternative way of creating a viewing condition that does not favor one hemisphere or the other. In fact, we considered the possibility that the qualitative error pattern on center trials would be similar to the pattern obtained on RVF trials. Accordingly, we conducted two experiments in which the CVC stimulus on different trials was presented to the LVF, the RVF or to the center of the visual field (see Fig. 12.1). In one experiment, the three conditions were intermixed randomly; in the other experiment, all of the center trials were given in a block at the beginning of the experiment, followed by LVF and RVF trials intermixed randomly. In each of these experiments, stimulus duration was titrated separately for center trials and for off-center (i.e., LVF and RVF) trials. Thus, overall error rates were approximately 50% for center trials and for the average of LVF and RVF trials.

Hellige, Cowin, & Eng (1994) reported very similar results from both of these experiments. As would be expected, we found a significantly lower overall error rate on RVF trials than on LVF trials and, as a consequence of the separate titration of duration on center trials, the overall error rate on center trials was intermediate. With respect to the qualitative pattern of errors, the results were very similar to those reported by Hellige et al. (1989) using LVF, RVF and redundant bilateral trials. The lower panel of Fig.12.2 illustrates this for the experiment in which the LVF, RVF, and center conditions were intermixed randomly. Note that the LVF and RVF patterns differ in the same way as reported by Levy et al. (1983) and by Hellige et al. (1989; see also Hellige, Cowin, Eng and Sergent, 1991). Note also that the qualitative error pattern obtained on center trials is very different from the pattern obtained on RVF trials and very similar to the pattern obtained on LVF trials. In this sense, the counterintuitive error pattern obtained earlier for redundant bilateral trials extends to center trials. This rules out interpretation of the earlier results as an artifact of using bilateral presentation.

Taken together, the results obtained by Hellige et al. (1989) and Hellige, Cowin, and Eng (1994) indicate that in neurologically intact individuals there can be a dissociation between hemispheric superiority for a task (e.g., an RVF advantage for recognizing CVCs) and which hemisphere's preferred mode of processing is favored when viewing conditions do not bias perceptual analysis toward one hemisphere or the other (e.g., the mode of processing characteristic of LVF trials). With respect to processing CVC stimuli, it is possible that the brain is biased toward using a mode of processing that can be utilized by both hemispheres. To the extent that the mode of processing characteristic of RVF trials involves phonetic mechanisms that are unavailable to the right hemisphere, it is unlikely that the use of these mechanisms would permit the right hemisphere to contribute much to performance on redundant bilateral or center trials. In contrast, both hemispheres can process individual letters so that the use of a letter-by-letter mode of processing would allow both hemispheres to participate on redundant bilateral and center trials. From this perspective, a mode of processing that is inferior on unilateral trials becomes superior when viewing conditions permit both hemispheres equivalent access to the stimuli.

An alternative possibility is that, in the natural environment, a letter-by-letter mode of processing is usually superior to a more linguistic/phonetic mode of processing for a vertical arrangement of letters. This is plausible because in English it is unusual to find words with the letters arranged vertically and, if vertically arranged letters do not form a word or CVC nonword, there may be some cost associated with trying to use a linguistic/phonetic mode of processing. Perhaps the brain has a bias toward what would be a more ecologically valid mode of processing, even though the CVC patterns used in the experiments by Hellige et al. (1989) and Hellige, Cowin, and Eng (1994) represent exceptions. From this perspective, a more linguistic/phonetic mode of processing vertically presented letters is restricted to those trials that stimulate only the left hemisphere directly by presenting the CVC to the RVF.

An interesting way to distinguish these hypotheses would be to conduct experiments similar to those that have been done, but using CVC stimuli with the letters arranged horizontally. Changing the letter arrangement from vertical to horizontal would not suddenly endow the right hemisphere with phonetic processing ability. Thus, the hypothesis that the brain prefers modes of processing that can be utilized by both hemispheres predicts that the pattern obtained on bilateral and center trials should be similar for vertical and horizontal arrangements. However, the hypothesis that the results obtained to date are related to the fact that vertical presentation is unusual in English predicts that the results obtained on bilateral and center trials will be very sensitive to the arrangement of the letters. Specifically, the difference between normalized FEs and LEs on those trials should be smaller with a typical horizontal arrangement of letters than with the vertical arrangement that has been used, and the qualitative pattern of errors on bilateral and center trials should move away from the pattern characteristic of LVF trials and become similar to the pattern characteristic of RVF trials.

Unfortunately, appropriate experiments remain to be carried out with horizontal presentation of CVCs. However, recent studies using upright and rotated displays of CVC stimuli provide a preliminary indication that the arrangement of letters is very important when the CVC is presented in a way that does not bias perceptual analysis toward one hemisphere or the other. It is to these studies that I now turn.

STUDIES OF ROTATED CVC DISPLAYS

Hellige, Cowin, Eng, and V. Sergent (1991) investigated the role of perceptual reference frames in producing visual field asymmetries for CVC recognition. To do so, we presented CVC stimuli in three conditions: (a) a standard upright condition, (b) with the stimulus display rotated 90 degrees clockwise and (c) with the stimulus display rotated 90 degrees counterclockwise (for examples, see Fig. 12.3). The goal in conducting these experiments was to determine whether there would be any effects of relative visual field in the two rotated conditions. There were none.

It is interesting to note that each of the two rotated conditions presents the letters of the CVC horizontally, albeit with the letters rotated either clockwise or counterclockwise. In addition, in those conditions the CVC is centered around the visual midline, appearing either above or below the fixation point. That is, the conditions of stimulus presentation do not favor one hemisphere or the other. Accordingly, the pattern of results from the two rotated conditions provide at least

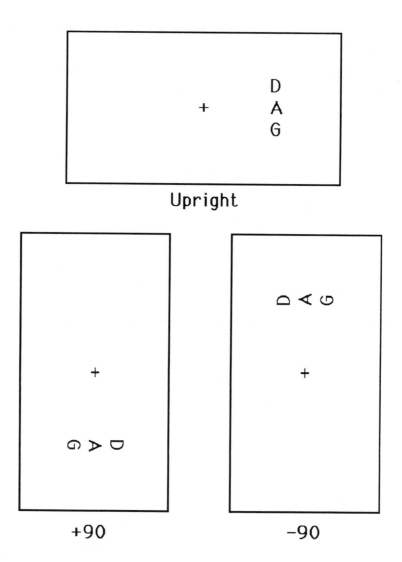

FIG. 12.3. Illustrations of the same CVC stimulus presented in an Upright condition, with the display rotated 90° clockwise (+90) and with the display rotated 90° counterclockwise (-90). Note that the sample CVC appears in the RVF in the upright condition and in the relative RVF in the two rotated conditions.

some preliminary information about the qualitative pattern of errors obtained with horizontal displays centered around the visual midline. Furthermore, the clockwise and counterclockwise rotation conditions differ from each other in an interesting way. In both conditions, subjects were to pronounce the CVC and to report the letters, beginning with the rotated "top" of the display. Note that for counterclockwise displays this results in the letters being processed from left to right, the order that is typical of English and that might be expected to favor a linguistic/phonetic mode of processing. However, for clockwise displays the letters had to be processed from right to left, an order that is atypical of English and that is likely to favor a letter-by-letter mode of processing.

With these things in mind, it is instructive to examine the qualitative patterns of errors obtained in the clockwise and counterclockwise rotation conditions (averaged across upper and lower locations) and to compare each of these patterns to those obtained on LVF and RVF trials in the upright condition. These comparisons are shown in Fig. 12.4 for one of the experiments reported by Hellige et al. (1991). The normalized percentages of FEs, OEs and LEs are shown for LVF and RVF trials with the results of the clockwise rotation in the upper panel, and the results of the counterclockwise condition in the lower panel.

Note that the different patterns obtained on LVF and RVF trials replicate the effects of earlier studies. That is, the difference between the normalized percentage of FEs and LEs was significantly smaller on RVF trials than on LVF trials. Interestingly, the qualitative error pattern obtained in the clockwise (+90

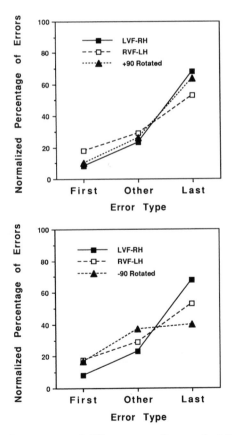

FIG. 12.4. Normalized percentages of different types of errors for LVF, RVF and clockwise rotation (+90) trials in the upper panel and for LVF, RVF and counterclockwise rotation (-90) trials in the lower panel. The data are taken from Hellige et al. (1991), Experiment 2. (First = first-letter errors; Last = last-letter errors; Other = other errors)

deg) rotation condition (upper panel of Fig. 12.4) is very similar to that obtained in earlier studies with vertical CVC stimuli presented in redundant bilateral or center conditions. That is, the qualitative error pattern was far more similar to the pattern obtained on LVF trials than on RVF trials. However, the clockwise rotation condition is the one that required the CVC to be processed from right to left, so that the preference to use a letter-by-letter mode of processing is not surprising. Note that the qualitative error pattern obtained in the counterclockwise (-90 deg) condition (lower panel of Fig. 12.4) is quite different. In this case, when the letters must be processed from left to right, the qualitative error pattern is far more similar to the pattern obtained on RVF trials than to the pattern obtained on LVF trials. In fact, the difference between the percentage of normalized FEs and LEs is even smaller on counterclockwise trials than on RVF trials, perhaps because the CVC is oriented horizontally on counterclockwise trials but vertically on RVF trials.

Of course, these results can only be suggestive because the LVF and RVF trials continued to use vertically presented CVCs and the individual letters were rotated in opposite directions for the +90 and -90 conditions. However, what they suggest is very interesting: That is, it is not always the case that the mode of CVC processing characteristic of LVF trials is applied when a single stimulus is centered about the visual midline. To the contrary, it appears that the more linguistic/phonetic mode of processing, which is characteristic of RVF trials, is applied when a single, horizontally oriented CVC is centered at the visual midline and the letters are processed in the left-to-right order that is typical of English. This possibility needs to be tested in experiments that use horizontally oriented CVCs for LVF and RVF trials, as well as for bilateral and center trials. To the extent that such studies confirm the importance of CVC orientation, they would support the hypothesis that the counterintuitive results reported in earlier studies were a result of using vertical displays. Furthermore, they would indicate that under more ecologically valid conditions, the mode of processing used when viewing conditions do not create a bias in favor of either hemisphere is the mode associated with the hemisphere having greater ability to perform the task.

INDIVIDUAL DIFFERENCES

Even when CVCs are oriented vertically, there is individual variation in whether the qualitative error pattern on redundant bilateral and center trials is more similar to the pattern obtained on LVF trials or to the pattern obtained on RVF trials. Of course, some of this individual variation is likely the result of random error. However, we have recently found that at least some variation of this sort cannot be dismissed so easily. Specifically, it appears that the qualitative error pattern on redundant bilateral trials is related to ear differences obtained in dichotic listening.

Hellige, Bloch, Cowin, Eng, Eviatar, and V. Sergent (1994) had right-handed and left-handed subjects attempt to identify dichotically presented (consonant-vowel) CV nonsense syllables. On each trial, two different stimuli from the set /ba/, /da/, /ga/, /pa/, /ta/, and /ka/ were presented simultaneously, one to each ear. Subjects chose two syllables from the set as their best guesses about which two syllables had been presented. This task typically produces a right-ear advantage (REA) for most people, a result that is thought to be related to LH superiority for phonetic processing. The direction and magnitude of the ear difference for an individual is also thought to be related to the individual's characteristic arousal asymmetry in favor of one hemisphere or the other (e.g., Kim, Levine, and Kertesz, 1990). Thus, an arousal asymmetry in favor of the left hemisphere could magnify the REA that results from LH dominance for phonetic processing, whereas an arousal asymmetry in favor of the right hemisphere could serve to reduce or reverse the REA.

The same subjects also performed the visual CVC recognition task using vertically oriented CVC stimuli presented to the LVF, RVF or to both visual fields simultaneously (redundant bilateral trials). One purpose of the study was to determine whether there was any relationship between the ear advantage shown by an individual during dichotic listening and whether the qualitative error pattern obtained on bilateral trials was more similar to the pattern obtained on LVF trials or the pattern obtained on RVF trials.

Figure 12.5 shows the percentage of right-handed subjects in our sample who produced ear advantages of different magnitudes (from a total of 120 dichotic listening trials). As shown in Fig. 12.5, the number of correct responses was higher for right-ear than for left-ear stimuli for most of the subjects, but there was considerable individual variation. In order to examine the relationship between the ear difference and performance on the CVC task, we focused attention on those subjects whose ear advantage score was at least one standard deviation from the group mean. As shown in Fig. 12.5, this produced a group of individuals who showed a left-ear advantage of at least one item (LEA group) and a group who showed a REA of at least 26 items (large REA group).

Figure 12.6 shows the normalized percentages of FEs, OEs, and LEs for each of the three visual field conditions in each of these two extreme groups. The first thing to note is that, for both groups, the qualitative error patterns on LVF and RVF trials were consistent with the results of earlier studies. For the LEA group, the qualitative error pattern on bilateral trials was more similar to the pattern obtained on LVF trials than to the pattern obtained on RVF trials, although the results are noisier than those obtained in earlier studies. Although not shown in Fig. 12.6, a similar pattern was obtained for the group whose ear difference was within one standard deviation of the group mean, a result that is consistent with the results of earlier experiments using vertically oriented CVCs. In marked contrast, for the large REA group the qualitative error pattern on bilateral trials was virtually identical to the pattern obtained on RVF trials and different from the pattern obtained on LVF trials. Hellige et. al. (1994) report similar results for left-handers.

At the very least, the relationship between the ear advantage on the dichotic listening task and the qualitative error pattern on redundant bilateral trials suggests reliable individual variation in bias toward the mode of processing

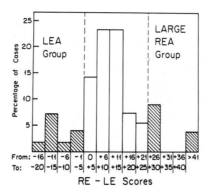

FIG. 12.5. Percentages of subjects with right-ear minus left-ear (RE-LE) scores of different magnitudes, from Hellige et al. (1994).

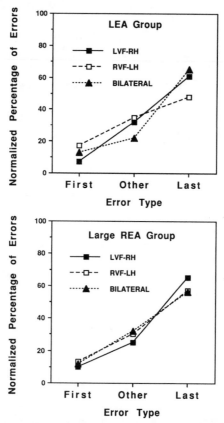

FIG. 12.6. Normalized percentages of different types of errors for LVF, RVF and bilateral trials. The results shown in the upper panel are from the LEA Group and the results in the lower panel are from the large REA group identified by Hellige et al. (1994). (First = first-letter errors; Last = last-letter errors; Other = other errors)

associated with one hemisphere or the other. Beyond that, the results suggest that such biases are related to hemispheric asymmetry for phonetic processing or to characteristic arousal asymmetry. In either case, this dimension of individual variation appears to be independent of variation in the direction of differences between LVF and RVF trials. For example, both the LEA group and the large REA group showed a RVF advantage for CVC recognition, and the two groups showed the same difference between the two visual fields in qualitative error pattern (see Fig. 12.6).

CONDITIONS THAT FAVOR THE APPLICATION OF METACONTROL MECHANISMS

This chapter began with the observation that, for many tasks, the left and right cerebral hemispheres of humans are biased toward qualitatively different modes of processing, which led to questions about the mode of processing that emerges when both hemispheres have an equal opportunity to process incoming stimulus information. The results reviewed here indicate that one way our brains deal with this situation is to utilize the mode of processing characteristic of one hemisphere, with the dominant mode of processing not always being the one associated with the hemisphere that has greater ability to perform the task. Furthermore, the mode of processing utilized on bilateral and center trials varies with specific task demands and may differ reliably from person to person (see also Hellige, 1987, 1991).

The emergence of a dominant mode of processing on bilateral and center trials is reminiscent of the metacontrol results reported for split-brain patients by Levy and Trevarthen (1976). Of course, when the brain is intact, it is very unlikely that either hemisphere is ever completely uninvolved in ongoing processing. For example, virtually all tasks involve the physiological activation of many regions of both hemispheres, as well as many subcortical structures (see Hellige, 1993). However, it is possible that the same neural metacontrol mechanisms that sometimes lead to a dramatic dominance of one hemisphere in split-brain patients lead to the more subtle dominance of one hemisphere's preferred mode of processing in neurologically intact subjects.

It is important to note that the relatively complete dominance of one hemisphere's preferred mode of processing is only one of the ways that the brain might coordinate the different processing biases of the two cerebral hemispheres when both of them have equivalent access to the relevant stimulus information. In fact, when I first discussed the potential of the redundant bilateral paradigm, I outlined several other alternatives that seemed at least as plausible (Hellige, 1987). For example, there are certainly conditions that would permit the two hemispheres to process the same stimulus information in parallel, with each hemisphere using the mode of processing that it prefers. In addition, there are likely to be conditions that encourage the emergence of new modes of processing on bilateral and center trials, modes that are different from either of the modes of processing favored on unilateral trials (see Banich, this volume, chapter 9; J. Sergent, 1991a). A major issue for the future study of interhemispheric interaction is the identification of factors that determine which of these several varieties of interhemispheric interaction will apply in a given situation.

At present, it is at least possible to begin identifying conditions that might favor the application of metacontrol mechanisms. One important condition seems to be whether or not the separate processing of the two hemispheres must converge on a common set of neural structures that underlie the preparation and organization of a motor response. As noted by J. Sergent (1991b), the earlier studies of split-brain patients reported by Levy and Trevarthen (1976) found evidence of metacontrol mechanisms using, for example, such things as the free-response paradigm described earlier, and other paradigms that created a kind of response competition between the two disconnected hemispheres. Sergent's own studies of split-brain patients illustrate that both hemispheres can contribute to overall performance when only a single, more integrative response is required. That is, simultaneous stimulation of both of the disconnected hemispheres need not eliminate either one of them from influencing the response generated by the individual.

In her split-brain studies, J. Sergent (1991b) examined the processing of different types of spatial relationships. Included in her studies were trials that presented the same information to both visual fields (and hemispheres), with the patients required to produce a single response (e.g., Is a dot to the right or left of the center of a circle?). Interestingly, performance on these redundant bilateral trials was superior to performance on either LVF or RVF trials. Note that this result, by itself, indicates that both hemispheres contributed to overall performance. Furthermore, certain qualitative aspects of the results were different on bilateral trials than on either of the two types of unilateral trials. For example, when subjects decided whether an item was to the left or right of another, a spatial compatibility effect was present on unilateral trials. That is, patients responded faster with the hand ipsilateral to the visual field stimulated. On bilateral trials, the response hand effect was different from that of either unilateral trial. That is, certain characteristics of processing on bilateral trials could not be predicted in a straightforward way from the mode of processing characteristic of either individual hemisphere.

When the split-brain studies of Levy and Trevarthen (1976) and J. Sergent (1991b) are considered together, they suggest that competition between the hemispheres at the response production level can lead to blocking of processing by one hemisphere. Similar blocks may occur at other levels, as well. In a general sense, blocking of one hemisphere's processing (or, at least, one hemisphere's preferred mode of processing) may occur to the extent that the left and right hemispheres' preferred modes of processing require certain neural structures to engage in mutually inconsistent processing. For example, Levy and Kueck (1986) argued that the phonetic mode of CVC processing favored by the left hemisphere leads to a very rapid or global distribution of attention across the three letters of the stimulus, but that the letter-by-letter mode of processing favored by the right hemisphere leads to a relatively slow, sequential distribution of attention. Perhaps it is so difficult (or impossible?) to simultaneously distribute attention in these two very different ways that it would be cumbersome (or impossible?) to use both modes of processing simultaneously on bilateral or center trials. That is, in the CVC experiments, the blocking of one hemisphere's preferred mode of processing may occur because both hemispheres must converge on the same set of neural structures that control the distribution of attention across space. Perhaps, when the modes of processing preferred by the two hemispheres are not mutually inconsistent, the two hemispheres will process the same information in parallel, with each hemisphere able to utilize fully whatever mode of processing leads it to perform optimally.

REFERENCES

Hellige, J. B. (1987). Interhemispheric interaction: Models, paradigms and recent findings. In D. Ottoson (Ed.), *Duality and unity of the brain.* (pp. 454-465). Hampshire, England: Macmillan Press.

Hellige, J. B. (1990). Hemispheric specialization. *Annual Review of Psychology, 41,* 55-80.

Hellige, J. B. (1991). Cerebral laterality and metacontrol. In F. Kitterle (Ed.), *Cerebral laterality: Theory and research.* (pp. 117-132). Hillsdale, NJ: Lawrence Erlbaum Associates.

Hellige, J. B. *Hemispheric asymmetry: What's right and what's left.* Cambridge, MA: Harvard University Press.

Hellige, J. B., Bloch, M. I., Cowin, E. L., Eng, T. L., Eviatar, Z., & Sergent, V. (1994) Individual variation in hemispheric symmetry: Multitask study of effects related to handedness and sex. *Journal of Experimental Psychology: General, 123,* 235-256.

Hellige, J. B., Cowin, E. L., & Eng, T. L. (1994). *Recognition of CVC syllables from LVF, RVF and central locations: Hemispheric differences and interhemispheric interaction.* Manuscript submitted for publication.

Hellige, J. B., Cowin, E. L., Eng, T. L., & Sergent, V. (1991). Perceptual reference frames and visual field asymmetry for verbal processing. *Neuropsychologia, 29,* 929-940.

Hellige, J. B., Jonsson, J. E., & Michimata, C. (1988). Processing from LVF, RVF and bilateral presentations: Metacontrol and interhemispheric interaction. *Brain & Cognition, 7,* 39-53.

Hellige, J. B., & Michimata, C. (1989a). Categorization versus distance: Hemispheric differences for processing spatial information. *Memory & Cognition, 17,* 770-776.

Hellige, J. B., & Michimata, C. (1989b). Visual laterality for letter comparison: Effects of stimulus factors, response factors and metacontrol. *Bulletin of the Psychonomic Society, 27,* 441-444.

Hellige, J. B., Taylor, A. K., & Eng, T. L. (1989). Interhemispheric interaction when both hemispheres have access to the same stimulus information.

Journal of Experimental Psychology: Human Perception and Performance, 15, 711-722.

Kim, H., Levine, S. C., & Kertesz, S. (1990). Are variations among subjects in lateral asymmetry real individual differences or random error in measurement? Putting variability in its place. *Brain and Cognition, 14*, 220-242.

Levy, J., Heller, W., Banich, M. T., & Burton, L. A. (1983). Are variations among right-handed individuals in perceptual asymmetries caused by characteristic arousal differences between hemispheres? *Journal of Experimental Psychology: Human Perception and Performance, 9*, 329-359.

Levy, J., & Kueck, L. (1986). A right hemispatial advantage on a verbal free-vision task. *Brain and Language, 27*, 24-37.

Levy, J., & Trevarthen, C. (1976). Metacontrol of hemispheric function in human split-brain patients. *Journal of Experimental Psychology: Human Perception and Performance, 2*, 299-312.

Levy, J., Trevarthen, C., & Sperry, R. W. (1972). Perception of bilateral chimeric figures following hemisphere deconnexion. *Brain, 95*, 61-78.

Sergent, J. (1991). Judgments of relative position and distance on representations of spatial relations. *Journal of Experimental Psychology: Human Perception and Performance, 17*, 762-780.

Sergent, J. (1991). Processing of spatial relations within and between the disconnected cerebral hemispheres. *Brain, 114*, 1025-1043.

uthor Index

3 - Descartes on unifying role of pineal.
4 - Fechner's prediction of split consciousness
8 - animal spirits in ventricle and brain
9 - corpus callosum as seat of soul
13 - no C.C. in marsupials
15 - Zinn cut cc in cats & dogs - little effect,
     soul 'extended' through brain.